FROM THE OFFICE OF
KEITH SEBELIUS, M.C.
1st DISTRICT, KANSAS

WITHDRAWN

STEPHEN SCROPE

THE EPISTLE OF OTHEA

_____

EARLY ENGLISH TEXT SOCIETY

No. 264

1970

THE EPISTLE OF
OTHEA

TRANSLATED FROM THE FRENCH TEXT OF

CHRISTINE DE PISAN

BY

STEPHEN SCROPE

EDITED BY

CURT F. BÜHLER

Published for
THE EARLY ENGLISH TEXT SOCIETY
by the
OXFORD UNIVERSITY PRESS
LONDON NEW YORK TORONTO
1970

Oxford University Press, Ely House, London W. 1

GLASGOW NEW YORK TORONTO MELBOURNE WELLINGTON
CAPE TOWN SALISBURY IBADAN NAIROBI LUSAKA ADDIS ABABA DAR ES SALAAM
BOMBAY CALCUTTA MADRAS KARACHI LAHORE DACCA
KUALA LUMPUR SINGAPORE HONG KONG TOKYO

SBN 19 722263 3

Grateful acknowledgement is made to the American
Council of Learned Societies for a generous grant
to the Society towards the cost of printing this edition
of *The Epistle of Othea*

PRINTED IN GREAT BRITAIN
AT THE UNIVERSITY PRESS, OXFORD
BY VIVIAN RIDLER
PRINTER TO THE UNIVERSITY

PREFACE

THE present edition of Stephen Scrope's translation of the *Épître d'Othéa* was first taken in hand immediately after the publication of my edition of the same writer's *Dicts and Sayings of the Philosophers* (E.E.T.S., o.s. 211, 1941). The delay of some twenty-five years in the completion of it was due to a great variety of causes, some of which were quite beyond my control. In the interval, however, a number of preliminary studies resulting from my work on this text were published and these are listed in the proper places. The entire work was completed, save for some necessary revision and final typing, by the spring of 1966.

It is a great pleasure to record my deep gratitude to the Master and Fellows of St. John's College, Cambridge, for the kind permission to print here the text of their manuscript. The Marquis of Bath most graciously permitted his manuscript to be deposited for my benefit in the British Museum on two separate occasions and allowed me to have a microfilm made of it. I am grateful to the Trustees of the Pierpont Morgan Library for granting me permission to make full use of the Morgan text.

The Warburg Institute of London, in providing me with desk space for the greater part of a year and granting me the privilege of using its invaluable library, deserves a special note of recognition. The fact that I was able to avail myself of this hospitality was entirely due to a Fellowship awarded to me by the John Simon Guggenheim Memorial Foundation in 1965; without this most welcome support, my edition would never have been finished.

It is a pleasant duty to thank the authorities of the following libraries for placing their resources so freely at my disposal: British Museum, Bibliothèque Nationale, Bibliothèque Royale, Biblioteca Apostolica Vaticana, Bodleian Library, University Library, Cambridge, Bayerische Staatsbibliothek, and the Pierpont Morgan Library.

The work of my predecessors in the study of the *Epistle of Othea* (Sir George F. Warner, P. G. C. Campbell, and James D.

Gordon) has immensely simplified my task. The extraordinary care which Professor Norman Davis and Mr. Robert Burchfield of the E.E.T.S. have bestowed on this edition requires special mention; their assistance, so generously given, has been deeply appreciated. My most sincere thanks for valuable help are also due to Professors Charity Cannon Willard, (the late) Rosemond Tuve, Gianni Mombello, Astrik L. Gabriel, and Joseph B. Trapp. I should like to express my very real appreciation to my colleagues on the staff of the Morgan Library (especially Miss Felice Stampfle and Dr. John Plummer) for their unfailing help and always useful suggestions.

Lastly, it is my sad duty to record here the understanding support and continuing encouragement over many years of my wife, for which these few words of thanks are entirely inadequate acknowledgement. It is just one of many sorrows that she did not live to see the publication of this volume.

C. F. B.

The Pierpont Morgan Library
December 1966

CONTENTS

INTRODUCTION

GENERAL REMARKS

THE *Épître d'Othéa la déesse à Hector*, judging from the number of surviving manuscripts and extant early printed editions, may well have been Christine de Pisan's most popular and successful (though perhaps not, according to our standards, her most skilful or rewarding) composition. For this critical edition of an English translation, there will be no need to give an account of Christine's life and works; the pertinent facts are available in a great many special studies devoted to her biography and to her *opera*,[1] including of course the *Othéa*.[2] It may here suffice to say that this work is now dated *circa* 1400,[3] or roughly half a century before the first English translation (that here printed for the first time in complete form) was undertaken. This translation, too, is not unfamiliar to students of the period. It was first shown by Sir George Warner[4] that this was the work of Stephen Scrope (*c.* 1396–1472), the stepson and ward of the well-known Sir John Fastolf (1380–1459).[5] Scrope's translations[6] appear in

---

[1] For the chief studies on Christine and her writings, see Robert Bossuat, *Manuel bibliographique de la littérature française du moyen âge* (Melun, 1951; with supplements: Paris, 1955, and Paris, 1961), nos. 4437–82, 6834–45, and 7888–92, 7900. Further, Pierre Le Gentil, 'Christine de Pisan, poète méconnu', *Mélanges d'histoire littéraire offerts à Daniel Mornet* (Paris, 1951), pp. 1–10; Félix Lecoy, 'Note sur quelques ballades de Christine de Pisan', *Fin du moyen âge et renaissance: Mélanges de philologie française offerts à Robert Guiette* (Antwerp, 1961), pp. 107–14; and recent works cited below.

[2] See especially Mombello (see List of Books), with extensive and important bibliography.

[3] Cf. Mombello, pp. 414–17.

[4] *The Epistle of Othea to Hector* (London, 1904), pp. xxv–xxxiii.

[5] The best biographical accounts of Fastolf and Scrope are given by G. Poulett Scrope, *History of the Manor and Ancient Barony of Castle Combe* (London, 1852); Warner, op. cit.; James Gairdner's introduction to *The Paston Letters* (London, 1904), i. 153–6; Margaret Schofield, *The Dicts and Sayings of the Philosophers* (Philadelphia, 1936), pp. 1–22; and K. B. McFarlane, 'The Investment of Sir John Fastolf's Profits of War', *Transactions of the Royal Historical Society*, 5th ser., vii (1957), 91–116.

[6] On Scrope's other translations, see my *The Dicts and Sayings of the Philosophers* (E.E.T.S., o.s. 211; London, 1941), pp. xxxix–xlvi, and Schofield, op. cit., pp. 35–39.

several specialized accounts of English literature,[1] and our translator can lay claim to be regarded as a writer of some distinction in the mid-fifteenth century, a period not particularly luminous in the annals of British literary history.

There can be, perhaps, no better way to judge the importance of any early text to its own era (and thus, also, to historians of literature) than to record the number of manuscripts of it which have either survived or which can be shown to have once been extant. By this criterion, the *Othéa* must rank high, for no fewer than forty-three located manuscripts[2] of the French text are listed by Dr. Gianni Mombello.[3] Another test of popularity (and, consequently, of stature) is the impact which a work had upon a culture beyond its own linguistic boundaries. Besides the translation of Christine's piece here printed, we have the one perhaps made (in the second half of the fifteenth century) by Anthony Babyngton[4] and that assigned, with excellent reason, to the printer Robert Wyer (*c.* 1540).[5] Not many French con-

---

[1] Cf. H. S. Bennett, *Chaucer and the Fifteenth Century* (Oxford, 1947), pp. 297–8; Albert C. Baugh, *A Literary History of England* (New York and London, 1948), p. 302; Samuel K. Workman, *Fifteenth Century Translation as an Influence on English Prose* (Princeton, 1940), pp. 177, 188–9, 202; Clarissa P. Farrar and Austin P. Evans, *Bibliography of English Translations from Medieval Sources* (New York, 1946), nos. 2817–17a and 3194; etc.

[2] In addition to the manuscripts, a number of early printed editions are also recorded. The *editio princeps* is Paris: Philippe Pigouchet [*c.* 1499], GW 6646. Three early sixteenth-century editions are listed by Jacques-Charles Brunet, *Manuel du libraire et de l'amateur de livres* (Paris, 1860–5), i. 1856, viz.: Paris, [sine nota]; Lyon, 1519; and Paris: Philippe Le Noir, 1522 (PML 41003). These have the title *Cent histoires de Troye*. There is an undated edition, printed at Rouen by Raulin Gautier, at the Biblioteca Colombina, Seville; this is entitled 'Lepistre de othea'. Two more undated editions, with the same title, are credited to the Parisian press of Jehan Trepperel's widow by Campbell (see next note), p. 17.

[3] The manuscripts were first listed by P. G. C. Campbell, *L'Épître d'Othéa; Étude sur les sources de Christine de Pisan* (Paris, 1924), pp. 9–16, with additions in my 'Sir John Fastolf's Manuscripts of the *Épître d'Othéa* and Stephen Scrope's Translation of this Text', *Scriptorium*, iii (1949), 124. These have been superseded by Mombello's list (pp. 401–4 and 12). Note also Mombello's chapter 'Lettori e imitatori dell'opera' (pp. 408–9) for the influence of the *Othéa* on French literature of that day.

[4] James D. Gordon, *The Epistle of Othea to Hector . . . edited from the Harleian Manuscript 838* (Philadelphia, 1942). He suggests (p. xliv) that the translator possessed 'something less than an intimate knowledge of French'.

[5] The colophon reads: 'Thus endeth the C Hystories of Troye, translated

tributions of so early a date aroused sufficient interest to call
forth three separate English translations within the space of a
hundred years, so that on this basis, too, the *Othéa* must be
regarded as a work of considerable literary significance.

A brief word should, however, be said about the structure of
the *Othéa*.[1] Following a short Prologue (to be discussed later),
the work proper is divided into a hundred chapters or sections,
each comprising a Texte, a Glose, and an Allegorie. Save for the
first five, each Texte is formed of a single quatrain, the purpose
of these Textes being, according to Warner,[2] to 'serve as a
medium for instilling into the mind of the pupil as many moral
precepts or rules of behaviour, wrapped up in an allusion to
some story from mythology, from the history of Troy or, very
rarely, from other sources, without the least regard for chrono-
logical propriety'. In the Glose, the material of the Texte is
enlarged and explained; further, it is usually fortified by some
saying attributed to an ancient philosopher. The Allegorie con-
cludes each chapter. This concerns itself with the spiritual
implications of what has been set forth; it, too, receives con-
firmation from some 'authority', a quotation from a patristic or
later theological source, with a final verse from Holy Scripture.
This division of each section into three parts recalls the arrange-
ment of the text in the *Chapelet des vertus* (which we shall
return to later, p. xxviii). There each chapter is divided into
an 'exposition (definition of the virtue or vice), the simile
(identification of the virtue or vice with some animal or bird,
followed by quotations from the Fathers and philosophers), and
the exemplum (a story illustrative of the matter discussed)'.[3]
A very convenient summary of the *Othéa*, analysing the hundred
sections according to their concern with Narrative, Chivalric
Virtue, and Morality has been printed by Dr. James D.
Gordon.[4]

out of Frenche in to Englysshe, by me. R. W. ¶ Imprynted by me Robert
Wyer, dwellyng in S. Martyns parysshe, at charyng Crosse. at the sygne of
s. John Euangelist besyde the Duke of Suffolkes place' (*STC* 7272; PML
40646). See also Warner, *Othea*, pp. xli–xlii.

[1] For a thorough and detailed account of the structure of *Othea*, see
Gordon, pp. vii–xxix.   [2] *Othea*, pp. xix–xx.

[3] Curt F. Bühler, 'The *Fleurs de toutes vertus* and Christine de Pisan's
L'Épître d'Othéa', *PMLA* lxii (1947), 41.

[4] *Othea*, pp. ix–xiii; also Warner, p. xx.

DESCRIPTION OF THE ENGLISH MANUSCRIPTS

Three manuscripts of Stephen Scrope's version of the *Epistle of Othea* have come down to our day:

MS. H. 5 (James no. 208),[1] *St. John's College, Cambridge* (S)

Vellum, $11\frac{1}{4} \times 8$ inches, middle of the fifteenth century; 2 fly-leaves (first stuck to upper cover), folios 61, 2 fly-leaves (last stuck to lower cover). Slightly imperfect; $1-7^8$ (wants 7_8) 8^6; that gathering 8 is a ternion is certain since 8_{3-4} is a single sheet with the string in the middle.[2] The manuscript thus lacks f. 56, the *Othea* being on the present folios 1–60[a].

The manuscript is fully rubricated, initials have been supplied where needed and six miniatures of unusually high quality survive.[3] A few signatures (mostly cut away) and catchwords at the end of each quire. Writing space (ruled with prickings) is about $7\frac{1}{4} \times 5$ inches (on f. 44) with 28–29 lines to the full page. For the numerous manuscript entries and scribblings, see the description given by M. R. James. Bound in old stamped brown leather over boards.

The manuscript is very clearly and carefully written; the hand appears to be the same throughout, though beginning with the penultimate line on f. 35 there is a change in the orthography. Here begins the regular use of *thorn* and the much more fre-

---

[1] Montague Rhodes James, *A Descriptive Catalogue of the Manuscripts in the Library of St. John's College Cambridge* (Cambridge, 1913), pp. 238–40. The *Othea* ends on f. 60, not f. 61 as given by James. See also O. Elfrida Saunders, *English Illumination* (Florence, 1928), p. 119 and pl. 128; Fritz Saxl and Rudolf Wittkower, *British Art and the Mediterranean* (London, 1948), pl. 34, 5; Fritz Saxl and Hans Meier, *Verzeichnis astrologischer und mythologischer illustrierter Handschriften des lateinischen Mittelalters* (Heidelberg and London, 1915–53), iii. 426, and pl. XLVIII; etc.

[2] The collation according to James is: 2 fly-leaves (1 stuck to cover), 1^8-7^8 (wants 8) 8^8 (wants 1, 2), 2 fly-leaves. This suggests that *three* leaves are wanting at the end of the seventh and beginning of the eighth gatherings, whereas only one leaf of the *Othea* is lacking. Folio 57 bears the faint (old) signature 'hij' (or 8_2).

[3] According to Eric G. Millar, *English Illuminated Manuscripts of the XIVth and XVth Centuries* (Paris and Brussels, 1928, p. 38), the manuscript contains 'six pictures in good English style of the first half of the fifteenth century'. The St. John's manuscript is no. 303 (p. 92) of Millar's list and is illustrated on plate 96. See also Appendix B.

quent appearance of *yogh*, both of which had been sparingly
employed before. From then on, too, a stroke over *o* and *u*
serves for an omitted *i* or *n*, which was previously rare. In
ff. 30[b] through 35 the scribe writes a heavy flourish over *th*, *ch*,
ll, etc., which had previously been but lightly crossed. With the
frequent use of *thorn* after f. 35, the opportunity for a decorative
stroke or flourish on *th* was diminished, and perhaps in con-
sequence the practice was largely abandoned elsewhere. There
seems to be no certain evidence, however, that more than one
scribe worked on this manuscript.[1]

MS. M 775. *The Pierpont Morgan Library,*
New York (M)

Vellum, $9\frac{3}{4} \times 6\frac{3}{4}$ inches, middle of the fifteenth century; a
composite volume (*Sammelband*) of 320 folios, the *Epistle of
Othea* appearing on the folios now numbered 200–74. Slightly
imperfect; 1–9^8 10^4 11^2, wanting three leaves, viz. $1_{1, 4-5}$ (or the
first, fourth, and fifth leaves of the *Othea*); f. 205 is torn, with
loss of miniature and some text.

The folios containing the *Othea* are carefully written by a
professional scribe, fully rubricated and with initials supplied.
The volume now contains three miniatures, nearly identical with
those in the St. John's manuscript and similar to those in the
French MS. Laud Misc. 570 of the Bodleian Library.[2] No
signatures; catchwords at the end of each quire. Writing space
(ruled with prickings) is $7\frac{1}{4} \times 4$ inches (f. 206); 28 lines. English
stamped calf (*c.* 1545), with the motto ('Ich dien') of Edward VI
as Prince of Wales (his arms having been removed).

[1] That professional scribes could write in a great number of amazingly
different styles of writing is well known, and this may sometimes account for
the varying 'hands' often identified in a single (otherwise homogeneous)
manuscript. See, for example, the facsimile edition (with introductory
study) of Leonhard Wagner's hundred different hands by Carl Wehmer,
*Leonhard Wagner. Proba centum scripturarum; ein Augsburger Schrift-
musterbuch aus dem Beginn des 16. Jahrhunderts* (Leipzig and Frankfurt,
1963).
[2] On the miniatures in the Laud manuscript and in the English ones
related to it, see Rosemond Tuve, 'Notes on the Virtues and Vices', *Journal
of the Warburg and Courtauld Institutes*, xxvi (1963), 264–303, and xxvii
(1964), 42–72 (especially pp. 264 and 281 ff.). M 775 was clearly mutilated
by some one wanting the pictures, which originally probably numbered six,
as in S.

As Dr. A. I. Doyle has shown,[1] the text of the *Othea* must have been written before the early owner, Sir John Astley (d. 1486), was created a Knight of the Garter (nominated 21 March 1461/2),[2] since his armorial bearings (lacking the Garter) occur on f. 274^a.

For the contents of M 775,[3] see my 'Sir John Paston's *Grete Booke*, a Fifteenth-Century "Best Seller"', *Modern Language Notes*, lvi (1941), 345–51, together with the works cited there and by Doyle, loc. cit.

MS. Longleat 253, Collection of the Marquis of Bath (L)

Vellum, $9\frac{1}{2} \times 7$ inches, middle of the fifteenth century, folios 95. Imperfect: 1^6 2^8 3^6 4–14^8, wanting 13 leaves, viz. 1_2, 2_5, 6_{1-8}, 12_2, and 14_{4-5}. The manuscript therefore lacks folios 2 (blank), 11, 37–44, 86, and 105–6, the *Othea* being found on folios 2–75^b of the modern numbering.

Written in one hand, very neat and regular, of which Warner (p. ix) says: 'it is hardly the hand of a professional book-scribe, the type being that more commonly found in correspondence and business documents of the period'. There is no ornamentation, spaces being left for rubrics (headings and Biblical quotations), initials, and (occasional) miniatures.[4] The manuscript thus appears to have been left unfinished. Original signatures,

---

[1] 'The Work of a late Fifteenth-Century English Scribe, William Ebesham', *Bulletin of the John Rylands Library*, xxxix (1957), 306–7.

[2] George E. Cokayne, *The Complete Peerage of England, Scotland, Ireland, Great Britain and the United Kingdom* [ed. Vicary Gibbs] (London, 1910–), ii. 543 (*in* Appendix B. The Order of the Garter, pp. 527–96).

[3] See also Seymour de Ricci and William J. Wilson, *Census of Medieval and Renaissance Manuscripts in the United States and Canada* (New York, 1935–40), ii. 1501–2, and Supplement (ed. C. U. Faye and W. H. Bond; New York, 1962), pp. 356–7. The manuscript is also noted by Francis L. Utley (*The Crooked Rib* (Columbus, Ohio, 1944), p. 312), Rossell H. Robbins (*Secular Lyrics of the XIVth and XVth Centuries* (Oxford, 1952), p. xxxi), Rosemond Tuve (op. cit., p. 282), and *The Pierpont Morgan Library, Report of the Activities and Acquisitions of the Library from 1930 through 1935* (New York, 1937), pp. 25–6 and 91–2.

[4] A space has been left, presumably for a miniature, on folios 2, 4^b, 7^b, 8^b, and 11. Assuming that a similar space was left on the folio now wanting (i.e. sig. 2_5), it was apparently planned that the manuscript would receive six miniatures, no doubt corresponding to those preserved in the St. John's manuscript and in the French Laud Misc. 570. It seems improbable that a manuscript in such an unfinished state would have been suitable as a presentation copy.

each quire being cited as a quaternion even when only a ternion; early arabic numbering on the verso of the last leaf in each gathering; no catchwords. Writing space (ruled with prickings) is about 6 × 3¼ inches; 31–36 lines to the page. There are a good many scribblings of no importance for the text, the most significant of these being cited by Warner (pp. x–xi). Bound in nineteenth-century dark-brown leather, with the remains of the old parchment cover preserved as the first leaf in the volume.

The second text (or texts) in the volume consists of rhymed couplets, in which love is likened to a tree, together with a debate between Reason and Love. This portion is incomplete at the end. The couplets are clearly not original compositions but copies, for on f. 78 (lines 13/14) the rhyme is 'appyltree: have' which suggests that one or more lines have been omitted by the scribe.[1] Similarly, on f. 95ᵇ a line is written in the lower margin below the ruling (with proper insertion marks) which supplies the text omitted before the last line on that page, as the rhyme makes clear.

It seems likely that other manuscripts of Scrope's translation must once have existed, namely: Scrope's working copy (as postulated below); the actual presentation copy to Fastolf (the 'unfinished' Longleat one could hardly have served for this purpose);[2] the similar presentation copy to Buckingham (unless this was the St. John's manuscript, for which there is no evidence); and probably the copy destined for the 'High Princess', since the Morgan text was written for Sir John Astley. Sir John Paston[3] certainly owned one copy of the *Othea* (if not two),

---

[1] Thus, lines 7–8 of f. 83ᵇ have the rhyme 'dede: bere' (the latter rhyming with the 'here' of l. 9). In l. 6 (up) of f. 84, 'hevy' has been corrected (by interlineation) to 'besy', and (f. 86, l. 9) 'dede' to 'dere' (to rhyme with 'there'). The poem is listed in Brown–Robbins *Index*, no. *65, and in the *Supplement* (Robbins–Cutler, no. 3553.8). See also Warner, p. ix.

[2] The presence of a second—and unrelated—text in Longleat MS. 253 seems also to argue against the assumption that it was the actual copy intended for presentation to Fastolf. One would expect that Scrope, in offering his translation as a gift to his penurious step-father, would want to present him with a volume that contained only his own work—and at that only the *Othea*, since he would wish to save any other work for separate presentation (and hoped-for largess).

[3] A copy was listed in the inventory of Sir John Paston's English books (Gairdner, op. cit. vi. 66). William Ebesham had written a copy for inclusion in Sir John Paston's 'Grete Booke' (*Paston Letters*, v. 1–5), and this

which cannot be identified with any of the manuscripts noted above.

THE DEDICATIONS AND DATE OF TRANSLATION

As Warner (p. xix) has pointed out, 'it was Christine's habit to send her works with a separate dedicatory preface to her several patrons as new-year's gifts for no other reason probably than the hope of a tangible acknowledgment'. Thus it was with the *Épître d'Othéa*,[1] and we now have copies of this work with prefatory lines addressed to King Charles VI, Louis (Duc d'Orléans), Philippe le Hardi (Duc de Bourgogne), and Jean (Duc de Berry). Scrope, of course, was not likely to have been aware of this; but (doubtless) with the same objective in mind as Christine, he dedicated his translation to three different persons, though probably not simultaneously.

The prologue in the Longleat manuscript is printed in Appendix A and provides much information, which Sir George Warner skilfully exploited in his entirely admirable Introduction; to this the reader is urged to refer. In this preface Stephen Scrope presents his translation to Sir John Fastolf (then aged about 'lx yeeres'), a labour which he had undertaken at his step-father's specific 'commaundement'. There is no reason to question the truth of this statement, since Fastolf was necessarily familiar with the facts. The old warrior returned from France about Michaelmas 1439 at the age (apparently) of fifty-nine.[2] If we assume that it was in the following year, or very shortly thereafter, that Scrope made his translation, this would accord reasonably closely with the statement made by Scrope in his prologue. Such an assumption would place the translation *circa* 1440; it was certainly not made after 5 November 1459, the date of Fastolf's death.

copy may—or may not—have been identical with the one noted in the Inventory. Compare my *Dicts*, pp. xlv–xlvi, and Doyle, 'Ebesham', p. 302.

[1] For manuscripts with these dedications, see Mombello, *Studi francesi*, xxv. 1–9.

[2] 'His retirement is generally fixed in 1440, but there is evidence of his being in Maine in the following year' (Warner, *Othea*, p. xxix, who goes on to point out that, on 12 May 1441, Fastolf was granted a pension of £20 yearly for his past services). McFarlane (see p. xi, n. 5) states that Fastolf returned to England in the autumn of 1439.

The *Othea* in the St. John's manuscript is dedicated to Humphrey Stafford,[1] who was created Duke of Buckingham on 14 September 1444 and was slain at the battle of Northampton on 10 July 1460.[2] This dedication must consequently be fixed within these limits. The versified prologue unfortunately provides no further clues, since (with only a few, very minor, adaptations) it is an almost literal translation from the French original. The statements[3] made therein thus apply to the Duc de Berry and Christine de Pisan rather than to the Duke of Buckingham and Stephen Scrope. The surviving English manuscript with this dedication may (or may not) have been the original presentation copy; either way, if Millar's judgement[4] be correct that the manuscript belongs to the first half of the fifteenth century, Scrope must have written this preface (to an obviously completed text) early in Humphrey's career as duke.

If Scrope had originally made his translation for Buckingham, one must assume that the translator made two deliberate misstatements in the preface to the Longleat manuscript, both quite needlessly: namely, that the translation was made at Fastolf's request and that Fastolf had 'lx. yeeres growyn vpon [him] at this tyme'. It seems more reasonable to assume that Scrope, having met with Fastolf's customary lack of generosity, wished to try his luck elsewhere—and thus wrote out the dedication to Buckingham. This would then represent Scrope's second prologue.

Who the 'hye princesse' of the dedication in the Morgan manuscript may have been—and how this version of the preface found its way into the manuscript written for Sir John Astley[5]—

---

[1] Perhaps about the time of this dedication, Buckingham may have had a brief (but threatening) encounter with the greatest prose writer of that day. Sir Thomas Malory was accused of lying 'in ambush with other malefactors for the purpose of murdering' the duke on 4 January 1450 (Eugène Vinaver, *The Works of Sir Thomas Malory* (Oxford, 1947), I. xvi).

[2] There is a good biographical sketch of him in *DNB* liii, 451–3.

[3] The text of the French dedication to the Duc de Berry is printed *in toto* from MS. Laud Misc. 570 (ff. 24–25) by Mombello, pp. 7–8.

[4] Cf. p. xiv, n. 3, above.

[5] It is possible, of course, that the 'High Princess' permitted Astley to borrow her manuscript in order to have a copy of it made for his volume. Alternatively, the version with this dedication may have been the one released by Scrope 'for publication' and would then have been found in the Paston manuscript(s).

must remain a mystery. So far as is known, only three members of the higher aristocracy[1] played a part in Scrope's life. He had sought, on at least two occasions,[2] to enter the service of the 'Good Duke Humphrey' of Gloucester,[3] but this nobleman's wife (the notorious Eleanor Cobham)[4] was hardly a suitable candidate for such a dedication. Scrope had had some dealings with the 'Kingmaker' (Richard Neville, Earl of Warwick),[5] and Anne Beauchamp, his wife, outlived Scrope by nearly a score of years. Buckingham's widow, Anne Neville, lived until 20 September 1480—but neither of these Annes was particularly noted as a patron of the arts. Lastly, a third Anne might be suggested, namely Buckingham's eldest daughter, with whom Scrope may have been acquainted before 1462 (the *terminus ante quem* of this copy of the translation, as determined by M 775). By a second marriage[6] Anne became the wife of Sir Reynold de Cobham of Sterborough ('Lord Cobham', 1460–71),[7] with

---

[1] For biographies of most of the individuals here named see the *Dictionary of National Biography* (= *DNB*).

[2] Cf. Poulett Scrope, *Castle Combe*, pp. 266 and 270, and Schofield, *Dicts*, pp. 11–12.

[3] Dedicating the same book to more than one person sometimes got the author into hot water. Note Pier Candido Decembrio's difficulties with Humphrey of Gloucester concerning his translation of Plato's *Republic*; see Roberto Weiss, *Humanism in England during the Fifteenth Century* (Oxford, 2nd edn., 1957), p. 55.

[4] For Eleanor, Duchess of Gloucester, see Kenneth H. Vickers, *Humphrey, Duke of Gloucester: A Biography* (London, 1907), *passim*.

[5] According to Poulett Scrope (pp. 285–6), Stephen Scrope, on 12 November 1466 'sold to the Earl of Warwick the wardship and marriage of his only son and heir, John Scrope, then about six years of age'. Furthermore, 'the Earl of Warwick was the lord paramount of [Scrope's manor of Oxendon], as held of the honour of Gloucester'. Finally, it is noted (p. 287) that Stephen had 'a will deposited in the hands of the Earl of Warwick'. These records suggest that Stephen Scrope had more than a passing acquaintance with Warwick.

[6] William B. D. D. Turnbull (*Compota domestica familiarum de Bukingham et d'Angoulême* (Edinburgh, 1836), p. iii) has a note on 'Anne, eldest daughter of the Duke, who was married first to Aubrey de Vere, and afterwards to Sir Thomas Cobham, Knight'. *DNB* liii. 453, concurs with this statement.

[7] According to *The Complete Peerage* (iii. 354–5), Anne Stafford's second marriage was to 'Sir Reynold de Cobham, of Sterborough Castle'. The facts seem to be these: Apparently the Sir Reynold who died in 1446 had two sons, of whom the elder was Sir Reynold, who had a daughter Margaret, Countess of Westmorland. Sir Reynold (the son) died in 1441–2, and the family estates were settled by Margaret's grandfather 'on her and her issue,

whose family Scrope had long been acquainted,[1] since Scrope's
lands in Kent were held of the father, also Sir Reynold (until
the latter's death in 1446). However, until 1462[2] Anne was still
married to Aubrey de Vere, the heir apparent to the Earl of
Oxford, who was executed (with his father) shortly after
Edward IV's accession. But this is all highly speculative—and
the identity of the 'high princess' remains problematical.[3]

From this short survey it becomes evident that Stephen
Scrope must have translated the *Épître d'Othéa* between 1440
and 1459,[4] with the very strong probability that the work was
undertaken in the earliest years of the first decade.

RELATIONSHIP OF THE MANUSCRIPTS AND CHOICE OF TEXT

The variant readings and the remarks made in the notes will
make it clear that of the three surviving manuscripts of the
Othea none has been copied from another. At this place it will
no doubt suffice to point to just a few of the special faults in the
several texts to establish this fact beyond question. L alone omits
all the Biblical quotations (but see note to 69/7–8) and has

with rem. to her uncle, Sir Thomas de Cobham'. This would seem to
establish the fact that the name of Sir Reynold's younger son was Thomas.
Margaret appears to have died in 1460 and was succeeded by her 'uncle and
h., being 2nd but 1st surv. s. and h. of Sir Reynold de C.' (in the Cokayne-
Gibbs shorthand). However, his name is here given as Sir Reynold, and he
married Anne Stafford. To explain this apparent contradiction, one could
perhaps assume that, though Sir Reynold's younger son was originally
named Thomas, he took the name of Reynold (there had always been a Sir
Reynold since the thirteenth century) when he succeeded to the estates.
His sister was, of course, the Eleanor Cobham who was the wife of Duke
Humphrey of Gloucester.

[1] Cf. Poulett Scrope, pp. 273–5, and Schofield, p. 15.

[2] Since she married Cobham fairly soon after the death of her first
husband, one may infer that she had known him quite well for some time.

[3] It seems almost certain that this dedication is the third in point of date.
One would think it most unlikely that Scrope would dare to dedicate this
work to the powerful Buckingham *after* having already dedicated it to a lady,
however exalted in rank.

[4] P. G. C. Campbell ('Christine de Pisan en Angleterre', *Revue de littéra-
ture comparée*, v (1925), 666) suggests that the translation of the *Othéa*
preceded that of the *Dicts*. Schofield (*Dicts*, p. 35) also dates Scrope's trans-
lation *circa* 1440. If Scrope had translated the *Othéa* after the *Dicts* (1450),
one might expect the philosopher quotations, drawn from the *Dits moraulx*,
to be more correct.

special *lacunae*[1] at 7/24, 9/30–10/1, 22/26–27, 74/31–75/1, 106/32–107/2, and 119/13–14. M, in turn, omits at 55/11–13, 99/13–14, 100/13–14, 105/21–22, 108/24, and 117/9–10. The following omissions and other slips are peculiar to S: 13/21, 65/13, 72/28, 80/20, and 85/14, as well as many of the other words and phrases which are supplied with parentheses throughout the text (as printed below).

Furthermore, each manuscript shows mistakes or misreadings which it has in common with one or the other of the extant copies:

> L = M (S is correct): 11/23, 32/14, 49/17, 62/6, 63/14, 86/7, 104/11,[2] and 104/28.
>
> L = S (M is correct): 31/12, 41/4, 44/26, 69/1–3, 74/15, 90/27, 100/5, and 118/18.
>
> S = M[3] (L is correct): 23/15, 24/10, 27/7, 37/28, 66/30, 76/2, and 82/21.

As this comparison shows, each manuscript uniquely has certain correct readings, according to the evidence afforded by the French original.

What may be deduced from these facts? The following reconstruction appears to provide the only plausible solution. Scrope must, of course, have had a 'working copy' of his translation, and this autograph copy he retained, entering into it (perhaps even from time to time) such corrections and emenda-

---

[1] Some years ago, I suggested that 'the text of the Longleat manuscript is further removed from the French original than that found in the two manuscripts not dedicated to Fastolf' ('The Revisions and Dedications of the *Epistle of Othea*', *Anglia*, lxxvi (1958), 270). However, the present edition shows that most of the many and serious *lacunae* in L are not the fault of Scrope (later corrected) but probably the slips of the copyist. L, of course, also omits the rubrics (Texte, Glose, and Allegorie) and lacks the miniatures.

[2] The example cited under 104/11 is a curious one. There was, apparently, an omission in the holograph copy (so L), which was filled in by conjecture in M and with reference to the French text by S. In connection with the examples cited here, one should also note a significant number of instances where S has the correct reading, and L and M (though differing from one another) are both incorrect: 30/8, 36/22, 70/29, 81/15, 101/3, 115/18, 117/6, etc.

[3] The miniatures in M and S are, of course, 'related' to each other and to those in the Laud manuscript. Further, S and M often have identical slips in the Biblical quotations (cf. 25/16–17, 27/25, etc.; in 118/20 they both (following Laud) omit the quotation). It will be recalled that both miniatures and quotations were not supplied in L.

tions as occurred to him. There is no evidence to show, as I once suggested,[1] that a deliberate and systematic review of Scrope's translation was ever undertaken by him or by anyone else. When a fair copy of the text was wanted, Scrope's autograph[2] was given to a professional scribe (with whatever prologue was appropriate). The scribe would then make his copy, selecting such readings (either Scrope's original wording or his alteration) as he judged to be the best ones. Clearly, the copyist also made his own errors and omissions; on occasion he was doubtless further responsible for still other emendations or deteriorations. The extent to which scribes could make free with their prototypes (and in practice actually did do so)[3] is a subject which has not been sufficiently investigated, but it is quite certain that they allowed themselves considerable liberty, sometimes bolstered by a very high opinion of their own critical talents.

In this fashion, then, the original presentation copies for Fastolf (F), for Buckingham (B), and for the Princess (P) had their origin. But we cannot assume, with any degree of certainty, that the extant *text* of the Longleat manuscript corresponds to that of F, or that that in the Morgan manuscript is identical with P—though the St. John's copy may be the actual presentation one (B).

As has been suggested above (p. xvii), the Longleat manuscript clearly is not F, because it is both so unfinished and because the volume contains a second text (an integral part of the volume) almost certainly *not* an original composition by Scrope[4] nor on

---

[1] Cf. my *Dicts*, p. xli; K. B. McFarlane, 'William Worcester: A Preliminary Survey', *Studies Presented to Sir Hilary Jenkinson* (London, 1957), pp. 196–221; and my *Revisions and Dedications*.

[2] That the three manuscripts are closely related and descend from a common ancestor seems to be indicated by the slips they all have in common, viz. Marcisus (27/15), Percival (for Perseus), Oan (for Pan; Chapter XXVI), Colus (for Eolus: Chapter LXXIX), etc. These errors may be safely attributed to Scrope himself and go to show that neither he nor the scribes of S, M, and L were sufficiently well read to make the necessary corrections.

[3] See my *The Fifteenth-Century Book: The Scribes, the Printers, the Decorators* (Philadelphia, 1960), pp. 37–8 and applicable notes.

[4] The subject matter of the second text is completely alien to Scrope, so far as we know his interests and character, as indicated by his writings and biography. Though this poem may be of no great literary value, the verse is infinitely better than what we find in the *Othea*.

a topic in any way appropriate for Fastolf. Similarly, the Morgan manuscript was written for—or at least came into the possession of—Sir John Astley before 1462, and forms part of a composite volume in which other tracts (possibly written out by the same scribe),[1] quite inappropriate for a lady, were included. This, then, could hardly be the original P. Lastly, there is nothing to show that the St. John's *Othea* is actually B.

In conclusion, it seems impossible to determine whether L was copied from F, M from P, or S from B,[2] nor whether the extant texts (if so copied) correspond exactly to their archetypes. To the contrary, the three manuscripts which have come down to our day may well have been written out afresh from the holograph, provided with that dedication believed to be most suitable and supplied (in the case of S and M)[3] with miniatures copied from those found in the French original. Such considerations would suggest a *stemma* as shown opposite.

The choice of a manuscript to provide the basic text did not prove to be particularly difficult. L could be eliminated at once,[4] since it was easily the most corrupt and obviously the

---

[1] Like the Paston 'Grete Booke', this volume was obviously designed (as a unit) to be a suitable item for a gentleman's library. The hand which wrote the *Othea* appears also to have written the *Sailing Directions* (ff. 131–8) and possibly the English *Secreta secretorum* (ff. 139–95). The decorative initials throughout the volume seem certainly to be the work of a single artist.

[2] So far as I am aware, there is no thorough study available of the extent of the practice, in fifteenth-century England, of owners lending their manuscripts for the purpose of having copies made of them. Is it likely that so mighty a person as the Duke of Buckingham would simply hand over a manuscript, dedicated to himself, to a commercial scribe for the purpose of copying it? Conceivably, a Sir John Astley might have persuaded a 'high princess' to part with her manuscript (if he knew of its existence) long enough to have a transcript of it made for his personal use. But is it probable that the scribe of L could have persuaded the notoriously tight-fisted and suspicious Fastolf to lend his manuscript even temporarily? In Italy, of course, the humanists were usually very generous with their codices—but to what extent such lending of manuscripts for copying purposes was prevalent in England would seem to be a topic worth investigating.

[3] The origin of the miniatures is traced back to BM Harley 4431 and BN fr. 606 by Rosemond Tuve, *Journal of Warburg and Courtauld Institutes*, xxvi. 281–2. For a general discussion of the illustrations of Christine's works, see Lucie Schaefer, 'Die Illustrationen zu den Handschriften der Christine de Pisan', *Marburger Jahrbuch für Kunstwissenschaft*, x (1937), 119–208 (without mention of the Laud or Scrope manuscripts).

[4] It is convenient, of course, to have the entire Longleat text in print in Warner's edition.

least complete of the surviving manuscripts, wanting some 15 per cent of the text. Of the remaining two S was slightly the better and was somewhat more complete than M, preserving also the important dedicatory lines. The text of the present edition has, therefore, been set up from MS. H. 5 of St. John's College, Cambridge, with such corrections from the other manuscripts as were made imperative by a comparison with the French original.

Scrope's autograph

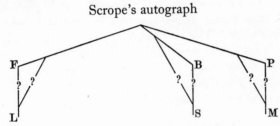

THE SOURCES AND THE TRANSLATION

The French original just referred to is, of course, the direct and immediate source of the English *Othea*. By this original is here meant that French manuscript of the *Épître d'Othéa* from which Stephen Scrope made his translation. In the hope of identifying this codex, I scrutinized thirty-two[1] of the forty-three surviving French manuscripts. This investigation, which is set forth in detail elsewhere, resulted in the conclusion that the particular manuscript[2] that Scrope must have used had not

[1] Twenty-nine such manuscripts were listed in my *Fastolf's Manuscripts* (p. 124), and three more were examined after publication: BN fr. 5026; Stockholm, Kungl. Bibl., Vu 22; and Cambridge, Fitzwilliam Museum, MS. CFM 22.

[2] Since Scrope's translation, as represented by S, was obviously based on a manuscript having the dedication to the Duc de Berry, the three surviving manuscripts with this preface (Laud Misc. 570, BN fr. 12438, and BN nouv. acq. fr. 6458) could easily be judged to be the most likely candidates. However, the search could not be confined to these three since it was quite possible that dedications might have been switched about, with the result that a manuscript with the body of the text closest to Scrope's exemplar might have had one of the other dedications. For full details, see my *Fastolf's Manuscripts*, where (p. 125) the French manuscripts with the dedication to Jean de Berry are listed. Mombello (p. 6) cites only two such manuscripts, omitting MS. fr. 12438. On this, see Henri Omont, *Catalogue général des*

INTRODUCTION

come down to this day, but that one so close to it as to justify
calling it a 'sister-manuscript' is now MS. Laud Misc. 570 of
the Bodleian Library.¹ This manuscript was either copied from
the one used by the English translator, or both these manu-
scripts had a common parent. In any event, Laud Misc. 570,
though once owned by Fastolf,² was not the French text which
Scrope had used but was sufficiently close to it to provide a
constant check on Scrope's translation.³

The ultimate sources⁴ of the French and English texts of
Othea are, of course, those used by Christine de Pisan in com-
piling her work.⁵ The texts which provided her with the bulk
of the information and details she needed were correctly
identified many years ago in a masterly study by P. G. C.
Campbell.⁶ The chief sources (lesser ones will be pointed out
in the notes) may be roughly listed thus:

manuscrits français [*de la Bibliothèque Nationale*]. *Ancien supplément français*
(Paris, 1895–6), ii. 524.

¹ *Catalogi codicum manuscriptorum Bibliothecae Bodleianae* (pt. 1–3;
Oxford, 1853–85), ii. 408–9 (with date 1450). From a smudged photo-
copy, I had suggested, quite erroneously (*Fastolf's Manuscripts*, p. 127,
n. 27), that the date might be 1454. Dr. R. W. Hunt kindly assures me that
the date is undoubtedly 1450. It is not unlikely, then, that Laud Misc. 570
was copied from Scrope's archetype *after* he had completed the translation
of it.

² This was clearly established by Kathleen Chesney, 'Two Manuscripts of
Christine de Pisan', *Medium Ævum*, i (1932), 35–41. Professor Chesney
correctly states (p. 38): 'Moreover there is the final inscription with the date
1450, and this was evidently contemporary with the execution of the
manuscript.'

³ It is probable that Robert Wyer made his translation from the edition
printed at Paris by Philippe Le Noir in 1522.

⁴ The final account of the sources of the *Othéa*, its structure, and its place
in literary history must await the publication of the critical French text,
promised to us by Dr. Gianni Mombello.

⁵ It is, of course, common knowledge that Christine borrowed freely from
many works and was not above copying her own words. Compare the notes
to the present text and Tuve, p. 297, n. 55; my *Fleurs de toutes vertus*, p. 40;
Christine's 'Le Débat de deux amants' (*Œuvres poétiques de Christine de
Pisan* (SATF, ed. Maurice Roy; Paris, 1886–96), ii. 40–109, especially the
notes, pp. 306–7); Gustav Gröber, *Geschichte der mittelfranzösischen Lit-
eratur* (Berlin and Leipzig, 1933–7), ii. 15, 17, 23, 24, etc.; Mathilde Laigle,
Le Livre des trois vertus (Paris, 1912), pp. 74–103; Suzanne Solente's notes
to her edition of Christine's *Le Livre de la mutacion de fortune* (Paris,
1954).

⁶ See his important study cited in n. 3 on p. xii, above, and Ghisalberti's
comments (pp. 74–76 in the article listed in the next note).

Ovide moralisé (for mythology)[1]
Histoire ancienne jusqu'à César (for history and mythology)[2]
Thomas de Hibernia, *Manipulus florum* (for quotations from Christian writers)[3]
Dits moraulx des philosophes (for quotations from the ancient philosophers)[4]
Flores Bibliorum (for Biblical extracts)[5]

To these sources, I have been able to make one significant

[1] Compare Bossuat, nos. 5311–18, 6990–8, and 7987–8: Fausto Ghisalberti, 'L' "Ovidius Moralizatus" di Pierre Bersuire', *Studj romanzi*, xxiii (1933), 5–136; and the early printed editions of the prose *Ovide*: Bruges, Mansion, 1484; Paris, Vérard, 1 March 1493/4; and Paris, Vérard [c. 1507]. See also the note on this text in the *Catalogue of Books Printed in the XVth Century now in the British Museum* (London, 1908–62), ix. 134, all three editions being in the BM. Manuscripts and printed editions of the chief source-books are listed in the Bibliography, below.

[2] Bossuat, nos. 3797–9 and 7833–4. For a recent and highly valuable addition to the bibliography on the *Hist. anc.*, with special reference to BM MS. Additional 19669, see David J. A. Ross, 'The History of Macedon in the "Histoire ancienne jusqu'à César"; Sources and Compositional Method', *Classica et Mediaevalia*, xxiv (1963), 181–231. See also his *Alexander Historiatus* (cf. note 4 below), pp. 18–20, and Solente's *Mutacion*, i. lxvi. Machaut (*Font. amour.*, line 2695) cites the 'Istoire des Rommains', apparently the continuation of the *Hist. anc.* now usually called the *Faits des Romains* (Bossuat, nos. 3800–15, etc.; for Machaut, see notes to Chapter LX). Christine herself praises these texts in her *Enseignemens moraux*, no. 78 (*Œuvres*, iii. 39).

[3] For the sake of tradition and convenience, the *Manipulus florum* is here assigned to Thomas de Hibernia, though his authorship of the work is doubtful. It is now thought probable that this compilation was begun (and largely completed) by John Walleys and only finished by Hibernicus. On this see Berthold L. Ullman, 'Joseph Lang and his Anthologies' (reprint from the *Festschrift* for John G. Kunstmann, 1959, p. 2), and Robert A. Pratt, 'Jankyn's Book of Wikked Wyves', *Annuale mediaevale*, iii (1962), 17–20. For a note on the *editio princeps*, see my 'The Two Issues of the First Edition of the *Manipulus florum*', *Gutenberg Jahrbuch 1953*, pp. 69–72.

[4] For short accounts of this work, see my *The Dicts and Sayings of the Philosophers*, pp. ix–xiii, and David J. A. Ross, *Alexander Historiatus: A Guide to Medieval Illustrated Alexander Literature* (London, 1963), pp. 7–8, with notes. The French text was printed by Robert Eder, 'Tignonvillana inedita', *Romanische Forschungen*, xxxiii (1915), 851–1022.

[5] Cf. Campbell, *Othéa*, pp. 169–70, Ullman, loc. cit., F. Stegmüller, *Repertorium Biblicum* (Madrid, 1950–61), no 8128. I have consulted the BM editions of: Antwerp, 1567; Antwerp, 1568; and Dillingen, 1574. The extracts are gathered under such headings as Castitas, Fides, Oratio, Peccatum, Sapientia, and this work (or some other like it) supplied Christine with her Biblical quotations.

addition,[1] as well as providing further information concerning the history of the legend which attributes to the apostles the formation of the Creed.[2] This new source is a French text of the late fourteenth century,[3] based on the Italian *Fiore di virtù*,[4] for which the name *Chapelet des vertus (CdV)* has been suggested and is here used. Further study of this text has shown that Christine, in writing the *Othéa*, was even more dependent on it than was at first apparent. The degree of this dependence will be more graphically set forth in the notes to the text. It may here be pointed out, however, that in certain chapters of the *Othéa* (for example II, IV, XVII, XVIII, XXI) the same philosophical, theological, and Biblical extracts will be found together as in the comparable section of the *CdV*. There are an even greater number of instances where *Othéa* and the *CdV*, in parallel sections, share the same patristic and Biblical quotations (thus: VI, XII, XX, XXII, LIV, LX, XC, etc.).[5] This could hardly be coincidence. Finally, as has already been suggested (p. xiii), the quite comparable structure of the *CdV* may well have influenced the form which Christine's *Othéa* ultimately assumed.

It is to be regretted that, in the notes, not every quotation or reference has been traced to its source—but, as is well known, the citations of medieval writers are not invariably correct and, even when most explicitly set forth, cannot always be depended on. There remain, therefore, a number of unlocated 'waifs and

---

[1] For Christine's use of a common proverb, see my 'Wirk alle thyng by conseil', *Speculum*, xxiv (1949), 412.

[2] Curt F. Bühler, 'The Apostles and the Creed', *Speculum*, xxviii (1953), 335–9.

[3] See my 'The *Fleurs de toutes vertus* and Christine de Pisan's *L'Épître d'Othéa*', *PMLA* lxii (1947), 32–44, and the additional note 'The *Fleurs de toutes vertus*', *PMLA* lxiv (1949), 600–1. A further note on this source is in my 'Christine de Pisan and a Saying Attributed to Socrates', *Philological Quarterly*, xxxiii (1954), 418–20.

[4] Surely it is a mere coincidence that the *Fiore di virtù* was extremely popular in Venice, where Christine was born (cf. her *Lavision*, 149/27); but it is interesting to note that, according to Lessing J. Rosenwald's compilation (*The Florentine Fior di Virtu of 1491* (Washington, 1953), pp. xxiv–xxix), twenty-four editions of this work were printed there between 1470 and 1501. On the *Fiore*, see also the note to 9/25. Christine praises Venice in her *Mutacion* (lines 4753–826; Solente, ii. 19–21).

[5] Occasionally one also finds the identical philosopher's apophthegm and Biblical extract in parallel sections of the *CdV* and the *Othéa*. For examples see notes to Chapters III, V, XIX.

strays', awaiting a more erudite scholar than the present editor to identify them.

In 1904, Sir George Warner[1] concluded that Scrope's 'rendering of Christine de Pisan's French may claim on the whole to be fairly well done,' and this opinion is more than confirmed by the present text. Warner's judgement was based on the very inferior copy preserved in the Longleat manuscript, with its careless omissions, atrocious orthography, and senseless misreadings—a major part of which, as is now clear, was the fault of the scribe and not of the translator. That Scrope occasionally misunderstood the French text, that he was insufficiently well read to correct certain obvious and elementary slips in his exemplar[2] or to remove his own errors when he reviewed his work, that his excessively literal rendering of the French into English (frequently word for word) sometimes destroyed the sense—all this cannot be questioned and is amply set forth in the annotation. But some of these faults were those common to his age (and may even be discovered in the Wyer translation of a century later); others may be attributed to his inexperience as a translator. With all its faults, Scrope's translation can be judged to be closer to the original and more attractively phrased than the version now connected with the name of Anthony Babyngton (if, indeed, it is not actually the work of a person so named).[3]

PRINCIPLES OF EDITING

A. *The Text*

The text of the *Othea* has been printed according to the Society's practice. The typical fifteenth-century flourishes over *ll*, *h*, *ch*, *th*, etc., and the tails on *m*, *n*, *g*, *p*, and the like, have been ignored. Exception to this rule has been made in the case of the flourished *r*, used finally and elsewhere to represent *re*, and this is so printed. All contractions have been silently

---

[1] *Othea*, p. xxxix. On p. xxxiii, however, Warner states that Scrope's style 'is so involved that in places it is hardly intelligible'.

[2] See p. xxiii, n. 2, above.

[3] Gordon (*Othea*, pp. xxxi, xxxvii) expresses some hesitation as to the authorship of this translation. 'Whatever claim he [Anthony Babyngton] may have to the translation edited here attaches only to the copy in the Harleian MS.' (pp. lxii–lxiii).

expanded, without the use of italics. Capitalization and punctuation are editorial.

The variant readings naturally record every textual variation found in the manuscripts. Every variant spelling of a proper name is recorded once—and but once only, this being judged sufficient to establish the existence of such a form. Such variations are numerous and display, if anything, little more than the ingenuity of the scribes in devising new spellings or a zealous desire on their parts to depart from the established norms. However, every variant spelling is again cited in the Index of Names, as a possible help towards identifying unfamiliar forms not only in the present text but in Middle English literature in general.

In the *variae lectiones*, asterisks are used to mark words or forms that may be presumed to have dialectal or orthographical significance. Such variants are noted only occasionally, but sufficiently often to remind the reader of the (often habitual) appearance of such forms in the other manuscripts.

No linguistic analysis of the *Othea* is here undertaken, for several reasons. First of all, the peculiarities of the three surviving manuscripts are such that whatever analyses might be attempted would expose the dialectal characteristics of the several scribes rather than those of the author. It has been pointed out elsewhere[1] that, in view of Scrope's life, it would 'be expected that his text would display the East Midland or London dialect'. Furthermore, any study of Scrope's language would necessarily have to begin with an examination of such autograph materials as his 'Schedule of Grievances' against Fastolf.[2] It would then be necessary to compare the results obtained from such an analysis with the linguistic characteristics of the dozen textual manuscripts still extant, those of the *Dicts*

---

[1] Compare Schofield, *Dicts*, pp. 46–7, and Bühler, *Dicts*, pp. lxiv–lxv. The rhymes in the *Othea* are mostly very pedestrian (often quite crude) and frequently represent no more than a direct 'carry-over' of the French rhyme-words into English. Rhyme-tests, therefore, fail to provide satisfactory evidence of any sort.

[2] Cf. BM MS. Additional 28209, f. 21, and Poulett Scrope, *Castle Combe*, pp. 279–83. See also Scrope's autograph copy of a letter from his father-in-law (Sir Richard Bingham) in MS. Add. 28212, f. 26; etc. There may well be other examples of Scrope's hand in the Castle Combe papers in the BM (MSS. Additional 28205–13; cf. Scrope's 'Replycacions' in 28212, f. 22).

as well as the *Othea*. Clearly, such a study, desirable as it may be for the history of the language, would require very extensive annotation and would be of limited value for the study of this particular text.

Asterisks in the Glossary mark words which, in the *Othea*, make an earlier or a later appearance than the dates cited by the *Middle English Dictionary* (in progress; Ann Arbor, 1952; cited as *MED*) or by the *Oxford English Dictionary* (Oxford, 1884–1933; *OED*). An asterisk can also mark the occurrence of a meaning not recorded by these dictionaries. As in the case of Scrope's translation of the *Dits moraulx des philosophes*,[1] the number of words so starred is very impressive. Again the explanation is that these words are, to a great extent, merely the first anglicizings of the corresponding French words appearing in the *Épître d'Othéa*.

B. *The Notes*

The notes are intended:

1. To explain, wherever possible, all obscure passages in the Scrope text. Since these were frequently the result of errors in his French exemplar rather than of simple mistranslation by Scrope, pertinent passages are cited from MS. Laud Misc. 570 (which, as we have seen, was closely related to his exemplar) and occasionally, for illustrative purposes, comparable lines from other French texts as well.

2. To indicate some of the chief textual differences between the present translation and those attributed to Anthony Babyngton and to Robert Wyer.

3. To cite the sources of the several stories and, to the extent that these could be determined,[2] those of the very numerous extracts and quotations given in the *Othea*, with more detailed

---

[1] Cf. my *Dicts*, p. lxv. Asterisks can also indicate the earliest use noted by *MED*.

[2] The problem of tracing the sources of Christine's quotations is often complicated by the fact that she seems to be quoting, here and there, from memory; see Campbell, *Othéa*, pp. 63–70 and Charity C. Willard, *The 'Livre de la paix' of Christine de Pisan* (The Hague, 1958), pp. 189 and 197. Mrs. Willard, too, has found it impossible to identify all the quotations in her edition (e.g. pp. 194 and 214). Lastly, Christine was also not over-generous in acknowledging her sources (p. 214).

particulars provided in the case of those not previously identified.

4. To quote identical or analogous passages from Christine's other works and from English and continental literatures of the fourteenth, fifteenth, and sixteenth centuries, thus emphasizing the central position held by the *Othea* in the culture of that period. A few examples of the continuity of that tradition into later epochs also have been given, as evidence for the permanent value inherent in the civilization from which the *Othea* (both French and English) evolved. The great number of surviving French manuscripts, and the (relatively) numerous English texts known to have been in existence, point to the obvious conclusion that the *Othea* was exceedingly popular in its own day and consequently of importance in the literary history of France and England.[1] 'Many early books', the late Rosemond Tuve reminded us,[2] 'were also still current, lively and useful to sixteenth-century writers.' It is hoped, therefore, that these notes may help to show how Christine de Pisan and her writings influenced (and were influenced by) the prevalent ideas and traditions current at that time.

[1] Warner (p. xx) somewhat understates the case when he remarks that the *Othea* 'is not without interest as a reflection of the taste of the time, but which contains, it must be confessed, little either to attract or to edify the modern reader'. The same remark, alas, would be applicable to the great bulk of the surviving fifteenth-century literature. But the very fact that the *Othea* was prized in its own day makes it an object of great value and significance to the literary historian and to the student of the period in general. Christine's work supplied her contemporary readers, of whom there appear to have been many, with what surely seemed to them an extraordinary variety of intellectual fare: a large stock of classical stories and allusions, the maxims of 'esteemed' philosophers (some of whom are not otherwise known!), Biblical and theological opinions on every likely subject, and a store of moral teachings to serve almost every daily—and, one is tempted to add, knightly— need. The chief virtue (and claim to fame) of Scrope's *Othea* is that it epitomizes the culture of the noble and wealthy classes of mid-fifteenth-century England, though no trace of that humanism so soon to flourish can be discovered in this translation. 'But by 1520 the English humanists were in full flower. Grocyn was dead, Linacre had published his *Galen*, Colet had founded his school, Lily had been teaching there eight years, More had published his *Utopia*, and Erasmus had become a world figure' (John M. Berdan, *Early Tudor Poetry, 1485–1547* (New York, 1920), p. 158). On Christine and her audience, see the recent article by Charity C. Willard, 'The Manuscript Tradition of the *Livre des trois vertus* and Christine de Pizan's Audience', *Journal of the History of Ideas*, xxvii (1966), 433–44.

[2] *Virtues and Vices*, p. 264.

TABLE OF ABBREVIATIONS AND
LIST OF FREQUENTLY CITED BOOKS

A NUMBER of abbreviations here used are familiar: BM (British Museum); BN (Bibliothèque Nationale, Paris); BR (Bibliothèque Royale, Brussels); STC (Short-Title Catalogue); Migne (*Patrologia*, the Latin series unless marked Gr for the Greek); and O.S. (Original Series) and E.S. (Extra Series) of E.E.T.S.

SCROPE'S *EPISTLE OF OTHEA*

L = Longleat, Marquis of Bath's Library, MS. 253.
M = New York, The Pierpont Morgan Library, MS. M 775.
S = Cambridge, St. John's College, MS. H 5.
B = Buckingham, Duke of, text with dedication to.
F = Fastolf, Sir John, text with dedication to.
P = Princess, text with dedication to an unidentified.

OTHER ENGLISH EDITIONS

Bab. = Babyngton, Anthony. *The Epistle of Othea to Hector* (ed. James D. Gordon). Philadelphia, 1942.
Warner = Sir George F. Warner. *The Epistle of Othea to Hector . . . by Stephen Scrope, Esquire.* London: Roxburghe Club, 1904.
Wyer = Robert Wyer. *The C. Hystoryes of Troye.* London [*c.* 1540]. (*STC* 7272).

THE FRENCH *OTHÉA*

Harley = London, British Museum, MS. Harley 4431, ff. 95–141.
Laud = Oxford, Bodleian Library, MS. Laud Misc. 570, ff. 24–93.
Le Noir = *L'Épître d'Othéa* [*Les Cent hystoires de Troye*]. Paris: Philippe Le Noir, 1522.
Pigouchet = *L'Épître d'Othéa* [*Les Cent histoires de Troye*]. Paris: Philippe Pigouchet [*c.* 1499].
Campbell = P. G. C. Campbell. *L'Épître d'Othéa: Étude sur les sources de Christine de Pisan.* Paris, 1924.
Mombello = Gianni Mombello. 'Per un' edizione critica dell' "Epistre Othea" di Christine de Pizan', *Studi Francesi*, xxiv (1964), 401–17 and xxv (1965), 1–12.

OTHER TEXTS BY CHRISTINE DE PISAN

Book of Fayttes of Armes and of Chyualrye (trans. W. Caxton; ed. A. T. P. Byles). E.E.T.S., o.s. 189, 1937.

Chemin = *Le Livre du chemin de long estude* (ed. R. Püschel). Berlin, 1887.

Cité = *Le Trésor de la cité des dames*. MS. Harley 4431, ff. 292–375.

Cyte = *The Boke of the Cyte of Ladyes* (trans. B. Anslay). London: Henry Pepwell, 1521 (*STC* 7271)

Lavision = *Lavision—Christine, Introduction and Text* (ed. Sister Mary L. Towner). Washington, 1932.

L'Épistre = Suzanne Solente. 'Un Traité inédit de Christine de Pisan: *L'Épistre de la prison de vie humaine*', *Bibliothèque de l'École des Chartes*, lxxxv (1924), 263–301.

Mutacion = Suzanne Solente. *Le Livre de la mutacion de fortune*. Paris, 1954. (Vols. i–ii; vol. iii (Paris, 1964) became available only after the Munich MS. had been consulted.)

Mutacion—MCG = München, Bayerische Staatsbibliothek, Codex Gall. 11 (for part vi of the *Mutacion*), ff. 102ᵇ–140ᵇ.

Œuvres poétiques (ed. M. Roy). Paris: (SATF), 1886–96.

Paix = *The 'Livre de la paix'* (ed. C. C. Willard). The Hague, 1958.

OTHER TEXTS CONNECTED WITH SIR JOHN FASTOLF

The Boke of Noblesse (ed. J. G. Nichols). London, 1860.

The Dicts and Sayings of the Philosophers (trans. S. Scrope; ed. C. F. Bühler), E.E.T.S., o.s. 211, 1941.

HISTOIRE ANCIENNE JUSQU'À CÉSAR
[= Hist. anc.]

(First redaction)

Add. 19669 (or Add.) = London, British Museum, MS. Additional 19669.

Egerton = London, British Museum, MS. Egerton 912.

Royal 16 = London, British Museum, MS. Royal 16 G. vii.

(Second redaction)

Royal 20 = London, British Museum, MS. Royal 20 D. 1.

Stowe = London, British Museum, MS. Stowe 54.

THE *METAMORPHOSES* OF OVID

Ovid = *Metamorphoses* (ed. F. J. Miller). London, Loeb Classical Library, 1916.

Ovide = Cornelis de Boer. *Ovide moralisé. Poème du commencement du quatorzième siècle.* Verhandelingen der Koninklijke Akademie van Wetenschappen. Afdeeling Letterkunde. Nieuwe reeks. Deel xv, xxi, xxx³, xxxvii, xliii. Amsterdam, 1915–38.

Caxton's *Ovyde* = William Caxton. *Ovyde: hys Booke of Methamorphose* (ed. S. Gaselee and H. F. B. Brett-Smith). Oxford, 1924.

Prose Ovide = London, British Museum, MS. Royal 17 E. iv [see entry in BM Catalogue].

[Printed editions]. Paris: Antoine Vérard, 1 March 1493/4. Paris: Antoine Vérard [c. 1507].

Cornelis de Boer. *Ovide moralisé en prose (Texte du quinzième siècle)*. [Verhandelingen d. K. Nederl. Akad. v. Wetenschappen. Afd. Letterkunde. N. R. D. LXI²]. Amsterdam, 1954. [From Vatican MS. Reg. 1686; a different text from Vérard's.]

OTHER ABBREVIATIONS

Add. 9785 = London, British Museum, MS. Additional 9785 (*Ystoire de Troye*).

Baldwin = William Baldwin. *A Treatise of Morall Phylosophie.* London: Edward Whitchurch [c. 1550]. (*STC* 1255.)

Bodley MS. 283 = Oxford, Bodleian Library, *Summary Catalogue*, No. 2338 (*Mirroure of the Worlde* or *Vice and Vertu*; cf. Tuve, p. 64).

Boke = *The Boke of Wysdome* (trans. of the *Chapelet des vertus* by J. Larke?). London: Thomas Colwell, 1565. (*STC* 3358.)

Boke² = *The Boke of Wysdome*. London: Thomas Colwell [c. 1575]. (*STC* 3358ª.)

CdV = *Chapelet des vertus*. New York, The Pierpont Morgan Library, MS. M 771 [printed edition—Paris: Philippe Le Noir, c. 1520].

Dicts = *The Dicts and Sayings of the Philosophers* (see above).

Geber = Richard Russel. *The Works of Geber*. London, 1678.

Gordon = *see* Bab. (under Other English Editions).

Griffin = Guido de Columnis. *Historia destructionis Troiae* (ed. N. E. Griffin). Cambridge (Mass.), 1936.

Leber = *Dits moraulx des philosophes* [*La Forest et description des grands et sages philosophes du temps passé*]. Paris: Pierre Leber, 1533.

Les enseignemens = *see* Solente (in next section).

ME De claris m. = Gustav Schleich. *Die mittelenglische Umdichtung von Boccaccio's De claris mulieribus*. Leipzig, 1924.

ME Sermons = *Middle English Sermons edited from British Museum MS. Royal 18 B. xxiii* (by W. O. Ross), E.E.T.S., O.S. 209, 1940.

ODEP = *The Oxford Dictionary of English Proverbs* (2nd edn. 1948).

1509 Orosius = Orosius [French version; *Orose en françois*]. Paris: Antoine Vérard, 1509.

PML = The Pierpont Morgan Library, New York.

Sources and Analogues = W. F. Bryan and G. H. Dempster. *Sources and Analogues of Chaucer's Canterbury Tales*. Chicago, 1941.

TG = *see* Lydgate, *Temple of Glas* (in next section).

Tilley = Morris P. Tilley. *A Dictionary of the Proverbs in England in the Sixteenth and Seventeenth Centuries*. Ann Arbor (Mich.), 1950.

WORKS CHIEFLY CITED

Ashby, George. *Poems* (ed. M. Bateson), E.E.T.S., E.S. 76, 1899.

Ayenbite of Inwyt, Dan Michel's (ed. R. Morris), E.E.T.S., O.S. 23, 1866; revd. P. Gradon, 1965.

Boccaccio, Giovanni. *De claris mulieribus.* Ulm: Johann Zainer, 1473.

Bonaventura. *The Mirrour of the Blessed Lyf of Jesu Christ* (trans. N. Love; ed. L. F. Powell). Oxford, 1908.

Book called Cathon (trans. W. Caxton). [Westminster: Caxton, *c.* 1483.]

Book of Vices and Virtues (ed. W. N. Francis). E.E.T.S., O.S. 217, 1942.

Bouchet, Jean. *Les Regnards.* Paris: Antoine Vérard [*c.* 1503].

Bühler, Curt F. 'The *Fleurs de toutes vertus* and Christine de Pisan's *L'Épître d'Othéa*', *PMLA* lxii (1947), 32–44, and 'The *Fleurs de toutes vertus*', *PMLA* lxiv (1949), 600–1.

—— 'The Revisions and Dedications of the *Epistle of Othea*', *Anglia*, lxxvi (1958), 266–70.

—— 'Sir John Fastolf's Manuscripts of the *Épître d'Othéa* and Stephen Scrope's Translation of this Text', *Scriptorium*, iii (1949), 123–8.

Campbell, P. G. C. 'Christine de Pisan en Angleterre', *Revue de littérature comparée*, v (1925), 659–70.

Catalogue of Romances in the Department of Manuscripts in the British Museum (by H. L. D. Ward and J. A. Herbert). London, 1889–1910.

Chaucer, Geoffrey. *The Works* (ed. F. N. Robinson). Boston, 2nd edn. 1957.

—— *The Complete Works* (ed. W. W. Skeat). Oxford, 1894–7.

Columnis, Guido de. *Historia Troiana.* Strassburg: [Printer of Jordanus de Quedlinburg], *c.* 9 October 1486.

Constans, Léopold. *La Légende d'Œdipe.* Paris, 1881.

Dives et Pauper, Dialogue of. London: Pynson, 5 July 1493.

Doctrinal of Sapience (by G. de Roye; trans. W. Caxton). [Westminster]: Caxton, 1489.

Edipus, Le Roman de (reprint of a sixteenth-century edition, by A. Veinant). Paris, 1858.

Fiore di virtù. Venice: Dominico de' Franceschi, 1566 (other early editions cited in the notes).

—— PML MS. M 770.

Gesta Romanorum (ed. S. J. Herrtage). E.E.T.S., E.S. 33, 1879.

Gower, John. *The English Works* (ed. G. C. Macaulay). E.E.T.S., E.S. 81, 82, 1900–1.

Hibernia, Thomas de. *Manipulus florum.* Piacenza: Jacobus de Tyela, 5 September 1483.

—— [Another edition]. Paris [1887].

Hoccleve, Thomas. *Works* (ed. F. J. Furnivall and I. Gollancz). E.E.T.S., E.S. 61, 72, 73, 1892–7.

Le Fevre, Raoul. *Recueil des histoires de Troie*. British Museum, MS. Royal 17 E. II.

Legrand, Jacques. *Boke of Good Manners* (trans. W. Caxton). London: Wynkyn de Worde, 1507.

Lydgate, John. *The Assembly of Gods* (ed. O. L. Triggs). E.E.T.S., E.S. 69, 1896.

—— *The Fall of Princes* (ed. H. Bergen). E.E.T.S., E.S. 121–4, 1923–7.

—— *Reson and Sensuallyte* (ed. E. Sieper). E.E.T.S., E.S. 84, 89, 1901–3.

—— *Siege of Thebes* (ed. A. Erdmann and E. Ekwall). E.E.T.S., E.S. 108, 125, 1911–30.

—— *Temple of Glas* (ed. J. Schick). E.E.T.S., E.S. 60, 1891.

—— *Troy Book* (ed. H. Bergen). E.E.T.S., E.S. 97, 103, 106, 126, 1906–35.

Machaut, Guillaume de. *Œuvres* (ed. E. Hoepffner). Paris: SATF, 1908–21.

Mer des histoires. Paris: Pierre Le Rouge, 1488–9.

Motz dorees, Senecque des (*in* Orosius. French. Paris: Vérard, 1509).

Patch, Howard R. *The Goddess Fortuna in Mediaeval Literature*. Cambridge, Mass., 1927.

Royster, James F. 'A Middle English Treatise on the Ten Commandments', *Studies in Philology*, vi, viii (Chapel Hill, 1910–11).

Seege or Batayle of Troy (ed. M. Barnicle). E.E.T.S., O.S. 172, 1926.

Solente, Suzanne. 'Deux chapitres de l'influence littéraire de Christine de Pisan', *Bibliothèque de l'École des Chartes*, xciv (1933), 27–45 (for 'Les Enseignemens que une dame laisse à ses deulx filz, en forme de testament'—BN, MS. fonds fr. 19919).

Speculum Christiani (ed. G. Holmstedt). E.E.T.S., O.S. 182, 1933.

Speculum humanae salvationis (ed. J. Lutz and P. Perdrizet). Mulhouse, 1907, etc.

Speculum sacerdotale (ed. E. H. Weatherly). E.E.T.S., O.S. 200, 1936.

Telin, Guillaume. *Bref sommaire des sept vertus, sept ars liberaulx,* (etc.) Paris: [for] Galliot du Pre, 1533.

Tuve, Rosemond. 'Notes on the Virtues and Vices', *Journal of the Warburg and Courtauld Institutes*, xxvi (1963), 264–303, xxvii (1964), 42–72.

THE EPISTLE OF OTHEA

In the *variae lectiones*, asterisks are used to indi-
cate words or forms that may be presumed to have
orthographical or dialectal significance and import-
ance. Such variants are noted only occasionally, but
sufficiently often to remind the reader of the (often
habitual) appearance of such forms in the other
manuscripts. The symbol Fr is used to represent the
reading of *all* French texts consulted.

Prolouge of the Pistell Othea

Praisyng be to God at this begynnyng,
In alle my wordes and soo folowyng.
To the right noble, hiȝ, myghti lyon
In whome there deliteth right many oon,   5
And than to you excellent prynce of wisedom,
Full myghti duke, vertuous of custom,
Redoubted Homfray, cosin to the kinge
Of Englande, to whom longeth myche thinge.
Duke of Bokyngham he is with hole sovne,   10
Erle of Herford, Stafford, and Northamtovne.
Benygne and hiȝ prynce, louer of wisedom,
In the grete largenes I trust all and som.
Of mekenes, the which your noble persoon
Ledith, as in the worlde seith many oon,   f. 1ᵇ
I am brought vn-to you to make present   16
Of this litell newe book with hooll entent.
I had doon thus or this, saue myspent tyme
Letted me; but the more bold at this tyme
I am to do, as whan I perceyued   20
Had the meknes that in you is schewid.
Wurthi prynce, and thus am I desirous
To serue you, if I were so gracious.
I make you yifte of my litell laboure,
If it please you, to se how I endure   25
To my symple power for to aument
The wurthynesses well sette in good entent.
All though that in me be connyng to lite
Where thorugh any myght haue appetite,
In my wordes ought for to lerne or take.   30
Yit som tyme is seen that symple men make
Grete iournaye, the which they right well fulfille.
And therfore my desire, corage and wille
Is that noble hertis may this report

---

1 *One folio wanting in* M; *for the preface in* L, *see* Appendix A.

So welle, that to all it may be disport.
As I can, this book translated haue I,
Othea-is Pistell callid verily,
Feynyng that to Hector sent and schewid
It was, because that he was conveid   5
With wisedom and with right gret wurthynes,
As that the stories berith wittenes.
Rightwis prince, benygne and right lowable,
I, that to your seruyce wolde were able,   f. 2
Besechith mekely to your hiȝ noblesse   10
That dispraised be not the febilnesse
Of my small witte, the which can not ferre loke.
Wherfore the lak be youen to my book,
And of your mankyndlynes take at worthe,
Consideryng that wille puttith me forthe   15
More than effecte, be ought that can appere
In me grete witte, for neuer, or this yere,
Though I haue herd full many a wise tale,
I gedered but crommes yet thoo be smale.
But yet lernyng hath stered me to this,   20
And litell the richer I am i-wis.
I may not werke but such stuf as I take;
Who-so hath litell breed, smale schive most make.
Please you, ryght hiȝ prince, to take of this thyng
The poure effecte of my litell connyng.   25

I   f. 2

Here beginneth the Pistell of Othea, the goddes, the which
sent it to Hector whan he was xv yere of age.

O thea, of prudens named goddes,
   That settith good hertis in wurthynes,   30
To the, Hector, noble prince myghti,
That in armes is euer wurthi,
The son of Mars, the god of bataile,
That in deedis of armes which will not faile,

9 M *begins*   14 mankyndlynes] good ladishipe M   17 or] er
M   yere] ere M   19 yet] and M   24 ryght hiȝ prince] hye prin-
cesse M   27–8 Here . . . age] *om.* L   th Pistill M   30 hertis] *om.* L
34 That] *om.* ML   which] *om.* M

And of myghti Mynerve, the goddes,
The which in armes is hiȝ maistres,
Successoure of the noble Troyens,
Heire of Troye and of the ceteseyns,
Salutacion afore sette plenere   5
I send, with loue feyned in no manere.
O good lord, how am I desiryng
Thi grete availe, which I goo seking,
And that aumented and preserued
It may be, and euer obserued   10
Thi wurschip and wurthynes in olde age,
That thow hast gretly had in thi first age.
Now, for to schewe the my pistell pleynli,
I will the enorte, and telle verili,
Of thinges that be full necessarie   15
To hiȝ wurthynes and the contrarie,
To the opposite of wurthynes,
So that alle good hertis may them dresse.
For to gete be good besi lernyng,
The hors that in the eire is fleyng—   20
It is the named Pegasus truly—   f. 3
That alle loueris loueth highly.
And because that thi condicion
I knowe, be right inclynacion,
Habill to take knyghtli deedes on hande   25
More than is in other v score thousande.
For as a goddes I haue knowyng,
Not be the assay but be connyng
Of thinges the which be for to com.
I ought to thinke on the hooll and som;   30
For I knowe thou schalte be euer duryng,
Wurthiest of all the wurthi lyuyng,
And schalte afore alle othir named be,
So that I may be beloued of the.
Beloued, whi schulde I not be soo?   35
I am that the which araieth all thoo

---

4 Heire] Feyre L   12 *fryst L   21 named the Pegasus L
22 highly] trewly M   23 that] of L   25 *Abill M, Able L   *knythly L
29 for] on L   30 *owthe L   33 schall L   35 I not] not I L

That loueth me and holdith me dere.
I rede theme lessons in chaiere,
Which makith hem clyme heuyn vnto.
I pray the that thou be oon of tho,
And that thou wilte here-in beleue me well.   5
Now, sette it well than in thi mynde and fele,
The wordes that I wull to the endite;
And if thou hire me ought telle, seie or write
Any thing that for to come may be,
And if that I seie, vmbethinke the   10
As that thei were paste, so do thou oughte
Knowe right wele that thei be in my thoughte
In the spirit of prophecee.   f.
Vnderstand well now and greue not the,
For I schall nothing seie but that schall falle;   15
Think well the comyng is not yit at alle.

Glose

Othea vppon the Greke may be taken for the wisedome of
man or woman, and as ancient pepill of olde tyme, not
hauyng yit at that tyme lyght of feith, wurschipid many goddes,   20
vnder the which lawe be passid the hiest lordes that hath ben in
the worlde, as the reaume of Assire, of Perse, the Grekes, the
Troyens, Alexander, the Romaynes and many othir, and namely
the grettest philosophres that euer were, soo as yit at that tyme
God hadde not openyd the yate of merci. But we Cristen men   25
and wommen, now at this tyme be the grace of God enlumyned
with verrey feith, may brynge ayen to morall mynde the opyn-
yones of ancient pepill, and there-vppon many faire allegories
may be made. And as thei hadde a custom to wurschip all thing
the which aboue the comune course of thinges hadde prerogatif   30
of some grace, many wise ladies in theire tyme were callid
goddesses. And trewe it is, aftir the storie, that in the tyme that
grete Troie florisschid in his grete name, a full wise lady callid

3 *them M, theym L   5 That will here-inne be-leve me wele L
7 *will M, wyll L   10 And if] As L   19 or] & L   *hold L
22 *rewme M   23 Alexandre L   and namely] anamly L   24 that]
thas L   were] was L   30 comyn M, comon L   33 grete] Greke L
Troy M, Troye L

Othea, consideryng the faire yonghthe of Hector of Troye, the
which that tyme florissched in vertues, and that it myght be a
schewing of fortunes to be in hym in tyme comyng, she sent
hym many grete and notable yiftis, and namely the faire stede
that men callid Galathe, the which hadde no felawe in the 5
worlde. And be-cause that alle the worldli graces that a good
man ought for to haue were in Hector, moralli we may seye that
he took them be the councell of [f. 4] Othea, the which sent
hym this pistell. Be Othea we schal vnderstaunde the vertu of
prudence and of wisedome, where-with he was araide; and 10
be-cause the iiij cardinall vertues be necessarie to good policie,
we schal speke of them, sewing euerich aftir othir. And to the
firste we haue youen a name and taken a maner of speche in som
wise poetikly, the bettir to folowe oure matere according to the
verray storie, and to oure purpos we schal take some auctoritees 15
of ancient philisophres. Thus we schal seie that be the seide
ladi this present was youen or sent to good Hector, the which in
liche wise may be to all othir desiring bounte and wisedome.
And as the vertu of prudence ought greteli to be recommended,
Aristotill, the prince of philosophres, seith: Because that wise- 20
dome is moost noble of all othir thinges, it schulde be schewed
be the beste reson and the mooste behoueli maner that myght
be.

The prolouge of the allegorie

For to bring ayen to allegorie the purpos of our matere to oure 25
wordes, we schal applique Holi Scripture to edificacion of
the soule, being in this wrecchid worlde.

As [s] be the grete wisedome and hiჳ myght of God all thinges
that be resonabli made alle scholde strech to the ende of
hym, and be-cause that our spirit, made of God to his likenes, 30
is made of thinges moost noble aftir the angelis, it is behoueli
and necessarie that it be araid with vertues, be the which it may

---

1 feyre youthe M, fre thought L   2 myght] *om.* L   4 grete]
M *breaks off, two folios wanting*   5 Galathee L   in the] in all the L
6 the worldli graces] wordly grace L   9 the] by the L   11 iiij]
om. L.   12 euerich] ich L   13 *fryst L   15 purpoyse L
20 Aristotle L   21 moost] þe most L   24 The . . . allegorie]
om. L   prolonge(?) S   27 this wrecchid] wrecheed L   28 Aas S
30 lekenes L   32 be the which] whereby L

be conueid to the ende wherefore it was made. And be-cause it
may be lettid be [the] assautes and watches of the enemye of
helle, the which is his deedli aduersarie, and often he dis-
troubelith it [f. 4ᵇ] to come to his beaute, we may calle man-
kyndli lif verrai chyualrie, as the Scripture seith in many   5
partes; and standyng alle erthli thinges be deceyuable, we
[schulde] haue in contynuel mynde the tyme for to come, which
is withoute ende. And be-cause that this is the grete wisedome
of parfit knyghthood and that all othir be of no comparison to
regarde of victorious pepill the which be crouned in blis, we   10
schal take a maner of speche of goostli knyghthood, and that to
be don principalli to the preising of God and to the profite of
tho that will delite them to here this present ditee.

Allegorie

How prudence and wisedome be moderis and conditoures of 15
all vertues, withoute the which the tothir may not be well
gouernyd, it is necessarie to goostli knyghthood to be araid with
prudence, as Sent Austin seith in the book of the Singularite of
Clerkis that, in what maner of place prudence be, men may
lightli cesse and amende alle contrarious thinges; but there   20
where prudence is despited, alle contrarious thinges hath
dominacion. And to this purpos Salamon seith in his Prouerbis:
Si intrauerit sapiencia cor tuum et sciencia anime tue placuerit,
consilium custodiet te, et prudencia seruabit te.

II   Texte   f.
                                                                26
        And to the entent that knowen may be
        What thou scholdest doo, drawe vnto the
        Thoo vertues that moost may the restore,
        The bettir to come to that seid afore
        Of the wurschipfull cheualerous.   30
        All though it be auenterous,

1 wherefore] for the which L   2 may be] was L   [the], *so* L,
om. S   and] of the L   3 enemye and aduersarie L   he] *om.*
L   distourbeth L   6 thinges] kynges L   thesceyvable *corrected
to* desceyvable *in* L   7 [schulde], *so* L, schal S   8 that] *om.* L
10 the victorius L   11 and] *om.* L   12 profyth L   15 is modyr L
18 Seynte Austyn L   of the] of L   21 were L   despisyd L   contarius L
26 know L   28 The L   moost may the] may the moste L
30 chevalroures L   31 it] that it L

Yit schall I sei whi that I sei this:
A cosin germayn I haue, i-wis,
Fulfilled sche is beaute with alle;
But of all thing in especiall
She is ful softe and temperid full wele;   f. 5ᵇ
Of strook of ire felith sche no dele;   6
Sche thinkith no thing but of right balaunce;
It is the goddes of temperaunce.
I may not all-oonly but be here face
Haue the name of that hiӡ myghti grace;   10
For if soo were the weight that she ne made,
To the all were not worth oo leke blade.
Therefore I will that with me sche loue the!
If sche will, lete here not foryeten be;
For sche is right a well lernyd goddes,   15
Here witte I loue and praise mych in distres.

Glose

Othea seith that temperaunce is here sister germayn, the
which he schulde loue. The vertu of temperaunce may
verili be seide sister germain and likli to prudence, for tem- 20
peraunce is schewer of prudence and of prudence folowith
temperaunce. Therefore it is seide that he schulde holde here
for his loue, and euery good knyghte schulde do the same, that
desirith dewe praise of good pepill. As the philosophre
Democritus seith: Temperaunce moderatith vices and perfitith 25
vertues.

Allegorie

The good spirit schulde haue the vertu of temperaunce, the
which hath the propirte to lymytte and sette a-side super-
fluyteis. And Sent Austin seith in the book of the Condicions 30
of the Chirche that the office of temperaunce is to refreyne and

1 this] thus L   4 specyall L   9 *hyre L   10 hiӡ] by L
11 For yef the weghte ne were sche to the made L   12 To] Th L   oo] a L
14 note for-getyn L   18 sister] cosyn L   19 The] for the L
20 sister] cosyn L   likli to] lykonnd L   23 schulde do] M begins
again   25 Demetricus L   moderath L   29 hath] om. L
*lemyte L, limite M   sette a-side] to sede on syde L   30 And]
For L   30–10/1Condicions . . . appese the] om. L

appese the condicions of concupiscence, the which be contrarie
to us and lettith us fro Goddis [f. 6] lawe, and more-ouere to
despite fleschli delites and worldli preisinges. Seint Petir
spekith to that purpos in his first Pistell: Obsecro vos tanquam
aduenas et peregrinos abstinere vos a carnalibus desiderijs, que 5
militant aduersus animam. Prima Petri secundo capitulo.

III   Texte

A nd with us strength behoueth the yette,
     If that be grete vertues thou sette,
Thou most the turne toward Hercules   10
And beholde well his grete wurthynes,
In whome there was full mych bounte.
And to thi linage all though that he
Was contrarie and a grete name him gate,   f. (
For all that haue thou neuyr the more hate   15
To his vertu, strengthe and nobles,
Which opened the yatis of wurthynes.
Yit, though that thou wilte folowe his wey
And also his wurthynes, I sey
It nedith nothing for the to make   20
Werre with them of helle ne no strif take.
Ne for to werre with the god Pluto
For any fauoure Proserpin vnto,
The goddes doughter callid Ceres,
Whom he rauysschid on the see of Grece.   25
Ne vnto the it is no myster
That thou to Serebrus, the porter
Of helle, besie the his cheynes to breke,
Ne of them of helle to take any wreke
The which to vntrewe wynneris be.   30
Nor for his felawis as dede he,
Pirotheus and Theseus, in fere,
The which that nere hand deceyued were

    2 more-ouere] more also L   3 praysynge L   8 strength behoueth]
streygth be honesty L   yitte M, yete L   9 gretter L   13 *lenage L
16 nobylnese L   17 yate M   20 for] to L   21 Where L
23 Proserpyne M, Proserpyng L   25 Gres L   26 maystyr corrected
to mystyr in L   27 to] be L   portar L

To auenture them in that valey soo,
Where many a soule hath full mych woo.
Werre ynough in erthe thou schalte finde ful felle,
Though that thou go not to seke it in helle.
It is nothing necessarie to the   5
So to purchace or doo armes, parde,
To go and feight with serpentis stinging,
With boores wilde or beres ramping.
Whethir thou ymagin this I wote nought,   f. 7
Or ellis of wildenes it comyth in thi thought   10
Of wurthynes for to haue a name.
In distres, if it be not for this same,
As for thi bodi the to defende,
If that such bestis wolde the offende,
Than diffence if assailed thou be,   15
With-oute doute it is wurschip to the.
If thou ouercome them and the saue,
Bothe grete laude and wurschip thou schalte haue.

Glose

The vertu of strengthe is not oonly to vnderstande bodili 20
strength, but the stabilnes and stedfastnes that a good
knyght schulde haue in all his deedis be deliberacion of good
witte and strength to resiste ayens contrariousnesses that may
come vnto him, whethir it be infortunes or tribulaciones, where
strengthe and myghti corage may be vailable to the exhaunsing 25
of wurthynes. And a-legge Hercules for to yeue example of
strengthe, to the entente that it may be double auaile, that is to
seye, in as myche as touchith to this vertu and nameli in deedes
of knyghthoode, where-in he was ryght excellent. And for the
highnes of Hector, it is a behouely thing to yeue him hiȝ 30
example. Hercules was a knyghte of Grece of merueilous

---

1 To] *om. by erasure in* L   valy L, vale M   2 Were L   *moche M
3 For werre L   herthe L   ful] *om.* L   felle] well M   4 that] *om.* L
sekyt L   it] *om.* M   8 beerys L   10 ell L   thougth L
12 this] the L   13 to] for to L   diffende M   14 wolde] wylde L
22 *knygth L   23 contrariousnesse ML (les contrarietez, Laud f. 31)
24 *weythir L   25 exausynge M, exaussyng L (exaussement, Laud f. 31)
26 a-legge] alyche L   27 *strengh L   28 this] his L   nameli] anamly L
30 *hynes L   hiȝ] by L   31 *meruelyous L, meruelous M

strengthe and brought to ende many knyghtly wurthynesses.
A grete iourneyer he was in the worlde; and for the grete and
merueilous viages and thinges of grete strengthe that he dide,
the poetes, which spak couertli and in maner of fable, seide that
he wente in-to helle to fighte with the princes of helle and that 5
he faughte with serpentis and fers beestis, be the which is to
vnderstande the grete and strong entirprises that he dide. [f. 7ᵇ]
And therfore it is seide to a good knyghte that he schulde loke in
this, that is to seie, in his wurschip and wurthynes aftir his
possibilite. And as a philosophre seith be a good example: 10
Lich as the cleernes of the sonne is profitable to all thing and as
the whete-corne whanne it fallith in good erthe is profitable also,
on the same wise this may be a good example to all thoo that be
wurthi, the which desirith wurthynes. And therfore the wise-
man seith that the vertu of strengthe makith a man abiding and 15
to ouercome all thinge.

Allegorie

Liche as the good knyghte withoute myghte and strength may
not deserue price in armys, on the same wise the good
spirit with-oute that may neithir wynne ne haue the wagis ne 20
the duwe price þat longith to good victorious pepill. And Sent
Ambrose seith in the firste Book of Offices that the verray
strengthe of mankyndli corage is that the which is neuer broken
in aduersite, ne prided in prosperite; and that proueth him to
kepe, to defende the garmentes of vertues and to sustene iustice; 25
the which makith contynuell werre to vicis and that is neuer
crased in laboures, but is hardi in perelles and [royde] ayens
fleschli desires. And to this purpos seith Sent John the
euangelist in his firste Pistell: Scribo enim iuuenes vobis,
quoniam fortes estis, et verbum Dei manet in vobis, vicistis 30
malignum. Prima Johannis ij° capitulo.

---

1 worthines L   3 dide] made & dede L   4 which] the wyche L
5 *fygth L   6 he faughte] favth L   *fierse ML   7 vndirstonden L
entreprises] L breaks off, one leaf wanting   10 *philesofre M   11 Like M
15 abiding] stedfast M (permanable, Laud f. 31ᵇ)   19 prise M (pris,
Laud)   21 dewe M   23 broke M   27 royde] so M, rude S
(roide, Laud)   28 *Seynt M

IV Texte f. 8

Yit oon of us, if that ye will be,
Minos resemble nedes most ye,
Though that he be maister and iusticere
Of helle, and of alle the corners there. 5
For if soo be thou wilte thiself enhaunce,
To kepe trewe iustice thou most the avaunce.
Ellis arte not wurthi an helme to were,
Ne for to gouerne a reaume nowhere.

Glose f. 8ᵇ

Prudence seith to the good knyghte that if he will be on the 11
good mennes rowe, he most haue the vertu of iustice, that
is to sey, [rightwis] iustice. And Aristotill seith: He that
is a rightwis iustice firste schulde iustifie himself, for he that
iustifieth not himself is not wurthi to iustifie another. This is to 15
vnderstande that a man scholde correcte his owne defautis, soo
that thei be hoolli fordon, and than a man soo correctid may
well and scholde be a correcter of othir men. And to speke
moralli, we schall telle a fable to the purpos vnder the couuert-
oure of poetis. Minos, as poetis seyn, is a iusticer of helle, as a 20
prouost or a chef bailie, and a-fore him is broughte alle [the
soules] descending in-to that valeye; and aftir that thei haue
deserued of penaunce, as many degrees as he will that thei be
sette deepe, as ofte he turnyth his taile aboute him. And
because that hell is the iustice and the punyschment of God, 25
lete us take oure maner of speche verili to speke to that purpos.
O trouthe, ther was a kyng in Grece callid Mino[s] of meruey-
lous fersnes, and in him was grete [rigoure] of iustice. And
therfore the poetis seide that aftir his deth he was commyttid to
be iusticer of helle. And Aristotill seith: Iustice is a mesure 30

2 Yet M   5 corneris M   8 Elles] L begins again   not]
thou note L   11 on] on of L   13 [rightwis], so M L, right S
(droitturiere, Laud f. 32ᵇ)   14 rytewyse iusticer L   15 iustifieth]
iustifies L   19 Ve L   fable] tale M (fable, Laud)   to the] to this L
20 sey L   as] or L   21 [the soules], so M L, thoo S (les ames,
Laud)   22 vaylie L   24 *deipe L   25 hell] he L   25-14/7 iustice
and . . . to yeue] torn away in M   26 maner . . . purpos] maner to
speke oure speche veryly to that purpose L   27 Minor S, Mynos L
28 fersnes] fairnes L   [rigoure], so L, rightwer S (rigueur, Laud f. 32ᵇ)

that God hath sette in erthe for to lymytte there-bi thinges
riȝtwislye.

Allegorie

And evin as God is hede of iustice and of alle ordris, it is
necessarie to the chyualerous spirit that wil come to the   5
victorious blisse for to haue this vertu. And Seint Bernarde
seith in a sermon that iustice is not ellis but to yeue euery man
that is his. Yeue than, seith he, to iij maner of pepil that the
which is theires, that is to sey, to thi souereyne, to thi felawe
and to thi subiecte: to thi souereyne, reuerence and obeisaunce,   10
reuerence in herte and obeisaunce of bodi; to thi felawe, thou
scholdist yeue councell [f. 9] and helpe, councell in teching
hym where he is ignoraunt and helpe him in confortyng his
novn-power; to thi suget, thou scholdest yif him keping and
chastisyng, kepyng in kepyng hym from evil deedis, chastisyng   15
in chastisyng hym if that he haue doon amys. And to this
prouerbe Salamon seith in his Prouerbis: Excogitat iustus de
domo impii, vt detrahat impios a malo; gaudium est facere
iusticiam. Prouerbiorum xxjº capitulo.

V   Texte   20

Also remember the of Percyualle,
  Whos name is knowen ouer-alle
Through-oute the worlde, bothe softe and harde.
The swifte hors Pegasus aftirwarde
He rode him through the aire fleyng,   f. 9
And Andromeda in his goyng   26
Fro the bellue he hir delyuered,
And with his strengthe hire from him reued;
As a righte good errant myghti knyghte
Brought hir ayen to hir kyn ful ryghte.   30
This deede in your mynde loke that ye holde,
For a good knyght scholde kepe that is bolde.

6 Seynt Bernard L   7 *giffe L   8 is his] his is L   11 reuerence
in . . . obeisaunce] *om*. L   12 schulde L   *teschyng L   14 nown-
power M, owyn power L (non puissance, Laud f. 33)   keping and . . .
in] chastissyng & L   16 if that] yf M, forgiffeyng hym that L   hath L
doo ML   to this prouerbe] thus here-to L   17 seyth Salomon L
20–15/1 *torn away in* M   21 remenbre L Percyvale L   23 Thorow-
oute M   25 eyre L, worlde M (par l'air, Laud f. 33ᵇ)   31 ye] it L

This wey if that he wul haue expresse
Wurschip, which is myche better than rychesse.
His schynyng schelde than loke thou vppon,
The which hath ouercome many oon.
With his fauchon loke that thou arme the,   5
Bothe strong and stedfaste than schalte thou be.

Glose

And be-cause that it is acording thing for a good knyghte to
haue wurschip and reuerence, we schal make a figure aftir
the maner of poetis. Perciuall was a ful wurthi knyghte and 10
wanne many reaumes, and the name of the greete lande of Perce
come of hym. And poetis seide that he rode the hors that flawe
in the eire, the which was callid Pegasus; and that is to vnder-
stande a good name, the whiche fleith through the eire. He bare
in his hande a fauchon or a glayue, the which is seide for the 15
grete multitude of pepil that were disconfited be him in many
batailles. He delyuered Andromeda fro the bellue. This was a
kynges doughter, the which he delyuered from a monstre of the
see, the which be the sentence of the goddes scholde a deuoured
hire. This is to vnderstande that alle knyghtis scholde socoure 20
wommen that [f. 10] hadde nede of theire socoure. This
Perciualle and the hors the which fleeth may be noted for the good
name that a good knyghte scholde haue and gete be his
good desertes; and there sholde he ride, that is to seye, that his
good name scholde be borne in alle contrees. And Aristotil 25
seith that a good name makith a man schynyng to the worlde
and agreable in presence of princes.

Allegorie

The chiuallerous spirite scholde desire a good name among
the saintis of hevin geten be his good desertis. The hors 30
Pegasus that bereth him schal be his good angell, the which

2 *Worshipe M, Wyrchip L   4 hath] haue euer L   10 Per-
cevale L   11 wanne] whan L   *rewmes M   12 *poyetis L
15 honde L   gleyue M   16 discomfyte L, discomfitid M   19 a]
haue M   22 may] many L   25 Aristotile L   26 name makith a
man] name of a man maketh a name L   29 chiualrous M,
cheualerours L   among the saintis] among the felachipe of the seyntis L
30 hors] good hors L   31 bereth] *om*. L

schalle make good reporte of him at the day of dome. Androm-
eda that schalle be delyuered, it is his soule, the which he
delyuerith from the feend of hell be the ouercomyng of synne.
And that a man on the same wise scholde wilne to haue a good
name in this worlde to the plesaunce of God and not for 5
veinglorie, Saint Austin seith in the Book of Correccion that
ij° thingis be necessarie to serue welle, that is to sey, good con-
cience and good name, conscience for feith and good name for
his neghbourgh; and who-so trustith in conscience and despiteth
a good name, he is cruelle; for it is a signe of a noble corage to 10
loue the weel of a good name. And to this purpoos seith the
wiseman: Curam habe de bono nomine; magis enim permanebit
tibi quam mille thesauri preciosi. Ecclesiastici xvj° capitulo.

VI   Texte

And with thin inclinacions   15
Of Jouis softe condicions
Loke thou haue; the bettir thou schalt be,
Whan that thou kepiste theim ryghtfulle.

                            Glose   f. ﹜

As it is seyde, poetis, the which wurschipid many goddes, thei 20
heelde the planetys of hevin for special goddes and of the
vij planetis thei named the vij daies of the woke. Thei wur-
schipped and held Jouis or Jubiter for theire grettist god,
be-cause that he is sette in the hiest spere of the planetys vnder
Saturne. The day of Thursday is named of Jouis. And namely 25
the philosophres yaf and compared the vertues of the vij
metallis to the vij planetis, and named the termes of theire
sciences be the same planetis, as a man may see in Jeber and
Nicholas and in othire auctours of that science. To Jouis is
yoven copir or bras. Jouis or Jubiter is a planete of softe con- 30

3 delyuerith] delyueres L   *fende M   4 wise] maner wyse L
6 Austyne M   7 serue] be-leve L   8 feith and] feyth L   9 *neygh-
borow M, neyburwe L   ho-so L   *tristith M, trostyth L   10 a signe]
signe M, a synge L   11 *wele ML   *purpoise L   16 Joyus L
18 kepes L   22 named] made L   *weke L   25 Satorne M
*Thurseday L   namely] anamly M   27 teremys L   28 Geber L
29 *autoures M   Jouys L

dicion, amyable and ful gladde and figure to sangwen complexion. Therfore Othea seith, that is to seye Prudence, that a good knyghte scholde haue the condicion of Jubiter, and the same scholde euery noble man haue pursuwyng knyghthood. To this purpos seith Pictagoras that a kyng scholde be gracious- 5 lye conuersant with [his] pepill and schewe to theym a gladde visage, and on the same wise it is to vnderstand of alle wurthi pepille tendyng to wurschip.

Allegorie

Now lete us brynge to oure purpos in allegorie the propirtees 10 of the vij planetis. Jouis, the which is a softe and a mankyndely planete, of the which the good knyghte scholde haue condicions, may signifie to us mercy and compassion that the good knyght hadde, Jhesu Criste, that it is the which the spirite schold haue in hymselfe. For Seint Gregori seith in the 15 [Pistill] of Poncian: I remembre not, seith he, that euer I herde or redde that he dide of evill deth that hath wil to fulfille the deedis of merci, for merci hath many praieres and it is impossible but that many preiers most nedis be exhauncid. To this purpos oure Lord seith in the Gospell: Beati mise[f. 11] 20 ricordes, quoniam misericordiam consequentur.

VII   Texte

Of Venus in no wise make thi goddesse,
And for nothing set store be her promys.
To folowe here it is rauenous,   25
Bothe vnwurschipful and perlous.

Glose

Venus is a planete of hevin, aftir whom the Friday is named; and the metal that we calle tyn or peuter is yoven to the same. Venus yeueth influence of love and of ydelnes; and sche 30 was a ladi called soo, the which was quene of Cipre. And

---

1 compeccion L   5 Pitagoras M, Pictogoras L   6 [his], *so* ML,
the S (sa gent, Laud, f. 35)   7 wurthi] wordly L   8 *tentynge M
14 it] *om.* L   15 Gregory M, Gregorie L   16 [Pistill], *so* ML, *om.* S
17 *dyed M, dyyed L   evill] hevy L   19 exaused M, exauced L
24 *promes M   26 perilous M, peryllous L   29 pewter ML
31 Cippre L

because that sche excedede alle wommen in excellent beaute and
iolynes, and was right amorous and not stedefaste in oo love
but abaundoned to manye, thei callid hire goddes of love. And
because that sche yeueth influence of lecherie, Othea seith to
the good knyght that he make hir not his goddesse. This is to   5
vnderstande that in such lijf he scholde not abaundon his bodi
ne his entente. And Hermes seith: The vice of lecherie steyneth
alle vertues.

Allegorie

Venus, of whom the good knyghte scholde not make his   10
goddesse, it is that the good spirite in himselfe scholde
haue no vanite. And Cassidoire seith vppon the Psaulter:
Vanite made a voide degree to become a fende, and yaf deth
to the first man, and voided hym from the blissidnes that was
grauntid vnto him. Vanite is moder of alle yvelles, welle of   15
alle vicis and the veyne of wikkidnes, the which puttith a man
oute of the grace of God and settith hym in his hate. To this
purpoos [f. 11ᵇ] Dauid seith in his Psaulter, speking to God:
Odisti omnes obseruantes superuacue. Psalmo xxxᵐᵒ.

VIII   Texte   20

    If thou assemble the in iugement,
    Be like to Saturne in avisement;
    Ere that thou yeve thi sentence verili,
    Be-warre that thou yeve it not doutousli.

Glose   25

Satirday is named aftir Saturne, and the metalle that we calle
leede is yoven therto, and it is a planete of slowe condicion,
hevi and wise. And there was a king in Grece had the same
name, the which was ful wise, of whom poetis spake vnder
couerture of fable; and thei seide that his son Jubiter cutte   30

---

1 sche] *om.* L   2 amerous ML   3 but . . . love] *om.* L
7 And Hermes] Armes L   The] that the L   11 *speryth L
*hym-selphe L   12 Cassiodre M, Cassidodre L   Psauter M, Sawtyr L
13 deth] tethe L   14 voyeddid L   15 euelis M   16 weyne L
17 settih L   19 obseruantes] aduersantes M   22 leke L   23 Or L
26 Satyrday L that we calle] *om.* L   27 *led M, lede L   29 which] *om.* L
30 couuerteure L

from hym his preuy membres, the which is to vnderstande that
he took from him his myghte and disherited him and drof him
away. And because that Saturne is hevi and wise, Othea seith
that a good knyghte scholde peise a thing greetly ere that [he]
yaf his sentence, whethir it be in price of armes or of any othir 5
deede. And euery iuge may note this same that hath offices
longyng to iugement. And to this purpos Hermes seith: Thinke
well vppon alle thinge that thou haste for to do and in especiall
in iugement of othir.

Allegorie 10

As the good knyghte scholde be slowe in the iugement of
othir, that is to sey, to peise well the sentence or that he
yeue it, on the same wise the good spirite sholde do in that the
which longith to him; for to God longith the iugemente, the
which can discerne cau[f. 12]ses ryghtwisli. And Seint Gregor 15
seith in his Moralles that, whanne our freilnes can not compre-
hende the iugementis of God, we oughte not to discute theym
in bolde wordes, but we oughte to wurschip them with feerful
scilence; and how meruelous that euer we thoughte them, we
schulde holde them iuste. And to this purpos spekith Dauid in 20
the [Psauter]: Timor Domini sanctus, permanet in seculum seculi;
iudicia Domini vera, iustificata in semet ipsa. Psalmo xviij°.

IX   Texte

Lete thi worde be clere and trewe in kynde,
Appollo schall yeue it the in mynde, 25
For he be no mene may noon ordure
Suffre no wise vnder couerture.

Glose

Appollo or Phebus, that is the sonne, to whom the Sonday is
youen and also the metall that is callid golde. The sonne 30
be his clernes schewith thinges that be hidde; and therfore

---

1 priue M   2 drof] drwe L   4 [he], *so* M, ye L, *om.* S
5 yaf] shulde yefe L   weythir that L   6 not thes L   8 vppon]
on L   9 of iugement L   12 or] er M   15 Grigorye L, Gregore M
19 *mervelyous L   21 [Psauter], *so* M, Paulter S, Sawter-booke L
24 clere and trewe] trewe and clere M (clere et voire, Laud f. 36^b)
30 goolde M

trouthe, the which is clere and schewith secrete thinges,
may be youen to him. The which vertu scholde be in the
herte and in the mouth of euery good knyght. And to this
purpos seith Hermes: Loue God and trouth, and yeue good
councell.　　　　　　　　　　　　　　　　　　　　　　　　　　5

Allegorie

Appollo, the which is for to sey the sonne, be whom we notifie
trouth, we may take that man scholde haue in his mouthe
the trouthe of the verray knyghte Ihesu Crist and flee all falsnes.
As Cassiodor seith in the book of the Preysing of Seynt Paul:　10
The condicion of falsnes is such that, where as it hath no
geynseyng, yit it fallith [f. 12ᵇ] in him-self; but the con-
dicion of trouth is to the contrarye, for it is soo sette that
the more geynseyng of aduersaryes that it hath, the more
it encrecith and reisith hymself. To this purpos seith Holy　15
Scripture: Super omnia vincit veritas. Secundi Esdre iijᵒ
capitulo.

X　　　　　　　　　　　　Texte

Vn-to Phebe resemble not; for whi?
He is to chaungeable and enemy　　　　　　　　　　　　　2c
To stedfastnes and to corage stronge,
Malencolyous is and full of wronge.

Glose

Phebe is callid the mone, of whome the Monday hath his
name; and to him is youen the metall that we call siluere.　25
The mone restith noon houre in a ryght poynte and yeueth
influence of vnstedfastnes and foly; and therfore it is seyde that
a good kny3t schold kepe him from such vices. And to this
purpos Hermes seith: Vse wisedome and be stedfast.

---

2 yofe L　　　4 and trouth] trowthe euer L　　　7 Apollo L　for]
om. L　　　10 Cassiodore M, Cassiodyr L　　of the] of L　　Poule
M, Powle L　　12 him-self] him-self that seyeth it M (*not in* Laud f. 37)
14 geyneseynges L　　aduersytes L　　19 Pheble *corrected to* Phebe *in* L
22 is] *om.* M　　24 Moneday L　　27 vnstefastenes L　　28 such]
which L

Allegorie

Phebe the mone, that we note for vnstedfastnes, the which a
good knyght scholde not haue [nor], on the same wise, the
good spirite. As Seint Ambrose seith in the Pistill of Simpliciam
that a fool is chaungeable as the mone, but a wiseman is euer 5
stedfaste in oo state, where he neuer brekith for fere ne chaungith
for no myghte; he reisith him not in prosperite ne plongeth not
in heuynes. There where wisedome is, there is vertu, strengthe
and stedfastnes. The wiseman is euere of oo corage; it lessith
not ne encreceth not, [f. 13] for chaungyng of nothing; he 10
floterith not in diuerse oppiniones, but abidith perfit in Jhesu
Crist, groundid in charite and roted in feith. And to this purpos
seith Holy Scripture: Homo sanctus in sapiencia manet sicut
sol; nam stultus sicut luna mutatur. Ecclesiastici xxvij°.
capitulo. 15

XI   Texte

I doute not, in noo wise, Mars thi fader,
Thou shalte folowe him in euery [mater];
For thin hiȝ and noble condicion
Drawith therto thine inclinacion. 20

Glose

The Tuwisday is named aftir Mars; and the metall that we
calle yrin is youen to hym. Mars is a planete that yeueth
influence of werres and batailles. Therfore euery knyght that
loueth and suweth armes and deedis of knyghthode and hath a 25
greet name of wurthynes may be callid sone of Mars. And
þerfore Othea named Hector soo, not-withstandynge he was
sone to kynge Priant, and seide he wolde well folowe his fader,

2 vnstedfastnesse *by correction from* stedfastnesse *in* M   3 knygh L
[nor], *so* M, *om.* SL (et, Laud f. 37)   4 As] For as M (*not so in* Laud)
Symplician M   5 *schawnegeable L   6 neuer] neythir L   ne]
ner L   7 ner plangeth L   9 oon L   lessith] lessyth it L   10 for
chaungyng of nothing] for schawngyth notte in no maner wyse for no thyng L
12 groundid] gon growndid L   17 fadir M   18 heuery L   [mater],
so ML, maner S (pas, Laud f. 37ᵇ)   19 thy L   22 Tewesday M,
Twysday L   and the] and that L   23 callen L   25 seweth M,
schewyth L   26 the sone L   28 *knyng L   Pryant ML

in as mych as a good knyghte oughte for to do. And a wise man
seith þat be the deedis of man may be knowen his inclinacions.

Allegorie

Mars, the god of bataille, may wel be callid the sone of God,
þe which batailled victoriousli in this world. And that 5
the good spirit scholde, be example, folowe his fader Jhesu
Criste and feighte ayens vices, Seint Ambrose [seyeth] in the
first book of Offices that, who-so will be Goddes frende, he
most be the fendes enemye; who-so wull haue peas with Jhesu
Crist, he most [f. 13^b] haue werre with vices. And evin as in 10
veine men makith werre in the felde with foreine enemyes there
where the cite is ful of homely spies, on the same wise noon may
ouercome the evilles outewarde that will not werre strongeli the
synnes of theire soulis; for it is the most glorious victorie that
may be for a man to ouercome hymself. And to this purpos 15
spekith Seint Paule in the Pistill: Non est nobis colluctacio
aduersus carnem et sanguinem, sed aduersus principes &
potestates, aduersus mundi rectores tenebrarum harum, contra
spiritualia nequicie, in celestibus. Ad Ephesios vj° capitulo.

XII   Texte   20

Of thi faucon be thou boolde and pleyne,
And of thi word bothe clene and certeyne
Mercury schall teche the that, hole and sounde,
The which of good speche knowith wel the grounde.

Glose

The Wednysday is named aftir Mercury, and quyk siluere 25
is youen therto. Mercury is a planete that yeueth influence
of pontificalle behauynge and of faire langage arayed with
retorik. Therfore it is seide to the good knyghte that he scholde
be arayed theire-with, for wurschipful behauyng and faire 30

1 for] *om.* L   And] To this M   2 of] of a L   may] men may L
knowe L   5–6 And . . . scholde] *om.* L   6 folowe] folowynge L
7 [seyeth], *so* ML, *om.* S   8 who-so] how so L   9 *will ML
13 werre] were L   strongly wyth L   15 *hyme-selphe L   And to] &
tho L   16 spekith] seyth L   in] *om.* L   Pistill] Postyle L   21 faucoun M
23 Mercurye L   hole] holde L   26 Wednesday M   26–7 and . . .
Mercury] *om.* L   29 *rethorique M   *knyte L

langage is full behouely to all nobill pepill desirynge the hiȝ
price of wurschip, soo that they kepe theim from to mych
langage. For Diogenes seith that of all vertues the more the
bettir, save of speche.

Allegorie

Mercury, the which is callid god of langage, we may vnder-
stand that the knyghte of Jhesu Crist scholde be araid with
good prechinges and wordes of techinges, and also thei scholde
loue and wurschip the sche[f. 14]weres ther-of. And Seint
Gregor seith in his Omelies that men scholde haue the pre-
choures of Holi Scripture in greete reuerence, for thei be the
messengeres that gooth to oure Lorde and oure Lorde folowith
theim. Holi prechinge makith the weye, and thanne our Lorde
cometh in-to the dwellinge place of oure herte; the wordes of
[exortacion] makith the cours, and so trouthe is receyued in-to
our vnderstandynge. And to this purpos oure Lorde seith to
his apostolis: Qui vos audit, me audit, et qui vos spernit, me
spernit. Luce x^mo capitulo.

XIII   Texte

Of alle maner soortes of armure
For to arme the with, bothe wel and sure,
Be thi moder nowe signed schall be,
Minerve, the which is not bitter to the.

Glose

Minerve was a ladi of grete connynge and fonde the crafte
to make armure, for a-foore the pepill armed them not but
with cuirboille; and for the grete wisedome that was in this
ladi, thei called here a goddes. And because that Hector couthe
sette armure wel a-werke and that it was his ryghte crafte, Othea
callid him the sone of Minerve, not-withstandyng he was sone

---

2 price] preyse M, pris L (so Laud f. 38^b)   of] of of M   3 Dyo-
geneys L   6 Be Mercurie L   7 araid] armed(?) L   10 Omelyis
L   12 *masseyngeres L   gone L   1st Lorde] Lord God L
15 [exortacion] L (so Laud f. 38^v) correction SM   17 apostelis M
22 modus L   inough L   23 is not bitter] is not bater(?) L, must be
best M   26 peyl L   not] om. L   27 cuirboyle ML   28 cowde L
29 a] on L   30 he] that he L

to Quene Echuba of Troy; and in the same wise alle that loueth
armes may be named. And to this purpoos an auctor seith that
knyghtes yoven to armes be sugettes to the same.

Allegorie

Where it is seide that good armoures and strong i-noughe 5
schalle be delyuered to the good knyghte be his moder,
we may vnderstande the vertu of feith, the which is a diuine
vertu and [is] moder to [f. 14ᵇ] the good spirite. And that sche
delyuerith armoures i-nough, Cassidoire seith in the Exposicion
of the Crede that feith is the lighte of the [sowle], the yate of 1•
paradis, the wyndowe of lijf and the grounde of euerlastinge
helthe, for withoute feith noon may please God. And to this
purpoos seith Seint Paule the appostoll: Sine fide impossibile
est placere Deo. Ad Hebreos vj° capitulo.

XIV   Texte   1•

Joyne to the Pallas, the goddesse,
And sette her ryghte with thi wurthinesse.
If thou haue her, good fortune thou schalte fele;
Pallas with Minerve is sittyng full wele.

Glose   2•

Also where it is seide that Pallas scholde be ioyned with
Minerve, the which is wele sitting, men schall vnderstande
that Pallas and Minerve is all oo thing, but the names be
dyuerse and be taken to ij° vnderstandinges. For the ladi that
is callid Minerve was so surnamed Pallas of an ile that is callid 2•
Pallaunce, of the which sche was borne; and be-cause that
sche generally in alle thinges was wise and fond many newe
craftis feire and subtile, thei callid here goddes of connyng.
Minerve is callid thus in that the which longeth to knyghthod,
and Pallas in alle thinge that longeth to wisedome; and therfore 3•

1 Ecuba L   Troye L   2 *autoure M   5 i-newgh L
6 knygh L   8 [is] so ML, his S   9 i-nowe ML, i-nough3 S
Cassiodir L   10 lighte] lyth L   [sowle], so L (l'ame, Laud f. 39), sonne SM
11 lyve L   *gronde L   of] of the L   13 Poule in the Pystyll L   16 Joyne
thou L   21 that] thas L   24 diueres L   to] for M   26 Pallance L
of the which] repeated in L   28 hyr goodes L   29 the which] which L
30 thynges L

it is seyde that he scholde ioyne wisedome to knyghthode, the
which is ful wel according therto, and that armes scholde be
kepte may be vnderstanden be feith. To this purpos seith
Hermes: Joyne the loue of feith with wisedome.

Allegorie 5

And as that Pallas, the which is noted for wisedome, scholde
be ioyned with knyghthoode, the vertu of hoope scholde be
ioyned [f. 15] with good vertues of the knyghtli spirite, with-
oute the which he may not availe. For Origene seith in the
Omelies vppon Exode that the hoope of the goodes that be for 10
to come is the solas of theim that trauaylith in this deedli lijf
liche as to laboreris the hoope of theire payment softith the
laboure of theire besynesses, and as to champions that be in
bataille the hoope of the croune of victorie esith the woo of
theire woundis. And to this purpos seith Seint Paule the 15
apostill: Fortissimum solacium habemus, qui conf[u]gimus ad
tenend[a]m proposit[a]m; quam sicut anchoram habemus
anime tutam. Ad Hebreos vj° capitulo.

XV   Texte

Pantasselle haue thou fauour vn-to,   20
That for thi deth schal haue mychil wo;
Such a womman scholde be loued and knowe,
Of whom soo nobill a voyce is sowe.

Glose

Pantasselle was a ful faire mayden and quene of Damazoine, 25
and of merveillous wurthines in armes and in hardines; and
for the greete goodnes that the hi3 name witnessed through the
worlde of Hector the wurthi, sche loued him ryghte hertily, and
fro the partyes of the Est sche come to Troy in the tyme of the
greete seege for to see Hector. But whanne sche foonde him 30

1 ioyne] yeuen L   to] and L   3 vndrestonde L   7 vertu]
whiche vertue L   9 Orygene L   11 trauellyth L   deedli]
bodely L   12 there laboure L   13 besines ML   to] om. L   16 configimus
SM   17 tenendum SM (so Laud, f. 39ᵇ)   propositum S
20 Pantassale M, Pantassele L   21 moche ML   22 Such] Syth L
25 Damazoyne M, Damazonie L   30 *qwen L   *fonde ML

deede, sche was out of mesure heuy; and with a greete hoost of
fulle cheuallerous gentilwommen, vigorousli sche venged his
deth where sche dede merveilous worthinesses; and many grete
greuaunces sche dide to the Grekis. And because that sche was
vertuous, it is seide to the good knyghte that he scholde loue 5
here, and that is to vnderstande that [f. 15ᵇ] euery good knyghte
scholde loue and preise euery vertuous persone, and namely a
womman strong in vertu of witte and conscience. And this
womman, that is woful for the deth of Hector, is vnderstanden
be wurthines and valure, whan it is dulle and deedid in knyght- 10
hoode. And a wiseman seith: Bounte scholde be alowed where
that it is perceyued.

Allegorie

B e Pantasselle, that was socourrable, we may vnderstande þe
vertu of charite, the which is the iijᵈᵉ diuine vertu that the 15
good spirite scholde perfiʒtli haue in himself. Cassidoire seith
that charite is as the reyne the which fallith in the prime-temps,
for it distillith the dropes of vertues vnder the which greine
good wil groweth and good hope fructifieth, that is to be pacient
in aduersite, temporat in prosperite, paciente in meekenes, 20
ioyous in affliccions, welwillyng to his enemyes and frendis, and
namely to his enemyes to be communiall of his goodes. To this
purpos seith Seint Paule the apostill: Caritas paciens, benigna
est; caritas non emulatur, non agit perperam, non inflatur, non
est ambiciosa, non querit que sua sunt. Prima ad Corinthios 25
xiijᵒ capitulo.

XVI   Texte

Narcisus loke ye resemble not,
Nor in-to mych pride wynde you not;
For to ouer-wenyng hauʒteyn knyghte   30
Of many a grace is voide ful ryghte.

---

1 hoost of] oste L   4 that sche] she L   7 preise euery]
prayse euer L   and namely] anamely L   8 strong in] in strong L
& off concyens L   15 cherite L   16 *parfitly M
Cassyodir L   20 temperat M, tempered L   22 anamely L
23 Seint] *om.* L   Postel L   28 L *cancels* the *before* ye   *resembil M
29 moche M   wynde you not] knyt your knot L   30 havteyn M

Glose

Narcisus was a yong bachelere the which for his greete
beaute reised him in soo greete pride that he hadde alle
othir in dispraise. And be-cause that he preised noon but him-
self, it is seid that he was soo amorous and assottid of himself 5
that he dide, aftir that he hadde beholden him[f. 16]self in the
welle. This is to vnderstande be the ouerwenyng [or ouctrecui-
dez] man of himself, [where]-in he beholdith him. Therfore it
is defended the good knyghte to beholde himselfe in his good
deedis, where through he myghte be ouerwenyng. And to this 10
purpos seith Socrates: Sone, beware thou be not deceyued in
the beaute of thi yougth, for that is no durable thing.

Allegorie

Nowe lete us sette in allegorie appliking to our purpos to the
vij deedly synnes. Be [N]arcisus we schal vnderstande the 15
synne of pride, fro the which the good spirite scholde kepe him.
And Origene seith in the Omelies: Where-of is it that erthe and
asschis pridith him, or how dare a man reise him in arrogance,
whan he thinkith w[h]ere-of he is comyn and what he schal
be-come; and in how freel a vessell the lijf is inne al nakid, and 20
in what harlotries he is plonged, and what vnclene materis he
cecith neuere to caste from his flesch be alle the condites of his
bodye? And to this purpos seith Hooly Scripture: Si ascenderit
ad celum superbia eius, et caput eius nubes tetigerit, quasi
sterquilinium in fine perdet[ur]. Job x^mo capitulo. 25

XVII   Texte

Athamas ful of righte greete madnes,
The goddes verily of woodnes,
She feersly strangeled her childer tweyne;
Therfore greete ire I defende the pleyne. 30

2 was] om. L   the which] that L   3 reised] seysyd L   4 disprayes L
6 dide] dyed M, dyede L   7 [or ouctrecuidez], so L, om. SM
(cheualier oultrecuidez, Laud f. 40^b)   8 were in S   9 diffendyth L
12 thi beaute L   14 in] an L   applyyng L   15 Marcisus SML
17 is it] it is L   18 derre L   19 were-of S   20 the lijf] thi lyff L
inne] om. L   21 plongeden L   24 capud M   25 perdet[ur]; so
Laud, perdet SM   28 The goddes] The *goodes L   30 greete] om. L
defende] the fende L

Glose

Athamas was a kinge maried to Quene Ino, the which made sothen corne to be sowen forto disherite hire stepchildere, for sche with money corrumped the prestis of the lawe, the which reported the answeres of the goddes thus: seying to the 5 kinge and to theim of the contre [f. 16ᵇ] that the corne the which men had sowen profited not, [wherfore] it pleasid the goddes that ijᵒ fayre and gentil childer, the which the kinge hadde, were driven away and exiled. And be-cause that the kynge consentide the [exilynge] of the ijᵒ childer, al-though that he dide [it] ayens 10 his wille and with greete sorowe, the fable seith that the goddes Juno wolde take vengeaunce therefore and went in-to helle to compleyne to the goddes of woodenes that sche myȝt come to kinge Athamas. Thanne the horrible and the feerfull goddes come with alle here serpently heres and sette here on the 15 fumerell of the palais and strecchid here armes to bothe sides of the yate. And than there began such strife be-twene the kinge and the quene that nerehande eche of theim had sleyne othir. And when thei wende to haue ronne oute of the palais, thanne the wood goddes druwe oute of her righte foul herres ijᵒ 20 horrible serpentis and keste in theire lappes; and whan that thei sawe them so feerfull, thanne thei waxe bothe madde. Athamas slowe the quene for woodenes and than his ijᵒ childer, and him-self lepte in-to the see from an hiȝ roche. The exposicion of this fable may well be that a quene myghte be soo diuerse to here 25 steppe-childer that for some malice she myghte disherite them, for the which aftir peas myȝte not be hadde betwene the fader and the stepmodere, and it myghte be soo that at the laste he slewe them. And because þat ire is a deedly vice and soo ivill that he that is soore teynte therwith hath no reson, it is seide to 30 the good knyghte that he scholde kepe him from ire, for it is a to

2 Yno L   3 hire] hys L   4 sche] he L   6 and] or L   the which] that the L   7 hadden sowene L   [wherfore], so M, where SL 9 *dreven L   10 [exilynge], so M, exillyng L, exuling S   of tho L [it], so M, om. SL   12 Juno] Yno L   *vengaunce ML   14 the kyng L   16 *streged L   18 nerehande] werrant L   *hem L   19 to haue] a hade L   21 that thei] that the goodes L   23 *childerne L   24 leep L   from an hiȝ] of frome a hght L   25 here] om. L 29 *euyl M, evyle L   30 hath no reson] hath no knowyng of reson L 31 a to] too L

greete defaute in a good knyghte to be angry. And therfore
Aristotill seith: Kepe the from ire, for it troubleth the vnder-
standynge and distroubleth reson.

Allegorie

Be Athamas, the which was soo full of ire, we schall propirly 5
vnderstande the synne of ire, the which the good spirite
sholde [f. 17] voide from him. And Seynt Austin seith in a
Pistell: Liche as vynegre, where it is put in a vessell, corrumpith
the vessell that it is ynne, if it abide longe there-ynne, so ire
corrumpith the herte where-in it is sette, if it abide longe ther- 10
ynne, that is to sey, fro day to day. Therefore seith Sent Paul
the apostle: Sol non occidat super iracundiam vestram. Ad
Ephesios iiij° capitulo.

XVIII   Texte

Of al thing that thou maist see with iȝe,   15
Fle euer the fals goddes envie,
That made Aglaros grener than yvi,
The which to a stoon chaungid was therbi.

Glose

A fable seith that Aglaros was sister to Herce, the which was 20
so faire that for here beaute Mercurius the god of langage
wedded hire, and thei were Cicropos doughteris, kyng of
Athenes. But Aglaros had so myche envie to her sister Herce,
the which for here beaute was so avaunced as to be maried to a
god, that sche become through here enforcyng in envie drie and 25
discolourid and grene as an ivi leef for envie that sche had to
here sister. On a day Aglaros was sette on the thresscholde of
the dore and lettid Mercurius the entre in-to the hous, and for
no praiere that he praied here sche wold not suffre him to
entre. Thanne the god wexe wroth and seide that euyr mote 30

1 therefore] there L   3 distourbith M, destroubeth L   7 Austyne M
8 *poote L in a vessell] *om.* L   10 if it] yf that it L   12 postell L
15 may L   *ye M, ey L   20 flable L   22 Cycropos ML
24 here beaute] beaute L   25 enforgyng L   drie] dey L   26 as
an] as L   the envie L   27 thresshefolde ML   28 and for] ne
for L   30 *hentre L   mote] myght L

sche abide there stille, as harde as here corage was; and thanne
Aglaros become as harde as a stoon. This fable may be likenyd
in liche caas to falle to sum persones. Mercurius may be a
myghti man, wel spekyng, the which made his sister to be
prisoned or to dye for sum displesire that sche had doon to him, 5
and therfore it is seide that sche was chaungid to a stoon. And
because it is [f. 17ᵇ] to foule a spotte and ayens gentilnes to be
envious, it is seide to the good knyght that of all thinge he kepe
him there-froo. And Socrates seith: He that berith the fardel
of envie hath perpetuel peyne. 10

Allegorie

Liche as this auctorite defendith the good knyght envie, the
same vice Holi Scripture defendith the good spirit. And
Sent Austin seith: Envie is hate of othres felicite, for the deedis
of the envious man stretchith ayens thoo that be gretter than he, 15
be-cause he is not as grette as thei; ayens thoo that be evinli to
him, be-cause that he is not gretter than thei; and ayens tho
that be lesse than he, for fere that thei schulde waxe as grete as
he. To this purpos Holi Scripture seith: Nequam est oculus
inuidi, auertens faciem suam. Ecclesiastici xiiij° capitulo. 20

XIX   Texte

Ferre ne slowe be-ware that thou not be;
Froo the malice loke that thou kepe the
Of Vlixes, that the geauntes yȝe
Stale, though he loked neuere so cleerlye. 25

Glose

A fable seith that whan Vlixes retourned in-to Grece, aftir
the destruccion of Troye, grete rages of tempestis brought
his schippe in-to an ile, where a geaunt was that had but oon
yȝe in the myddes of his forhede, the which was of an huge 30
gretnes. Vlixes be his subtilte stale it and toke it from him, that

---

2 L *cancels* aha *before* aglaros   5 presound L   7 foule . . . ayens]
folow a aspotte ayens L   gentilesse M, ientylnes L   8 thynges L
kepe] kepte L, shulde kepe M (il s'en gard, Laud f. 42)   13 same] *om.* L
14 seith] seyth that L   othir L   16 by-cawse that L   so grete L
ayens] and ayens M (contre, Laud f. 42ᵇ)   22 ne] no L   23 Froo]
For L   24 Vlyxes L   25 looke L   29 *chip L   30 forred L
huge] hooges L   31 his] hy L

is to seye, he put it oute. This is to vnderstande that the good
knyght schulde be-ware that slouth ouertooke him not with
deceytis and wiles of malicious pepill, so that his yȝe be not
taken awey, that is to seye, the yȝe of his vnderstandynge in his
wurschip, in his getynge or in that [f. 18] the which is derere to 5
hym, as many inconueniencis falleth ofte throuȝ slouth and
lacchesse. And to this purpos seith Hermes: Blessid is he that
vsith his dais in dewe occupacions.

Allegorie

Where it is seide that the good knyghte schulde not be ferre 10
ne slowe, we may vnderstande the synne of slouthe, the
which the good spirite scholde not haue. For as [Bede] seith
[vp-on] Salamones Prouerbis: The slowe man is not wurthi to
regne with God, the which wil not laboure for the loue of God,
and he is not wurthi to receive the crowne promysed to knyghtis, 15
the which is a cowarde to vndertake feldes of bataile. Therfore
the Scripture seith: Cogitaciones robusti semper in habundancia,
omnis autem piger in egestate erit. Prouerbiorum xxj° capitulo.

XX   Texte

In no wise striue with no frosschis, 20
Ne defoule the not in theire brothis.
Ayens Lathonna thei assemblid sore,
And troubled the cleire watir here afore.

Glose

The fable seith that the goddes Lathonna was moder to 25
Phebus and to Phebe, the which is the son and the mone,
and sche bare them bothe in hire wombe. Juno chaced hire in
eueri contre be-cause sche was conceived be Jubiter, hir
housbonde. On a day the goddes Lathonna was trauailed
gretli, and sche arived on a waisch; and than sche aboode vppon 30

2 ouertooke] ouercome L   3 *ye M, eye L   6 in-
coniencies L   7 Hermes seythe L   11 slewthe L   12 [Bede],
so M, Bedeisus SL (probably from Bede sus [sic] in Laud f. 43)   13 [vp-on],
so M, in SL   14 the which] that M   *lowe L   16 the which] that L
20 frosshes M, frosses L   22 Latonna M   28 be] wyth L
30 *wasshe ML

the watir for to staunch hir gret thirst, there where a grete
felauschip of carles were for to bathe them in the watir for the
hete of the son, and began to chide Lathonna and troubled hir
watir that sche wende to a dronken of, and for no praiere that
sche made thei wolde not suffre hire drynke ne had no pite of 5
hire myschefe. Than sche cursid them [f. 18ᵇ] and seide that
euer aftir mote thei abide stille in the broth. Than were thei
foule and abhominable and cecid neuyre of braynge ne
chidynge. So the carlis become frosschis, the which neuyr
sithen cecid of braynge, as it schewith in somere tyme be ryueres 10
sides. This may be takin be communes that dide some dis-
plesere to sum grete maistres, the which made them to be caste
in a ryuere and to be drounyd, and thus become thei frosschis.
And it is to vnderstande that a goodli knyght schulde not soile
him in the broth of vilony; for liche as vilony may not suffre 15
gentilnes, on the same wise gentilnes in himself may not suffre
vilony, and nameli not to stryue ne to make debate with a
persone vilonous of condicions, ne to speke outragiousli. Platon
seith: He that ioyneth to his gentilnes nobles of good condicions
is to prayse, and he that holdith him content with the gentilnes 20
that cometh of his kynne with-oute addynge therto some good
condicions scholde not be hoolden noble.

Allegorie

Be the carles that become frosschis we may vnderstande the
synne of couetise, the which is contrary to the good spirite. 25
For Sent Austin seith that a couetous man is liche to helle, for
helle can not swolowe so many soulis to [that he] sey that he
had ynough; even so though al the tresoure of the worlde were
hepid to-gidere to the possession of the couetous man, he
schulde not be satisfied. To this purpos the Scripture seith: 30
Insaciabilis oculus cupidi in patrem iniquitatis non saciabitur.
Ecclesiastici xiiij° capitulo.

---

2 *feleshipe M, feleshyp L   4 wende] *om.* L   a] haue ML
7 *broththe L   8 cessid M   10 ryuer M   11 take M   14 goodli
knyght] knyght goodly L   soile] file M, fyll L (souillier, Laud f. 43ᵇ)
17 and nameli] anamely L   ne to] ne L   18 vylens M, vilens L
19 nobilnesse L   21 good] *om.* M   22 holdin ML   26 *like M
27 swolve L   [that he], *so* M, *om.* SL   28 hathe L   al the] all L
30 be] yette L

XXI   Texte

Accorde noo thinge with the god Bachus,
For his tatchis be foul and vicious.
Hijs disportes be neither good ne fyne,
For he makith the pepill turne to swyne.   5

Glose   f. 19

Bachus was the man that first planted vynes in Grece; and
whanne they of the cuntre felte the strengthe of the wyne,
the which made [them] dronken, thei seide that Bachus was a
god, the which had youen such strengthe to his plante. Be   10
Bachus is vnderstanden dronkenes, as that the which is a ful
vnbehouely thing to alle noble men and to a man that wolde vse
reson. And to this purpos Ipocras seith that superfluytes of
wynes and metis destroieth bothe body, soule and vertues.

Allegorie   15

Be the god Bachus we may vnderstande the synne of glotonye,
from the which the good spirite schulde kepe him. Sent
Gregory seith in his Moralles that, whan the vice of glotonye
hath the maistrie of a persone, he lesith al the good that he hath
don; for, whanne the beli is not restreyned be abstinence, alle   20
vertues be drowned to-gidere. And therfore Sent Paul seith:
Quorum finis interitus quorum deus venter est; & gloria in
confusione eorum qui terrena sapiunt. Ad Philipenses iij°
capitulo.

XXII   Texte   25

Pymalyones ymage for to fele,
If that thou be wise sette therbi no dele,
For of such an ymage so wel wroughte
The beaute therof was to dere boughte.

---

2 Acorde for L   3 *tacches M, tachys L   be bothe L
8 *qwan L   *felthe L   *streyngth L   9 [them] so M, thyme L, om. S.
10 planet M   11 vndirstonde ML   *drwnkkynnes L   13 Ypocras ML
sūfluites (sic) L   14 vynes L   bothe] om. L   17 from] for L
18 Grigory L   glotenye L   26 Pymaliones M, Pimaliones L
29 was] is L

Glose

Pymalion was a ful subtil werkman in makyng of ymages; and
a fable seith that, for the gret lewdenes that he sawe in the
women of Cidoyne, he dispreisid them and seide he schulde
make an ymage where-in there schulde be nothing for to blame. 5
He made an ymage after a womman of souereyne beaute. Whan
he had ful made it, loue, the which subtilli can rauysch hertis,
made him to be amorous vppon the ymage, so that [f. 19b] for
hire he was vexid with wois of loue, ful of clamoures and pitous
sighynges that he made to it; but the ymage, which was of ston, 10
vnderstoode him not. Pymalion wente to the temple of Venus,
and he made there so deuout prayers to hire that the goddes
had pite; and, in schewyng therof, the bronde that sche helde
be hire-self began to take fire and schewe flaume. And than the
louere was mery for that tokne, and went towarde his ymage, 15
and tooke it in his armys, and warmed it so sore with his nakid
flesch that the ymage had lijf, and began to speke. And so
Pymalion recoueryd ioye. To þis fable may be sette many
exposicions, and in liche wise to othir such fables; and the poetis
made them because that mennys vnderstandynge schulde be 20
the more scharpe and subtill to finde dyuers exposicions. It
may be vnderstanden also, be the dispreisinge, that [Pimalion]
dispraisid the lewednes of lewde wommen and enamoured him
on a mayden of righte grete beaute, the which wolde not, or
myght not, vnderstande his pitous pleyntes, no more than [the] 25
ymage of ston had doon; that is to sey, be thinkynge on the
faire beautes he was anamoured, but at the last he prayd hire so
much and kepte him so nere here that, at the last, the mayden
loued him at his wille and hadde hire to mariage. Thus the
ymage that was harde as ston recouerid lijf be the goddes Venus. 30
So it wolde be seide that the good knyȝte scholde not be assottid
of such a made ymage in such wise that he lefte to folowe the

---

4 Cydoyne M, Cidonie L   7 *sotely L   8 for] he for L
9 clamoures and] clamorous & full of L   13 had pite] of pete L
14 *flame L, flambe M   16 wyth hys his L   18 many] om. L
22 vnderstond L   [Pimalion], so M, Pilamyon S   25 [the], so
ML, om. S.   26 a ston L   sey] sey that L   28 that at the last]
that L   29 at his wille and] & at his wille L   And thus L   32 lefte]
lyst L (laisse, Laud f. 45)

crafte of armes, to the which he is bounde be the ordre of knyghthode. And to this purpos seith Abtalyn: It longith nothinge for a prince to assotte him on nothing that is to be repreuede.

Allegorie   5

Pymaliones ymage, on whome the good knyght schulde not be assottid, we schal take for the synne of lecherye, from the which the knyghtli goostli spirite schuld kepe his body. Wherefore Sent Jerom seith in a Pistil: O fire of helle, seith he, of whome the wode is glotonye, [f. 20] the flaume is pride, the 10 sparkis be foule wordes, the smoke is the evill name, the assches is pouerte and the ende is the turment of helle. To this purpos seith Sent Petir the apostill: Voluptatem existimantes delicias, coinquinacionis & macule, delicijs affluentes, conuiuijs suis luxuriantes. Secundem Petri ij° capitulo.   15

XXIII   Texte

Of Diane remembre besili,
For the honeste of thi bodi.
For hire pleasith no vileyns lijf,
Ne no dishoneste ne strijf.   20

Glose

Diane, that is the mone, and as there is nothinge so evill but that it hath some good propirte, the mone yeueth chaste condicion; and thei named it after a ladi that so was callid, the which was ful chaste and was euer a virgin. So it wolde be seide 25 that honeste of the bodi is ful wel longing to a good knyght. And to this purpos Hermes seith: He may not be of parfit witte that hath in him no chastite.

Allegorie

And, for to brynge to mynde the articules of the feith to oure 30 purpos, withoute the which a good spirite may litel avayle, for Diane we schal take God of hevyn, the which is withoute any

---

2 Abtalin L   *longghit L   4 reprouid ML   11 be] is L
the evill] evil L   12 turment] turnementes L   17 Dyane L
19 vilens M, violeyns L   20 no] non L   26 *knygh L

spott of vnclene loue, to whom a thinge foulid with synne may
not be agreable. To the knyghtli spirite, than, it is necessarye
to beleue vppon the makere of hevyn and of erthe, as the first
articule of the feith seith, the which Sent Petir the apostill sette:
Credo in Deum patrem omnipotentem, creatorem celi et terre. 5

XXIV   Texte

Be thou like to the goddes Ceres,
That took fro noon but yaf to corn encrees;
In such wise abandoned schulde be   f 2
The good knyghte, wel sette in his degre.   10

Glose

Ceres was a ladi that fonde the crafte to ere lande, for a-fore
gaineryes sewe withoute laboure; and because that the
lande bare the more plenteuouslye after that it was eried, they
seide that sche was a goddes of cornys; and thei callid the lande 15
after here name. Where[-fore] it wolde be seide that, as the
lande is habundaunte and [a] large yeuere of alle goodes, on the
same wise schulde a good knyghte be habundaunte to alle
persones and to yeue his helpe and comforte aftir his powere. And
Aristotill seith: Be a liberal yeuere and thou schalte haue frendes. 20

Allegorie

For Ceres, to whom the good knyȝt schulde resemble, we
schall take the Sone of God whome the good spirite schulde
folowe, the which hath youen so largeli to us of high goodes,
and in him schuld be beleued stedfastli. As the secunde articule 25
seith, the which Sent John sette: Et in Jhesum Cristum, filium
eius vnicum, Dominum nostrum.

XXV   Texte

Alle hiȝ vertues, as that be wel sette,
In the as in Isis let them be sette;   30

1 *onclen L   4 *article ML   9 *habaundoned M   10 The]
To L   12 erye the londe L   13 gaineyers L   swe L   14 plenteously
L   ered M, erryed L   a] om. L   16 Wherfore ML, Where S
17 lande] lawde L   habaundone L, habandoned M   [a], so ML, om. S
18 habaundonede LM   20 Arystotyl L   22 For] Afore M, Here L
24 goodnes L   26 Jon ML   29 Aalle M   be wel] he wyll L
30 be sette] b schette L

And al maner greynes fructifie;
In such wise schuldest thou edifie.

Glose

Ysis, as poetis seith, is goddes of plantis and graffis, and sche
yeueth them strengthe and growinge to multeplie. There-
fore it is seide to the good kny3t that so schulde he fructifie in
alle vertuis and eschewe alle [euyl] vicis. And Hermes to this
purpos seith: O man, if thou knewe the inconueniencie of vice,
what thou woldest be-ware [f. 21] there-of; and if thou knewe
the reward for wurthynes, what thou woldest loue it greetly.   10

Allegorie

There where it is seide that the good spirite schulde be like to
Isis, the which is a plantere, may be vnderstanden the
blessid concepcion of Jhesu Criste be the Holi Goost in the
blissid Virgin Marie, moder of all grace, of whom the grete   15
bounteis may not be ymagyned ne hoolly seide; the which
wurthi concepcion the good spirite schulde haue hoolly in hym,
and kepe this holy articule stedfastli, as Sent James the gretter
seith: Qui conceptus est de Spiritu Sancto, natus ex Maria
virgine.   20

XXVI   Texte

To the iugement in no wise holde the
Of Migdas, the which nothyng wisele
Jugede; be his councel set thou no store,
For eeris of an asse he hadde therefore.   25

Glose

Migdas was a kynge that had litel vnderstandynge; and a
fable seith that Phebus and Oan, the [god] of pasturis,
stroof to-gedere, and Phebus seide that the sowne of the harpe

5

2 L cancels wys before wyse   4 Ysys L   as] om. L   goodesse L
griffes M, gryffes L   7 [euyl], so ML, om. S (mal, Laud f. 46)
7 Harmes L   9 what] that L   12 *qwere L   spirite] knygh L
(om. in Laud)   13 be vnderstanden] we understond
L (pouons, Laud f. 46b)   16 holy ML   18 *article M, artecle L
23 Mygdas ML.   27 Mydas L   kynge] knyght L (roy, Laud)
28 [god], so L, goddesse SM (le dieu, Laud)   29 *strof M, strove L
* sownde L

is more to preise than the sowne of the pipe or of the floyte.
Oan helde the contrarye and seide that the sowne of the floyte
was more to preyse. Thei made Migdas juge of that discorde,
and aftir that thei were bothe ioyned afore Migdas, at longe
leiser he iugede that the sowne of the floyte was bettir and more 5
plesante than the sowne of the harpe. So the fable seith that
Phebus, the which was greued, hadde despite of his iugement,
made him rude eeris liche an asse in schewynge that he had
vnderstandynge of an asse, the which hadde iuged so folily.
It may be also that some iuged lewedly ayens a prince or a 10
myghti man, the which ponysschid him, makynge him to bere
[f. 21ᵇ] on him some signe of a foole, the which is vnderstanden
be the eeris of an asse. Also it is to vnderstande be this fable
that a good knyght scholde not holde him content with a lewde
iugement not grounded on reson, ne himself scholde be no iuge 15
of so defauty a sentence. A philosophre seith to this purpos that
a fool is liche a molle the which herith and vnderstandith not.
And Diogenes likenyth the fool to a stoon.

Allegorie

The iugement of Migdas, the which a good knyghte scholde 20
not kepe, we may vnderstande Pilate, the which iuged the
blessid Sone of God to be taken and streyned as an harpe and
to be honged on the gebet of the Crosse as a briboure, he the
which was pure withoute any spotte. Also it is to vnderstande
that the good spirite scholde be-warre how he schulde iuge an 25
innocent; and he schulde beleue the articule that Sent Andrewe
seith: Passus sub Poncio Pilato, crucifixus, mortuus et sepultus.

XXVII   Texte

As trewe felawes of armes dooth,
Vn-to helle, whither that soulis gooth, 30
Thou schuldest goo, them to socoure certeyne
At nede, liche as Hercules dede as men seyne.

---

2 seide that] seide L   *flowte L   7 greued] gevyd L
*dyspyte L, dispite M   12 *syngne L   12–13 vnderstanden be] to
vnderstond L   eres L, ere M   an] the L   16 fawty L   21 Pylate
L, be Pilate M   23 on] opon L   24 withoute] wyth L   26 Andrew M
30 *whedir L   32 At] And L   liche as] lich L

Glose

The fable seith that Theseus and Protheus went in-to helle
for to rescuwe Proserpine that Pluto rauysschid, and thei
hadde ben evill goon hadde not Hercules a been; for theire
felawes had not be socourid had he ne been, the which dide so 5
notable deedes of armys that he affraide alle the peple of helle,
and he smote assonder Acerberus the porterys cheynes. So it
is seide that a good knyghte schulde not fayle his felawe for no
maner of perill þat myȝt be, for trewe felawis schulde be as oo
thing and all on. And Pictagoras seith: Thou schuldest kepe the 10
loue of thi frende diligentlye.

Allegorie   f. 22

Be the auctorite that seith he schulde socoure his truwe
frendis in armys vnto helle, we may vnderstande the blessid
soule of Jhesu Criste, the which drewe oute the good soulis of 15
holi patriarkes and prophetis that were in limbo. And be this
example the good spirite schulde drawe to him alle vertues and
beleue the articule that Sent Philip seith: Descendit ad inferna.

XXVIII   Texte

Cadimus loue and yeue to him preisynge;   20
And that auctorised may his techynge
Be in the; for the welle in certeyne
He wan fro the serpent with grete peyne.

Glose

Cadimus was a ful noble man and founded Thebes, the 25
which was a cite of grete name. He sette there-ynne an
vniuersite, and himself was greteli lettred and of grete con-
nynge; and therfore the fable seith that he doutede the serpent
at the welle. This is to vnderstande connynge and wisedome,
the which riseth alwey, that is for the welle; the serpent is noted 30

2 Thesus L   4 goon] begone L   7 assonder] in soundir L
7 Cereberus L (a Cerberus . . . coppa, Laud f. 47ᵇ)   *chynnes L
9 as] evyn as L   10 shuld L   16 *profhetes L   18 Phelip L
23 whan L   27 kunnyng and wysdom L   28 and . . . he] the whiche
man after that the fabyl seith he L

for the peyne and the trauayle that a stodiere most doute ere
that he gete connynge. And the fable seith that he become a
serpent himself, the which is to be vnderstanden that he become
maister and correctoure of othir. So Othea wolde sey that a
good knyghte schulde loue and wurschip clerkes that be lettred, 5
the which be grounded in connynge. To this purpos Aristotill
seide to Alexander: Wurschip wisedome and fortefie it with
good maistres.

Allegorie

Be Cadimus that douted the serpent at the welle, the which 10
the good knyghte scholde loue, we may vnderstande the
blessid manhode of Jhesu Criste, the which douted the serpent
and wan the welle, that is to sey, the lijf of this worlde; the
which [he passid] with grete peyne [f. 22ᵇ] and with grete
trauayle, of whom he had the victorie be strengthe, whan he 15
roos the thirde day, as Sent Thomas seith: Tercia die resurexit
a mortuis.

XXIX   Texte

Delite the greteli in the connynge
Of Yoo, more than good or othir thinge;   20
For bi that thou maist lerne ful gretli
And of good ther-inne take largeli.

Glose

YOO was a yonge ientil womman and doughter to kynge
Ynacus, the which was righte connynge and fonde many 25
maneres of lettres that had not be seen afoore. Though that som
fablis sey that Yoo was Jubiter-is loue and that sche become a
cowe and aftir a womman as sche was. But as that poetis hath
hidde trouthe vnder couerture of fable, it may be that Jubiter

1 or L   3 be vnderstanden] vndirstond L   4 wolde sey]
seith L   5 and wurschip clerkes] clerkes and worshipe M   7 Alexaundre
M, Alysawndre L   12 the which] that M   14 [he passid], *so
ML, om.* S (il passa, Laud f. 48)   15 had the] hade L   16 *rose ML
*thridde M, thredde L   19 Delite the] Delyte L   20 Yo ML
22 goodes M (bien, Laud f. 48)   theryng L   27 Jupiteris L   becam L
28 knowe *corrected to* kowe L   as that] as the L

loued hire, that is to vnderstande, be the vertues the which were
in hire sche become a cowe; for as a cowe yeueth mylke, the
which is swete and norisschynge, [soo] sche be the lettres that
sche fonde yaf noryshschynge to vnderstandynge. [More-ouyr]
in that sche was a comon womman may be vnderstanden that 5
hire witte was comon to alle, as lettres be comon to alle pepill.
Therfore it is seide that the good knyghte schulde ful muche
loue Yoo, the which may be vnderstanden be lettres and scrip-
tures and stories of good pepill, the which the good knyghte
scholde here tolde gladlye and redde, the example of the which 10
may be vaylable to him. To this purpos Hermes seith: Who-so
enforceth him to gete connynge and good condicions, he
fyndith that the which schall please him in this worlde and in
[the] othere.

Allegorie 15

Yoo, the which is noted for lettres and scriptures, may be
vnderstanden that the good spirite scholde delite him to
rede or to here Holy Writte and note the Scriptures in his
mynde, and there-bi may he lerne [f. 23] to clyme to heuen with
Jhesu Criste be goode werkes and holy contemplacion. And he 20
scholde beleue the wurthi articule that Sent Bartholomewe seith:
Asscendit ad celos, sedet ad dexteram Dei patris omnipotentis.

XXX   Texte

Be-ware in what place so that it be,
In the noyse of floytes slepe not ye;   25
For Mercurius, that softe singeth,
With his floite the pepill enchaunteth.

Glose

A fable seith that, whan Jubiter loued faire Yoo, Juno had him
in suspecion and descended from heuyn in a skye for to 30
take hire housbonde with the deede. But whan Jubiter saugh

---

1 was L   3 [soo], so M, om. SL   4 [more-ouyr], so M, and
SL   8 Yoo] tho L   be lettres] þe letteris L   9 the which the] that
the M   10 telle L   the example of the which] that the example therof M
14 [the], so ML, that S (l'autre, Laud)   18 not L   20 he] om. L
21 worethi L, noble M (digne, Laud)   Barthilmew M, Bertylmw L
25 *flowtes L   29 hym gretly L   31 with] whit L

here come, he chaungede his loue to a cowe; yit for all that Juno
was not oute of suspecion, but asked him the cowe of yifte; and
Jubiter ayens his luste graunted it to hire, as he that dorst not
geyne-sey hire for doute of suspecion. Than Juno yaf Argus,
the which had an .C. yen, this cowe to kepe, and euere he wacchid   5
it. But the god Mercurius, be the commaundement of Jubiter,
toke his floite, the which sange softely, and blewe so longe in
Argus ere that alle his .C. yen were a-slepe; than he smote of
his hede and took the cowe. The exposicion of this fable may
be as that some myghti man loued a ientil womman that his wif   10
tooke to hire for to make wacche on hire housbonde, that he
deceyued hire not, and ther-vppon sette grete wacchis and
clere seers, the which may be notid for Argus yen. But the
louere, be a persone malicious and wele-spekinge, dede so
moche that the keperes consentid to yeue him his loue, and thus   15
were thei broughte a-slepe be Mercurius floite and had here
hedes smyten of. Therfore it is seyde to the good knyghte that
he schulde not suffre to be broughte a-slepe with no such
floite as to be robbed of that the which he schulde kepe. And
to this purpos Hermes seith: Kepe you fro thoo [f. 23ᵇ] that be   20
gouerned be malice.

Allegorie

Be Mercurius floite we may vnderstande that the good spirite
be not deceyued be the olde enemye through any mysbeleue
of the feith or othire wise. And he schulde beleue stedfastly the   25
articule that Sent Mathewe the euangelist seith, that God schal
come to iuge the quyk and the deede, where he seith: Inde
venturus est iudicare viuos et mortuos.

XXXI   Texte

Thinkith that Pirus schall resemble   30
His fader, and that he schall trouble

2 not] *om.* L   *yfte M   3 it] *om.* L   *durste M, dryst L
4 geyne-sey] ayens sey L   5 wchid L   7 song L   8 ere] eyre L
*eyne L   10 womman that] woman than L   12 weches L
13 *seerres M   15 *miche L   16 here] *þer ML   17 Therfore]
There L   18 on slepe L   20 you] thou L   20–1 is gouernede L
24 through] trowe L   25 And] than L   26 Mathew M, Matheu L
27 to iuge] and iuge L   *qweke L

His enemyes and put them to distres;
The dethe he schal venge of Achilles.

Glose

Pirus was Achilles son and resembled ful wel his fader in
strengthe and hardynes; and aftir the deth of his fader he 5
come to Troye and ful scharpeli venged his fader and hurted
greetli the Troyens. Therfore it is seide to the good knyghte
that, yif he haue mysdon to the fader, lete him be-ware of the
son whan he cometh to age; and, yif the fader be wurthi and
manly, the son schulde be the same. The wiseman seith to this 10
purpos that the fadris deth askith of the son the vengeaunce
there-fore.

Allegorie

There where he seith that Pirus schulde be liche his fader, be
that we may vnderstande the Hooli Goost, the which pro- 15
cedith of the Fader, in whome the good spirite schulde beleue,
as Sent James the lesse seith: Credo in Spiritum Sanctum.

XXXII   Texte

Haunte thou the temple and wurschip in tyme
The goddes of heuene, and at all tyme   20
After Cassandra kepe thou the gise,   f. 24
If that thou wilte be holden [for] wise.

Glose

Cassandra was kynge Priantes doughter, and sche was a ful
good ladi and a deuoute in theire lawe. Sche serued the 25
goddis and haunted the temple, and sche spake but litell
withouten cause; and whanne sche muste speke, sche spake
nothinge but that was trewe, ne sche was neuere founde with
lesynge; sche was ful connynge. Therfore it is seide to the good
knyghte that he schulde be like here, for lewde customes and 30
lesinges be gretli to blame in a knyghte, for he schulde serue

4 Pyrus L   5 hardynes] worthinesse M (hardement, Laud f. 49ᵇ)
6 hurte L   9–10 and manly] or manly L   10 which man L   11 of]
om. L   20 godesse L (les dieux, Laud)   21 Cassaundra L
22 [for], *so* ML, *om.* S   25 *there L, hire M   26 godesse L
28 with] with no L   30 *leke L   31 be]ys L   *knyte L

God and wurschip the temple, that is to seye, the chirche and
the mynystres therof. And Pictagoras seith: It is righte a
loueable thinge to serue God and to halowe his seintes.

Allegorie

The auctorite seith that the good knyghte schulde haunte the 5
temple. In liche wise the good spirite schulde doo, and he
schulde haue singulere deuocion in the feithful holi chirche and
in the communyon of seintes. As the articule seith that Sent
Symond made, the which seith: Sanctam ecclesiam catholicam,
sanctorum communionem.   10

XXXIII   Texte

If thou wilte often haunte the see,
Of Neptunus thou schulde remembre thee;
And thou schuldest greteli halowe his fest,
That he may kepe the euere fro tempest.   15

Glose

Neptunus vppon the paynymes lawe was callid the god of
[þe] see, and therfore it is seide to the good knyghte that
he schulde serue him, that is to vnderstande, that knyghtes, the
which gooth often many viages on the see or in othire dyuerse 20
perelles, haue more nede to be [f. 24b] deuoute and to serue
God and his seintes than othire pepill, to the entente that at
theire nede he may be the more socourable and helpely to
them. And thei scholde take a singulere deuocion to some
seinte be deuoute prayeres, be the which thei may calle to him 25
or hire in there besynessis. And that [the prayer of the] herte
is not al-oonly sufficient, therfore the wise man seith: I noyse
nat, seith he, God al-oonly to be serued be wordes but be good
deedis.

2 righte a] a ryght L   5 actorite L, autorite M   9 Symonde M
13 shuld ofte L   14 greteli halowe] halow gretly L   17 Neptimus (?) L
18 [þe], so L, om. SM (la mer, Laud f. 50b)   20 gooth] gosh L   in many L
22 *seyntens L   *peplyl L   that] om. L   23 the more] om. L   helpy L
26 besynes L   [the prayer of the], so M, prayere with SL (de cuer,
Laud)   27 therfore] om. L   27–28 I . . . serued] that God all only ys
not well serued L

Allegorie

Be Neptunus, to whom the good knyghte scholde calle if he go ofte be the see, we schall vnderstande that the good spirite, the which is contynuelly in the see of the worlde, schulde calle deuoutly vppon his makere and pray that he wul 5 yif him grace so to lyue that he may haue remyssion of al his synnes. And he scholde beleue the articule that Sent Jude seith: Remissionem peccatorum.

XXXIV   Texte

Loke that at al tymes thou take good hede   10
Bothe to Acropos crafte and to his spede,
Which smyteth and sparith noon in no kynde;
That schall make the to haue thi soule in mynde.

Glose

Poetes callid deth Acropos; wherfore it is seide to the good 15
knyȝte that he schulde thinke that he schall not euere lyue
in this worlde, but sone departe there-fro. Therfore he scholde
sette more store be the vertues of the soule than to delite him in
bodily delites; and alle Cristen peple scholde thinke ther-vppon,
to the entente that he myghte remembre to prouide for the 20
soule, the which schall endure withouten ende. And to this
purpoos Pictagoras seith that, liche as oure begynnyng cometh
of God, oure ende muste nedis be there.

Allegorie

There where it is seide to the good knyghte that he schulde f. 25
take hede to Accropos, the which is notid for deth, the same 26
schulde the good spirit haue, the which be the merytes of the
Passion of oure Lorde Jhesu Criste scholde haue stedfast hope,
with the peyne and diligence that he scholde put therto, to haue
heuene at the laste ende. And he scholde beleue stedfastly to 30
rise ayen at the day of dome and haue euer-lasting lijf, if he

4 which] *om.* L   5 schulde] he shulde L   6 al] *om.* L
10 that] *om.* L   11 Acropose L   and to] and L   15 calle L
16 *thynghe L   17 sone] some M   derefro L   20 to prouide] the
provide L   22 Pytagoras L   *comyht L   31 and haue] to haue L

deserue it. As Seint Mathi seith in the last articule, where he
seith: Carnis resurrexionem et vitam eternam. Amen.

XXXV   Texte

Belorophon, let him example be,
In all maner deedis that do will ye,   5
The whiche had moche leuer for to dye
Thanne supporte vntrouth be any weye.

Glose

Belorophon was a knyghte of righte grete beaute and ful of
trouth. His stepmoder loued him so wel & so hoote that   10
sche requyred it of him and, because he wolde not consente to
hir wille, sche dide so moche that he was condempned to be
deuoured with feers bestis; and he had more lust to chese deth
than to do vntrouth. To this purpos Hermes seith: Be gladder
to dey with-oute cause than to do vntrouth.   15

A prolouge to the allegorie

We schal now come to declare the commaundementis of the
feith, and therto we schal take an allegorie to oure
purpoos.

Allegorie
                                                                 20
Belorophon, the which was so full of trouth, may be noted for
God of heuene and, as his hiȝ mercy hath ben to us [f. 25ᵇ]
and is ful of trouth, we may take the first commaundement, the
which seith: Thou schalte wurschip no straunge goddes. To
this seith Seint Austin that [the] wurschip the which is callid 25
the decre thou scholdist not do it, neithir to ydole ne to ymage
ne to no liknes of no maner creature, for that is a dewe wurschip
al-oonly to God, and in this commaundement is defended all
ydolatrie. To that our Lorde seith in the Gospell: Dominum
Deum tuum adorabis et illi soli seruies. Mathei iiijᵗᵒ capitulo. 30

2 resurreccionem M   5 maner of L   ye] he L   6 for] om. L
7 Than to L   10 so wel & so hoote] soo hote ML   11 be-cause that ML
13 mo L   the deth L   15 vntrouth] a inconuenyence L (descouuenue,
Laud f. 51)   17 come now L   21 Berolophon L   23 all
trouth L   25 [the], so ML, we S   26 the decre] decre L   shulde L
*ydoile L   27 no maner] no interlineated in S   of creature L

XXXVI Texte

Maymon, thi owne trewe cosin in dede,
The which is thi neghboure at thi nede,
He loueth the so myche thou ought him loue,
And for his nede arme thi bodi aboue.

Glose

Kyng Maymon was cosin to Hector and of the Troyens lyne
and whan Hector was in feers bataylles, where he was often
gretly oppressid with his enemyes, Maymon, the which was a
ful worschipful knyghte, folowed him euer nere and socoured 10
Hector and brak the grete precis of pepill. And that schewid
well, for whan Achilles had slayne him be treson, Maymon
woundid Achilles sore and had slayne him had not socoure
a-comen to him in haste. Therfore it is seid to the good knyghte
that he schulde loue him and socoure him at his nede; and this 15
is to vnderstande that euery prince and good knyghte which
hath kyn, be thei neuer so litell or pore, so he be good and trewe,
he schulde loue him and supporte him in his dedis, and in
especiall whan he felith him trewe to him. And it happith som
tyme that a grete prince is bettir loued and more trewli of his 20
poore kyn than of a ful myghti man. And to this purpos seith
Rabion the philosophre: Encrece frendes, for thei schal be
socourable to thee.

Allegorie f. 26

Be Maymon, the trewe cosin, we may vnderstande God of 25
heuene, the which hath ben a ful trewe cosin for to take
oure manhod, the which benefete we may not gwerdon. Thus
here may we take the ij^{de} commaundement, that seith: Thou
schalte not take the name of God in vein, that is to seie, as
Seint Austin seith: Thou schalte not swere dishonestli, ne 30
with-oute a cause, ne for coloure of falsnes, for ther may no
gretter abusion be than to brynge to a fals witnes the chefe and

2 thine M, thyn L   4 louyd L   5 nede] cause M (besoing,
Laud f. 51^{b})   8 Hector was] Hector L   11 *presis M, presses L
12 Maymons L   13 had slayne] sleyne L   17 trewe] trwee L
19 happenyth L   22 Rabyon L   32 obusioun M   fals]
flasse L

the righte stedfast trowthe. And in this commaundement alle
lesinges be defendid, al periury and al blaspheme. The lawe
seith to this purpos: Non habebit Dominus insontem eum qui
assumpserit nomen Domini Dei sui frustra. Exodi. xx^mo
capitulo.   5

XXXVII   Texte

Avise the, or any worde be schewde
Of grete manacynges, nyce or lewde,
Comyng oute of thi mouth be to grete ire,
And loke well in Leomedon the syre.   10

Glose

Leomedon was kyng of Troye and fadir to Priant. And whanne
Jason, Hercules and their felawys wente to Colcos for to gete
the fleese of golde and were aryved and descendid at the porte
of Troye for to refresch them with-oute hurte of the cuntre,   15
Leomedon, not wel avised, sent boistous messangeris to voyde
them of the lande and to manace them gretely, if thei [voydid]
not in hast. Than the barones of Grece were so wroth for that
wrongeful conveyng that aftir that folowed the distroccion of
the first Troye. Therfore it is seide to the good knyghte that, 20
standyng the worde of manace is foule and vilenous, it schulde
be sadli peysid ere that it were spokyn, for many grete hurtys
often tymes folowith therof. To this purpoos the [f. 26^b] poet
Omer seith: He is wise that can restreyne his mouthe.

Allegorie   25

Howe the worde of grete manace comyth of arrogaunce, and
[that] to breke the commaundement it is also an ouir-
hope, we may vnderstonde be this that noon scholde breke the
holy-day, for that is ayenst the commaundement the which is

---

1 stefast L   trowhe *corrected to* trowthe L   8 *manasynges M, mani-
synges L   9 oute] forthe L   10 Leomedom L   syre] fire L
12 Leomemedon L   Priaunt M   13 felawys] feleshipe M (compaig-
nons, Laud f. 52^b)   15 ony hurte L   16 bostus L   17 [voydid], *so*
ML, voide S   19 *destruccion ML   21 velyens L   22 peysid]
passede L   24 restreyne] refreyne L (reffrener, Laud)   27 [that],
so ML, *om.* S   29 *halyday L   the which] þat L

seide: Vmbethinke the to halowe the Sabaoth day. Be the which
Seint Austin seith: It is commaundid us to hallowe the Sonday
in-stede of the Juwes Sabaoth, for thanne we scholde solempneli
take bodily reste, cessing solempneli also of all werkis of thral-
dom, and to be in reste of soule in cessing of all synne. And to 5
this purpos Isaie the prophete seith: Quiescite agere peruerse,
discite benefacere.

XXXVIII   Texte

Trust nothing to be in certainte
Vn-to that the trouth well knowen be;   10
For a litill [of] presumpcion
Piramus makith the mencion.

Glose

Piramus was a yonge ientilman of the citee of Babiloine, and
fro that he was but viij yere of age, loue wounded him with 15
his darte and was soore taken with the loue of Tisbe, the faire
gentil damysell, the which was like to him in kin and of age.
And, be the grete hauntyng of the ij° lovers to-geddir, the grete
loue was parceyued and be a seruant accusid to the moder of
the yonge ientill woman, the which toke hir doughtir and schette 20
hire in chambirs and seide sche scholde kepe hire wel ynough
fro the hauntyng of Piramus; and [f. 27] there-fore was gret woo
betwene tho ij° childer in full pitous compleyntes and weping.
That preson dured longe, but as thei wex in age the sparke of
loue encreced; for al theire longe absence, it quenchid not. 25
Be-twene the placis of theire kin was but a thin walle. Tesbi
parceyued the wal crased, where through sche sawe brightnes
on the tothir side. Than sche toke the pendant of hir girdell
and put it through the crevice to the entent that hir loue myght
parceyve it, as that he dide in schorte tyme, and there tho ij° 30

1 Sabat ML   day] om. L   3 the stede L   *Jewes M, Jues L   4 take]
all-so take L   bodily reste] reste bodyly L   also] om. L   6 Ysaie
M, Ysaye L   the prophete seith] seyth the profyte L   9 certeynete L
11 [of], so ML, om. S (pou de, Laud)   14 Pyramus L   Babiloyne M,
Babylonie L   15 viij] vij L (vij, Laud)   of age] olde L   16 Tysbe L
17 gentil damysell] yonge gentilwoman ML (belle damoiselle et gente, Laud
f. 53)   21 hir chambre L   seide] om. L   22 was] þer was L   23 tho]
the ML   25 not] neuer the more L   26 Thesbe L   27 *brygnes L
30 tho] thei L

loveris made ofte theire assembles with ful pitous compleintes. At the laste, as to sore constreined be [loue], there accorde was sich that at nyghte, in the first quarter of the nyghte, thei scholde parte fro there kin and mete withoute the cite at a welle vnder a white-thorn, where in theire childehode they were wont to pleye. Whan Tesbe was comen to the welle al aloone and feerful, sche herde a lyon come ful rudeli, for the which sche, ful of feere, fledde and leyde hire in a busch fast by; but in the wey felle from hire a white wympil. Piramus come, the which be the mone-schyne parceyued the wympil, but the lyon had fouled it and made it al blody, the which had vomyted ther-vppon the intrayle of a beste that he had deuoured. Than the sorowe of Piramus was out of mesure grete, the which wende his loue had ben deuourid with wylde bestis; and than aftir [his] pitous compleyntes & sorowe, he slowe himself with his owne swerde. Tesbi come out of the busch, but whan sche vnderstode and parceyued that hir loue was blodi and deying, and that sche sawe the swerde and the blood, than with grete sorowe sche fell vppon her loue, the which myghte not speke vnto hir. And þan, aftir many grete compleintes, weymenta-cions and swovnyngis, sche killed hir-silf with the same swerd. Soo the fable seith that than, because ther-of, the wal that was wonte to be white become blak. And be-cause that be litill occasion happith so grete mysaventurys, it is seide to the good [f. 27ᵇ] knyghte that he scholde [not] yeve grete feith to a litel tokene. And to this purpos the wiseman seith: Yelde the not to thingis the which ben in doute, a-fore that thou haue had dewe informacion.

Allegorie

There where he seith that he [wenith] not [to] be in certeine, we may not therbi the ignoraunce that we haue in childe-hode. And where we [be] vndir correccion of fadir and modir, in that we may vnderstande the iiij^th commaundement, the

2 be [loue]; *so* L, be bone S, with loue M   3 at] *om.* L   5 white] qwythe L   where] were L   8 *bosche L   11 fouled] sylyd L blody the] L *breaks off, one quire of 8 leaves wanting*   15 [his], *so* M, this S   21 *sownynges M   25 [not], *so* M, *om.* S   30 [wenith], *so* M, may S   [to], *so* M, *om.* S (il ne cuide point estre, Laud f. 53ᵇ) 31 note M   32 [be], *so* M, *om.* S

which seith: Wurschip fadir and modir. The which Seint
Austin expoundith, seying that we schold wurschip our kin in
ij° maneris, in doynge to theim dewe reuerence and in seruyng
theim in theire necessitees. And to this purpos the wiseman
seith: Honora patrem tuum, et gemitus matris tue ne obliuis- 5
caris. vij° capitulo.

XXXIX   Texte

Beleue, for the helthe of thi body,
Esculapyones answeris pleinly.
And nat oonly on the enchaunteresse   10
Circes, the which is to grete a trompresse.

Glose

Esculapion was a ful wise clerke, the which fonde the crafte
of phesik and made bookis therof. And therefore it is seide
to the good knyghte that he [shulde] trust his answeris for his 15
helthe; that is to vndirstonde, if he haue nede, he [shulde]
tourne to lechis and phisiciens and not to Circes, the which was
a stronge enchaunteresse. This may be seid for theim that in
theire seeknessis vsith sorceries, charmys and enchaunte-
mentis, and wenyth therby to be hool, the which is a thing 20
[f. 28] defendid and ayens the commaundement of holichirche,
and that no good Cristen man schold vse. Platon brent and
reproved the bookes of enchauntementis and of sorceries made
vppon medicynes, the which som tyme were vsid, and [he]
fordide theim and kepte him to thoo of resonable science and of 25
experience.

Allegorie

Be Esculapion, that was a phisicien and a leche, we may
vnderstonde the vth commaundement, the which seith:
Thou schalte not slee. That is to sey, seith Seint Austin, neithir 30
with herte, with tonge ne with hande. Also there is defendid all
violence, strokes and bodili hurtes. But yet it is nat so defendid

1 The which] *om.* M   2 *expownith M   11 to grete a] a
greet M (trop, Laud)   14 *phisik M   15 [shulde], *so* M, *om.* S
16 [shulde], *so* M, to S   21 ayens the the M   23 repreuid M
24 [he], *so* M, *om.* S

to princes, to iuges and to maastres of iustice to put to deth
yvell doers; but to theym all-oonly the which haue noon
auctorite, saue in caas of necessite, there where a man may not
ellis escape, in which caas ryght suffriþ oon to slee anothir, in
his body defendant and ellis nat. To this purpos the Gospel 5
saith: Qui gladio occiderit, oportet eum in gladio occidi. Luce
xiijº capitulo.

XL   Texte

> In him to whom thou hast to myche mysdoon,
> The which may not venge him the vppon,   1
> Trust not [to] him, for harme therof may falle.
> The deth of Achilles tellith the alle.

Glose

Achilles dide full mych harme to the citesyns and killed many
of [Priantes] childer, Hector, Troyles and othir, for the 1
which thei oughte to [hate] him. Notwithstandyng this
Achilles trustid [f. 28ᵇ] quene Ecuba, Priantis wif, whoos childer
he hadde slayne be treson, and went be nyght to speke with hire
for to trete of a mariage betwen Policene, hir doughtir, and him.
And there was Achilles slayn be Paris and his felauschip, be the 2
commaundement of the quene, his modir, in Appolynys
[temple]. Therfore it is seide to the good knyghte that he schuld
not truste his enemye to whom he hath to mych mysdoon, with-
oute a pees or amendis made to him. To this purpos a wiseman
seith: Be-ware of the wacchis of thin enemye the which may not 2
venge him.

Allegorie

As in him, to whom a man hath to myche mysdoon he schulde
not truste, in that we may take how that we schulde doute
the vengeaunce of God; and there-in it is necessarie to kepe the 3
commaundement, the which seith: Thou schalte do [no] mys-
chef, that is to seye, in auoutrie ne in fornicacion. And herein

---

1 *maystres M   to put] þer puttynge M   11 [to], so M,
om. S   15 [Priantes], so M, theire S (au roy Priant, Laud f. 54ᵇ)
16 [hate], so M, om. S   19 Polixene M   21 Apolines M
22 [temple], so M, tyme S   31 [no], so M, om. S   32 aduoutrie M

is defendid, as Isodre seith, al the filþe of fleschli defautis, the which is not in mariage, and al disordenat vsages of secrete membris. To this purpos the lawe seith: Morte moriatur, mechus & adultera. Leuitici xxᵐᵒ capitulo.

XLI   Texte   5

Like to Buissieres be not leef,
The which was worse than an arrant theef;
It is to reprove his cruelnes,
To such deedis the in no wise dres.

Glose   10

Buissieres was a king wondirful cruel and delited him gretlye in manslaughter; and in-deede he killed them himself in his templis with knyvis, and made sacrifices to his goddis. Therfore it is [f. 29] seide to the good knyghte that in no wise he scholde delite him in slauȝter of mankyndely nature, for such 15 cruelnes is aȝens God, aȝens nature and aȝens al bounte. And to this purpos Socrates seith to councel the good knyght: If thi prince be cruel, thou schuldest moderate him be good examples.

Allegorie

Be Buissieres, the which was a mansleer and contrary to 20 mankindeli nature, we may note it in the defence that we do aȝens the commaundement that seith: Thou schalte do no thefte. Seint Austin seith that in this is defendid al vnleifful vsurpacion of othir mennys thingis, as sacrilege, al raveine, al thing takin be force and be lordschip of the pepil withoute 25 reson. To this purpos Seint Poul the apostill seith: Qui furabatur, iam non furetur. Ad Ephesios iiij capitulo.

XLII   Texte

Sette the not to mych on thi plesaunce,
For it puttith in to grete balaunce   30
Thi lijf, which thou schuldist loue parde;
Leander perisschid in the see.

1 Ysidre M   3 Mortem M   6 Buissierres M   7 erraunt M
8 to] *interlineated in* S   12 manslaughte M   them himself] them M
13 templis] templis him-self M   23 *vnlefull M   24 *rauene M
29 *moche M

Glose

Leander was a yong ientilman that loued to hertili feire Hero; and, as there was an arme of the see betwene the ij° maners of the ij° louers, Leander passid it often be nyghtis, swymmyng for to see his ladi, the which had hir castell fast be the banke- 5 side, because theire loue schulde not be perceyved. But it felle on a tyme there roos a gret tempest vppon that watir, the which duryd many daies, that distourbed the ioye of the louers. But yit it hap[f. 29ᵇ]ped that Leander, constreyned with to grete desire, took the watir in the tyme of the tempest, and there he 10 was so longe possid with the perlyous wawes that he muste nedis perych pitously. Sche, the which was on the tothir side in gret thoughte for hir loue, whan sche sawe þe body come fletyng on the ryver-side, than sche was streyned with so mervelous a sorowe that sche caste hir-silf in-to the see, and in 15 taking the perisched bodi in here armys was drownyd. Therfore it is seyde to the good knyghte that he schulde not loue his delite soo myche to put his lijf therfore in-to gret aventure. Wherefore a wiseman seith: I merveile that y se so many perellis suffrid for bodili delite, and so litell purviaunce made for the 20 soule, the which is euerlasting.

Allegorie

How that auctorite defendith that a man schulde not sette soo mych be his plesaunce may be vnderstanden be the commandement that seith: Thou schalt bere no fals witnes 25 ayens thi neiȝebore. And Seint Austin seith that there is defendid also all fals accusacions, grucchinges, bakbityngis, and all fals reportes and dissymilacions to othir. And Isodore seith that a fals witnes doith velony in sondri partes: to God, whom he despitith in forsweryng him; to the iuge, the which he 30 deceyuith with his lesinges; and to his neghbore that he hurtith, in that he is falsly disposed ayens him.

---

7 that ther M   up-on the M   8 distroublid M   11 perilous M
12 the tothir] that othir M   26 *neighborow M   28 Isidre M
29 doith] doot vilenye M

XLIII   Texte

Yelde Helaine ayen if asked she be
For in gret trespace lyeth mendes parde.
Bettir it is soone to pees consente
Than to [hide] the vntrouthe badly mente.   5

Glose   f. 30

Helayne was king Menelaux wif and rauisched be Paris in
Grece. And wan the Grekis were comyn vppon Troye
with a gret armee for to venge that deede, a-fore ere thei dide
any mysdeede to the lande, thei required that Helaine myghte be   10
restored aȝen to theime; and amendis made for the offence, or
ellis thei wolde destroie the contre. And because the Troyens
wold not do it folowed the gret myschef that come aftir to them.
Therfore it is seide to the good knyghte that, yf he haue begonne
a debate folily, it is bettire for him to leve it and to make pees   15
than to pursewe it, that harme fall not to him therof. Wherfore
Platon the philosophre seith: If thou haue doon wrong, to whom
that euere it be, thou schuldest not be at eese to thou were
accordid with him and made peas.

Allegorie   20

Be Helayne, the which scholde be yolden ayen, may be
vnderstanden the commaundement the which seith: Thou
scholdist not desire thi neghboris wif. For the which Seint
Austin seith is defendid bothe thoughte and wil to do fornica-
cion, the which deede is defendid a-foore in the vth comaunde-   25
ment. For our Lorde seith in the Gospell: Qui viderit mulierem
ad concupiscendum eam, iam mechatus est in corde suo.
Mathei v° capitulo.

XLIV   Texte

Resemble thou not to the goddesse   30
Aurora, that yeueth grete lightnesse
To othir, whan that hir houre is comyng
And in hir-silf hath sorowe and wepyng.

2 Heleyne M   5 [hide], so M, om. S (encourir, Laud f. 56)
8 whan M   come M   11–13 and amendis ... to them] om. M
19 had made M (fait, Laud)   32 *oure M

Glose

Avrora is the spring of the day; and fables seith that it is a
goddesse, and that sche hadde a son of hires slayne in the
batay[f. 30ᵇ]le of Troye, the which was callid Tynus; and she,
that had myght as a goddes, chaungid the body of hir son in-to a 5
swanne, and fro thens come the first swannes. This [lady] was
of so grete beaute þat it reioiced all tho that sawe hir, but all hir
lijf sche bewaylid hir son Signus. Therfore it is seide to the
good knyghte that bi his good vertues he schulde be reioiced,
and [afore othir] he schuld not be hevy but gladde and behauyng 10
him graciosely. [Wherfore] Aristotill seide to Alexander the
grete: What maner of heuynes that thin herte haue, thou
scholdist schewe a glad visage to thi pepill.

Allegorie

Be Aurora that wepeth we may vnderstonde that no desire 15
schulde wepe in us for couetice of worldli thingis. And be
this we may note the xᵗʰ comaundement, the which seith: Thou
schalte not covete thi neghboris hous, his oxe, his asse ne nothing
that he hath. For the which Seint Austin seith that the will is
defendid to do thefte or raveyne, and this is defendid afore in 20
the vijᵗʰ commaundement. To this purpos Dauid seith in the
Psaultere: Nolite sperare in iniquitate, rapinas nolite concu-
piscere.

XLV   Texte

Knowing that this Pasiphe was a fool,   25
In no wise lerne thou not of here scool.
Though that som wommen do soo amys,
Yit right many goode there be, ywis.

Glose

Pasiphe was a quene; and some fables sein that sche was a 30
woman of grete dissolucion, and namely soo that sche loued
a bull, the which is to vndirstonde, that sche was aqueynted

---

4 Tinus M   6 [lady] *so* M, day S (dame, Laud f. 57)   10 [afore
othir], *so* M, for that othir S   11 [Wherfore], *so* M, Where S
Alisaundre M   17 seyeth þat M   32 *bole M

with a man of foul condicions, be whom sche conceyved a son
of grete cruelnes [f. 31] and mervelous of strengthe. And
because he had forme of man and nature of a bull, in that he was
stronge and of gret scharpenes and so yvell þat all the worlde
exilid him, poetis seide be ficcion that he was half man & half 5
bull. And therfore, though that lady were of such condicions,
it is seide to the good knyght that he scholde neithir sey ne
sustene that alle wommen schulde be like to hire, standing the
trouthe seith the contrarye. For Galien lerned the science of
lechecrafte of a womman notable and wise called Clempare, 10
the which lerned him to knowe many good herbes and the
propirteis of them.

Allegorie

For Pasiphe, the which was a fooll, may be taken a soule
retournyd to God. And Seint Gregor seith in his Omelies 15
that in hevin thei haue grettir ioye of a soule retourned to God
than of a rightwisman that euer was [rightwis]; liche as a cappi-
teyne loueth bettir a knyght that fledde and than [returnid], and
aftir his retourne wounded sorer his enemye, than he that neuer
dide auenture; and as a laborere loueth bettir the lande that, 20
aftir thornes, berith frute habundantly, than that the which had
neuer no thornes and berith no frute. To this purpos God seith
be the prophete: Reuertatur vnusquisque a via sua pessima, &
propicius ero iniquitati & peccato eorum. Jeremie xxvjº capitulo.

XLVI   Texte   25

> If thou haue doughteris for to marye,
> And thou wilte make them all redye
> To man, so that hurte come noon to the—
> Of kyng Adrastus vmbethinke the.

Glose   30

Adrastus was kyng of Arges, and a full myghti man and a f.31ᵇ
good. It fell that ijº errant knyghtes, the toon callid
Pollinites, the tothir Tidius, faughte in the derke nyght vnder

---

9 Galiene M   17 euer was] hath euyr bene M   rigthwis
S   18 retournyth S, returnid M   19–20 dide neuer a venture M
24 eorum] ipsorum M   33 Polimites M

the yatis of his paleis; for the tone chalangid the totheris
lodging, be-cause of a stronge tempest and a [greet] rayne, the
which had turmentid them all the nyghte, and thider were thei
sodeinly comen at aventure at that tyme. The king, the which
herd noyse of swerdes smytyng vppon scheldis, roos out of his 5
bed, and come and departid the ijᵒ knyghtes and made hem
accordid. Pollinites was the kinges son of Thebes and Tidius
anoþer kinges son of Grece, but thei were exilid out of there
contreis. Adrastus wurschipid gretly tho ijᵒ barons and yaf
them in mariage ijᵒ feire doughteris of his. Aftir that, for to sette 1
Pollinites in the ryghte of his lande, the which his brothir
Theocles held fro him, the kinge Adrastus made a gret armee
and went to Thebes with a gret ooste. But there-of fell so mych
harme that all that grete oost was disconfited, and deed and
taken euerychone, and the kingis ijᵒ sones-in-lawe deede. And 1
the brithir, which were at debate, euery of them slowe othir in
batayle, and there [lefte] of all but Adrastus and ijᵒ knyghtes with
him. And be-cause there is mych to do for to sette aȝen in
theire ryghte pepill the which is exilid, it is seide to the good
knyghte that in such case he ought to take conseill, and he 2
schold take hede to this aventure, and how Adrastus drempte oo
nyghte that he yaf his ijᵒ doughteris to be maryed to a lyon and
to a dragon, the which faughte to-gidere. The expositour of
dremys seith that dremys comyth of fantesies, and may be a
sweuenyng of good or yvell aventure that is to come to creatures. 2

Allegorie

f

Where it is seide whoo hath doughteris to marie, that he
schold take hede to whom he schall yeue theim, we may
vnderstande that the good Goddis knyghte scholde take good
hede with whom he schold felauschip him, if it happe that he 3
wul go in-to felauschip as good Tobie dide. On the same wise,
euery man scholde sette his thoughtes in holy meditacions. And
Seint Austin seith in a pistill that [tho], the which hath lerned
of oure Lorde to be debonayre and meeke, profiteth more in

---

2 [greet], *so* M, *om.* S (grosse, Laud)   14 discomfitid M
16 *brethir, M   the whiche M   17 [lefte], *so* M, leste S   20 not
partially erased after ought S   25 sweuenyng] shewynge M   28 hede]
good hede M   31 *feleshipe M   Tobi M   33 [tho], *so* M, *om.* S

meditacions and in prayers than some othir doo in reding and in hering. Therfore Dauid seith in the Psaulter: Meditabor in mandatis tuis, que dilexi.

XLVII   Texte

> With Cupido, the yong and the ioly,   5
> It plesith me that thou queynte the truly.
> The god of batayle it plesith also;
> Yit be good mesure it oughte to be do.

Glose

Cvpido is god of loue; and because it sittith not mych amys   10
for a yong knyghte to be amorous vppon a wise wurschip-
full lady, for his condicions may be mych the bettir so that he
can kepe the menewey, and also it is a disportefull thing in
armys, it is seide to the good knyghte that he may a-queynte
him well ynough with Cupido. For a philozophre seith that to   15
loue with good corage, it cometh of noblesse of herte.

Allegorie

That it pleasith well the god of bataill that thou aqueynt the
with Cupido, it may be take be penaunce. If the good
spirite repentaunte of his synnes and a feighter ayens vices be   20
ioyned and newe entred in-to the ryghte wey, it plesith righte
well to the god of bataill, the which is Jhesu Criste, that he
aqueynte him with [f. 32ᵇ] penaunce, and that Jhesu Criste,
be his wurthi bataill, was oure redemptoure. What word of
more mercy, seith Seint Bernard, may be seid to a synner, the   25
which was dampned, that there as where he was soolde be
synne to the fende of helle and had not where-with to bie him
ayen, than that the which God the Fadir seide to him: take my
Sone and yeve him for the; and the Sone seide: take me and
bye the ayen with me. Seint Petir remembrith this to the in his   30
first pistill: Non corruptibilibus auro vel argento redempti
estis, sed precioso sanguine quasi agni incontaminati & [im-
maculati] Jhesu Cristi. Prima Petri iᵒ capitulo.

---

15 *philesofre M   20 repentaunce M   26 solde M   32–33 [im-
maculati], so M, in maculati S

XLVIII   Texte

Corinis, the feire, note may thou noughte,
For the reporte of the message broughte
Be the ravin, for if thou it slee,
Thou schalte aftir gretly repente the.   5

Glose

Corinis was a gentilwoman, as a fable seith, that Phebus
loued [paramoures]. The ravin, which serued him at that
tyme, tolde him that he sawe Corinis, his loue, lie with anothir
yong man. Phebus was so sori of thees tydyngis that he killed   10
his loue as sone as sche came be-fore him. But aftir he repentid
him righte sore. Thanne the ravin, the which abood to haue
his guerdon of his lorde for that good deede, was cursid and
driven away; and his fedris, the which weren wonte to be white
as snowe, Phebus chaungid them in-to blak, in token of sorowe; 15
and ordeyned him fro thens-forth to be bringer and schewer [of]
yvell tidingis. The exposicion of this may be vnderstanden that
the seruaunt of some myghti man myghte reporte to him tidingis
liche for the which he was dryven away and vndoon. Therfore
it is seide to þe good knyghte that he scholde nat avaunce him   20
to tell tidingis to his [f. 33] prince be flaterie, the which myghte
meve him to anger or ire ayens the willfare of any othir, for at
the laste, in such reportes, commonly the rewardes be smale;
and also he scholde not beleue no reporte made to him be
flatrye. To this purpos Hermes the philosophre seith that a   25
reportoure or a contreuour of wordis, outhir he lieth to him to
whom he reportith them outhir he is fals to him of whom he
seith them.

Allegorie

Corinis, the which scholde not be sleyn, we may vnderstande   30
therbi oure soule, the which we scholde not slee be synne
but kepe it wele. For as Seint Austin seith: The soule scholde
be kepte as a cofre, the which is ful of tresoure, as a castell that

---

4 for] and M (car, Laud)
10 *tithingis M   11 come M   14 *fetheris M   16 [of], om. S
22 or] or to M   *welfare M   27 outhir] or M

8 [paramoures], so M, paramous S

is beseegid with enemyes, and as a king that restith in his
chambre of with-draughte. And this chambre scholde be
cloosed with v yatis, the which be the v wittis of kynde; and the
closyng of thes yatis is not ellis but for to withdrawe the
delectacions of the v wittis. And if it be so, that the soule 5
scholde go oute of thes yatis to his foreine werkis, he scholde go
oute demurely, wiseli and discreteli, liche as princes whan thei
go oute of theire chambris, where they haue vsscheris afore
them with macis for to make wey in the prees. On the same wise,
whan the soule scholde go oute to see, here, speke, fele or taste, 10
it scholde haue before him fere for his vsschere, the which
schulde haue for his mace the consideracion of the peynes of
helle and of the iugement of God. And to kepe thi soule thus, the
wise man counceilith the, seiyng: Cum custodia serua cor tuum,
quoniam ex ipso vita procedit. Prouerbiorum iiij^to capitulo.   15

XLIX   Texte

    Be Juno gretly thou ne set ne telle,
    Though that the note be better than the schell;
    Desire to haue wurschip and wurthynes,
    For it is mychell bettir than riches.   20

Glose   f. 33^b

J uno, vppon the fables of poetis, is the goddes of riches. And
because that to gete goodes and richesses longith mych
bisines and trauayle, and that such besinesses may torne a man
fro the geting of worschip, and standing worschip and worthines 25
is more to preise than riches, in as mych as the note is better
than the schelle, it is seide to the good knyghte that he schulde
not sette so his thoughte in felicite that the pursuyng of wur-
schip be lefte ther-fore. To this purpos Hermes seith that it is
better to haue pouerte in doyng good deedis than riches lewedly 30
or yvill gotyn, standing that wurthines is euer-lasting and
richessis voyde and deceyvabill.

3 *closid M   7 wiseli] vesili M   11–12 the . . . mace] and for
his mase he shulde haue M (qui doit auoir pour mace, Laud f. 60)
14 *seyinge M   20 *moche M   24 *turne M   26 in as
mych] L begins again   *nutte L   27 slelle L   28 so] om. L   par-
seyvyng L   wurschip] worthines L (vaillance, Laud f. 60)   29 lefte] leste
(?) L   30 *richesse M   31 *getyn L   that] om. L

Allegorie

Juno, whom we schulde not sette to mych bi, the which is taken for riches, we may vnderstande therbi that the good spirite schulde dispreise riches. And Seint Bernard seith: O sone of Adam, ligne couuetouse; wherfore louest thou so mych thees worldly rychessez, the which be not trewe neithir youris; and, whethir ye will or noon, at your deth ye moste nedis leve them? And the Gospell seith that a camell scholde sonner passe through a nedillis yȝe than a richman scholde entre in-to the kyngdome of hevin, for a camell hath but oo bocche on his bake and the yvill rich man hath ijᵒ, oon of yvill possessions and the tothir of synnes. He most nedis leue the first bocche at the deth, but the tothir, whethir he will or noon, he schall bere with him, if he leue it nat afore or that he dye. To this purpos oure Lorde seith in the Gospell: Facilius est camelum per foramen acus transire, quam diuitem intrare in regnum celorum. Mathei xixⁿᵒ capitulo.

L 　　Texte 　　f.

Ayens Amphoras sadde counsell, y seye,
Go not to distroye, for than thou schalte deye,
To Thebes ne the cite of Arges,
Assemble noon oste with schelde ne targes.

Glose

Amphoras was a full wise clerke of the cite of Arges and hadde mych connynge. And whan king Adrastus wolde goo vppon Thebes for to distroye the cite, Amphoras, the which knewe be connyng whate harme myghte falle there-of, counceylled the king not to goo; for, if he wente, all scholde be deed and distroyed. But he was not beleued; yit it fell as he seide.

2 we] he L　　to] *om.* L　　5 ligne couuetouse] leue couetyse L (lignee couuoiteuse, Laud)　　6 thees] this L　　ryches L　　not] neythir L　　neithir youris] ne they be not youres ML (ne vraies ne vostres, Laud)　　7 *non L, noo M　　8 *chamelle L　　9 *ye ML 10 kynddom L　　11 the bak ML　　14 if he leue it he leue it L　　or] er M 19 seye] þe sey L　　22 noon] not L　　26 *distrye L　　27 be konnynge knew ML　　28 thei all L　　29 and] ad L

[Wherfore it is seyde] to the good [knyght] that ayens the
councell of wise men he schulde take no grete emprice. But as
Salamon seith: The wise mannys councell availith litill to him
that will not do there-aftir.

Allegorie 5

Be Amphoras councell, ayens the which noon scholde goo to
bataill, we may take þat the good spirite scholde folowe holi
prechinges. And Seint Gregor seith in his Omelies that, liche
as the lif of the bodi may not be sustened with-oute that he take
his refeccion bodily, on the same wise the lijf of the soule may 10
not be sustened with-oute ofte hering the worde of God. Than
Goddes word, the which ye here with youre bodily eeris,
receyue them in your hertis; for, whan the worde is herde &
kepte in the wombe of mynde, than it may not profite but as a
seek stomak castith oute his mete; and as men be in dispeire of 15
him that brokith not but castith alle oute, evin so is he in perill
of euerlasting deth, that herith prechingis and doith not there-
aftir. Therfore the Scripture seith: Non in solo pane viuit
homo, sed de omni verbo quod procedit de ore Dei. Mathei
iiijᵗᵒ capitulo. 20

LI   Texte   f. 34ᵇ

Governe thou thi tonge aftir Saturne;
Lete noon yvill ther-in long soiourne.
To speke to mych it is a foull custome,
And grete folye ther-in is to presume. 25

Glose

Saturne, as I haue seid a-fore, is a planete hevy and slowe.
Therfore it is seide to the good knyghte that his tonge
scholde be like to him; for the tonge schulde not be to hasti in
speking to mych, but wise, soo that it speke noon harme of noon, 30

---

1 [wherfore it is seyde], *so* ML, *om.* S   [knyght], *so* ML, *om.* S
2 enterpryse L   3 Soleyne L, Solin M (*so* Laud)   vayleth L
7 þat] *interlineated in* S   11 worde] good worde L   12 the which
ye here] þe here the which L   13 herde] hed L   14 in the] in yowre L
not] *om.* ML   16 castih L   16 is] his L   17 prechyng L
23 noon] not L   27 before L   *planeth L   *sclowe L   30 wysyly L
no harme M

ne nothing that a man myghte ther-in presume folye. [For a
poete seyeth]: Be the word men knowith a wise man, and be the
looke a fooll.

Allegorie

Be the tonge, the which scholde be liche Saturne, is vnder-   5
standen the sadnes of speche. Huwe of Seint Victoure seith
to this purpos that the mouth, the which hath no keping of dis-
crecion, farith as a cite that is withoute a wall, as a vessell that
hath no bothom, as an horse that hath no bridell and as a schippe
that hath no rothir. An yvill kepte tonge glideth as an eell, it   10
perceth as an arwe; frendes soon torned therby and enemyes
multiplied. It is sclaundrous and sowith discordes; at oo strooke
it smytith and killith many persoones. Who-so kepith his
tonge kepith his soule, for deth and lijf is in the power of the
soule. And to this purpoos Dauid seith in the Psaulter: Quis   15
est homo si vult vitam, dies diligit videre bonos? Prohibe
linguam a malo, & labia ne loqua[n]tur dolum.

LII   Texte

Beleue the crowe and his trewe counceill,
And be nevir besy ne travaill   20
In yvill tydingis; to be the berere
Of thi demene thou maiste be the surere.

Glose

The fable seith that the crowe mette the ravin whan he   f.
broughte the tidingis [to] Phebus of his loue Corinis, the   25
which had doon amys, and he requyred him so soore that he
toolde him the cause of his iournay. But sche disealowid him
be-cause he went not to yeue him example of the same, the
which for a liche case had ben chaced out of Palles hous, where
somtyme he was wonte to be gretly avaunced. But he wold not   30

1 presun L   1–2 [For a poete seyeth], so ML, om. S   5–6 vndir-
stondens M   6 Hue ML   Victore L   7 no] not the L   9 *bottome
M   *chippe L   10 an eell] om. M   14 for] fro L   *poure
L   15 Sawter booke L   17 loquatur S, lequantur M
21 tithinges M, thyngges L   22 demene] deme L   25 [to], so ML,
of S   26 him] of hym L   soore] ferre L   27 this iurneye L
*disalowed M, dissalowed L   28 to] for to L   29 Palles] the pallas L
30 somtyme] some L

beleue here, for the which harme folowed to him. Wherefore it is seide to the good knyghte that he scholde truste the crowe. And Platon seith: Be no iangilloure ne to the kyng grete report-oure of tidinges.

Allegorie

How the crowe scholde be beleued, it is seide that the good spirite scholde vse such counceill. As Seint Gregor seith in his Omelies that strength valith not where counceill is not, for strengthe is soon ouerthrowen, if it be not restid vppon the yifte of counceill; and the soule, the which hath loste in him the seege of counceill outeward, he is disparbelid in dyuers desires. Therfore the wiseman seith: Si intrauerit sapiencia cor tuum, consilium custodiet & prudencia seruabit te. [Prouerbiorum ij° capitulo].

LIII   Texte   15

> If thou enforce the with eny wighte
> Strengir than thou to make pleies of myghte,
> Withdrawe the feire that hurte thou ne be.
> Of Ganymedes vmbethinke the.

Glose

Ganymedes was a yonge gentilman of the Troyens ligne, and a fable seith that Phebus and he strove to-gedir in casting of a barre of iryn. And, as Ganymedes myght nat withstand the strengthe of Phebus, he was slayne with þe reboundyng of þe barre, that Phebus launchid soo high þat he had lost þe sighte þerof. And þerfore it is seide [f. 35ᵇ] that þe strif is nat good wiþ a strenger and a myghtier þan hym-silf is, for þer may not come þerof but greet inconueniencie. Wherfor a wise man seith: To be bisi wiþ men þat vse vngraciose games, it is a signe of pride, and comonly þe ende is angre.

---

1 wherefore] where L   7 Grigorie L   8 *vaylith M,
vailet L   where . . . not] so S and L (reading when), om. M   11 *dys-
parbuled L   13 [Prouerbiorum ij° capitulo], so M, om. S   16 with]
which L   23 *myth L   25 barre, that] barre L   hade lawnchyd L
27 hym-silf is] a man is hym-selfe L   28 Wherfor] Where L
29 vngraciose] outragious M (malgracieux, Laud f. 62ᵇ)

Allegorie

For to seie þat a man scholde not enforce him ayens a stronger than he is him-silf, it is to vndirstande that þe good spirit scholde not take on him to stronge penaunce wiþ-oute counceill. Seint Gregori in his Morallis spekiþ here-of, and seith that 5 penaunce profitiþ not, if it be nat discrete; ne þe vertu of abstinence is not worth, if it be in such wise þat it be scharpir þan þe bodi may suffre. And þerfore it is to conclude þat no poore persoone schold take it on him wiþ-oute counceil of a more discrete þan himsilf. Wherfore þe wiseman seith in his 10 Prouerbis: Vbi multa, omnia fac cum concilio.

LIV   Texte

Resemble nat Jason, that man
The which thorugh Meede þe flees wan
Of goolde, for þe which soone aftirward   15
He yaf hir right yvil guerdon & harde.

Glose

Jason was a knyght of Grece, the which went in-to straunge contreis, þat is to seie, in-to þe ile of Colcos, be þe enorting of his vncle Pelleus, þe which of envie desired his deth. There 20 was a scheep þat hadde a flees of goold and it was kepte be enchauntement, but the conquest was soo stronge þat [noon] come þider but that loste þe lijf. Meede, the which was þe kingis doughtir of þat contre, took so greete loue to Jason that be þe enchauntementis þat sche couthe, of þe which she was a 25 souereyne maistres, made charmes & lerned Jason to enchaunte, be [f. 36] þe which he wanne the flees of goold; wherbi he had worschip aboue alle knyghtis lyuynge, and be Meede was reserued from deth, to whom he had promissid euer to be trewe frende. But aftir he fayled of his feiþ [& loued anothir], and 30 lefte hir hooly & forsooke hir, nat-wiþstandinge sche was [of]

4 Grigori L   7 not] nought M   be in] be sette in L   9 a] om. L
10 Wherfore] where L   13 not to L   Jasone L   14 Mede M,
Medee L   *fleze L, flese M   21 *chepe L   22 [noon], so ML,
om. S   23 there lyfe L   25 cowde L   26 made] she made L   to
enchaunte] enchauntementis L (enchantemens, Laud f. 63)   28 *knyt-
tes L   30 [& loued anothir], so L, om. SM (et autre ama, Laud)
31 [of], so ML, om. S

souereyne beaute. Therfore it is seide to þe good knyght that
he schold nat be like to Jason, þe which was to vnknowing and
to vntrewe to that the which had schewid [him] myche goodnes.
Wherfore it is to vileynose a thing for a knyghte or any noble
persoone to be rekeles or yvilknowing of goodnessis, if any he   5
haue receyved, be it of lady, of gentilwomman or of any othir
persoone; for he scholde evir þinke þeron and guerdon it to his
powere. To this purpos Hermes seiþ: Be not slowe ne delaiynge
to remembre of him that hath doon the good for þou scholdist
euere þinke þeruppon.   10

Allegorie

The good spirit scholde nat be like to Jason, the which was
rekeles, þat is to seie, he schold nat be rekeles ne vnknowing
of the beneficis receyved of his maker. And Seint Bernarde
seith vppon the Canticles that vnknowing is enemye to þe soule   15
and leser of vertuis, a dispreising of meritis and a lesing of
beneficis, and also ingratitude farith as nought, þe which drieth
þe welle of pite, þe dewe of grace and þe ryuer of merci. And
to this purpos þe wise man seith: Ingrati enim spes tanquam
[ibernalis] glacies tabescet, & disperiet tanquam aqua super-   20
vacua. Sapientie xvj^{mo} capitulo.

LV   Texte

> Kepe the wel fro [the] serpent Gorgon;
> Bewar þat thou loke not him vppon;
> Haue good sad mynde vppon Persyual   25
> And he schal the telle the story al.

Glose   f. 36^b

Gorgon, as þe fable seith, was a gentilwomman of souereyne
beaute. But bi-cause þat Phebus lay bi hir in the temple
of Dyane, þe goddesse was so soore greued þat sche torned hir   30

---

2 was to vnknowing] was vnknowyn L (trop fu descongnoissant, Laud)
3 [him], so ML, om. S   4 a] om. M   5 *recheles M   good-
nesse ML   6 hath L   lady or off L   7 þeron] therof M   vnto
his L   13 þat . . . rekeles] om. L   vnknowing] vncunnyng L
14 Barnarde L   15 vnkunnyng L   16 and leser] a lesser L   a dispreis-
ing] and dispraysyng L   20 [ibernalis], so M, infernalis S   23 [the],
so ML, om. S   25 Perciuall M, Percyualle L (Perseus, Laud f. 63^b)
30 greued] meved & grevyd L   turnid M, schawnged L

in-to a serpent of riȝt horrible figure; and þat serpent had such
a propirte þat euery man þat bihelde hir was chaungid sodenly
in-to a stoon. And for þe harme þat folowid of hir, Percivale,
þe worthi knyght, went for to fiȝt wiþ þat fers beste; and
bihelde him-silf in þe briȝtnes of his schelde, þe whiche was   5
al gold, because he schulde not beholde þe yvil serpent; and
he dide so myche þat he smote of his hede. Many exposicions
may be made vppon þis fable, and Gorgon may be vndirstanden
for a cite or a towne þat was wont to be of greet beaute; but,
thorugh þe vicis of þe dwellers þerin, it become a serpent and   1
venymose, þat is to vndirstande, þat it dide myche harme in þe
marchis to þeire neȝboris, as to robbe or to pulle hoolly alle þo
þat þei myȝte gete, as marchauntys and othir passeris forbi
were taken & holden and put in streite prisones, and þus were
þei chaungid in-to a stoon. Persival, þe which biheld himsilf in 1
[his] schelde, þat is to seie, in his strengthe and knyȝthode,
went to fiȝt ayens þe cite & took it and took þe power [fro] it, þat
it dide no more harme, myȝte be þat som man myȝte take a ful
faire ladi of yvil condicions, the which bi her couetise put many
from here goodes, but he put hir fro þat wil. And many oþere   2
vndirstandis may be sette her-in. Therfore it is seide to þe
good knyght þat he kepe him from biholding yvil þingis, þe
which myȝt drawe him to yvil. And Aristotil seith: Fle pepil
ful of wickidnes; folwe wise men and studie in there bookis;
and biholde þi-silf in there werkis.   2

Allegorie

How þat Gorgon scholde not be biholden vppon, that is to
seie, that þe good spirit schulde not biholde ne þinke in no
maner [f. 37] delite, but biholde him in þe schelde of þe state

2 bihelde] helde L   4 and] and he L   7 his] his his L, hire M
8 vppon] of L   and] as M (et, Laud)   *vndirstonde L   9 beaute]
bounte L (bonte, Laud)   12 pyll L, spoyle M (pillier, Laud)   hoolly]
Holy Chirche L   13 as] and L   forth-bi M   15 a stoon] stones L
(en pierre, Laud)   Persiuale M   þe which] that L   16 [his], so L, þis
SM (son escu, Laud)   17 went] and went L   cite &] cite he L   fro]
þer-fro S   18 myȝte] It myght L, That myght M   be] be seyde M
19 condicions] dedys L   20 here] there L, hire M   21 vndirstandynges
ML   therin M   22 shulde kepe M   24 folowe M, and befolowe L
25 werkis] dedes L   27 vppon that] that L, it M   28 ne þinke] no
thyng L (ne penser, Laud f.64)   in] on M   29 biholde] he holde L   *childe L

of perfeccion, and þat is for to fle delites. [Crisostom seyeth
that, as impossible as it is for fire to brenne in watir, as impos-
sible it is for the compunccioun of herte to be] amonge worldly
delites, for þei be ij° [contrary] þingis and þat distroieth ich of
þem oþir, for compunccion is modir of teeris and delite[s] 5
engendrith laughingis, compunccion restreyneth þe herte and
delites enlargith it. To þis purpoos seith the Scripture: Qui
seminant in lacrimis, in exultacione metent.

LVI   Texte

    If þat loue vn-to þe make schorte þe ny3te,   10
    Bewar Phebus noye þe not wiþ his my3t,
    Wherbi þou maist be take and teid
    In Vulcans lyemes and ouer-leid.

Glose

A fable seith that Mars and Venus loued to-gidere paramours. 15
  It fel on a ny3t þat þei were a-slepe arme in arme; Phebus,
þe which saugh cleerli, come vppon them and forþwiþ he accusid
hem to Vulcans, Venus housebonde. Thanne he, þat sau3 them
in that plite, forged a lieme and a cheyne of bras and bonde hem
bothe to-gidere soo that þei my3t not meve, as he þat is smyth 20
of hevin and can werke subtilly; and þus he come vppon þem,
and þanne wente he for þo oþere ij° and schewed þem his schame.
And þe fable seiþ that such rioterys þere be þat wolde ful fayne
falle in þe same mysdede. To this fable may be sette dyuers
exposicions, and it may ful souereynly touche som pointis of 25
astronomye to þo þat subtilly can vndirstande it. Mars to oure
purpoos seith that þe good knyght scholde kepe him þat in such
wise he be not ouerleyde be for3etilnes of tyme. And a wise

1 is] it is M   1–3 [Crisostom . . . to be], so M, Aristotil seith þat as
is impossible þat corrupcion of herte is S, Aristotyl seithe þat as it is impos-
sibyl þat compunccion of herte is L   4 contraries S   4–5 and . . . oþir]
and suche as eche of them distroyeth othir M   5 delites] so L, delite SM
7–8 seith . . . metent] seyth Holy Scripture: They þat sowyn in wepyng shal
repyn in lawyng L   10 make shorte to þe L   12 *tied ML
13 Vlnecans L, Vulcanes M   16 þat þei] that þat loueres L   17 forþwiþ] for
the which L   19 *lieme M, alyeine L   20 bothe] om. L   *smyght M
22 for þo] forth the L   23 sich rotters L   24 To To M   26 *sotely L
28 wise he] he L   be fore yetilnes L

man seith þat vnnethe is any thing soo secrete but þat of some it is perceyved.

Allegorie f.

There where þe auctorite seiþ: if loue schorte þe ny3t to þe, we schal sey þat þe good spirit schuld kepe him from þe 5 watches of þe feende. Seint Leo þe pope seith to þis þat þe oolde enemye, þe which transfigurid him in-to an angil [of] li3t, seceth not to stretche his snaris of temptacions ouer all and to aspie how he may corrumpe þe feith of [good beleuers]; he biholdiþ whom he schal embrace wiþ þe fire of couetise, whom 10 he schal enflamme wiþ þe brennyng desire of lecherie, and to whom he schal purpose þe likerousnes of glotonye; he examyneth of al customes discuti[th] of hertis, commytteþ affeccions; and þere where he findiþ a creature moost enclyned & li3te, he sekiþ cause of iniure and occupieþ him þere-in. Therfore seiþ 15 Seint Petir þe apostil: Sobrij estote & vigilate, quia aduersarius vester diabolus tanquam leo rugiens circuit, querens quem deuoret. Secundem Petri vltimo capitulo.

LVII   Texte

Thamarus dispreisid may not wel be,   20
Though a womman sche were of Femine.
Vmbethinke þe where taken was Cirus,
For right harde and dere he bou3t þat distres.

Glose

Thamarus was quene of Amazonie, a ful worþi ladi and ful 25 of greet worþines, of greet hardines and wise in armes [and] gouernaunce. Cirus, þe greete king of Perse, þe which had conquered many a region, wiþ a greete oost he meved for to go ayens þe reaume of Femene, of þe which he sette but litil be

1 seith þat] seith L   vnnethes L   soo] of L   4 if] þat if L
lowe schorte the myght L   7 *holde L   [of], so L, om. SM
9 [good beleuers], so ML, go beluerris S   11 and to] to ML
13 discutyth L, discutid SM   14–15 þere . . . þere-in] there seketh he
cause of iniure where he fyndeth hyme L   16 Petyr L   20 Thamaris ML
21 *voman L   Femene ML   22 Cyrus L   23 he] interlineated in S
brought L (compara, Laud f. 65)   distrus L   25 was] om. L   Amazoyne
M   26 [and], so ML, om. S   29 þe reaume] a grete reaume L, the
lande M (le regne, Laud)

þe strengþe. But sche, þe which was experte & subtill in crafte
of armes, suffrid him to entre in-to hir reaume wiþ-oute eny
meving of hir, vnto þe tyme þat he was comen in-to streite
passagis among hillis & greete mountaynes, where a ful strong
cuntre was. Thanne be Thamarus busschementis he was 5
assailid on euery partye wiþ þe wommenys oost and brought so
ferforth þat he was taken, and all his peple deed & taken. The
quene [f. 38] made him to be brouȝt before hir and made his
hede to [be] smyten of and to be cast in a tubbe ful of
his baronnys blood, the which sche had made to be hedid in his 10
presence. And Thamarus spak in þis wise: Cirus, þe which
had neuer ynough of mannys bloode, now maist þou drinke
ynough; and þus endid Cirus, þe greet king of Perce, þe which
was neuer ouercomen in bataile afore. Therfore Othea seiþ to
the good knyȝt þat he schulde neuer be so ouer-trusting in 15
him-silf, but that he schuld doute þat he myȝte happe amys
be som fortune and yet be sympiller þan he is. To þis
purpos Platon seiþ: Dispreise noon, for his vertuis may be
greete.

Allegorie 20

Thamarus, the which schulde not be dispreisid þough sche
be a womman, is to seie þat a good spirit schulde not dis-
preise ne hate þe state of meeknes, be it in religion or ellis
where; and þat meeknes is to preise. John Cassian seith þat in
no wise þe edifice of vertues in oure soule may not reise ne dresse 25
him-silf, if þe foundement of verry meeknes be not tastid first
in oure hertis, þe which, and it be righte stedfastly sette, may
sustene the highnes of perfeccion and of charite. Therfore
the wiseman seiþ: Quanto maior es humilia te ipsum in
omnibus, & coram Deo inuenies graciam. Ecclesiastici iijº 30
capitulo.

1 strengthe therof M   3 vnto] into L   4 passage L   6 euery]
euer L   7 and all . . . taken] om. L   8 quene] qwhen L
9 hede to] hede L   [be], so ML, om. S   *smetyn L   tobbe L   10 sheded
(with s cancelled by another hand?) L   14 no batayle L   15 so] om. L
16 *mytht L   17 infortune L   18 *wertues L   21 thowe þat L
23 ne hate] in hate L   24 Jon L   26 *fryst L   28 highnes]
lynes L (la haultesse, Laud)

LVIII   Texte

Thi witte to be enortid suffre noughte
To foli delites, ne ther-to broughte
Thi worschip; if it the askid be,
Anoon beholde þe wele in Mede.   5

Glose

Mede was oon of þe connyngist wommen of sorcerye þat
euere was and had moost connynge as that stories seiþ.
Not-withstanding sche suffrid hir witte to be enortid atte þe
owne wille for to [f. 38ᵇ] fulfille hir delite, as in lewde loue sche   10
suffrid hir to be maistried, so þat sche sette hir herte uppon
Jason and yaf him worschip, bodi and goodes; for þe which
aftirward he yaf hir a ful yvil reward. Wherfore Othea seiþ þat
þe good knyȝte scholde not suffre reson to be ouercomen with
lewde delite in no maner caas, if he wil vse of þe vertu of   15
strengthe. And Platon seiþ þat a man of liȝt corage is soon meved
wiþ þat þe which he loueth.

Allegorie

That a man schulde not suffre his witte to be enortid to lewde
delite may be vnderstanden that þe good spirit schulde not   20
suffre his propir wille to haue dominacion; for, if dominacion of
propre wille ceced not, þer schold be noon helle ne þe fire of
helle schulde haue no dominacion but uppon þe persoone þat
suffriþ his propre wille to be lord of him, for propre wil feightith
ayens God and emprideth þe silf; that is þe which despisith   25
paradijs and clotheth helle and voidith þe valew of þe blood of
Crist Jhesu and submittith þe worlde to þe þraldom of þe
fende. [To this purpos the wise man seyeth]: Virga atque
correccio tribuent sapientiam; puer autem qui dimittitur
proprie voluntati confundet matrem suam. Prouerbiorum   30
xxixᵒ capitulo.

3 herto L   4 the askid be] be asked of the L   8 as that] as the
M, and þat L   13 aftirward] aftir that ML   17 louede L
21-2 dominacion of propre wille] propir will of dominacion L   22 schold]
schold not S   24 *feythyt L   25 that is] that is he M   despisith]
dispoilleth L (despoille, Laud f. 66)   26 clothit L   27 tharledom L
28 To . . . seyeth] so ML, om. S   Virgo M   29 dimittitur] diunctum
M

LIX   Texte

If þou be suget to god Cupido,
The wode giaunt loke þou kepe þe fro,
That þe harde roche in no wise may put be
Vppon Acis and vppon Galathe.   5

Glose

Galathe was a fairye and a goddes, þe which had a yong
gentilman þat sche loued and was deede. þer was a giaunt
of a foul stature þat loued hir, but sche lust not to loue him; but
he aspied hir soo bisily þat he parceyued þem boþe in þe crevis 10
of a roche; þanne were þei ouerleid wiþ a sodeyne rage, and the
roche tremblid in such wise [f. 39] that it hooly brak and clave
a-sondir. But Galathe, þe which was a fairye, dressid hir in-to
the [see] and ascapid þerbi. This is to vndirstande þat þe good
knyȝte schulde be-ware in such caas to be ouerleid wiþ such as 15
hath myȝte and wille to greve him.

Allegorie

How he schulde be-ware of þe giaunt, þe which is yoven to
Cupido, it is to vndirstande þat þe good spirit be wel ware
þat he haue noon ymaginacion to þe worlde ne to noo þing 20
þerof, but euer þink þat alle worldly þingis may litil while
endure. For Seint Jerom seiþ vppon Jeremye þat þer is no þing
þat may be noised long amonge þoo þingis þe whiche schal
haue ende; so al oure tyme is of litil regarde to þe euerlasting
terme. To þis purpos the wise man seith: Transierunt nam velud 25
vmbra et tanquam nuncius percurrens. Sapientie v° capitulo.

LX   Texte

Fleeth euer the goddesse of discorde;
Evil be hir lynes and hir corde.
Pellus mariage ful sore sche troublid   30
For þe which aftir myche folke assemblid.

---

3 *geaunt M, giant L   5 Galatee L   7 phayrie M   fairye
and a] fayre L (vne nimphe ou vne, Laud f. 66ᵇ)   8 he was L
10 a creues M   12 clave] raffe L   13 *asownedyr L   14 [see],
so ML, *space left in* S   21 *woordly L   litil] litill auayle (*with latter
word cancelled*) M   22 Jerome M   23 þat may] may L   þe whiche]
which L   24 is] is as L   29 lyenis L

Glose

Discorde is a goddesse of yvil deedis; and a fable seith þat, whanne Pellus weddid the goddes Thetis, of whom Achilles was aftir þat borne, Jupiter and alle þoo oþer goddes & goddessis were at þe maryage, but þe goddesse of discord was not praid 5 þerto. And þerfore for envie sche come vnsent fore; but she come not al for noughte, for sche did verily hir office. Whanne þei were sette at dyner at oo bord, þo iij myghti goddessis, Pallas, Juno and Venus, there come Discorde and cast an appil of goolde vppon þe boorde, where-on was writen: Lete þis be 10 yoven to þe faireste. Thanne þe feest was troublid, for euery of them seide þat þei oughte to [f. 39b] haue it. Thei went a-fore Jupiter for to be iuged of þat discorde, but he wolde not plese oon for to displese anothir. Wherfore þei put þe debate vppon Paris of Troye, þe which was an herdman [at that time]. þan as 15 his modir drempte, whan she was greet wiþ him, that he schulde be cause of þe destruccion of Troye, he was sent þerfore to the herdman to þe forest, wenyng to him that he had ben his sone. And þere Mercurius, þe which ledde þe ladies, tolde him whos sone þat he was; than he lefte keping of schepe & went to Troye 20 to his greete kyn. The fable witnessith þus, where þe verrey storye is hid vndir poetikly couerture; and because þat often tymes many greete myschevis hath fallen and falliþ þrough discorde and debate, Othea seith to þe good knyght þat he schulde be-warre of discorde, soo as þat it is a foul þing to be a debatour 25 and to meve riotis. Pictagoras seiþ: Go not, seiþ he, in þat wey where hates growith.

Allegorie

Where it is seide þat discorde schold be fled, on þe same wise þe good spirit schold flee alle lettingis of conscience, 30 and eschewe strives & riottis. Cassidore seith vppon þe

2 Dyscorde L   4 þoo] the L   6 *invie L   8 dyner] dynne L   þo] the L   11 Thanne] & than L   euery] yche L 12 seide þat þei] sey thei L   13 but he wolde] *repeated in* S   14 for to] to L   15 Paaris L   which] *om.* L   [at that time] *so* M, *om.* SL (adonc, Laud)   16 drempthe M   17 of þe] off L   to the herdman] *om.* M to the forest to the herdeman L   18 *venyng L   19 ledde] *om.* L 21 *witneschit L   25 soo as þat] so that as L   27 where hate M, where that hattes L   growes L   31–1 Cassidore ... Psaulter] *om.* L

Psaulter: Souereynly, seiþ he, fleeþ strives and riottis; for to
strive ayens pees, it is woodnes; to strive ayens his souereyne,
it is madnes; to strive ayens his sogette, it is greet vilonye.
Therfore Seint Poul seiþ: Non in contencione & emulacione.
Ad Romanos xiij° capitulo.   5

LXI   Texte

Thin yvil mysdede foryete þou noughte,
If thou to any hast so mys-wroughte,
For þe reward he wil wel kepe for þe.
Distroied was Leomedon, parde.   10

Glose   f. 40

Leomedon, as I haue seide afore, was king of Troye; and he had
doon grete velonye to þe barons of Grece to voyde þem
from his lande, þe which þei forȝate noughte. But Leomedon
forȝate it whanne þe Grekis ran on him, þe which ouercome   15
him, he vncouerid & dispurveide; soo þei destroied him and
killed him. Therfore it is seide to þe good knyȝte þat, if he
haue mysdon to any, þat he kepe him weel, for he may be sekir
it schal not be forȝeten, but raþer vengid, whan he may haue
tyme and [place]. And to þis purpos Hermes seith: Be-ware   20
þat þin enemyes come not vppon þe and þou dispurveied.

Allegorie

That he schulde not forȝete þe mysdede þe which he hath do
to anothir may be vndirstanden þat, whan þe good spirit
feelith him in synne for defaute of resistence, he schulde þinke   25
þat he schal be ponyssched, as þei be þat be dampned, if he
amende him not. And þere-of spekith Seint Gregori þat þe
doom of God gooþ now feire and softeli & a slowe paas, but in

3 his sogette] his *interlineated in* S   4 Powle L   contempcione M   8 to
any] aniy L   haue L   mys-wroughte] myche wroughte L   9 *2nd* fro the L
12 afore] *om.* L (deuant, Laud f. 67ᵇ) '   14 lande] lawde L   Leomedon
hathe foryeten L   15 ron L   16 vncouerid] vnware M   and
killed him] *om.* L (et [le] occirent, Laud)   20 [place], *so* ML, space S
(lieu, Laud)   21 *thynne L   23 þe which] that L   done ML
25 defaute] fawte L   26 schal] shuld L   27 spekith] seith L

tyme comyng it schal recompence more greuously; the mercy
schal tarye of his acte. To þis purpos [the prophete] Joel seith:
Ad Dominum Deum vestrum quia benignus & misericors est,
paciens & multe misericordie, prestabilis super maliciam. Joelis
iij° capitulo.   5

LXII   Texte

If it happe thou be of loue dotid,
Be-ware at þe leest to whom þou telle it.
That thi deedis discouered not be,
Vmbethinke well of Semelle.   10

Glose

The fable seith þat Semelle was a ientilwomman þat Jupiter
loued paramours. Juno, þe which was in gelozie, took þe
liknes of an auncient womman and come to Semelle, and wiþ
feire wordis [f. 40ᵇ] bigan to reson hir in so myche that Semelle   15
knowliched to hir al þe loue of hir and of hir loue; and to be
welbeloued and knowin of him, sche vauntid hir. The god-
desse þan seide to hir, þe which tooke noon hede of þe deceite
ne perceyued noo þing, yit of þe loue of hir loue whanne þat
sche scholde be nexte wiþ him, þat sche scholde aske him a   20
yifte; and, [whan] sche had wel required him and þat he had
grauntid it, þe which sche scholde desire of him, þat he wolde
vouche-saaf to halse hir in such wise as Juno halsed his wijf,
whanne þat he wolde solace him wiþ hire; and in such wise
myȝte he perceyve þe loue of hir loue. Semelle forȝate it noughte, 25
and whan sche had made þe request to Jupiter, the which had
promyssid to hire, and as a god þat myȝt not calle it ayen, he
was ful sory and wist wel þat sche had ben deceyued. Than
Jupiter took liknes of fire and halsid his loue, þe which in a litil
while was al broiled and brente, for þe whiche Jupiter was ful   30
hevi of þat aventure. Vppon þis fable may be taken manye

1 the more L   2 [the prophete], so L, om. SM (le prophete, Laud)
Jouel M   4 Joelis iij° capitulo] om. M   7 doited L   10 the
welle L (toy, Laud f. 68)   13 *ielousie M, ialoucie L   14 *lekenes L
cam L   16 be] om. L   17 *knowe M   19 whanne þat] when L
21 [whan], so ML, om. S   22 it, þe which] that L   desire of him] om. M
23 halsed Juno L   25 she perceyue L   27 to hire] it hyre L
29 of fire] of hir L   30 bruled L

vnderstandinges, and namely vppon þe science of astronomye,
as maystres seiþ. But it may be also þat be some wey a gentil-
woman myghte be deceived be þe wife of hir loue, wherþorugh
him-silf made hir die be inaduertance. And þerfore it is seide to
þe good knyghte þat he schulde be-warre, whanne he spekiþ 5
of a þing þe which he wolde were secrete, afore er þat he speke
his word, to whom he seiþ it and what he seiþ, for be circum-
stauncis þingis may be vnderstanden. Therfore Hermes seith:
Schewe not þe secretnes of þi thoughtis but to þoo þe which
þou hast wel proued. 10

Allegorie

How he schulde take hede to whom he spekith, we may
vnderstande that þe good spirit, what-so-euer his thoughte
be, scholde be-warre in euery caas where yvil suspecion myghte
falle [f. 41] to any oþer. As Seint Austin seiþ in þe book of 15
Schepe þat we schulde not al-oonly sett store to haue good
conscience, but in as myche as oure infirmite may, and as myche
as þe diligence of mankindeli freelnes may, we schulde take
good heede þat we dide noo þing þe which my3te com to yvil
suspecion to oure stedfast breþir. To þis purpos seiþ Seint Paul 20
þe apostil: In omnibus prebe te exemplum bonorum operum.
Ad Titum secundo capitulo.

LXIII   Texte

The disporte trust not mychel vppon
Of Dyane, for þere is disporte ri3t noon 25
For þem þat be in kny3thode pursuyng
That schulde cause theym to haunte to mych huntyng.

Glose

Dyane is callid goddesse of þe wode and of huntyng; soo it is
seide to þe good kny3t pursuyng þe hi3 name of armys þat 30
he schulde not muse to myche in þe disportes of huntyng, for

1 and namely] anamly L   2 seyne L   3 myghte] may L
4 to die L   6 þe which] that L   were] that it were L   er þat]
or L   7 for by the L   8 may be] ma ben L   9 secretetes L
þe which] that L   13 thoughte] thowtys L   14 be he L   15 Aus-
tine M   of Shepe M, of *interlineated* S, of Job L   17 and] *inter-
lineated* S   17–18 myche as] myche L   19 þe which] that L   20 brother
ML   24 to mychyll L, moche M   25 disporte] sporte M   30 hi3] hight L

it is a þing þat longiþ to ydilnesse. And Aristotil seith þat
idilnes ledith a man to alle inconueniencies.

Allegorie

That a man schulde not folwe to myche Dianes disporte, the
which is take for ydelnes, þe good spirit may note þe same 5
and þat it is to eschewe. Saint Gregori seiþ: Do euer som good
þing, þat þe fende may alwey finde þe occupied in som good
occupacion. To þis purpos þe wiseman seith: Considerauit
semitas domus sue, & panem ociosam non commedit. Prouerb-
iorum xxxjᵒ capitulo.   10

LXIV   Texte

Auaunte þe nought; for greete harme folwiþ þerfore
To Yragnes, þe which mystooke hirre sore,
That aȝens Pallas hir so avauntid,   f. 4
For þe which þe goddesse hir enchauntid.   15

Glose

The fable seiþ that Yragnes was a gentilwomman ful subtile
& kunnyng in schaping, weving and sewing, but sche was
to presumptuous of hir connyng, and in deede sche vauntid hir
aȝens Pallas; for þe which þe goddesse was greued wiþ hir, þe 20
which for þat foli vauntyng sche chaungid hir in-to an yraigne.
And, seide sche: þou vauntid þe so mych in weving and spyn-
nyng þat þou schalte euer weve and spynne werke of no value;
and fro þens come þe yraignes þat be ȝit, þe which cecith not of
spynnyng and weving. It may be so vnderstonden þat some 25
persoones vauntid them aȝens hir maystres, for þe which in som
wise þei took harme. Therfore it is seide to þe good knyȝte þat
he schulde not vaunte him, standing þat it is a foul þing to be a
vauntour, for it may abesse to myche [the] preise of his bounte.

4 not] *om.* M   5 *noote L   6 it] *interlineated* S, *om.* L
Grygori L   12 folwiþ þerfore] fell thereoff L   13 To] *so by
correction from* The S, The M, To L   þe] *interlineated* S   hirre] *by cor-
rection from* him S   20 þe which] that L   21 *schawneged L   in-to
in-to L   22 And than L   sche] sith M, *om.* L   vauntest M   spyn-
nyng] sewyng L   23 þat þou] thou M   euer aftir this L   24 sessyth
L, cesse M   26 persone L   vauntid them] wanted L   28 þat it]
that is M, it L   þing] thyng for a knyght L (laide chose a chevalier, Laud)
29 abuse L   [the], *so* ML, to S

And in þe same wise Platon seiþ: Whanne þou doost a þing,
seiþ he, bettir þan anoþir, be-war þou avaunte not þer of; for if
þou do, þin availe is mych þe lesse.

Allegorie

For that a man schulde nat vaunte him, we may seie that þe 5
good spirit schulde be-war of vauntyng. For Saint Austin
spekiþ aȝens vaunting in þe xij book of þe Cite of God, þat
vaunting is no mankindely preising, but it is a tourned vice of
þe soule, þe which loueþ mankindely preising and dispitith þe
verry witnes of propre conscience. To þis purpos þe wiseman 10
seith: Quid profuit vobis superbia, aut diuiciarum iactancia
quid contulit vobis? Sapiencie vᵒ capitulo.

LXX   Texte

If to greete desire wil þe in bring
To loue mychel disport of hunting,   15
Dadomus þan remembre may the,   f. 42
For wiþ a wood wilde bore deed was he.

Glose

Dadomus was a ioli gentilman and of greet beaute. Venus
loued him paramours, but be-cause þat he delitid him to 20
myche in hunting, Venus, þe which doutid þat some hurte myȝt
come to him be som aventure, sche praid him ofte þat he wolde
be-war how he huntid at greet bestis. But Dadomus wolde nat
be-ware, and þerfore he was slayne with a wilde bore. Wher-
fore it is seide to þe good knyȝt þat, if he wil algatis hunte, lete 25
kepe him fro such hunting as may do him harme. To þis
purpos þe prophete Sedechias seith that a king schulde nat
suffre his sone hunte to myche ne be idill, but he schulde make
[him] to be enformed to good condicions and to fle vanite.

1 þing] tyng L   2 he] the L   6 *wauntyng L   8 no]
not L   it is] is L   turnid M, aturnyd to L (peruerse, Laud)   9 pray-
synges L   *dispithet L   10 his propyr L   12 qui M   14 þe
in] them L (te, Laud)   15 moche M, mechell L   16 Dadonius
(?) L   19 Dadamus L   20 þat] om. L   22 þat he wolde] to L
23 at] to L   24 Therfor L   26 as] that L, as as M   27 king]
knyght L (vng roy, Laud f. 70)   29 [him], so ML, om. S   in good M

Allegorie

How he schulde þinke on Dadomus may be vndirstandin
that, if þe good spirit be in any wise oute of þe wey, at the
leste he schulde þinke on the greet perel of perseueraunce. For,
as þe fende hath greet myȝte vppon synners, Seint Petir seiþ 5
in þe secunde Pistil þat synners be bounde to corrupcion and þe
feend hath power ouer þem, for he þat in bataille is ouercomen
of a-nothir is become bonde to him. And in token þerof it is
seide in þe Pocalipse: Data est bestie potestas in omnem tribum
& populum. Apocalipsis xiijᵒ capitulo.   1

LXVI Texte

If soo be þat þere assaile þe any,
Beware þou ne þi men [isse] not liȝtly
Aȝens þem, þat þi towne of strength not slake;
Of þe first Troie example þou mayst take.   1

Glose

f.

When Hercules wiþ myche pepill come vppon þe first Troye
and þat king Leomedon herde seie of þeire comyng,
thanne he, wiþ alle þe pepill þat he myghte gete in þe cite, issed
oute and wente [ayens them] to þe watir-side; and þere þei   2
assemblid wiþ ful fierse bataile, and þe cite was lefte voide of
peple. Than Thelamen Ayaux, þe which was embuched wiþ
a greet oost nere þe wallis of þe cite, entrid in-to it, and þus þe
first Troie was taken. Therfore it is seide to þe good knyȝt þat
he scholde kepe him þat in such wise he be not deceyved wiþ his 2
enemyes. And Hermes seith: Kepe þe froo the pepil of thin
enemyes.

Allegorie

Where it is seide þat a man schulde kepe him, if he be
assailed, þat his cite be not voide, it is to seie þat þe good 3
spirit schulde kepe him euer sesid & fillid wiþ vertues. And

3 weye that (*with* at *interlineated*) L   5 *opon L   7 ouercome L
12 þat] thette L   13 [isse], *so* M, vse S, ryse L (saillent, Laud)
19 issed] yode L   20 [ayens them], *so* ML, *om.* S (contre eulx, Laud)
22 Thelamenayaux M   enbushed L   23 *cete L   31 euer kepe
hym L

here-to seith Saint Austin that, liche as in tyme of werre men of
armys schulde not be vnsesid of þeire armys ne oute of hem,
nyȝt nor day, on þe same wise duryng þe tyme of þis present
lijf he schulde not be dispoilid of vertues, for he þat þe feende
fyndith wiþoute vertues farith as he þat þe aduersarye findith 5
withoute armes. Therfore þe Gospell seith: Fortis armatus
custodiet atrium suum. Luce xj^{mo} capitulo.

LXVII   Texte

Vppon þe harpe assot þe not to soore
Of Orpheus; if thou sette any stoore   10
Be armys, if þou wilte [therin] wel spede,
To sewe instrumentis þou hast noon nede.

Glose

Orpheus was a poete; and þe fable seith þat he couthe pley
so well vppon þe harpe, þat þe rynnyng watris torned 15
theire course, & the briddis of the ayre, þe wilde bestis and þe
fiers serpentis foryat theire cruelnes and restid to here þe sowne
of his harpe. This is to vnderstande [f. 43] he pleid so wel þat
al maner of peple, of what condicions þat þei were, delited them
to here þe poet pleye; and because þat such instrumentis assot- 20
tith often þe hertis of men, it is seide to þe good knyȝt þat he
schulde not delite him to myche þer-inne, for it longith not to
þe sones of knyȝthode to muse to myche in instrumentis ne in
othir ydilnessis. To þis purpos an autor seith þat þe sowne of
þe instrument is þe snare of þe serpent. And Platon seiþ: He 25
þat settiþ hooli his plesaunce on fleishli delites is more bonde
þan a sclave, þat is to sey, þan a man þat is boughte and soolde.

Allegorie

Orpheus harpe, vppon þe which a man schulde nat be assot-
tid, we may vndirstande þat þe knyȝtly spirit schulde nat 30
be assottid ne mused in no maner of worldly felauschip, be it

2 theyme L   3 ner L   4 thate L   6 Godspell S   10 any]
interlineated S   11 if]*om.* L   [therin], *so* ML, *om.* S   12 sewe] fre L
14 cowde L   pley . . . vppon] welle pleye on L   15 þat] so that L
rennynge watir M, ryngyng wateres all only L   16 theire] his M   *coruse L
17 fres L sowne] songge & the swete sounde L (le son, Laud f. 71)
18 pleyith L   20 poietis L   sotted L   24 ydylnes L   auctorite L
(*so* Laud) þat] *om.* L   sowne] soule L (le son, Laud)   26 on] of L

C 5326   G

kyn or oþir. Seint Austin seith, in þee book of [the] Singularite
of Clerkis, that þe solitary man felith lesse prikkinges of his
fleisch þat hauntiþ not voluptuosenesses þan he that hauntiþ it,
and lesse is sterid to couetice þe which seeth not worldly rich-
esses þan he þat seeth it. Therfore Dauid seith: Vigilaui & 5
factus sum sicut passer solitarius in tecto.

LXVIII   Texte

    Grounde nat vppon noon avisiones,
    Ne vppon noon lewde illusiones
    Grete emprises, þough þei be riȝt or wrong;   1
    And of Parice remembre you among.

Glose

B e-cause þat Parice had dremed þat he scholde rauisch
  Helayne in Grece, a greete armye was maade and sent from
Troye in-to Grece, where þat Parice rauischid Helayne. Thanne 1
for þat wrongful deede þei come aftir þat vppon Troye wiþ al þe
power of Grece, þe which was so grete a cuntre at þat tyme that
it lastid to þe cuntre þat we calle now Puille and [f. 43ᵇ] Calabre
in Itaille, and at that tyme þat was callid Litil Grece. And of
þat cuntre was Achilles and þe Myrundois, þe which were so 2
wurþi fiȝtteris; [that] greet quantite of pepill confoundid Troie
and al þe cuntre. Therfore it is seide to þe good knyȝt þat he
schulde nat vndertake to doo no greete þingis vppon avisiones,
for greete harme and greete bisines may come þerof. And þat a
greete emprise schulde not be doon wiþ-oute good deliberacion 2
of counceill, Platon seiþ: Do noo þinge, seiþ he, but þat þi
witte hath ouerseen a-fore.

Allegorie

T hat a greete emprise scholde not be taken for avision, þat is
  to seye þat þe good spirit schulde in noo wise presume ne 3
reise him-silf in arrogance, for [noo] maner of grace þat God

1 [the], *so* L, *om.* SM   2 prikkynge M   3 voluptuousenesse L
4 it sterith L   riches L   8 Grownde yow L   *aduisiones M,
avysyons L   9 no L   10 Of grete ML (*not in* Laud)   emprise
L (*so* Laud)   þough þei be] be they M, though it be L   13 Paryis L
17 þe which] there L   18 Callabre M, Calebre L   19 Ytalie M, Ytaly L
at] *om.* L   þat was] it was L   20 Mirondois M, Mirmedewes L
21 [that], *so* L, wiþ SM (celle, Laud)   23 thynge L   31 [noo], *so* ML, in S

hath youen him. And Seint Gregor seiþ in his Morallis that
þer be iiij spices in þe which alle bolnyngis of arrogansis be
schewid. The first is whan þei noise them-silf of þe goodnesse
þat þei haue; the secunde is whanne thei wene wele þat þei
haue deserued and receyued it for þeire merites, þee goodnes 5
þat þei haue; the iij^de is whanne þei avaunte to haue þe goodnes
þat þei haue not; the iiij^th is whanne þat þei dispraise oþir and
desire þat men schulde knowe þe goodnes þat is in them. Aȝens
this vice þe wise man spekiþ in his Prouerbis: Arroganciam &
superbiam & os bilingue detestor. Prouerbiorum viij° capitulo. 10

LXIX   Texte

    If ye loue wel houndis and birdis, than
    Of Antheon, þe feire yong ientilman,
    The which become an hert, vmbeþink wel þe,
    And loke þat such fortune come not to þe.   15

              Glose   f. 44

Antheon was a ful curteys yonge ientilman and of gentil
condicions, but he loued houndis & birdis to myche. For,
as þe fable seith, þat on a day as he huntid al aloone in a thik
forest, where-in his men had loste him; thanne as Dyane, þe 20
goddesse of þe wode, hadde huntid in þe forest to it was þe
houre of noon, sche was soore chaufed and hoot for þe greet
heete of þe sunne, for þe which sche had a lust to bathe hir in
a feire welle and a cleer, þe which was þere fast by; and as sche
was in þe welle, al nakid, envirouned wiþ feiriys and goddesses 25
þe which serued hir, Antheon, þe which took noon hede, come
sodeinly vppon hir and sawe alle þe [goddesse]; of whom, for
hir greet chastite, þe visage waxe reede for schame and was ful
soori. And thanne sche seide: Be-cause þat y knowe weel þat þees
yonge gentilmen wul vaunte þem of ladies and gentilwommen, 30

2–3 be made shewde M   3 noise them-silf of] noyse they haue of
them-selfe L   7 the] and the L   8 goones L   9 *vyse L
12 ye] thou L   and] an L   13 On Anteon L   17 *corteis L
yonge] om. L   18 but he] and L   For, as] fore L   20 whein M
22 chaffede L   23 lyste L   24 feire] fyre L   25 *fayries M,
fayreis L   godes L   27 [goddesse], goddesses SM, godes L (la deesse,
Laud)   28 *castite L   29 þees] thysse L   30 gentilman L (les
damoiseaulx, Laud f. 72)   þem] hym L

to þe entent þat þou schalt not mowe vaunte þe þat þou
hast seen me nakid, y schal take þe myȝte of þi speche fro þe.
Thanne sche cursid him; and anoon Antheon become a wylde
herte, and noo-þinge was lefte him of mankindely schappe but
al-oonly vndirstondinge. Thanne he, ful of greet sorowe and 5
of sodein feere, went fleyng þrough þe busschis, and anoon he
was receyved wiþ his owne houndis and halowid wiþ his owne
men, þat serchid þe forest for him; but now thei haue founde
him & knewe him nat. There Antheon was drawe dovne, þe
which wepte greete teeris afore his owne men, and fayne wold a 1
cried them mercy if he myȝte haue spoken; and sen þat tyme
hider-too hertys wepith euer at þeire deeth. Antheon was slayn
& martired wiþ greet woo wiþ his owne meyne, þe which with-in
a litil while had al deuourid him. Many exposicions may be made
vppon þis fable, but to oure purpos it may be seid of a yong 1
man þat habandoneth him hooly to ydilnes, and dispendith his
goodis and his getinges in þe delite of his bodi and in disportes
of huntyng, and to kepe ydel meyne. Here-by it may be seide þat
he was hatid of Diane, þe which is notid [f. 44ᵇ] for chastite, and
deuourid of his owne meyne. Therfore it is seide to the good 2
knyȝt that he schulde beware he be not deuourid in liche wise.
And a wise man seith þat ydelnes engendrith ydelnes and erroure.

Allegorie

Be Antheon, þe which become an hert, we may vndirstande
the verry repentaunt man þat was wont to be a synner, and 2
now hath ouercomyn his fleisch and made it boonde to þe good
spirit and taken þe state of penaunce. Seint Austin seith in þe
Psaulter þat penaunce is an eesi deede and a light charge; it
ouȝt not to be callid a greete charge for a man but wingis of a
brid fleinge, for, as a brid in erþe here beriþ þe charge of theire
wingis and þeire wingis [berith] them to hevin, on the same

1-2 þou hast] hathe L   see L   7 *halwed M, halewed L
9 knowe L   10-11 haue a cried M, haue cryed L   *sene L, syne M
12 euer at there dethe wepyn L   13 *menye L   with-in] in ML
16 to] in L   17 in þe] in L   18 it may] may it L   21 be] were L
22 þat] om. L   26 *fleyssch L, flesshe M   27 and taken] takyn L
28 Sawtyr L   deede] thyng or dede L (vng fais, Laud f. 72ᵇ)   29 but]
but as ML   *wenges L   30*herth L   31 [berith], so ML, om. S
(portent, Laud)

wise, if we bere here in erthe þe charge of penaunce, it schal
bere us to hevin. To þis purpos þe Gospel seith: Penitenciam
agite; appropinquabit enim regnum celorum. Mathei iijᵒ
capitulo.

LXX   Texte   5

> I sey: goo nat to þe yatis of helle
> For to seke Euridice, be my councelle.
> Litil he wan there with his harpe and pley,
> Orpheus, as þat y haue ofte herd sey.

Glose   10

Orpheus þe poete, þe which harpid so weel, a fable seith þat
he maried him to Euridice, but þat day of mariage they
wente disportynge in a medewe bare-fote for þe greete heete of
þe sunne. [An herde coueyted] þat faire womman and ranne
to a rauisschid hir, and as sche fledde a-fore him, for feere of 15
him, sche was biten wiþ a serpente þat was hid vndir þe grasse,
of þe which the mayden diede in a litil while. Orpheus was
riȝt hevy of þat mys-aventure. Orpheus took his harpe and
wente to þe ȝatis of helle in þe derke valey afore the helly paleis,
and [f. 45] þanne he began to harpe a pitous lay, and he pleide so 20
sweetly þat alle þe turmentis of helle seecid and alle þe helly
offices lefte there besinesses, for to here þe sowne of þe harpe;
and namely Proserpine, þe goddesse of helle, was meved with
greete pyte. Than Pluto, Lucifer, Cerebrus & Acharon, the
which for þe harpour saugh þat þe officers of þe helly peynes 25
lefte and ceecid, took him his wijf vpon a condicion þat he
scholde goo afore and sche aftir; and þat he schulde not loke
behinde [him] to he come out of þe valey of helle; and if he
lokid behinde him, he schulde lese here. Vppon þis condicion
sche was delyuered to him aȝen. So Orpheus went afoore and 30

1 in (on L) erthe here ML   7 Eruridice M   12 but þat] but
on the L   13 disportynge] to disporte theyme L   *medowe M,
medwe L   14 sonne and L   [An herde coueyted], so ML, And
herde couetise S   ranne for L   15 a] haue M   16–17 grasse . . . while]
gresse of the medwe and within a litell while after the mayden dyed L
18 Orpheus took] yit he tooke L   19 *dyrke waly L   20 a pitous lay]
pytously L (vng piteux lay, Laud f. 73)   22 besynes L   23 namely]
anamly L   24 Lucifere L   Acharoun M, Acaron L   25 offices L
the helly] hell L   28 [him], so ML, om. S   29 lese] lefe (?) L

his loue aftir; but he þat was to hoote in love, þe which desired
to beholde hir, myght not kepe him fro lokinge aȝen aftir his
love; and anoon, as he lokid behind him, Euredice departid
from him and was aȝen in helle, so þat he myȝt no more haue
hir. This fable may be vnderstanden in many maneres. It 5
myȝt be so þat som man had his wijf taken from him and he had
gete hir aȝen and ȝit aftir lost hir aȝen. On þe same wise, it may
be of a castel or of oþir þingis. But to oure purpos it may be
seide þat he seekiþ verrily Euredice in helle, þe which seekith
an impossible thinge; and, þough he may [not] recouere þat, he 10
oughte not to be wroþe. Salamon seiþ þe same: It is a foly
þinge, he seith, to seke þat þe which is impossible to be hadde.

Allegorie

Be þat a man schulde nat goo to seeke Euredice in helle, we
may vndirstande þat þe good spirit schulde nat aske, ne 15
require of God, noo þinge þat is merveilous ne þat is merveil to
þink on, that is to seye, to tempte God. And Seint Austin seith
vppon Seint Johannis Gospel þat Goddis creature is nat ex-
aunced whan he requirith a þinge þat is impossible to be doon
or schulde not be doon, or a þinge þe whiche he wolde vse amys 20
ȝif it were grauntid him, or a þinge þe which schulde hurte
[f. 45ᵇ] the soule if it were exauncid. And þerfore it cometh of
þe grace of God yif þat he ȝeve not a creature a þinge þe which
he knowith þat he wolde vse amys. To þis purpos Seint Jamys
þe apostle seith in his Pistil: Petitis, & non accipitis, eo quod 25
male petatis. Jacobi iiijᵒ capitulo.

LXXI   Texte

If þou wilte verrily knowe a knyȝt
In cloister or cloos wheþir he be diȝt,

3 as he] as L   partyd L   7 getten L   and ȝit . . . aȝen], om.
ML (et puis la reperdi, Laud)   8 oþir þingis] anothir thyng L (autre
chose, Laud)   10 þough he] thowgh a man L   [not], so ML,
om. S   14 a] interlineated in S   15 schulde not] shulde L
16 is merveil] mervell L   17 þink on] be thyng oon L   18 Jones M
19 þinge . . . doon] thyng the which may not be doone L (qui ne se peut
faire, Laud)   21 yf that L   or ell L   þe which] that L   23 grace]
mercy L (misericorde, Laud f. 73ᵇ)   yif þat] if L   he . . . þinge] thinge
be not yeuen to a creature M   not] not to L   24 knowith þat] knowyth L
28 will L   29 wheþir] where L

The say þat was made to Achilles
Schal lerne þe to prove them douȝtles.

Glose

The fable seiþ þat Achilles was sone to þe goddes Thetis, and
because þat, as a goddesse, sche knew yif hir sone hauntid 5
armys þat he schulde die, sche, þe which loued him wiþ to
greete loue, hidde him in maydenys cloþinge and made him
were a vaile like a nonne; in þe goddes abbey he lyved soo, and
Achilles was hid so longe vn-to some persoones parceyued him.
And þe fable seith þat þere he begat Pirus vppon þe kingis 10
doughter, þe which was aftir þat ful chyualrous. Thanne began
þe Troyens greete werrys, and þe Grekis knewe wele þat þei
hadde nede of Achilles for to strengthe þem; he was souȝt
oueral, but þei myȝt not heere of him. Vlixes, þe which was ful
of gret malice, souȝte him ouerall and come to þe temple, but 15
yit he myȝt not parceive þe trouth. He avised him of greet
malice & sotilte; and þan Vlixes tooke kercheues, girdelis and
of al maner of iuellis longing to ladies, and þer-wiþ faire armure
& bright, and kest al dovne in þe myddis of þe place in presence
of þe ladies, and praid ech of þem to take þat the which plesid 20
them best. And þanne, as euery þing drawiþ to his nature, þe
ladies ranne to þe iewellis and Achilles seesid þe armure; and
þan Vlixes ran and took him in his armys and [seyde]: þis is he
þat y seeke. And be[f. 46]cause þat knyȝtis schuld be more
enclyned to armys þan to plesaunces, þe which longiþ to 25
ladies, the auctorite seiþ þat þerbi a man may knowe þe verry
knyȝt. And to þis purpos Legmon seiþ þat a knyȝt is not
knowen but bi his deedis of armys. And Hermes seiþ þat
[thou] scholdist prove a man afore er þat þou trust him to
greetly.   30

2 *Sall L   6 *shud L   9 hid so longe] long hydde L   vn-to
that ML   10 kingis] thyn kynges (with first word cancelled) L
15 *sowgth L   and] om. L   17 keuercheffes L   girdill L   18 of
al] all L   iowell L   20 take] make L   22 iowell L
23 [seyde], so ML, om. S   25 plesaunce ML   þe which] which L
27 Legaron L (Legmon, Laud)   29 [thou], so ML, om. S   preue L
or ML

Allegorie

Where it is seide: if þou wilt knowe a good knyȝt, we may vndirstande þat þe good knyȝt, Crist Jhesu, schulde be knowen be þe deedis of armys in good werking, and þat such a knyȝt schulde haue þe dewe preise þat longiþ to good men. 5
Seint Jerome seiþ in a Pistil þat, as þe riȝtwisnes of Godde leeueþ noon yvil þing vnponysschid, on þe same wise it leeueþ noo good þing vnrewarded; so þan to good pepill no laboure scholde be thought to harde, ne no tyme to longe, standinge þat þei abide þe euerlastinge hire of blisse. Therfore Hooly 10
Scripture seiþ: Confortamini et non dissoluantur manus vestri; erit enim merces operi vestro. Secundi Paral[i]pomenon xv^{mo} capitulo.

LXXII   Texte

> With Athalenta strive þou not now,   15
> For sche hath grettir talent þan þow.
> It was hir crafte for to renne fast;
> To such a rennyng haue þou noon hast.

Glose

Athalenta was oon of þe phayrie and like a gentilwomman of 20
greet beaute, but hir destenye was dyuerse, for because of hire many lost þeire lyves. This gentilwomman, for hir greet beaute, was coveitid of many oon to be had to maryage. But þere was made such a covenaunte that noon schulde haue hire but if þat he ouer-ranne hire; and if sche ouer-ranne him, he 25
scholde dye. Athalenta was merveilously swifte, [f. 46^{b}] so þat noon myȝt strecche to hir in rennynge, and þat causid many oon for to dye. This rennynge may be vndirstanden in many maneres. It may be as some þing may be coveitid of many persoones, but it may not be geten wiþ-oute greet traveile; þe 30
rennyng þat sche made is þe defence or þe resistence of þe same

---

4 dede L   7 leeueþ] lovyth L   10 abide] abydyng L
hire and blys L   12 Paralpomenon S, Paralopomenon M   xv] v M
20 *fayrie M, fayre L   lyche to L   21 but but L   *destonye L
25 if þat] *om.* L   26 mervelious L   28 for to] to M   29 þing
may be] thyng that is gretly L (moult, Laud)   30 but yit L   geten]
hadde L

þing. And also þe fable may be noted namely for þoo þat makiþ greete strif and neded not. Also þe auctorite seiþ þat an harde man and a coragious oughte not to myche to strive for vnprofitable þinges, þe which he schulde not sette by, standinge þei touche not his worschip, for many greete hurtes folowith such 5 strives. And Thessille seith: þou schuldist do þat þe which is most profitable to þe body [and] moost behovely to þe soule, and flee the contrarie.

Allegorie

That we schulde nat strive wiþ Athalenta may be vnderstanden 10 þat þe good spirit schuld nat be lettid wiþ nothing þat þe worlde doith, of what gouernaunce it be. And Seint Austin seiþ to þe same in a Pistil þat þe world is more perlious to creaturis whan it is esy þan whan it is scharpe; for þe softir he seeth it, þe lesse it schulde lette him, and lesse he scholde drawe it to his 15 loue þan whan it ʒeueth him cause to dispite it. To þis purpoos Seint John þe euangelist seith in his first Pistill: Si quis diligit mundum, non est caritas Patris in eo. Prima Johannis ijᵒ capitulo.

LXXIII   Texte   20

> As þat Parys iuged, iuge þou nought,
> For many men hath ben ful hard brought
> Be grauntyng of yvil sentences,
> And had þerfore right greuous wages.

Glose   25

The fable seith þat iij goddessis of greet myghte, þat is to seye, Pallas goddes of kunnyng, Ju[n]o goddes of goode, and Venus [f. 47] goddes of love come before Paris holding an appil of goolde, the whiche seide: Lete þis be ʒouen to þe fairest & þe myʒtiest. þere was greete discorde for þis appil, 30 for ych of them seide þat þei ouʒt to haue it, and at þe laste alle

1 thynges L   anameli ML   2 nedith L   4 stondyng that L
5 his] to his L   a greet hurte M   such] of suche ML   7 [and], so
L, om. SM (et, Laud)   11 non thyng L   12–13 And ... same] And
to the same Seynt Austyn seyth L   *perilous M   22 hath] hau L
23 sentence L   24 wages] recompence L   27 Juvo S
30 myghttyest of vs L (not Laud)   31 þat] om. L   alle] om. L

þei took Paris for to iuge þe cause. Paris sought diligently þe
strengþe and þe myȝte of euery of them be þe silf. Than seide
Pallas: I am goddesse of cheualrie and of wisedom, for be me
armes be departid to knyȝtis and konnyng to clerkis; and if þou
wilte ȝeve me þe appil, trust verrily þat y schal make þe to passe 5
alle oþir in knyȝthode and connyng. Aftir þat Ju[n]o, þe goddes
of good, seide: And be me is departid þe greet lordschipis and
tresoris of þe worlde; if þou wilte ȝif me þe appil, y schal make
þe myȝtier and richer þan any oþer. And þan spak Venus wiþ
ful loving wordis and seide: I am sche þat kepith scolis of loue 10
& of iolynesse, & makiþ foolis to be wise and wise men to do
folye; I make riche men pore & þoo þat be exiled riche. There
is no myȝte þat may compare wiþ my myȝte. If þou wilte ȝeue
me þe appil, be me þou schalt haue þe loue of fayre Helene of
Grece, þe which may availe þe more þan any maner of rich- 15
esse. And þan Paris yave his sentence and forsoke boþe
knyȝthode and wisedom and riches for Venus, to whom he ȝaf
the appil; for þe which aftir Troye was distroied. This is to
vndirstande, be-cause þat Paris was not chiualrous ne riche, he
sett be no þing, but alle his thouȝt was on love, and þerfore ȝaf 20
he þe appil to Venus. Wherefore it is seide to þe good knyȝt
þat he schulde not demene him soo. And Pictagoras seiþ: The
iuge þat iugeth not iustly deserveth myche yvill.

Allegorie

Be Paris þat iugeþ folily is vndirstanden þat þe good spirit 25
schuld be-ware how he iuged oþir. Seint Austin spekiþ
þerof aȝens the [Manytheiens] þat þer be ij° þingis þe which in
special we schuld eschewe: first, to iuge oþir persoones, for we
knowe not of what corage þinges be doon, þe which to condempne
it is þerfore greete presumpcion, for wee [f. 47ᵇ] scholde take 30
them to þe bettir party; secundly, be-cause we be not in certeyne

2 euery] ich L 4 armes is L 6 in koonyng & in knytehode L
Juvo S þe goddes] godes L 8 also tresowrys L wyl L, wolte M
9 recher and myghier L 11 wise] wyse men L 12 and I L
17 and wisedom] wisdom L 18 aftir that ML *dystryyd L
23 iugede L 25 iugeþ] iugid ML 26 iuged] iugeth M
27 [Manytheiens], so M, om. (with space) SL (Manicheiens, Laud f. 76)
28 especiall ML 29 contempne L 30 þerfore] om. M it is þerfor
it is L 31 for because L

what þei schal be, þat now be good or now yvil. Oure Lord to þis
purpos seith in þe Gospell: Nolite iudicare, & non iudica-
bimini; in quo enim iudicio iudicaueritis, iudicabimini.
Mathei vij° capitulo.

LXXIV   Texte   5

> In Fortune, þat greet myghti goddesse,
> Trust not to myche ne in hir promesse;
> For in a litil space sche chaungith,
> And þe hiȝest ofte ouer-throwith.

Glose   10

Fortune, aftir þe speking of poetis, may wel be callid þe greet
goddesse, for be hir we see þat worldly þingis be gouerned.
And be-cause þat sche promissith to many prosperite ynough—
and, in-deede, to some sche ȝivith it and in litil space takiþ it
away, whan it pleasith hir—it is seide to þe good knyȝte þat he   15
schulde nat trust in hir promysses ne disconfort him not in his
aduersitees. And Socrates seiþ: The cours of fortune fariþ as
engins.

Allegorie

The cause whi þat he seiþ þat he schulde not trust in fortune,   20
we may vndirstande þat þe good spirit schuld flee & dis-
preise worldly delites. þerfor Bois seiþ in þe thirde book of
Consolacion þat þe felicite of þe Epituriens schuld be callid
vnfelicite, for þe ful & perfitȝ felicite is þat þe whiche makiþ
man sufficiently myȝti, reuerende, solempne & ioyeux, þe   25
which condicions resist not þe þingis where-vppon worldly
pepill settiþ þere felicite. Therfore God seiþ be þe prophete
Isaie: Popule meus, qui te beatum dicunt, ipsi te decipiunt.
Isaie iij° capitulo.

1 þei] the L   or] and M (ou, Laud f. 76)   4 vij] vj M   7 *Trist L
11 wel be] be wele L   12 *wordly L   13 þat sche] she L   *inowght L
14 takiþ] she yeuith M   20 The cause] Becavse L (Parce que, Laud)
22 Boys L, Boyce M   *thridde M   24 infelicite M   the full
and the perfyȝth L, the profite M (plaine et parfaitte, Laud)   is] it is L
makiþ] make L   25 myghtly corrected (?) to myghty L   26 tho
thingis M, to thynges L   28 Isaye M   decipient M

LXXV   Texte   f.

To vndirtake & to avaunce werre,
Make þou not Paris þe begynner.
Bettir he coude, I take witnes above,
Disporte in þe feire armys of his love.   5

Glose

Paris was noþing condicioned to armys but al to love. There-
fore it is seide to þe good kny3t that he scholde not make a
cheuentayne of [his ost, ne] of his bataillis, a kny3t þe which is
not apte to armys. And þerfore Aristotle seide to Alixander: 10
Thou schuldist make him constable of þin ooste þat þou knowest
is wise & expert in armys.

Allegorie

That 3e schulde nat make Paris to beginne 3oure werres is to
vndirstand þat þe good kny3t goostli, tending oonly to þe 15
knyghthode of heven, schulde be holly drawen fro þe worlde
and chese co[n]templatijf lijf. And Seint Gregori seiþ vppon
Ezechiel þat þe lijf contemplatijf is of ri3te preferrid afore þe
actijf lijf as for þe worthiere & þe grettere, for þe actijf lijf
trauailith himsilf in þe laboure of þis present lijf, but þe con- 20
templatijf lijf farith as he þat tastith þe sauoure of þe
reste þat is for to come. Wherfore þe Gospell seiþ of Marie
Magdalene, be whom contemplacion is figurid: Optimam
partem elegit, que non auferetur ab ea in eternum. Luce x^mo
capitulo.   25

LXXVI   Texte

Set þe not to be a spye, y sey,
But loke þou kepe euer þe hi3 wey.
Cephalus, with his scharpe iaueloth,
Leerith it þe, and þe wijf of Loth.   30

2 vndirstande M   & to] to L   3 not *interlineated in* L   Paris be
thi gynner M   4 couthe M   I] *om.* L   *vittenes L   9 [his ost
ne], *so* ML, noon S (de son ost ne, Laud)   10 Aristotyl seith L   Ali-
zaunder L   11 *connestable ML   knowes L   14 is] it is L   15 tentynge
M   17 comtemplatijf S   Grigore L   18 Ezeciell L   21 tastith]
tristith L (gouster, Laud)   22 Mary Mawdeleyn M   27 I the seye L
29 Sephalus L   scharpe] harpe L   *iauyloth M   30 lerneth the soo M

Glose

The fabill seiþ þat Cephalus was an auncient knyȝt, the whiche delitid him greetly al his lijf in þe disporte of hunt-yng, and hee [f. 48ᵇ] coude cast a darte þat he hadde merveil-ously, þe which darte hadde suche a propirte þat it was nevir cast in veyne but killid al þat it touchid; and, because þat he had a custome to rise in þe morneyng and to go to þe forest to aspie þe wilde beestis, his wijf was ielous ouer him & supposed þat he loued othir þan hire; and for to knowe þe trouthe, sche went aftir to aspie him. Cephalus, þe which was in þe wode, whan he herde þe leves make noise where þat his wijf wente, supposid it had ben a wylde beeste, caste his iauelott & killed his wijf. He was hevy of þat mysaventure, but þer myȝt no remedye be had. The womman [Lothis] wijf, as þat Holy Scripture witnessiþ, torned aȝen, aȝens þe commaundement of þe aungel, whan sche herde þat þe v citees sanke behinde hire, and þerfore anoon sche was chaungid in-to a gobet of salte. And to alle such figuris may be sett many vndirstandingis. But, for to take it in example for þe trouthe, no good man schulde delite him to aspie anoþer in þingis þat longith not to him. And to þe entent þat noon wolde be aspied, Hermes seiþ: Do not to thi felowe þat þe which þou woldist not were doon to þe, and stretche no snaris for to take men wiþ-all, ne purchace no harme to þem be aspiyng ne be willes, for at þe laste ende it wil turne vppon þi-self.

Allegorie

That a man schulde not sette him for to spie may be vndir-standen þat þe good spirit schulde not peyne him to knowe oþer mennys deedis, ne to enquere tidingis of oþer. For Seint John Crisostome seith vppon þe Gospel of Seint Mathew: How

---

2 kyngh (*cancelled*) knyght L   4 kouthe M   4–5 þat . . . darte] *om.* L   6 but it L   12 supposed that L   a] some L   kest L, he keste M   14 remedies M   Lothes ML, Lothtis S   17 gobet of salte] salte ston L   18 And to] And be L   18–19 But . . . trouthe] For the trwthe & for to take it in example for the trowthe L   20 spye L   21 entend that no man L   wolde] shulde M   23 noon harme LM   24 wiles M, wyles L   ende] *om.* ML   27 aspie M   29 *tithingis M   30 John] *om.* M   Mathieu L

takist þou so greete heede, seith he, of so many litell defautis
of oþer men and letist passe so many greete defautis in þin owne
deedis? If þou loued þi-silf bettir þan þy neȝbore, whi empech-
ist þou his deedis & levest þin owne? Be þou diligent to con-
sidere þin owne deedis firste, and þan considere þe deedis of 5
othir. To þis purpos oure Lorde seith in þe Gospell: Quid
autem vides festucam in occulo fratris tui, trabem in oculo tuo
non vides? Mathei vijⁿ capitulo.

LXXVII   Texte   f.

> Dispreise not of Helene þe conceill;   10
> I conceill þe so, wiþ-outyn faill,
> For ofte many hurtys falliþ then,
> Be-cause [þat] we beleue not wise men.

Glose

Helene was broþir to Hector & king Priantis son of Troye. 15
He was a ful wise clerk & ful of kunnyng. As myche as he
myȝt, he counceilid þat Paris schuld not go in-to Grece to
rauysch Helayne; but þei wold not do aftir him, for þe which
þe Troyens were hurte. Therfore it is seide to þe good knyȝt
þat he schuld beleue wise men & þere counceill. And Hermes 20
seiþ: Who-so worschipiþ wise men & vsith þeire counceill, þei
be euerlasting pepill.

Allegorie

Helene, þe which counceiled aȝens þe werre, that is to seye
þat þe good spirit schuld eschewe temptacions. And Seint 25
Jerome seiþ þat a synner hath noon excusacion wherbi he ought
to suffre temptacions to ouercome him, for þe temptyng fend is
so feble þat he may ouercome noone but þoo þat wul be ȝolden
to him. And þere-vppon Seint Poul þe apostle seith: Fidelis
deus, qui non pacietur vos temptari supra id quod potestis; sed 30
faciet eciam cum temptacione prouentum, vt possitis sustinere.
Primo ad Corinthios xᵐᵒ capitulo.

---

1 takys L   2 latyst L   3 *neyghburght L   empechist] em-
ployest M (empesches, Laud f. 77ᵇ)   4 leuys L   þou] om. ML
10 Helayne M   13 [þat], so ML, om. S   16–17 ful of . . . myȝt] a full
konnynge as any myght be M   17 Paarys L   in-to] to M   21 so]
interlineated S   26 excusaciones M   *howght L   28 wol M, wyll L

LXXVIII Texte

Be not to mery ne to sory
For þi dremys, though þei be hevy,
Morpheus biddith, the messangere
Of þe god of slepe and dremys sere.   5

Glose

A fable seiþ þat Morpheus is son to þe god of slepe; & he is
his messangere, and he is god of dremys & makiþ dremys
& causiþ [f. 49ᵇ] men to dreme. And because þat dremes [be]
a troubelous þing and a derke, and some tyme be-tokeneth   10
noþing and some tyme it may signifie the contrarie of þe dreme,
þer is noon so wise þat may propirly speke liche as þe exposit-
ours seiþ of theim. Therfore it is seide to þe good knyȝt þat he
should not be to hevy ne to mery for such avisions, by the
whiche man may not shewe no certeyne knowlech ne to what   15
thing thei shall turne, and namely that a man shoulde not be to
mery ne to hevy for thingis of fortune, þe which be transitorie.
Socrates seiþ: þou þat arte a man, thou shouldist not be to hevy
ne to mery for no maner cause.

Allegorie   20

T here it is seide þat a man shoulde not [be to] mery ne to
hevy for no [avisions], we shall sey þat þe good spirit
shoulde not be to mery ne to hevy for no maner cause þat
comyth to him, and þat he should suffre tribulacions paciently.
Seint Austin seith vpon þe Psauter: Feire son, seith he, if þou   25
wilte wepe for þe sores þat þou felest, wepe vndir þe correccion
of þi Fadir; yf þou wepe for tribulacions þat comeþ to þe,
be-ware þat it be not for indignacion ne for pride, for þe
aduersite þat God sendith to þe it is a medicine & no peyne, it

8 his] *om.* M   & makiþ dremys] *om.* L   9 [be], *so* ML, is S
10 trobolous thynges L   10–11 some . . . and] *om.* L (aucune fois riens
ne segnefie, Laud f. 78ᵇ)   it betokenith M   11 the contrarie] contrarie L
of] to L   12 speke] that may speke L   liche liche S   13 theim] tyme L
15 a man ML   16 anamely L   that] *om.* M   18 thou] *om.* M
shuld L   21 Where ML   [be to], *om.* S, be M (trop, Laud)   21–22 heuy
ne to mery M (*not* Laud)   22 ma-avisions S   23 heuy ne to meri L (*not*
Laud)   25 Awstyn L   26 thi sorres L   *veepe L   29 þe it] the M

is a chastisement & no dampnacion. Putte not fro þe þi Fadris
rodde, but yf þou wilte þat he put þe from his heritage; and
þinke not on þe peyne þat þou ouȝtist to suffre of his scourge,
but considere what place þat þou hast in his testament. To þis
purpos þe wise man seith: Esse quod tibi applicatum fuerit 5
accipe, & in dolorem sustine, & in humilitate pacienciam habe.

LXXIX   Texte

    Be the see, yf þou wilt vndertake
    Perlious viagis for to make,
    Of Alchion beleve þe counceill.   10
    Ceys therof þe sooþe may þe tell.

Glose   f.

Ceys was a king, a ful good man, & loued wel Alchion, his
wijf. þe king took a deuocion for to goo a perlious passage
on þe see. He took þe see in a tempest, but Alchion his wijf, þe 15
which loved him right hertily, dide greetly hir bisines to meve
him fro þat viage and wiþ greete teeres of weping praid him
ful bisily; but it myght not be remedied be hir, ne he wolde not
suffre hir to go with him, standing þat she wolde algatis a goon
wiþ him; and at þe departing she stirte in-to þe shippe. But 20
Ceys þe king confortid hir and with forse made hir to abide, for
þe which she was ful anguishous & hevi & in right greet woo.
Neuer-þe-lees Colus, þe god of wyndes, meved them so greetly
vpon þe see þat þe king Ceys with-ynne fewe daies perishid on
the see, for þe which, whan Alchion knewe þat aventure, she 25
kest hir-silf in-to þe see. The fabill seiþ þat þe goddes had pite
þerof and chaungid þe bodies of þe ijᵒ louers in-to ijᵒ birdis, to
þe entent þat þeire greet love myȝt be had in perpetuel mynde.
And ȝit þe same birdis fle vpon þe see-side, þe which be callid
Alchiones & þeire fedris be white; and whanne þe maryners see 30
þeim come, þan be þei sikir of a tempest. The ryght exposicion

---

2 yf that L   wolte M   he] *om.* L   þe from] fro the M   3 *owghtes L
4 þat] *om.* ML   5 man] *om.* L   10 Alcheon M   13 Ceis M   he
louid M   Alchyon L   15 he took þe see] *om.* L (se mist en mer,
Laud f. 79)   in] on M   16 to] for to M   17 fro] for L
wepinges M   19 haue gone L   20 *sterte M, styrte L   on-to L
*shepe L   21 with forse] *om.* M   22 & hevi] heuy M   23 god]
goddes M   27 of þe] of tho ML   28 in in M   29 tho same M

here-of may be þat in mariage ij° lovers loued to-gidir in liche
wise, þe which poetis likneth to þe ij° birdis þat had such a caas
& aventure. Therefore it is seid þat þe good knyȝt schoulde not
put him in no perlious passage ayens þe counceil of his good
freendes. And Assaron seiþ þat þe wise man enforcith him to   5
drawe him from hurtys, & the fool doith his diligence to finde
hurtis.

Allegorie

For to beleve Alchion, it is to vndirstande þat þe good spirit
be some yvil temptacion is empechid wiþ some errour or   10
doute in his þought, in þe which he shoulde reporte him to þe
oppinion of the chirche. For Seint Ambrose seiþ, in þe secunde
book of Offices, þat he is from him-silf, þat dispiseþ þe counceil
of þe chirche, for Joseph helpid kinge [f. 50ᵇ] Pharaoo more
profitabli wiþ þe counceil of his prudence þan þough he hadde   15
yoven him eithir goold or siluer, for siluer myȝt not a purueid
for þe famyn of Egipte þe space of vij yere. And þerfore it is
concludid: Trust counceil & thou shalte not repente þe. To
þis purpos þe wiseman seiþ in his Prouerbis to þe persone of
holichirche: Custodi legem meam atque consilium et erit vitam   20
anime tue. Prouerbiorum iij° capitulo.

LXXX   Texte

Of a childe beleve not þe counceill,
For of Troilus remembre the well.
Truste ye may men agid & proved,   25
That in armys hath sore been chargid.

Glose

Whan king Priant had repaired Troye ayen, þe which was
destroyed be-cause of þe greving of theim þat wente in-to
Colcos, than Priant thouȝt to take vengeaunce for þat destruccion   30
and assemblid his counceil, where þat were manye hiȝ barones

---

1 liche] suche M   3 seid þat] seide to L   schoulde] that he shulde L
4 *perilous M, perlyous L   12 openyon L, opiniones M   13 2nd þat]
the whiche M   14 Pharao M, Pharaon L   15 his prudence] the
chirche M (de sa prudence, Laud f. 79ᵇ)   17 Egypte L   yere, and]
yere L   20 vitam], so SM, vita Laud   21 tuee M   24 Troylus L
25 Trest L   26 be M   29 þe greving of] om. M

& wise men, for to wite whedir it were good þat Paris, his sone,
shoulde go in-to Grece to rauysh Helene or noon in a chaunge
for Esiona, his sister, þe which was takyn be þe Thelomonaialles
& ledde in-to thraldom. But alle þe wise men seide nay, be-
cause of prophecies & of scriptures, þe which seide that, þrough   5
þat rauishing, Troye shoulde be distroyed. Than Troylus, þe
which was a childe & þe yongist of Priantys sones, seid þat men
should not in counceil of werre beleve olde men ne þere
prouerbes, þe which þrough her cowardice counceilith euer to
reste; so he counceilid þat þei shoulde go thider. Troylus   10
counceill was holden, of þe which folowid myche harme.
Therfore it is seide to þe good knyȝt þat he schoulde not holde
ne beleve þe counceil of a childe, þe which of nature is full light
& litil to considere. An auctorite seith to þis purpos þat, where
a [f. 51] childe is kinge, the lande is vnhappy.   15

Allegorie

That a good spirit shoulde not agree him to þe counceil of a
childe is to vndirstande that he shoulde [not] be ignorant but
knowing & ful lerned in þat þe which may be profitabil to his
helþe. For ayens ignorant peopill Seint Austin seiþ þat ignoraunce   20
is a ful yvill modir, þe which hath right yvill doughters, þat is to
sey, falsnes & doute; þe firste is myschaunce, þe secunde is wrec-
chidnes; þe firste is vicious, but þe secunde is softer; and þese ijᵒ is
drawen awey be wijsdom. þerefore þe wise man seiþ: Sapienciam
pretereuntes non tamen in hoc lapsi sunt vt ignor[e]nt bona, sed   25
insipiencie fuerunt hominibus memoriam. Sapiencie xᵒ capitulo.

LXXXI   Texte

Hate Calcas & his fals deceites,
Of whom þe infinite malicis
Betraieth many reaumes expres;   30
Of worldly peopill þere is noon wers.

---

  2 Eleyne M, Elen L   3 Esyona L   Thelomonailes M, Thelo-
monailles L   5 of proficies L, of the prophecies M   that] om. L
7 & þe] and M   9 þrough] threwe L   10 thider] togedir L
11 folowid] felle L   15 *onappy L   18 is] it is ML   [not], so M,
om. SL   19 profitable M, prophyte L   20 þat] om. L   21 right]
full ML   22 secunde is] secunde M   23–4 be drawen M   25 ig-
norant S   31 no ML

Glose

Calcas was a soutil clerk of þe cite of Troye; and, whan king Priant knewe þat þe Grekis come vpon him wiþ a greet ooste, he sent Calcas in-to Delphos to wite of þe god Appolin how þe werre shoulde fortune. But aftir þat þe god had 5 answered, þe which seide aftir x yere þe Grekes shoulde haue þe victorie, Calcas turned toward þe Grekes & aqueynted him wiþ Achilles, þe which was comen in-to Delphos for þe same cause, and with him he wente to þe Grekis, whom he helpid for to counceill ayens his owne cite; and ofte tymes distourbled þe 10 peas betwene þe Grekis & þe Troyens. And because he was a traitour, it is seide to the good kny3t þat he shoulde hate such yvil sutill pepill, for theire tresones so doon by wylis may hurte greetly reaumes & empires & alle maner [f. 51ᵇ] of pepill. Therfore Platon seith: A sutil enemy, thou3 he be poore and not 15 my3ti, may greve more þan an enemye myghti & riche vnknowing.

Allegorie

Calcas, þe which sholde be hatid, may be vndirstande þat þe good spirit should hate all fraudelouse malice ayens his neghbore, for he should in no wise consent þer-to. For Seint 20 Jerome seiþ that a traitour will not be souplid, neiþer for fam- iliarite of feleship ne for homlynes of mete & drinke, ne for grace of seruice, ne for plente of benefices. Of þis vi[ce] seiþ Seint Paul þe apostil: Erunt homines cupidi, elati, superbi, proditores, proterui. ij° ad Ethemologeum [iij°] capitulo. 25

LXXXII   Texte

Be þou nat hard [for] to graunt, y say,
Such a thing as wele emplye þou may.
To Hermofrodicus haue tending,
The which took harme for his denying.   30

2 *subtill M, sootyl L   4 Delphas M   Appoline M, Appolonie L
6 ansqweryd L   8 comme L   9 hepid *corrected to* helpid M
10 oftetymes and ofte tymes L   distourbid ML   12 that that L
13 yvil] *om.* M (soubtilz et mauuais, Laud f. 80ᵇ)   13–14 for...pepill] *om.* M
willes L   15 soothel L   16 vnknowyn L   19 *fraudulous M
23 vi- S   25 proterui] prorrem(?) M   Ethimologeum M [iij°],
so M, iiij° S   27 [for], *so* ML, *om.* S   28 employe M, enploy L
29 tendyynges L

Glose

Hermofrodicus was a beuteuous yong thing, and oon of [the] fayrie was soore enamoured on him; but he in no wise hadde liste to loue hire, & she pursued him ouer-all. It fel on a tyme þat þe yong [gentilman] was ful wery of þe pursuet where-inne he had trauayled all þe day. þan he come to a welle-spring sette a-boute wiþ salewes, be þe which was a fayre stanke, stille & cleer, for þe which a liste he hadde to bathe him. He dide of his cloþis & went in-to þe water. Whan she of þe fayrie sawe him uncloþid & al nakid, she went in to him & for greet loue took þat yong þing in hir armys; but he, the which was full froward, put hir fro him riȝt rudeli, ne she myȝt not wynne his hert for no prayere. Than she of þe fayrie, ful of woo, praied to þe goddes þat she myȝt neuer parte from hir love, þe which put hir soo fro him. The goddes in pitie herde hir deuout preyre; þan sodeinly þei chaungide þe ijᵒ bodies in-to oone, [f. 52] þe which were of ijᵒ sectes. This fabill may be vndirstandin in manye maners, liche as sutil clerkis and philosophris hath hidde theire greete secretis vnder couerture of fable. Therto it may be vndirstandin sentence longing to þe science of astronomye, & as weel of nygromancye, as þat maistris seith. And because þat þe mater of love is more delitable to here þan othir, gladly þei made theire distincciones vpon love for to be þe more delitable and namely to rude pepill, þe which take but þe barke, & þe more aggreable to sutile, þe which sokeþ þe liquour. But to oure purpos we may vndirstand þat it is vileine & a foul þing to refuse or to graunte wiþ greet daungere þat þe which may not turne to vice ne to preiudice, þough it be grauntid. For Hermes seiþ: Make no longe delay to put in execucion þat þe which þou shouldist doo.

---

2 [the], *om.* S   3 on] of L   4 luste M, leste L   5 [gentilman], *so* M, þing SL (le damoiselle, Laud f. 81)   *purswte L   7 salowes M, salwes L   7–8 fayre stanke] stangne M (bel estanc, Laud)   8 he had a luste M   12 ne] *so* L   13–14 of . . . woo] *om.* M   15 goddes of ML (les dieux . . . en pitie, Laud)   17 sectes] seytis L (sexes, Laud) 23 delectable M, delictable L   ghadely L   24 þe more] *om.* M   delectable to here L (*not* Laud)   and namely] anamly L   26 souketh ML 30 put it in L   shuld L   doon M

Allegorie

The good spirit sholde not be harde to graunte there where
it seeth necessite, but recomfort þe nedi to his power. As
Seint Gregori seith in his Morallis that, whan we wille recom-
fort any þat is afraied in heuynes, we shoulde firste make 5
heuynes wiþ theim, for he may not verily recomfort þe hevy
persoone which cordith him not wiþ his hevynes. For, liche as
men may not ioyne on iren to anoþir if þei be not hoote boþe
ij° & softid wiþ þe fire, on þe same wise we may not redresse
anothir if oure hertis be not softid be compassion. To þis 10
purpos Holy Scripture seiþ: Confortate manus dissolutas, &
genua debilia roborate. Ysaie xxxv° capitulo.

LXXXIII Texte

Thou maist with þe pleies the solas
Of Vlixes, whan þou hast tyme & spaas 15
In the tyme of trwes & of feeste,
For þei be bothe sutill & honeste.

Glose f.52ᵇ

Vlixes was a baron of Grece & of greet sutilte; & during þe
longe seege afore Troy, þe which lastid x yere, whan that 20
trwes were, he fond pleies ful sutil and faire for to disporte
knyȝtis therwiþ in þe tyme of [soioure] & reste. And some sey
þat he fonde þe game of þe chesse & such othir liche. Therfore
it is seide to þe good knyȝt þat in dwe tyme men may wele pley
at such games. For Solin seiþ: All þingis þat is sutil & honest is 25
leeful to be doon.

Allegorie

The pleies of Vlixes may be vndirstanden þat, whan þe
knyȝtly spirit shall be wery of preyere and of being in
contemplacion, he may wele disporte in reding Holy Scriptures. 30
For as Seint Jerome seiþ in his Morallis: Holy Scripture is sette

2 *speryte L   3 it] he L   seet M, seyth L   5 affrayed M   * fryst L
7 as] a L   9 on] one M   16 *trewes M   feste ML   20 afore]
of M (deuant, Laud f. 82)   whan that] whan the M, that L   22 [soioure],
so ML, socour S (a seiour, Laud)   seyne L   25 Solyn ML   thinge M
30 redynge of ML   31 in his Morallis] om. L (Saint Gregoire es
Morales, Laud f. 82)

in þe yen of oure hertis as a myrrour, to þe entent þat we shoulde þere-in see þe erthly face of oure soule; for þere may we see oure lewedenes, þere may we see how mych we profite & how fer we be from profite. To þis purpos oure Lorde seiþ in þe Gospell: Scrutamini scripturas, quibus putatis vitam eternam habere. Johannis v° capitulo.

LXXXIV

Texte

If thou wilt yeve þe to Cupido,
Thin hert and all abaundon hir-to
Thinke on Cresseidis newfangilnes,
For hir herte hadde to myche doubilnes.

Glose

Cresseide was a gentilwoman of grete beaute, and yit she was more queint & sotill to drawe peopill to hir. Troilus, þe yongist of Priantys sones, was ful of grete gentilnes, of beaute & of worthines, loued hir right hertily, and she hadde yoven him hir loue & promissid to him þat it shoulde nevir faile. Calcas, fadir to þe gentilwoman, þe whiche knewe be science þat Troye should be distroied, dide so myche þat his doughtir [f. 53] was delyuerid to him & brouȝt oute of þe cite & ledde to þe sege among þe Grekis, where hir fadir was. Greet was þe sorowe & ful pitous the compleintis of þe ij° lovers at þeire departing. Neuerþe-lesse, with-in a while aftir, Diomede, þe which was a hiȝ baron and a ful worthi knyȝt, aqueinted him wiþ Cresseide & labored so sore to hire þat she loued him & holly foryate hir trewe loue Troylus. And be-cause þat Cresseide had so light a corage, it is seide to þe good knyȝt þat, yif he wil sette his herte in any place, lete him be-ware þat he aqueinte him not wiþ such a lady as Cresseide was. And Hermes seiþ: Kepe þe from yvil feleship, þat thou be not oon of theim.

---

1 oure] yowre L   *merowre L   2 þere-in] om. L   erthly] herdly L
for þere] & therefor L   3 the lewdenes L (nostre, Laud)   how mych]
who myche that L   4 fer] fayre L   from] om. L   9 Thy L
therto M   13 Cresseyde M   was] om. L   and yit] an L   14 more] yit
more L   15 gentilesse M   16 hertily] well M   17 nevir to S
20 & brought & browght L   22 petous of L   þeire] the L   23 Dyomed L
25 so] interlineated S   that that M   26 holly] only L   And] om. L
27 had] was L   a] of L   29 queynte him not M, be not aqwauyntyd L

Allegorie

Cresseide, of whom a man shoulde be-warre to aqueinte him, is veinglorie, wiþ þe which þe good spirit shoulde not aqueinte him, but fle it vnto his power, for it is to light & cometh to sodeinly. And Sent Austin vpon þe Psaulter seith 5 þat he, þe which hath wel lerned & assaied be experience to ouer-goo þe degrees of vices, he is comen to þe knoulech þat þe synne of veinglorie is holli or mooste specialli to eschewe of parfit men, for among all oþer synnes it is hardist to ouercome. Therfore þe apostle Seint Paul seith: Qui gloriatur, in Domino 10 glorietur. Secundem ad Corinthios.

LXXXV   Texte

Whan þou hast killid Patroclus,
Ware of Achilles, I counceil þus,
If þou leve me, for þei be al oone,   15
Theire goodes betwen þem be comone.

Glose

Patroclus & Achilles were felawes to-gedir and right dere frendes, so þat þer was neuer ij° brethir loved bettir to-gider; and þei and þeire goodes was comone as all oo þing. And 20 because þat Hector slewe [f. 53ᵇ] Patroclus in bataille, Achilles hadde greet hate to Hector and fro þens-forþ swore his deeth. But because þat he douted myche his greet strengthe, he lefte neuer aftir to waite how he myȝt finde him discouered to be-traye [him]. Therfore Othea seid to Hector, as be prophecie of þat 25 which was for to come, þat, whan he had slayn Patroclus, it were nede for him to be-ware of Achilles. This is to vnder-stande þat eueri man, þe which hath sleyne or mysdoon to anoþer mannes trewe freende or felawe, þat his felaw wul take

5 to sodeinly] sodeynly M   7 þe degrees] degrees L   he] om. M coume L   8 to eschewe] to be shewed M (a eschiuer, Laud) 9 oþer] othir thingis with latter word cancelled M   10 Seynt Poule the apostill M   þe] þe a S   14 þe thus L   19 were neuer ML 20 were comon ML   21 slow M   22 the greet M   23 þat] om. L greet] om. M (grant, Laud)   24 aftir] om. L   25 [him], so ML, om. S 27 This] That L   28 mysdone to moche M (not Laud)   29 þat his felaw] om. L

vengeaunce yif he may. Therfore Magdirge seiþ: In what [caas]
þat euer þou be wiþ þin enemy, holde him euer in suspecte,
þou3 þat þou be my3tier þan he.

Allegorie

Where it is seid þat whan þou haste slein Patroclus, thou   5
shouldist be-ware of Achilles, we may vndirstande þat,
yif þe good spirite suffre him be þe fende to bowe to synne, he
oughte to doute euerlastinge deeth. As Solin seiþ: þis present
lijf is but a kny3thode, and in tokin þerof þis present lijf is
callid a werre in difference of þat above þe which is callid   10
victorious, for it hath euere þe victorye of enemyes. To þis pur-
pos the apostle Seint Paul seith: Induite vos armatura Dei, vt
possitis stare aduersus insidias diaboli. Ad Ephesios vjº capitulo.

LXXXVI   Texte

Be-ware thou voide not fro the Eccho,   15
Ne [hire] pitous compleintes also;
Susteyne al [hire] will, yif it may be,
For þou woste not what may come to þe.

Glose

The fabill seiþ þat Eccho was a womman of fayrie, and   20
because she was wonte to be to greete a iangeler and be hir
iangeling on a day accusid Juno, þe which for ielousie on a day
lay in awayte on hir housbonde, þe goddesse was wroth and
seide: Fro hens-forth þou shalte no [f. 54] more speke firste,
but aftir anothir. Eccho was enamoured on feire Arcisus, but,   25
neithir for preiere ne for signe of love that she made to him,
him liste not to haue pite of hire, in so myche þat þe faire
creature diede for his love. But dying she preyde to þe goddes
þat she my3t be venged on him, in whom she had founde so

---

1 Magdarge M, Magdare L   [caas], so M, om. SL (lieu, Laud f. 83)
5 *slayne M, sleyne L   6 shulde L   7–8 he howte L   As] And L
9 and] an L   10 a] om. L   deference L   11 þe victorye] bene full
M, om. L (victoire, Laud)   15 fro the] from M   Hecco M, Echo L
16 and 17 [hire], so M, his SL   18 wote ML   20 Ecco M
womman of fayrie] fayre woman L (vne nimphe, Laud)   22 2nd on a]
on L   25 anamored L   Arcysus M, Archsus L   27 him luste M,
he lyst L   28 goddesse ML (aux dieux, Laud)   29 on] of L

myche cruelnes, þat onys yit þei myȝt make him to fele þe
sharpnes of love, where-by he may prove þe gret woo þat verrey
lovers haue, þe which in love be refused; and þan she died. Soo
Eccho made an ende, but hir voice remayneth, which lastith
yit; & þere þe goddes made it perpetuel for memorie of þat 5
aventure, and yit it answerith to peopill in valeis and on ryuers
aftir þe voice of othir, but it may not speke first. Eccho may
signifie a persone þe which of gret necessite requireth þe vois
þat is yoven to a-nothir, þat is to seie, of nedi peopill þere is
abiden ynowe, for þey may not helpe þeim-self wiþoute helpe 10
of othir. Therfore it is seide to þe good knyȝt þat he shoulde
haue pite of nedi pepill þat requireth [it]. And Zaqualcum seith:
Who-so wul kepe wel þe lawe, schulde helpe his frende wiþ his
good, & lene to nedi peopill & be gracious, not denying iustice
to his enemy, and kepe him from vice and dishonoure. 15

Allegorie

Be Eccho, þe which shoulde not be refusid, may be noted þe
mercy þat þe good spirit sholde haue in himsilf. And Seint
Austin seiþ, in þe book of oure Lordis Sermon þat he made on
þe hill, þat blessid be þoo þat willyngly socoureþ poore peopill, 20
þe which be in penurie, for þei deserue mercy of God vpon
theim þat is in penurie; and it is a iuste þing þat who-so wull be
holpen of a souereyne more [myȝti] þan he to helpe a simpeler
þan he is, in as myche as he is myȝtiere þan he. Therfore þe
wise man seiþ in his Prouerbis: Qui primus est ad misericordiam 25
benedicetur. Prouerbiorum xxijᵒ capitulo.

LXXXVII	Texte	f.54ᵇ

If thou wilt haue a crowne of victory,
Which is bettir þan any good worldly,
Damee þou moste folwe and pursuwe 30
And þou shalte haue hir, yif þou wilte wel suwe.

2 *charpenesse L   he may he may S   3 and] om. L   5 god-
desse M   6 answheris L   10 abydyng L   12 [it], so ML, om. S
Zaqualcuin M, Zaqualquin L   14 leene M, leue L (prester, Laud)
15 but kepe M   19 Lodis L   20 1st þat] om. M (que, Laud)
2nd þat] the whiche M   21 þe which] that M   *penowrye L   21–22 for
... penurie] om. M   23 myȝtiere S   24 as he] as that he M, that he L
*mythyer L   29 *wordly L   30 folue L, folow M   31 And
þou] And L   swe L, pursue M

Glose

The fable seiþ that Damee was a gentilwomman þat Phebus loued hertily, & he pursued hir sore, but she wold not agre to him. It befelle on a day þat he sawe þe feire creature go in a wey, & he folowed and, whan she sawe him come, she fledde & þe god aftir. And whanne he was so nere þat she sawe wele she myȝt not scape, she made hir praier to þe goddes Diane þat she wolde saue hir virginite, and þe bodi of the mayden chaungid in-to a grene lourere. And whanne Phebus was comen nere þerto, he tooke of þe braunchis of þe tre & made him a chapelet in signe of victorie. And namely in þe tyme of þe Romaynes gret felicite, þe victorious peopill of þem were crowned wiþ laurere. This fable may haue many vndirstandingis. It myght happe þat some myȝti man wiþ longe traveill suwed a lady, in so myche þat with his greet pursute he come to his will vndir a laurere, and for þat cause fro þens-forth he loued þe laurere & bare it in his deuice, in signe of þe victorie þat he had of his loue vndir þe laurere. And also þe laurere may be take for golde, þe which betokenyth worship. It is seid to þe good knyȝt þat he moste pursuwe Damee, yif he wull haue a crowne of laurere, þat is to seie, peine & trauaile, yif he wull come to worship. To þis purpos Omer seiþ: Be gret diligence a man cometh to perfeccion.

Allegorie

That Damie wolde be pursued for to haue a crowne of laurere, we may vndirstande þat, yif þe good spirit wil haue a glorious victorie, he moste haue perseueraunce, þe which shal lede him to the [f. 55] victorie of paradise, of þe which þe ioies be infinite. As Seint Gregori seiþ: Who hath þat tonge þat may suffice to telle it, and where is þe vndirstanding þat may or can comprehende it, how many ioies be þere in þat souereigne cite of paradise, euer to be present wiþ þe ordris of aungelis,

2 that] *om.* L   4 fell ML   5 folowid hire M   7 scape hym L
prayers L   8 wolde] shulde L   9 *lorier ML   11 *syngne L
anamly L   in] *om.* L   þe tyme] tyme M, to theyme L   18 vndir
that tre M (soubz le lorier, Laud f. 84ᵇ)   20 yif] if that L   21 seyne L
23 grete perfeccion L (*not in* Laud)   26 *speryth L   27 *sall L
29 Grygory L   31 how] who L   bene there M   32–107/3 present
. . . be-holde þe] *om.* L (*by homoeoteleuton*)

with þe good spirites, assistid to þe blis of þe leder, to be-holde
þe present visage of God, to se þe vnscribeable lighte, to be in
suerte never to haue fere of deith, to be mery wiþ þe yifte of
euere-lasting clennes. To þis purpos Dauid seith in his Psaulter:
Gloriosa dicta sunt de te, ciuitas Dei.   5

LXXXVIII   Texte

To þe, also, y make mencion
Of Andromathais vision.
Dispite not þi wijf, y counceil þe,
Ne oþir wommen that [wise] be.   10

Glose

Andromatha was Hector-is wijf; and þe nyghte afore þat he
was slayn, þer come to his wijf in a vision þat þe nexte day
þat Hector wente to þe bataille wiþouten [doute] he shoulde
þere be slayne. For þe whiche Andromatha, wiþ grete sighes &   15
weping, dide hir power þat he shoulde not goo to þe bataille;
but Hector wolde not beleue hire, and þere he was slayne.
Wherfore it is seide þat a good knyȝt shoulde not holly dispreise
þe visiones of his wijf, þat is to seye, þe avice & þe counceill of
his wijf, yif she be wise & wel condicioned, and namely of oþir   20
wise wommen. For Platon seiþ: þou shouldist not dispreise þe
counceill of a litil wise persone, for, þough þou be neuere so
olde, be not ashamed to lerne, þough a childe wolde teche þe,
for some tyme þe ignorant may avise þe wise man.

Allegorie   25

The avision of Andromatha, þe which shoulde not be dis-
preised, is þat a good purpos, sent be þe Holy Goost, Jhesu
Cristes knyȝt shoulde [f. 55b] not sette it at noughte, but anoon
sette it in effecte vn-to his powere. Therof spekith Seint Gregori
in his Morallis þat þe good spirit for to drawe us to goodnes   30

3 *surte L   deeth and M (not so Laud)   4 his] þe L   8 Andro-
mathus M   10 *wemen L   [wise], so L, vici S, visi M   12 Avdro-
matha L   Hectoures L   13 in] om. M   14 [doute], so ML, om. S
there he L   15 þere] om. L   *seghens L   16 vepynges L,
wepynges M   no goo L   to] in to L   17 þere] therfore M   19 þe]
om. L   þe avice] in avice L   20 she] he L (elle, Laud)   and anamly L
21 shuld L   24 *ingnorant L   29 vn-to] to M

admonestith us, meveth us & techeþ us; he admonestith oure
mynde, he mevith our will and techiþ oure vndirstanding; þe
spirite, softe & swete, suffrith no maner of litil spotte of chaf to
abide in the habitacion of þe herte where he inspiriþ but broileþ
it anoon wiþ his sutil circumspeccion. Therfore þe apostle 5
Seint Paul seith: Spiritum nolite extinguere. Ad Hebreos xjᵐᵒ
capitulo.

LXXXIX   Texte

> If þat thou haue greete werre & besy,
> In Babiloines strengthe verily   10
> Troste not; for be Minous, & þat soone,
> It was take; trustith not þan þer-oone.

Glose

Greete Babiloine was founded be þe gret giaunt Nambroit,
and it was þe strengist cite þat euer was made; but not- 15
wiþstanding it was take be king Ninus. Therfore it is seide to
þe good knyȝt þat he shoulde not so myche troste in þe strengþe
of his cite or his castell in tyme of werre, but þat it be ful
purueied of pepill and of al þing þat behoueth for dewe defence.
For Platon seiþ: Who-so trustith al-oonly in his strengþe is 20
often ouercomen.

Allegorie

Be þe strengthe of Babiloine, where-inne men shoulde not
trust, is to vndirstande þat þe good spirit shoulde not truste
ne attende to thingis þat þe worlde promisith. And Seint 25
Austin spekiþ þerof in þe book of þe Singularite of Clerkis þat
it is to lewde a truste to name his lijf to be sure ayens þe perellis
of þis worlde; and it is a folich hope to wene to be saaf among þe
bitingis of synnes; yit þe victorie in-certayne is as [f. 267ᵇ of M]

---

    1 & monychit L   *techitht L   2 vndirstandynges ML   3 of litil]
litill M   3–4 to abide] abydyng L   5 postile L   10 Babilonies L
11 Minos L   12 þan] om. M   14 Babilon M, Babilony L   Nam-
broth L   15 made] om. L (fust faitte, Laud f. 85ᵇ)   16 king]
knynght L   Minos LM   17 good] good spirit with latter word cancelled M
18 or] or off L   19 *diffence M   21 ouercome M   24 is] it is L
is . . . þe] om. M (with space)   25 thinge M   26 of þe] of L
27 þe] om. M   perell L   28 worde M   saue L   29 bitynge M

[longe as men be amonge the dartes of ther enemyes and kepith
them vnhurte; but who-soo is enuyroned with flawmes is not
lightli delyuerid with-oute brennynge. Truste to him that hath the
experience; though the worlde laugh on the, truste it not; lete
thine hope be sette in God. Therfore seyeth [the prophete Dauid]: 5
[Bonum est confidere in Domino, quam confidere in homine].

XC   Texte

Hector me must pronounce thi deeth smerte;
Wherfore greet sorow bitith myne herte.
That shall be as whan Priaunt, the kynge,   10
Wilte not truste, whiche shal goo the prayinge.

Glose

The day that Hector was slayne in the batayle, Andromatha,
his wif, come to pray kynge Priaunt, with full greet com-
pleyntis and wepinges, that he wolde not that day suffre Hector 15
[to] goo to the batayle, for with-oute doute he shulde be slayne
yf he went thider. Mars, the god of batayle, and Minerue, the
goddes of armes, had verili [f. 268 of M] shewid it hire in hire
sleepe, where they apperid to hire. Priaunt dide all that he
myghte he shulde not feighte that day, but Hector stale fro his 20
fader and sterte oute of the cite be a wey vndir erthe and went
to the batayle, where he was slayne. And be-cause he neuer
disobeyed [his fadir] but that day, may be seyde that the day
that he shulde disobeye his fader than shulde he die. And it
may be vndirstanden that [noon] shulde disobeye his souereyne 25
ne his good frendes, whan they be wise as in resoun. And
therfore Aristotill seyde to Alisaundre: As longe as thou trustest
to the counsell of them that vsith wisdom and that louith the
trewli, thou shalt reighne gloriously.

1 longe] S *breaks off, one folio wanting; text supplied from* M   3 *Trost L
4 laugh] lawith L   5 thi L   5–6 *Two line space in* M; *English from*
L; *Latin from* Harley   10 be as] *om.* L   that Priant L   11 Wilte]
Woldest L   shal goo] come L   13 in the] in L   16 [to], *so* L,
om. M   to the] to L   18 it hire] it there L   19 sleepe] shepe L
20 myghte for L   21 vndir the L (soubzterraine, Laud)   22 And for L
23 *dishobehed L   [his fadir], *so* L, *om.* M   seyde that] seide L
24 *dishabey L   25 [noon], *so* L, he M (nul, Laud f. 86^b)   shulde not M
26 be wise] awyse hym L (ilz sont sages, Laud)   27 Alexandir L
28 to the] the L   loued L   29 salt L   glorously L

Allegorie

Where she seyde to Hector that she must pronounce his
name, is þat the good spirit shuld haue continuel mynde
on the oure of dethe. Therfore seyeth Seynt Bernarde that in
mankyndeli thingis men fynde no thinge more certeyne than   5
dethe; for deeth hath noo mercy of pouerte ne dooth noo wor-
shipe to riches; it spareth neyþer wisdom, condicions ne age;
men hath noon other certeyne of dethe but that it is at the dores
of agid men and it is [in] the medwis of yonge men. To this
purpos the wise man seyeth: [Memor esto, quoniam mors non   10
tardabit].

XCI   Texte

  I purpose yit to make the sadde and wise,   f.
  That thou vse, in batayles, for no gise   of
  Of thine armes discouerid for to be;   15
  For thi deeth it will open to the.

Glose

In the batayle Hector was founde discouerid of his armes, and
than he was slayne. And therfore it is seyde to the good
knyght that he shulde not in batayle be discouered of his armes.   20
For Hermes seyeth þat deeth farith as the strok of an arowe and
lyf fareth as an arowe sette to shotte.

Allegorie

There where it is seyde that he shulde kepe him couered with
his armes, it is to vndirstande þat the good spirite shulde   25
kepe his wittes cloos and not voyde. Seynt Gregore seyeth herof
that a persone the whiche departith his wittes fareth as a
iogeloure the whiche fyndeth no worse house than his owen;
therfore he is euer oute of his house, liche as a man that kepith

  2 Where he L (elle, Laud)   that he L   4 Thereof L   6 dethe]
deth ne lesse incerteyne than is the owre of deth L (not in Laud; see note)
ne] & L   9 [in], so L, om. M   mydwes L   10–11 Two line
space in M; Latin from Harley; om. Laud   15 harneis L (armes, Laud;
so below)   16 it] than it L   18 harneis L   20 harneis L
21 strok] stokke L   22 that is sette L   shoote L   25 harneis L   to]
om. L   27 *departhit L *vittis L   28 *iowgolowre L   29 liche] euen L

not his wittis cloos is euer vagaunt and oute of the house of his
conscience; and also he farith as an open halle wherin men may
entre on eueri side. Therfore oure Lorde seyeth in the Gospell:
Clauso hostio, ora Patrem tuum.]

XCII   Texte   f. 56

> Of Polibetes coveite not hastili   6
> His armys, for thei be vn-happi.
> Of his dispoiling folowed, parde,
> Thi woful deeth be þem þat suwed þe.

                        Glose   10

Polibetes was a ful myȝti king, þe which Hector slowe in þe
bataile aftir many othir greet deedis þat he hadde doon þat
day. And because þat he was armyd wiþ faire armys & riche,
Hector coveited theim & stouped doun vppon his hors necke
for to dispoile þe body. And þanne Achilles, þe which suwed 15
aftir him with hole will to take him discouerte, smote him
beneþe for faute of his armure & at a strook killed him, of whom
it was greet harme for a worþier knyȝt was nevir girde wiþ
swerde of þe which þe stories makiþ mencion. And þat such
[couetises] may be noyous in such places, it shewith bi þe seid 20
caas. Therfore þe philozophre seith: Disordinat covetise ledeth
a man to deeth.

                      Allegorie

That we shoulde not coveite Polibetes armes, we may vndir-
stand þat þe good spirit shoulde haue no covetise to no 25
maner of worldly thing. For Innocent seith þat it ledith a man
to deeth, for covetise is as a fire þat may not be staunchid. þe
covetous persone is nevir content to haue þat which he desirith;

---

2 also he] *om.* L (aussi, Laud f. 87)   wherin] where L   3 oure]
om. L   5 Texte] S *begins again*   6 Pollibetes L   7 harmes L
9 *sewed ML   11 Polibethes M   13 *harmede L   14 coveite L
doung L   vppon his] vp-on the M, of his L   16 discouered M
17 defaute M   *harmure L   18 wiþ] whyth L   19 *swerte M   þe
stories] stories L   maken L   20 [couetises] *so*, ML, curtesies S   noyous]
no noyens L   21 þe] this M   Disoordnet L   24 Polibetis L
26 thinges M, tynges thynges L   27 is as] it is L   28 that the
whiche ML

for, whanne he hath þat which he desired, he desirith euer more.
Euer he setteþ his ende in as myche as [that] he tenteth to haue
more and not to that þe which he hath. Auarice & couetice be
ij° saus makers, þe which ceeceth neuer to seye: Bring, bring;
and to þe valew þat þe money wexeth, þe love of þe money   5
wexeth. Couetice is þe wey to þe goostly deeth and ofte tymes
to bodily deeth. Therfore þe apostil Seint Paul seith: Radix
omnium malorum est cupiditas. Prima ad Thimotheum vj^to
capitulo.

XCIII   Texte   f

 Assot þe not in loue of straunge kinde;   1
 The deede of Achilles haue in mynde,
 Which wende to make of his enemy
 His verray loue and þat entierly.

                            Glose   1

Achilles was assottid in loue of Polixene, the faire mayden, þe
 which was sistir to Hector, as he sawe hir in þe begyn-
nyng of þe yere at þe seruice of Hectoris yeris mynde in þe
trewes tyme, where many Grekis wente to Troye to se þe
noblesse of þe cite & of þe riche tierment, that was þe moost 2
solempnely made þat euer was made for þe bodi of a knyȝt.
There Achilles sawe Polixene, where he was sore taken wiþ hir
loue þat he myȝt in no wise endure. And therfore he sent to
Ecuba, þe quene, þat he wolde trete of mariage; and he wolde
make þe werre to sece, and þe siege to departe & he shoulde   2
euer be þeire frende. It was longe aftir or Achilles was armed
ayens þe Troyens be-cause of þat loue, and dide gret peyne to
make þe oste to departe; but he myȝt not do it, and þerfore þe
mariage was [not] made. Aftir þat Achilles slowe Troylus, þe
which was so ful of worthines þat he was riȝt like to Hector, his 3

 1 that the whiche M, that L   2 [that], *so* L, *om.* S, þat that M
4 Bring bringer S 5 and to to S 6 to þe] þe *interlineated in* S
7 postyll L 7–9 *Latin text omitted, with space, in* M 13 enmye L
14 loue] lyffe L 16 Polexene L 18 yeris meynde L 20 nobilnes L
terment M, terrement L that] the whiche M þe moost] most M
21 solemny L was made] was M 22 Polixenne L 23 in] *om.* L
24 Eccuba M, Hecuba L 26 was armed] armed L 27 lowe L
29 [not], *so* ML, *om.* S slowe] sawe M

brothir, standing þe yong aage þat he hadde. But þe quene
Ecuba was so ful of woo for him that she sente for Achilles to
come to hir to Troye for to trete of þe mariage. He wente
þidir, & þere he was slayne. Therfore it is seide to þe good
knyȝt þat he shoulde not assotte him vpon straunge loues, for 5
be ferre loues comyth myche harme. And þerfore þe wiseman
seith: Whan þin enemyes may not venge þeim, than hast þou
nede to be-ware.

Allegorie

That a good spirit shoult not assotte him vpon straunge loues, 10
that is to vndirstande þat he shoulde chaunge nothing but
if it come holly of God and determyned in him. All straunge
is þe worlde, þe which he shoulde flee. That he shoulde flee þe
worlde Seint Austin seiþ in expounyng [f. 57] Seint Johannis
pistil: þe worlde passith concupiscence. O resonable man, þan 15
seith he, whethir haddist þou levir loue þe temperell worlde &
passe with þe tyme, or be with Crist Ihesu & lyve perpetuelly
with him. To þis purpos Seint John seiþ in his firste pistill:
Nolite diligere mundum, neque ea que in mundo sunt. Prima
Johannis ijᵒ capitulo.   20

XCIV   Texte

Vndir-take noon armes folily;
It is perell, for soule and bodi,
A naked arme & no shelde to take.
Of Aiaux may þou example make.   25

Glose

Ayaux was a ful proude knyȝt of þe Grekis & trustid to myche
on him-silf, but yit he was a good knyȝt of his hande. And
for pride & sollennes he vndirtook to do armes with his arme
nakid discouerid wiþoute a shelde, so he was borne thorugh & 30

2 sente for] sent M   3 *treite L   of] for M, of of *with second cancelled*
S   4 And þerfor L   6 myche] *om.* L   man] *om.* L   7 þin] tyme M
11 that is] it is M   12 holly] oonli M   straunge] strange loues L
(estrange, Laud)   14 expownyng of L   Jone M, Jonis L   16
wherther M   had L   17 passe therwith M   18 Jon L   *fryst L
Latin text supplied by another hand in S   22 *harmes L   29 soleyn-
nesse ML   30 *chelde L   so] & so L   *boron L

ouer-þrowen deed. Therfore it is seide to þe good knyȝt þat,
to do such armes, þei be neiþer profitabill ne worshipfull, but
rathir þei be named lewde & proude, and þei be to perlious.
Aristotill seiþ þat many erreth be ignoraunce & faute of know-
ing, & wote not what is to do ne to leve; & some faille be arro- 5
gance & pride.

Allegorie

How armes should not be vndirtaken folyly is þat þe good
spirite shoulde not truste in his owne fragilite. As Seint
Austin seith in a sermon þat noon shoulde presume in his owne 1
herte whan he pronounceth a worde ne noon shoulde truste in
his strengthe whan he suffrith temptacion; for, whanne we
speke wisely good wordes, þei come of God & not of our witte;
and whanne we endure aduersitees stedfastly, it cometh of God
& not of oure pacience. To þis purpos þe apostle Seint Paul 1
seiþ: Fiduciam talem habemus per Cristum ad Deum, non
quod sumus sufficientes aliquid cogitare ex nobis tanquam ex
nobis. Secundem ad Corinthios iijᵒ capitulo.

XCV   Texte   f.

Authenor exile and chace awey,   2
Which purchaced ayens his contrey
Bothe treson, falsnes & greet vntrouthe;
But yif he were yolden, it were routhe.

Glose

Avthenor was a baron of Troye; and whanne it come at þe 2
laste to greet Troyenne batailles, þe Grekis, þat had longe
kepte sege afore þe cite, þei wiste not how þei myȝt haue a
conclucion to take þe cite, for it was of right greete strengþe.
þanne, be þe tising of Authenor, for angre þat he had to king
Priant, he confortid þeim & seide þat þei shoulde make a pes 3

1 þat] for M   3 *perilous M   4 faute] for defaute M (faulte, Laud
f. 88ᵇ)   5 is] it is L   8 *vndertake L   10 Tawstyn L
11 shoulde truste] susde L   12–13 we speke] he speketh M (nous
parlons, Laud)   14 we endure] he endureth M (nous endurons, Laud)
18 nobis] vobis M   20 Athenor M, Antenor L (Anthenor, Laud)
25 Anthenor L   25–26 at . . . greet] to the ende of the greet M   27 they
wost L, wiste M   29 he] om. M   30 Pryaunt M

wiþ þe king, and be þat mene þei may put þeim-self in-to þe
cite and þei shall be youen wey. Thus þei dide, be þe which
Troye was be-traied. And be-cause þat þe treson here-of was
to greete & to yvill, it is seid to þe good knyȝt þat all such
semblable, where he knowith theim, he shoulde exile & chace 5
þeim awey, for such peopill be greetly to hate. Platon seiþ that
disceit is capteyn & gouernoure of shrewes.

Allegorie

Be Anthenor, þe which shoulde be chaced awey, we may
vndirstand that þe good spirit should drive awey alle þingis 10
wherby any inconueniencye myȝt come to him. To þis Seint
Austin seiþ þat he, þat is not besy to eschewe iij inconueniencies,
is liche a botirflie, [the whiche] torneth so ofte aboute þe fire
of þe lampe þat he brenneth his wingis and þanne he is drowned
in þe oyle; and to þe birde, þat fleith so ofte aboute þe glewe 15
þat he lesith his federis. Example of Seint Petir, [the whiche]
abode so longe in þe princes courte of þe lawe þat he fell in
such an inconueniencye to reneye his maister. And þe wise
man seith: Fuge a via malorum, ne transeas per eam. Prouerb-
iorum iiijᵒ capitulo.   20

XCVI   Texte

> In Mynervez temple to suffre
> Thou shoulde not thin enemy to offre.
> Take þou good hede of þe hors of tre;
> Troye had ben yit, yif þat had not be.   25

Glose

The Grekis had made a feint peas wiþ þe Troyens be
Anthenores treson. They seide þei hadde avowed a yifte
to Mynerve, þe goddesse, þe which þei wolde offre; and þei had

---

2 wey] awey L   6 that] *om.* M (*also* Laud)   10 drive awey]
dryue M   thinge M   12 he þat] he the whiche M   13 *btyrflye L
[the whiche], *so* M, that L, he S (qui, Laud)   14 birneth L   wenges L
he is] is ML   15 oyle] oyle of the lampe M (en l'oille, Laud)   16 Petir]
pepill M   [the whiche], *so* ML, he S   17–18 into sich L   18 to reyne L,
that he renyed M (de renier, Laud f. 89ᵇ)   And] Therfore M (Et pource,
Laud)   22 suffre] offir L   23 shuldest M   to offre] suffre L
24 *1st* of] to ML   25 yet bene had that L   28 Anthemores L
seyde that M   hadde avowed] vowed M   29 þei had] the hadde L

made an hors of tre of an huge gretnes, þe which was ful of men of armes; and it was so grete þat þe yate of þe cite most be broken for to lete it come in. And þe hors was sette vpon whelis, þat rollid it forth to þe temple; and whanne nyȝt come, þanne þe knyȝtis lepte out & wente aboute in þe cite, þe which brente 5 & killed & distroyed þe towne. Therfore it is seide to þe good knyȝt that he should not truste in such fantesies ne offringis. To þis purpos a wise man seith: A man shoulde doute þe sotiltees & þe spies of his enemy, yif he be wise; & his shrewed- nes, yif he be a foole.

Allegorie

Be Mynerves temple we may vndirstande holi chirche, where sholde not a been offred but preier. And Seint Austin seith in þe book of Feiþ that, wiþoute þe felauship of holichirch & bapteme, noo þing may avayle, ne þe deedis of mercy may not vayle to euerlasting lijf; for, withoute þe lappe of þe chirche, noo helpe may be. Therfore Dauid seith in þe Psaulter: Apud te laus mea in ecclesia magna.

XCVII   Texte

Trustith not to haue a sure castell;
For Ylion, the faire stronge castell,
Was take and brent, & so was Thune.
All is in þe handis of fortune.

Glose

Ylion was þe maister dongeon of Troye, & þe strengist & þe fairest castell þat euer was made of þe which stories makeþ mencyon; but not-wiþstonding it was take & brent & brouȝt to nouȝt, and so was þe cite of Thune, þe which was somtyme a greet þing. And be-cause þat such cases falleth be þe chaunge- abilnes of fortune, it is desired þat þe good knyȝt should not be

3 wheles the whiche M   4 come] come and when the tovne was most in rest L   5 lepte out] lepid owt of the hors L (*not in* Laud) *vent L   6 Thefor L   7 no sich L   9 of his of his L   13 not] nought M   15 *baptym L   16 vayle to] auayle to M   17 Therfore] There L (pource, Laud)   Dauyd M   Sauter booke L   20 Trost L 21 For Ylyones towre sette full well L   25 Ylyon L   the faryst and the strengest L (le plus fort & le plus bel, Laud f. 90)   27 & brent] brent M   28 *soom-tyme M   29 cases] causes L

proude in him-silf ne think him-silf sure for no strengþe. Therfore Tholome seith: þe hiჳer þat a lord be reised, þe perlioser is þe ouerthrowe.

Allegorie

That a man should not wene to haue no sure castell, we may 5 vndirstande þat þe good knyჳt, þe spirit, should take noon hede to no maner of delite. For, as delites be passing & not sure & ledith a persoone to dampnacion, Seint Jerome seiþ þat it is impossible for a persoone to passe fro delites to delites, [that is to sey], for to passe and lepe fro þe delites of this worlde to 10 þe delites of paradis, þe which fillith þe wombe here & the soule þere. For þe diuine condicion is vnbounde, for it is not yoven to thoo þat weneth to haue þe world euerlasting in delites. And to þis purpoos is writen in þe Pocalipce: Quantum glorificauit se & in delicijs fuit, tantum date ei tormentum & 15 luctum. Apocalipsis xviijº capitulo.

XCVIII   Texte

Eschewe þou should þe swyne of Circes,
Where þat þe knyჳtis of Vlixes
Were torned to swyne as to þe ye.   20
Vmbethink þe wel on þis partie.

Glose

Circes was a quene [whose] reaume was opon þe see of Ytaile, and she was a grete enchaunteresse & knewe myche of sorcerie & wich-crafte. And whanne Vlixes, þe which wente 25 be þe see aftir þe destruccion [f. 59] of Troye, as he wende to a retourned in-to his contre þrough manye grete & parlious tormentis þat he hadde, he arived at an haven of þe same lande. He sente to þe quene be his knyჳtis to wite whethir he myჳte suerly take haven in hir lande or noone. Circes resceyved his 30

3 *perliouser ML   5 a] om. L   no] a L   6 knyჳt þe] knyghtli M, om. L (le bon esperit, Laud)   9–10 to delites . . . delites] om. M [that is to sey], so L, om. S   10 fro þe] fro L   of this] of the M   12 condicions L   14 *wreetyn L   15 tormentum] tortum M   19 *knyttes L 21 on] of L   23 Cyrces L   [whose], so ML, was S   24 Ytailie M enchauntouresse M   25 which craft L   wente be] wente to L 26 as] and M   went L   a] haue M   27 perilous M, perlyous L 28 *hauyn M   30 suerly] om. M (seurement, Laud f. 90ᵇ)   taken L

kny3tis ful gentilly and of curtesie made ordeyne for þeim a
potage ful delicious to drinke, but þe potage had such a strengthe
þat sodeinly þe kny3tis were chaunged in-to swyne. Circes may
be vndirstanden in many maners. It may be vndirstande be a
lande or a contre where þat kny3tis were put in foul & vileynes   5
prison; and also she may be likened to a lady ful of wantonnesse
& ydelnes, þat bi hir many erraunt kny3tis, þat is to sey, suwing
armes, þe which namely were of Vlixes pepill, þat is to vndir-
stande, malicious & noyous, were kepte to soiourne as swyne.
And þerfore it is seide to þe good kny3t þat he should not reste   10
in such a soiournyng. For Aristotil seith: He þat is holly [set]
to fornicacion may not be alowed in þe ende.

Allegorie

Circesis swyne may we take for ypocrisye, þe which þe good
spirit sholde eschewe of al þing. Ayens ypocrites Seint   15
Gregori seiþ in his Morallis þat þe lijf of ypocrites is but as a
fraudelous vision and as a fantesie ymagened, þe which shewith
outwarde likenes of an ymage, þe which is not [soo] in verry
deede inwarde. To þis purpos oure Lorde seith in þe Gospell:
[Ve vobis ypocrite, qui similes estis sepulchris dealbatis, que a   20
foris apparent hominibus speciosa, intus vero plena sunt ossibus
mortuorum. Mathey xxiij° capitulo].

XCIX   Texte

Thou shoulde no grete reson shewe to þe man,
The which as þat þeim vndirstande ne can.   25
Yno, the which þe sodeyn corne dide sowe,
Noteth it to þe wele y-nough, y trowe.

Glose

Yno was a quene, þe which made sodein corne to be sowen,
the which come not vp. And þerfore it is seid to þe good   30
knyghte þat good resones & wele sette & wise auctoritees shoulde

---

2 deliciously M   4 vnderstond L   may] ma L   5 veleyns L,
vilenous M   6 wantonnesse] voydenes M   9 noyens L   11 Arystotill L
[set], so M, om. SL   12 to] in L   *aloved L   14 we] be M (pouons,
Laud)   15 thinges ML   16 but as] but L   18 [soo], so M,
om. SL   20 Biblical quotation omitted in S and M; see note.   24 resons
M (raisons, Laud f. 91)   25 as] interlineated in S   þeim] tyme L (les,
Laud)   26 soddyn L, soþen M   29 þe which] that M

not be toolde to peopil of rude vndirstanding and þat can not
vndirstande þeim, for þei be loste. And þerfore Aristotil seith:
As reyne availith not to corne þat is sowen on a stoon, no more
availith argumentis to an vnwise man.

Allegorie   5

That faire and wise wordis shoulde not be tolde to rude &
ignorant peopil, þe which can not vndirstonde þeim, is to
seye þat it is as a thing loste, and þat ignoraunce is to blame.
Seint Bernard seiþ in a book of xv Degrees of Meekenes þat for
nought þoo escuse þeim of fragilite or of ignoraunce, standing 10
þat such as synne moost freely be gladly freel & ignoraunte, and
many þingis þe which shoulde be knowen be some tyme
vnknowen, outhir be negligence to conne it, or be slownes in
asking it, or be shame to serche for it. Alle such ignoraunces
hath noon excusacion. Therfore Seint Paul þe apostil seith: 15
Si quis ignorat, ignorabitur. Prime ad Corinthios xiiij° capitulo.

C   Texte

Autoritees y haue writen to þee
An C; lete þem be take a-gree,
For a womman lerned Augustus   20
To be worshipid & taught him þus.

Glose

Cesar Augustus was emperour of þe Romaynes and of alle
þe worlde; and because þat in þe tyme of his reigne pes
was in alle þe worlde & þat he regned pesibilly, lewde peopil & 25
mysbelevers thouȝt þat þe pes was because of his goodnes; but
it was not, for it was Crist Jhesu, þe which was borne of þe
Virgine Marie and was þat [f. 60] tyme on þe erþe, and as longe
as he was on erþe, it was pes ouer all þe worlde. So þei wolde
haue worshipid Cesar as god. But þan Sibille bad him to be 30

1 to] to the L   can] con M   7 con not M   is] it is L   8 and þat] and
than L (mais que, Laud)   10 þoo] þey M   *ascuse L   13–14 or
be slownes . . . for it] om. L (not om. Laud)   14 axinge M   a shame M
15 excusaciouns M   the postil Seynt Povle L   þe apostil] om. M (in
Laud)   16 Prime] om. M (in Laud)   24 th tyme L   26 the
cause pes (with cause cancelled) L   27 not] not soo M   for it was] it
was for M (mais non estoit car ce estoit, Laud f. 92)   30 haue] a M
Sebille L   to be] be M

well ware þat he made him not to be worshipid, and þat þer
was no god but oone aloone, þe which had made all thinge.
And þanne she ledde him to an hiȝ mountaigne wiþ-oute þe
cite, and in þe sonne, be þe wil of oure Lorde, aperid a Virgine
holding a Childe. Sibille shewid it to him and seide to him þat 5
þere was verry God, þe which shoulde be worshipid; and þanne
Cesar worshipid him. And be-cause þat Cesar Augustus, þe
which was prince of all þe worlde, lerned to knowe God and þe
beleue of a womman, to þe purpos may be seide þe auctorite
þat Hermes seiþ: Be not ashamed to here trouthe & good 10
teching of whom þat euer seiþ it, for trouthe noblith him þat
pronounceth it.

Allegorie

There where Othea seiþ þat she hath writen to him an hun-
drith auctorites and þat Augustus lerned of a womman, is 15
to vndirstand þat good wordis & good techingis is to preise, of
what persoone þat seith it. Hewe de Seint Victor spekiþ here-of
in a book callid Didascolicon þat a wise man gladly heriþ al
manere of techingis; he dispisith not þe Scripture; he dispiceth
not þe persone; he dispiceth not þe doctrine; he seekith indiffer- 20
ently ouer all, and al þat euere he seeth of þe which he hath
defaute; he considerith not what he is þat spekith, but what
þat is þe which he seiþ; he takith noon hede how myche he
can himself, but how myche he can not. To þis purpos þe wise
man seith: Auris bona audiet cum omni concupiscencia 25
sapienciam. Ecclesiastici vjº capitulo.

---

1 þat þer] þer M   2 *on ML   5 2nd to him] om. M   7 þat
Cesar] that Ceesar L   8 which] om. L   worde L   11 teching]
techyngges L, techinge of a woman or M (not in Laud; see note)   15 woman
it is L   16 is] be M   17 Howe L   18 Didascalicon ML   20 sekeþ
not (with not cancelled) M   21 of] om. L   22 but what] but L
23 noon] no L   24 con M   him-sef M   con not M

APPENDIX A

PREFACE TO L

The Boke of Knyghthode

Noble and worshipfull among the ordre of cheualrie, renom-
meed ffor in as much as ye and suche othir noble knyghtes &
men of worchip haue exerciced and occupied by long contin-
uaunce of tyme the grete part [f.2ᵛ] of yowre dayes in dedys of
cheualrie and actis of armis, to the whic[h]e entent ye resseyved 5
the ordre of cheualrie, that is to sey, principaly to be occupied
in kepyng and defendyng the Cristyn feythe, þe rigth of the
chirch, the lond, the contre and the comin welefare of it. And
now, seth it is soo that the naturel course off kynde, by reuolu-
cion and successyon of lx yeeres growyn vpon yowe at this tyme 10
of age and feblenesse, ys comen abatyng youre bodly laboures,
takyng away yowre naturall streyngtht & power from all such
labouris as concernyth the exercysing off dedis of cheuallrie, be
it yowre noble courage and affeccion of such noble & worchip-
full actis and desirys departyth not from yow, yet rygth neces- 15
sarie [it] now were to occupie the tyme of yowre agys and
feblenes of bodie in gostly cheuallrie off dedes of armes spirit-
uall, as in contemplacion of morall wysdome and exercisyng
gostly werkyys which that may enforce and cavse yow to be callid
to the ordire of knyghthode that schal perpetuelly endure and 20
encrese in ioye and worship endelese. And therefor I, yowre
most humble son Stevyn, whiche that haue wele poundered
and consideryd the many and grete entreprises of labouris &
aventuris that ye haue embaundoned and yovyn youre selph to
by many yeeris contynued, as wele in Fraunce [and] Normandie 25
as in othir straunge regions, londes & contrees. And God,
which ys souuerayn cheueten and knyght off all cheualrie, hath
euer preseruyd and defendid yow in all yowre seyde laboures off
cheualrye in-to this day, ffor the which ye be most specyaly

5 whice L   16 [it] *om.* L   25 [and] *om.* L

obliged and bownden to be-com hys knyght in yovre auncient
age, namely for to make ffyghtyng ayen youre goostly ennemyes,
[f. 3] that all-wey be redy to werre wyth youre sovle, the which,
and ye ouere-com hym, shall cawse yow to be in renomme and
worchyp in Paradis euerlastyng. I, consideryng thees pre- 5
misses wyth othir, have, be the suffraunce off yowre noble and
good ffadyrhode & by yowre commaundementes, take vp-on me
at this tyme to translate ovte off French tong, ffor more encrese
of vertu, and to reduce into owre modyr tong a Book off Knyght-
hode, as wele off gostly and spirituell actis off armys for the 10
sowle-hele as of wordly dedys & policie gouernaunce, and which
is auctorised and grounded fryst vp-on the iiij Cardinal Vertous,
as justice, prudence, ffors and temperaunce, also exempled vpon
the grete conceytys and doctrine off fulle wyse pooetys and
philosophurs, the whiche teche and covnesell how a man schuld 15
be a knyght for the world prynspally, as in yeftis off grace vsyng,
as the Cardinalle Vertuus make mencion, ffryst in iustice
kepyng, prvdently hym-self gouuernyng, hys streynght bodely
and gostly vsyng, and magnanimite conseruyng, and all-so
gouuernyng hym-self as a knyght in the seyde Cardinall Vertu- 20
ouse kepyng. Which materis, conseytys and resons be auctorised
and approued vp-on the textys and dictes off the holde poetys
and wyse men called philosophurs. And all-so ye schal fynde
here in this seyde Boke off Cheuallry how and in whatte maner
ye, and all othir off whatte astate, condicion or degre he be off, 25
may welle be called a knyght that ouercomyth and conqveryth
hys gostly ennemyes by the safegard repuignand defence off
hys sovle wich among all othir victories [and] dedys off worchip
is most expedient and neces[f. 3ᵛ]sarie, where as dayly in grettest
aventures a man puttyth hym inne and most wery he is to be 30
renommed in worchip & callid a knyght that dothe exercise
hys armes and dedys off knyght-hode in gostly dedys in con-
qveryng his gostly ennemees and ouyr-comyng þe peple and
aventure off the world. And this seyde boke, at the instavnce &
praer off a fulle wyse gentyl-woman of Frawnce called Dame 35
Cristine, was compiled & grounded by the famous doctours of
the most excellent in clerge the nobyl Vniuersyte off Paris, made

to the ful noble famous prynce and knyght off renovnne in his
dayes, beyng called Jon, Duke of Barry, thryd son to Kyng Jon
of Frawnce, that he throwe hys knyghtly labourys, as welle in
dedys of armes temporell as spirituell exercisyng by the space
and tyme of C yeerys lyvyng, flowrid and rengnyd in grete 5
wor-chip and renovnne of cheualry. And in thre thyngges
generaly he exercisyd his knyghtly labowris: there-of oon was in
victories, dedis of cheualrie and of armys, in defendyng the
seyde Royalme of Frawnce from his ennemyes; [the second was]
in grete police vsyng, as of grete cowneseylles & wysdomys, 10
yevyng and executing the same for the conseruacyon of iustice
& transquillite and al-soo pease kepyng for all the comon welle-
ffare of that noble Royaulme; the thredde was in spirytuell and
gostly dedys yovyn ontoo for the helthe and well-fare of hys
sovle. And in euery of these thre thynggys the seyde prynce 15
was holden ful cheualrouse and suremounted in his dayes above
all othir. Wych schewyth welle opyn[f. 4]ly to euery vnder-
stander in the seyde booke redyng that it was made acordyng
to hys seyde victorius dedis and actis of worchip exercysyng.
And the seyde booke ys diuidyd in thre partys gederid in a 20
summe of an C textys, drawen vpon the dictis and conceytys of
the seyd most famous poetys off olde tyme beyng as Vyrgyl,
Ouyde, Omer & othir; and al-so with an C commentys there-
vpon, callid exposicyons or glosis vpon the seyde textys, of
exemplys temporell of policie govuernaunce & worldlye wys- 25
doms and dedys, grovndyed and also exempled by experiens &
by auctorite of the auncient philosophurs and clerkes as Hermes,
Plato, Salomon, Aristotiles, Socrates, Ptholome and suche
othir. And vp-on thies exemplis & glosis is made and wretyn
al-so an othyr C allegories & moralizacions, applied & moralized 30
to actis and dedys of werkyng spirituell, for to doctrine enforme
and to lerne euery man nov lyvyng in this world how he schuld
be a knyht exercisyng and doyng the dedys of armys gostly,
for euer-lastyng victorie and helthe of the sovle. Which alle-
gories and moralizacions ben grovnded and auctorised vp-on 35

the iiij holy doctorus of the chirche as Austyn, Jerom, Gregorie, Ambrose, al-soo vpon the Bible, the Holy Ewaunngelistes and Epistollys and othyr holy doctorus, as here textis more opynly schalle appere here-afftyr. ffiat. ffiat. Amen.

APPENDIX B

A NOTE ON ST. JOHN'S COLLEGE, CAMBRIDGE, MS. H. 5

The writing of St. John's College MS. H. 5 is apparently all by one calligraphic bastard secretary hand (cursiva anglo-gallicana formata) of the middle of the fifteenth century, though varying somewhat in size and slant.[1] After the first few pages it is smaller and less showy but very much in the same style as the writing of Laud misc. 570, the copy of the French original which was made in 1450 for Sir John Fastolf, and of several other English manuscripts of the third quarter of the century.[2] Like them it also has pink ruling and illuminated border decoration in a Franco–Flemish style (with coloured acanthus and gold ivy-leaves) though from an English workshop, as is clear from a vernacular note at the end. Not only are the miniatures from the same model (perhaps the actual exemplar used by Scrope for his translation) as that of the Pierpont Morgan and Laud ones,[3] but also from the same school as the last-named, themselves by a French artist working more than once for Fastolf and more than once in association with the same scribe or scribes.[4]

The quality of the St. John's manuscript, on finely prepared matt membrane, is very compatible with it being the dedication copy for Humphrey Stafford, first Duke of Buckingham. Sir Sydney Cockerell surmised that this copy 'perhaps passed to

[1] This script is directly influenced by contemporary continental *bâtardes*, besides its more remote ancestry.

[2] Cf. O. Pächt and J. J. G. Alexander, *Illuminated Manuscripts in the Bodleian Library*, i (Oxford, 1966), vii, 54–5, 57, pls. LIII, LVII; Harley 4775 of the English *Golden Legend*, translated 1438, is another in this script.

[3] See Bühler, *Scriptorium*, iii (1949), 123-8; R. Tuve, *Journal of the Warburg and Courtauld Institutes*, xxvi (1953), 282, 284–5, pls. 32, 34.

[4] Ibid.; Pächt and Alexander, loc. cit., and p. 52. Professor Pächt has attributed the St. John's miniatures to William Abel, who illuminated the Consolation Charter for Eton in 1447–48: *Eton College Quincentenary Exhibition Catalogue* (1947), add. nn. p. 13.

Henry Stafford, son of the above Duke of Buckingham and second husband of Margaret Countess of Richmond, mother of Henry VII and foundress of St. John's College'. But that it did not reach the College direct from her is clear from the end-leaf additions made by members of the Bremschet family at the end of the fifteenth century.[1]

In 1472 the Duke's daughter Anne, widow of Aubrey de Vere and Thomas Cobham, bequeathed to her sister-in-law the Countess of Richmond 'my boke with the pistilles of Othea'.[2] This could have been her father's original copy, or the version re-dedicated to a 'high princess' (perhaps herself or her mother), or even the French.[3] Her mother, Anne Neville, may have a better claim to the re-dedication than Dr. Bühler suggests. It was to her (as a granddaughter of John of Gaunt) that Skeat attributed the note 'neuer foryeteth anne neuyll' in Corpus Christi College, Cambridge, MS. 61, the copy of Chaucer's *Troilus* with the celebrated frontispiece of the author reading to a courtly gathering; though there are other contemporary candidates for the identification.[4] She may also be the person intended by another marginal note, in the unique manuscript of the *Romant of the Rose*, Glasgow University Library, Hunterian V. 3. 7, f. 139ʳ, 'my lorde monjoy my lady your wyffe', since after the Duke of Buckingham's death, she married, in 1467,

[1] M. R. James, *Descriptive Catalogue*, pp. xx, 238–9, quoting Sir Sydney Cockerell, *Exhibition of Illuminated MSS* (Burlington Fine Arts Club, London, 1908), p. 78. The notes of births and baptisms (significantly naming the Queen, members of the nobility and prelates as god-parents) appear to have been written at several times circa 1488–1500, not all at one much later date, as often happens with such memoranda.

[2] Testament 12 April 1472, proved 2 May: Prerogative Court of Canterbury, 6 Wattys; the summary by Sir N. H. Nicolas, *Testamenta Vetusta* (London, 1826), p. 325, does not mention this bequest, nor that of 'a cup with Gloucestre Armes' to the same legatee.

[3] Anne, widow of John, fifth Lord Scrope of Bolton, in 1498 left 'to my lorde of Surrey a Frenche booke callid the Pistill of Othia': *Testamenta Eboracensia*, iv (Surtees Society 53, 1868), 152.

[4] M. R. James, *A Descriptive Catalogue of the Manuscripts in the Library of Corpus Christi College* (Cambridge, 1912), i, pp. lxiv, 126–7. As the book appears to have been in the hands of John Shirley, one may wonder if this Anne was not rather the daughter of Richard Beauchamp, Earl of Warwick (Shirley's chief patron), who married Richard Nevill the Kingmaker; or their daughter, wife of Edward, Prince of Wales and afterwards of Richard III. But these were not the only ladies of the name at that time.

Walter Blount, first baron Montjoy, who died in 1474.[1] According to M. R. James the Wingfield Psalter, the second part of New York Public Library Spencer MS. 3, must have been made for her.[2] In 1480 she bequeathed the Countess of Richmond, her daughter-in-law, a book of English called Legenda Sanctorum (possibly the 1438 prose version of the *Golden Legend*), a book of French called Lucum, another of the Epistles and Gospels, and a Primer.[3] Although she does not mention *Othea, Troilus,* or the *Romant*, she could have parted with them in her lifetime, and in any case it is not uncommon for particular books, and other valuable possessions, to be unspecified in their owners' wills.[4]

A. I. Doyle

[1] Cf. J. Young and P. H. Aitken, *A Catalogue of the Manuscripts in the Library of the Hunterian Museum* (Glasgow, 1908), pp. 330–1, where the inscription is incomplete, and the dating and identification later than the writing requires.

[2] *Descriptive Catalogue of Fifty Manuscripts from the Library of Henry Yates Thompson* (Cambridge, 1898), no. 28, p. 130; S. de Ricci. and W. J. Wilson, *Census*, ii, 1335–6.

[3] *Testamenta Vetusta*, p. 357.

[4] Anne Scrope's legacies, cited on p. 126, n. 3, above, do not include Harley MS. 4012, the *Cleansing of Man's Soul* and other English writings, which she owned before her marriage to Lord Scrope.

NOTES

For editions of texts referred to by title only see List of Books, pp. xxxiii–xxxvii.

3/1 See my article 'The Revisions and Dedications of *The Epistle of Othea*', *Anglia*, lxxvi (1958), 266–70. This English dedication is a very literal translation of Christine's presentation of her work to Jean, Duc de Berry (as found in MS. Laud Misc. 570, ff. 24–5), with only the most elementary alterations to make the text applicable to Buckingham. The line-for-line style of translation is entirely comparable to the other renderings of French verse in the volume, and this strongly suggests that the dedication to Buckingham was also the work of the translator of the rest of the book. The French prologue in Laud is printed by Mombello, pp. 7–8.

3/8 For Humphrey Stafford, first Duke of Buckingham, see *DNB* liii, 451–3, and the Introduction, pp. xix–xxi. His grandfather, Thomas of Gloucester, was the brother of John of Gaunt, Henry VI's great-grandfather. His wife, Anne Neville (perhaps the 'high princess' of the Morgan text?), was a grand-daughter of John of Gaunt, so that Buckingham (both directly and by marriage) was 'cosin to the kinge'.

3/17 Me suy meue a vous faire, en present,
     De ce petit liuret nouuel present. (Laud, f. 24^b)
Since it is Christine's adjective rather than the translator's, it does not follow that the 'newe' implies a recent English translation.

3/22–30 Prince digne, & comme desireuse
     De vous seruir, se feusse si eureuse.
     Je vous fais don de mon petit labour,
     Afin que vous voyez com ie labour,
     A mon pouoir, a l'augmentacion
     De vaillantise en bonne entencion,
     Combien qu'en moy ait sauoir trop petit
     Parquoy aucun peust prendre appetit
     En mes dittiez, pour doctrine y aprendre. (Laud, f. 24^b)

4/9   Moy, vostre serue, nommee Christine. (Laud)

4/18–20 . . . car iadis, de mon pere,
     Je ne cueilli, de ses tressages tables,
     Fors mietes, tout eust il mes notables. (Laud)

P. G. C. Campbell ('Christine de Pisan en Angleterre', *Revue de littérature comparée*, v (1925), 666) suggests that the comparable

English lines imply that the *Othéa* was translated before the *Dits des philosophes*, that is between 1444 and 1450. However, since these lines are merely an adaptation of the French original, no special value can be attached to their meaning so far as Scrope is concerned.

4/23   qui pou a pain fait tenue lesche. (Laud)

This does not seem to be recorded as an English proverb.

I

4/29 The 58 lines correspond, almost line for line, with the French.

4/33 For Hector's 'parents', see also Chapters XI and XIII.

5/18 Compare Warner (p. xl and p. 5, n. 4): 'Affin que ton bon cuer sadrece, H[arley]. The translator no doubt read "tout bon cœur".' (But this *is* actually the text in Laud, f. 26.)

5/21–2   C'est Pegasus le renomme
          Qui de tous vaillans est ame. (Laud; cf. Warner, p. 6, n. 1)

6/8–16 Christine's explanation for the anachronisms which occur.

6/18 For Othea (ὦ θεά), see Warner (p. xix), Campbell (pp. 31–3), Mombello (p. 409) and Gordon (pp. i–ii). Note that Othea also appears in *The Assembly of Gods*, where the editor (Triggs, note to l. 249) remarks: '*Othea*. I have retained the spelling in the text, though I am confident that Athena is the right reading.' Similar Greek forms may be seen in the Alitheia (for ᾿αλήθεια) of the *Ecloga Theoduli* (ed. Joannes Osternacher, Linz, 1902) and perhaps in the *TYM* ωθεος (for Tymo-theos) in Jan van Eyck's 'Leal Sovvenir' portrait (cf. Erwin Panofsky, 'Who is Jan van Eyck's "Tymotheos" ', *Journal of the Warburg and Courtauld Institutes*, xii (1949), 80–90). Note especially ll. 304–5 in *The Assembly of Gods*:

          . . . Othea, chyef grounde of polycy,
          Rewler of knyghthode, of Prudence the goddese.

'A theos', see MS. Rawlinson C 101, 4 (*Notae grammaticales*), f. 144: 'Deus dicitur a theos grece quod signat metum latine . . .'

6/25 On the rehabilitation of the classical gods, see the *Fulgentius metaforalis* (ed. Hans Liebeschütz (Leipzig, 1926), especially Chapter I: Ydolatria) and Thomas de Walleys, *Metamorphosis Ouidiana moraliter . . . explanata* (Paris, 1509), who explains the text (f. 1): 'litteraliter, moraliter, historialiter, nec non spiritualiter'.

7/1 For Christine in praise of Hector, see also *Mutacion*, ll. 5256–61.

7/5   Galathee, qui n'ot pareil ou monde, (Laud, f. 27)

7/20–3 Aristotle = *Dicts*, 150/29–30 and 151/33–5. See also Christine's *Chemin*, where the following lines are attributed to Aristote:

> Pour ce que sapience est mere
> De toutes vertus non amere,
> Par les meilleurs raisons monstree
> Elle doit estre et demonstree. (ll. 5415–18)

7/28–8/1 This passage has been borrowed directly from the *Chapelet des vertus* (*CdV*). On this, see my 'The *Fleurs de toutes vertus* and Christine de Pisan's *L'Epître d'Othéa*', *PMLA* lxii (1947), 32–44, and (especially for the title) my additional note 'The *Fleurs de toutes vertus*', *PMLA* lxiv (1949), 600–1.

8/4 beaute] so in all manuscripts; beatitude (Laud and other French texts).

8/15 Ceste discrection [prudence] est dicte mere des vertus (S. Solente, 'Un traité inédit de Christine de Pisan: l'Epistre de la prison de vie humaine', *Bibliothèque de l'école des chartes*, lxxxv (1924), 293).

8/18–22 Warner (p. 9, n. 1) points out that the *De singularitate clericorum* is 'attributed to Cyprian and Origen as well as to St. Augustine' (cf. Migne, iv. 866 for the Latin quotation).

8/22–4 Prov. ii. 10–11, as in *CdV*. Warner (p. 9, n. 3) remarks that the 'quotations from the Vulgate . . . [were] omitted by the translator, possibly with the intention of filling them in from the Wycliffite English version'. This may be true of the scribe of L but not of Scrope, since the Latin texts are present in S and M. On the unfinished state of the Longleat MS., see Introduction, pp. xvi–xvii.

Following the Bible quotation, Harley 4431 (f. 96ᵇ) adds: 'Attrempance estoit aussi appellee deesse; et pour ce que nostre corps humain est compose de diuerses choses et doit estre attrempe, selon raison peut estre figure a l'orge [*sic*; so in BN fr. 606, f. 2ᵇ], qui a plusieurs roes et mesures; et toutefoiz ne vault rien l'orloge s'il n'est attrempe, semblablement non fait nostre corps humain se attrempance ne l'ordonne.' This is followed by a miniature of the Goddess Temperance with a clock, a picture (leaf wanting in M) that is repeated in Laud and S (though without this explanatory text). See Charity C. Willard, 'Christine de Pisan's "Clock of Temperance"', *L'Esprit créateur*, ii (1962), 149–54, and Eleanor P. Spencer, 'L'horloge de sapience', *Scriptorium*, xvii (1963), 277–99.

II

8/26 Again, the 22 lines of English verse agree line for line with the French text.

9/2 seur germaine (Laud. f. 28ᵇ; also below, l. 18).

9/12 Compare *OED* under *leek*, sense 3, and *ODEP*, p. 360. French has 'ung pois' (Laud, f. 29) or 'sept pois' (Pigouchet, sig. a3). Cf. Tilley O 66 ('not worth a leek') and P 135 ('not worth a pea').

> Car s'elle n'en faisoit le pois
> Tout ne te vauldroit pas vn pois. (Harley, f. 97)

9/18 *CdV* (M 771, f. 6ᵇ): 'Atrempance est seur de prudence car de prudence descent atrempance.' Compare also Hoccleve, *Regement of Princes* (E.E.T.S., E.S. 72, 1897), pp. 171–5.

9/24–6 The quotation from Democritus is apparently not in the *Dicts* (cf. 284/26). Neither *CdV* nor its English version (*Boke*, ff. 16ᵇ–17) assign the saying to a particular philosopher, though the latter has: 'Temperaunce dothe moderate the Vyces, & maketh the vertues perfecte.' Not in the Italian *Fiore di virtù*. For additional bibliography to that in the articles cited above (note for 7/28), see my 'Studies in the Early Editions of the *Fiore di virtù*', *Papers of the Bibliographical Society of America*, xlix (1955), 315–39, and Lucia Kliem, 'Das "Fiore di virtù" und "Die Pluemen der Tugent", eine kurze Gegenüberstellung', *Cultura Atesina*, viii (1954), 95–103.

9/30–10/3 *CdV* (M 771, f. 7), under Atrempance, reads: 'Saint Augustin dit que la vertu de atrempance est refraindre et contrarier aux concupiscences qui nous sont contraires et qui nous destournent de la foy de nostre seigneur. Et ad ce propos parle mon seigneur Saint Pierre disant en sa premiere epistre: Obsecro vos . . .' (as in *Othea*). Cf. Warner's note (p. 10, n. 5) and my explanation for the omission in L in my *Revisions*, pp. 268–9. This quotation, also cited by Hibernia (Temperantia a), comes from Augustinus, *De moribus ecclesiae*, Lib. i, cap. 19 (Migne, xxxii. 1326).

10/3–6 I Petr. ii. 11. Note that all the quotations in the *Othea* are also found in the corresponding section of the *Chapelet des vertus*.

III

10/8 The 44 lines of English verse quite literally parallel the French. See *Ovide*, vii. 1681–1951, for the story of Hercules as known to Christine.

10/27 'Cerberus, the porter of hell, with hys cheyne' appears in *The Assembly of Gods*, l. 37. See also Chapter XXVII.

10/30 Qui trop sont desloyaulx gaignons (all Fr. texts. See Godefroy, iv. 204: Gaignon = mâtin [mastiff]). Scrope must have thought that 'gaignon' equalled mod. Fr. 'gagneur'.

11/8 aux lyons ne aux ours rapans (Laud, f. 30ᵇ); aux lyons ne aux loups rauissans (Pigouchet, sig. a4).

11/21-4 *CdV* (M 771, f. 21) speaks of: 'pacience . . . qui est soustenir doulcement les assaulx d'angoisse'.

11/26-7 et pour donner exemple de force allegue Hercules (Laud, f. 31); and for to gyue materiall example of force, we shall alledge vs vpon Hercules (Wyer, sig. B6); and for to gyve a materiall example of the verteu of strenthe, Othea allegeth Hercules (Bab., p. 17).

12/11 The source for this saying has not been found; compare Joan. xii. 24.

12/15-16 Socrates dit que la vertu de force fait l'omme pardurable quant il met sa force a resister contre les vices (*CdV*, f. 21^b; similarly Telin, f. 60, but not attributed to any philosopher).

12/21-8 Cited by Hibernia (Fortitudo c); cf. Migne, xvi. 80 (beginning of cap. xxxix).

12/26-7 the which . . . laboures] omitted by Harley (f. 98) but in Laud (f. 31^b): 'qui fait continuelle guerre aux vices qui n'est oncques recreue en labeurs' (so Pigouchet; cf. Gordon, p. xl).

12/28-31 I Joan. ii. 14. This extract also included by *CdV* (M 771, f. 21^b) under Force.

IV

13/2-9 Corresponds line for line with Christine's verse. For Minos, see *Ovide*, ii. 5074-80, where he is also called a 'justisier'.

13/13 Aristotle. Compare *Dicts*, 155/35 and *CdV* (Le Noir, f. 20): 'Salomon dit / ne desire d'estre iuge se tu ne peuz bien faire iustice.' See also Tilley C 552.

13/23-4   cignesi con la coda tante volte
                 quantunque gradi vuol che giù sia messa

(Dante, *La divina commedia* (Milan, 1938), p. 36. Christine cites 'Dant de Florence' in her *Livre de Prudence*, BR MS. 11072, f. 243^b).

13/30-14/2 *CdV* (M 771, f. 30), under Justice: 'Aristote dit que iustice est une mesure que Dieu a establie en terre pour limiter les choses' (cf. *PMLA* lxii (1947), 43; thus *Boke*, f. 71). Compare *Dicts*, 158/15-18; Telin, f. 61^b; Baldwin (*STC* 1255, sig. N3, attributing the saying to Plato); and my article 'The Newberry Library MS. of the *Dictes and Sayings of the Philosophers*', *Anglia*, lxxiv (1956), 288. Also Nicholas Ling, *Politeuphuia* (London, 1598; *STC* 15686, f. 82^b): 'Iustice is a measure which God hath ordaigned amongst men vppon the earth, to defend the feeble from the mighty, the truth from falshood, and to roote out the wicked from among the good.'

14/6-16 Following directly on the Aristotle quotation, *CdV* continues:

'Et dit que iustice n'est autre chose fors que a rendre a chascun ce qui est sien. Tu dois rendre a trois manieres de gens ce qui est leur. C'est assauoir a ton souuerain, a ton pareil ou a ton subget. A ton souuerain dois rendre reuerence de ceur et obedience du corps. A ton pareil ayde en le secourant en sa non puissance. A ton subget dois rendre garde et discipline en le chastiant s'il fait mal' (so *Boke*, f. 71^b, though fuller and closer to *Othea* but without attribution to St. Bernard). See Bernardus Claraevallensis, *De adventu Domini sermo III, 4* (Migne, clxxxiii. 45). Not in the *Fiore di virtù*.

14/16–17 Et a ce propos (Pigouchet, sig. a4^b); and to þe same purpos (Bab., p. 20); (*but*) a ce prouerbe (Laud, f. 33).

14/17–19 Prov. xxi. 12 (+15), with Laud and Scrope omitting 'iusto' before 'facere'. This quotation also in *CdV* under Justice.

V

14/21–15/6 The eighteen lines correspond exactly to the French text, except that Scrope has substituted Percival for Perseus. Ovid. iv. 610 sq. and *Ovide*, iv. 6586 sq.; Campbell, pp. 123–4. For a cut of Perseus riding Pegasus, see Boccaccio, *De mulieribus claris* (Ulm, 1473), f. xxij. See also Chapter LV; Bab. has Perseus in both places, as has Wyer. Rosemond Tuve ('Spenser and some Pictorial Conventions', *Studies in Philology*, xxxvii (1940), 169) cites the miniature in the St. John's MS., but apparently did not note that the name was 'Percyualle' there.

15/10–12 *Hist. Anc.* (Add. 19669, f. 57): 'Perseus . . . uainqui les genz & desconfit & apela le regne Perse & le pueple Persanz.' In *Mutacion* (MCG, f. 90^b), Christine speaks of Perseus 'duquel nom Perse fu nommee'.

15/17 Belue est un moustre de mer (*Ovide*, iv. 6620).

15/21–5   Par Pegasus est entendus
             Bons renons, qui est espandus
             D'aucun home par sa proesce,
             Par son sens ou par sa noblesce.
             Renomee est tost espandue. (*Ovide*, iv. 5808–12)

15/25–7 *CdV* (M 771, f. 27) under Bonne renommee: 'Aristote dit que la bonne renommee fait l'ome reluisant au monde et agreable en la presence des princes.' So in *Boke* (f. 63^b) but apparently not in *Dits*.

16/6–11 Augustinus, *Sermo CCCLV: De vita et moribus clericorum suorum* (Migne, xxxix. 1569). Used by Chaucer in the *Tale of Melibee* (Robinson, p. 183, l. 1643; his note, p. 744, says this 'is not in Albertanus'. It is, however, in the French text; see *Sources and Analogues of Chaucer's Canterbury Tales*, ed. W. F. Bryan and G. Dempster (Chicago, 1941), p. 604, ll. 927–9. Also used by Christine elsewhere;

cf. Mathilde Laigle, *Le Livre des trois vertus de Christine de Pisan* (Paris, 1912), p. 84.

16/12–13 Eccli. xli. 15. Scrope and Laud (f. 34^b) agree in incorrectly citing chapter sixteen. *CdV* also has this quotation at this point but correctly gives 'xlj' as Harley, Pigouchet, Le Noir, and Wyer. Harley (f. 99) then inserts a passage on the Planets not in the other texts.

VI

16/15 For Jupiter and Thursday, see *Ovide*, i. 721–6.

16/25 De Iouis est le iour du Ieudi nomme (Harley, f. 99^b; Laud, f. 35, omitting the first two words). The identification of the day of the week with a particular god, self-evident in the French, is lost in the English translation.

16/25–8 On this, see Richard Russel, *The Works of Geber, the most famous Arabian Prince and Philosopher* (London, 1678), pp. 75–83; also Chaucer's *House of Fame*, ll. 1430 sq. (Robinson, p. 295, and notes, p. 786) and notes to the next chapter.

16/28 Ieber, or Geber, is Jābir ibn Ḥaiyān; cf. George Sarton, *Introduction to the History of Science* (Baltimore, 1927–48), i. 532–3.

16/29 Nicholas. Campbell (p. 54, n. 2) suggests Nicolas de Farnham (cf. *DNB* xl. 416), who is not listed by Sarton (op. cit.), Lynn Thorndike (*A History of Magic and Experimental Science* (New York, 1923–58)), or Thorndike and Kibre, (*A Catalogue of Incipits of Mediaeval Scientific Writings in Latin* (Cambridge, Mass., 1963)). Warner (p. 17, n. 3) cautiously proposes Nicholas of Lynne, a more likely identification; see Sarton (iii². 1501), Thorndike (iii. 523), Thorndike–Kibre (col. 1871) and my note in *Speculum*, xxi (1946), 229, n. 5. Nicholas is omitted by Bab. (p. 23), though found in all French texts consulted.

16/30 Jupiter's metal is tin, according to Geber (p. 79), Bab., *The Assembly of Gods* (l. 271), Wyer ('tyn or pewter'), etc. All French texts have 'le cuiure ou arain' as Laud (f. 35).

17/3–4 and . . . knyghthood] omitted Bab.; 'et de mesmes doiuent auoir tous nobles poursuiuans cheualerie' (Harley, f. 99^b).

17/5–8 Pictagoras = *Dicts*, 60/24–6 and 61/26–8. See also Chapter XLIV (56/13).

17/10–11 Sentence omitted by Bab. (p. 23).

17/14–15 Jhesu . . . hymselfe] omitted by Bab.

17/15–19 *CdV* (M 771, f. 36^b): 'Saint Gregoire parlant de misericorde dit: Je ne me recorde point auoir iamais veu ne leu ne ouy que celluy soit mort de male mort qui ait voulentiers acompli les oeuures de misericorde de car misericorde a moult de prieres; et est impossible que la priere d'aucuns ne soit ouye et essaulcee.' Similarly Telin (f. 117ᵇ) and *Boke* (f. 85ᵇ), though Warner (p. 18, n. 2) says this passage is not in St. Gregory nor in St. Jerome's epistle to Nepotianus. Legrand's *Book of Good Manners* (*STC* 15398, Lib. I, cap. iii) also cites Gregory's letter 'to Nepocyan'. Hibernia (Misericordia n), assigning this to Jerome's letter has: 'Non memini me legisse mala morte mortuum, qui libenter opera caritatis exercuit; habet enim multos intercessores & impossibile est multorum preces non exaudiri.' The Latin text is also found on sig. o4 of the *Ordinary of Christian Men* (*STC* 5198), there attributed to St. Ambrose's *De officiis*. Slightly different texts are found in the *Stella clericorum* (*STC* 23244, sig. A4: 'Non memini me legisse aliquem esse damnatum in hoc seculo qui vitam duxit liberalem, Hieronymus') and the *Doctrinal of Sapience* (Duff 127 = PML 699), sig. C3ᵇ: 'Seynt Jherome saith that he remembreth not to haue seen a persone to deye of an euyll deth that gladly dyde the werkes of merry [*sic*].' The *Speculum Christiani* (48.29 and 208.2) has the similar extract from St. Augustine: 'He may not dye euyl that has lyuede wele (etc.)'; see the *De disciplina Christiana* (Migne, xl. 676) and *Sermo CCXLIX* (Migne, xxxviii. 1162). Compare Tilley L 391 ('He that lives well shall die well').

17/20–1 Matth. v. 7, with the same extract appearing in *CdV* under Misericorde. Scrope omits 'ipsi' which is found in all the other texts, including Laud (f. 35ᵇ).

VII

17/23 Venus and Friday in *Ovide*, i. 727 sq.

17/28 Venus est planette du ciel dont le iour du Vendredi est nomme (Laud, f. 35ᵇ; cf. note to 16/25).

17/29 estain ou piautre (Laud and Harley); copure (Bab. and Wyer). In *The Assembly of Gods* (l. 379), Venus wears 'a rede copyr crowne'. Copper is assigned to Venus by Geber (p. 80) and by Chaucer (*House of Fame*, l. 1487). For gods and their metals, see also Chaucer, *CYT*, ll. 826–9, and Robinson's note (p. 761, referring to *Confessio Amantis*, iv. 2462 sq.) as well as Skeat's notes (iii. 492–500, and v. 426–7).

18/7–8 Hermes dit que le vice de luxure estaint toutes vertus (*CdV*, M 771, f. 20ᵇ); Hermes saithe, that the Vyce of Lechery doth quenshe al vertues (*Boke*, f. 49ᵇ). Not in the Italian *Fiore*.

18/13 Vanite fist l'ange deuenir deable (Laud, f. 36). See Warner, pp. xl and 19, n. 2. It is probable, however, that the quotation from Cassiodorus comes from his *Expositio* on Psalm 18, as suggested by Hibernia (Superbia ay): 'Quantum enim in malo magna sit, hinc datur intelligi, quae ex angelo diabolum fecit, quae homini mortem intulit, et concessa beatitudine vacuavit. Omnium malorum mater, scelerum fons, vena nequitiae' (Migne, lxx. 113).

18/16 et la veine de iniquite (Laud, f. 36, and other Fr. texts); omitted by Bab. (p. 25).

18/19 Ps. xxx. 7 (Scrope omitting 'vanitatis', present in Laud).

VIII

18/21 Saturday, see *Ovide*, i. 640–3 (with the history of Saturne, 513–718, and exposition, 719–826). For a Texte and Gloze on this subject, see Amos Parducci, '*Le Tiaudelet*: Traduction française en vers du *Theodulus*', *Romania*, xliv (1915–17), 43–4.

18/27 Lead is the metal of Saturn (Geber, p. 78), and he wears a crown of this in *The Assembly of Gods* (l. 287). Chaucer (*House of Fame*, ll. 1448–9) has:

> And the led, withouten faille,
> Ys, loo, the metal of Saturne. (Robinson, p. 296)

18/27 According to the *Fulgentius metaforalis* (Liebeschütz, p. 71), Saturn is identified with the 'virtutem prudencie'.

19/1 According to Lydgate's *Reson and Sensuallyte* (E.E.T.S., E.S. 84, ll. 1299–1300), Jupiter

> Made him lese, I yow ensure,
> Hys membres of engendrure.

There is a curious woodcut portraying this in Vérard's 1509 Orosius (sig. a4).

19/7–9 Hermes; compare *Dicts*, 13/24–5.

19/15–20 Gregorius, *Moralia*, xxvii. iii (Migne, lxxvi. 401-2).

19/21–2 Ps. xviii. 10.

IX

19/30 Geber (p. 75) also identifies gold with the sun.

20/4–5 Hermes = *Dicts*, 14/15–16 and 15/15.

20/10 Warner (p. 21, n. 1) states: 'No such work appears under the name of Cassiodorus.' The Latin text will, however, be found in Hibernia (Veritas x), where it is correctly attributed to Chrysostomus, as in Bab. (p. 27). It is printed by Migne (*Gr.* l. 496) in *Homilia IV: De laudibus S. Pauli Apostoli*, though Hibernia erroneously cites the Third Homily.

20/12 dechiet elle en soy mesmes mais (Laud, f. 37.; compare M).

20/16 III Esdr. iii. 12 (although Laud, Pigouchet, etc. all cite the second book). In the *Mutacion* (ll. 5683/4), Christine seems to have adapted this proverb to read: '. . . verite si est la somme | Des vertus'. Bab. here quotes Eccli. xxvii. 12. Gordon's note (p. 148) on the Scrope text has gone awry.

X

20/20 'The translator, not Christine de Pisan, is responsible for making Phoebe masculine' (Warner, p. 21, n. 3).

20/22 Malencolieuse et lunage (Laud, f. 37); Merancolieuse [*sic*] et lunage (Pigouchet, sig. a7ᵇ).

20/25 Geber (p. 77) also assigns silver to the moon.

20/29 Hermes; compare *Dicts*, 12/22 and 13/22–3, and Campbell, p. 181.

21/4 Warner (p. 22, n. 1) cites the *Epistola ad Simplicianum* as printed by Migne (xvi. 1085). In the *Chemin* (ll. 5185–95), we find these lines attributed to Ambrosius:

> Que le sage point ne se brise
> Pour paour de nulle maistrise,
> Ne pour puissance ne s'esmuet
> Ne se change ne se remuet,
> Pour prosperité ne s'eslieve,
> Ne s'abaisse pour joie brieve
> Ne pour adversité aucune.
> La ou sapience est commune,
> La est vertu, la est constance,
> La est force et grant habondance
> De sagece . . .

21/13–15 Eccli. xxvii. 12. This extract is found in *CdV* under Folie (M 771, f. 6ᵇ).

XI

21/22 De Mars est nomme le iour du Mardi (Laud, f. 37ᵇ; see comment to 16/25). Iron is also identified as the metal of Mars by Geber (p. 81). Chaucer, *House of Fame*, ll. 1446–7, has:

> For yren Martes metal ys,
> Which that god is of bataylle.

22/2 This saying is not found precisely in this form in the *Dicts*, but see 8/15 and 292/1–6. Compare also : 'Esprouue les hommes a leurs œuures & non pas a leurs dictz' (Telin, under Absalon, f. 110).

22/5–6 According to Warner (p. 23, n. 1), 'there is some confusion here in the translation'—but the confusion is due solely to the *omissio ex homoeoteleuto* of the scribe of L.

22/7–15 Not found in Migne, xvi. 23–184, but see Hibernia (Bellum m) where the following is attributed to 'Ambrosius de officijs': 'In cassum contra exteriores inimicos in campo bellum geritur: si intra ipsa vrbis menia eius insidians habetur.' It occurs in Gregorius, *Moralia*, xxx. 18 (Migne, lxxvi. 556) with 'civis' for 'eius'.

22/16–19 Eph. vi. 12. Warner (p. 23) prints 'non est vobis', but the reading is 'nobis' in Laud (f. 38) and Vulgate.

XII

22/21 Soies aourne de faconde (Laud, f. 38). Warner (p. 23) supplies the note: 'The translator seems to have misinterpreted "faconde", eloquence, speech, as "falchion".' Wyer (sig. D4[b]) has:

> Be thou aourned, of perfyte eloquence
> And of speche clene & plesaunt influence.

22/23 hole = wholly. Warner explains the *holde* of L as 'old'.

22/26 De Mercurius est nomme le iour du Mercredi (Laud, f. 38; cf. comment to 16/25).

22/26–9 In *The Assembly of Gods*, Mercury holds a 'box with quyksyluer' (l. 370) and 'In eloquence of langage he passyd all the pak' (l. 368). See also Gordon's note (p. 149) and Schick's (*TG*, pp. 80–1).

23/3–4 Diogenes = *Dicts*, 66/13–14 and 67/14–15, and notes. Compare Campbell (p. 180) and Newberry MS. f. 36, Ry 20 (f. 225): 'The prophyte of spech ys lesse þan þe prophyte of sylens' (see my article on the Newberry *Dictes and Sayings*, referred to in the note on 13/30, p. 288). Bab. (p. 30) has: 'For Diogenes seyth þat, among al verteus, feyr eloquent langage not excessiuely vsed is muche commendyd.'

23/10–18 Saynt Gregorye saith, that we ought to haue those in greate reuerence, whiche do preache the Holye Scrypture, for they be cursers that go before our Lorde, & our Lord doth folowe them. The holy preachinge commeth before, and our Lord cometh after in the vision of our heartes and courages, the words make the curse before: and trueth is spred abroade in our vnderstandynge; to this purpose, God saithe to his Apostles, ¶ Qui vos audit, *etc.* (*Boke*, f. 101; similarly in Telin, 'De sainct Gregoire', f. cxviii, and in the final chapter of *CdV*, Le Noir edition, sig. f5). See my article in *PMLA* lxii (1947), 39, n. 41.

23/17–18 Luc. x. 16; so *CdV* (M 771, f. 44[b]).

XIII

23/23 Minerue qui ne t'est amere (Laud, f. 38[b]); Whiche (doubtles) is thy frende and not frowarde (Wyer, sig. D6). The text in M is obviously a scribal emendation.

23/25–7 Gordon (p. 149) cites Boccaccio's *De claris mulieribus* (ch. 5), though he adds 'there is no proof that Christine used this source', for the statement that Minerva invented the making of arms.

> Armour also oute of yrne and stele
> She forged firste the body to defende,
> That mannys lyf hath savyd many a sele.
> (*ME De claris m.*, ll. 680–2)

In the *Cité* (Harley 4431, f. 314) Christine wrote: 'car elle trouua l'art et la maniere de faire le harnois', and in this chapter she cites: 'si que dit Bocace'. Compare A. Jeanroy, 'Boccace et Christine de Pisan, Le *De claris mulieribus* principale source du *Livre de la cité des dames*', *Romania*, xlviii (1922), 92–105. So, in *Les Enseignemens* (BN fr. 19919, f. 20ᵇ), we find: 'Minerve trouve la maniere d'armer'. Compare *Le Livre des fais d'armes* (BN fr. 603, f. 2ᵇ and Caxton's *Fayttes*, sig. A1ᵇ); also in Christine's *Mutacion* (Solente, ii. 282, 11986–98).

23/27 in cuyrboyle, þat is to sey, in sothen ledder (Bab., p. 31). Compare *The Assembly of Gods*, l. 617 and notes (p. 77), and Chaucer, *Tale of Sir Thopas* (*CT* vii. 875).

24/2 autorite off scripture (Bab.). Apparently a proverb based on Matth. xxvi. 52. Compare Willi Haeckel, *Das Sprichwort bei Chaucer* (Erlangen, 1889), no. 55: 'For sothly Salamon saith: He that loveth peril, schal falle in peril.'

24/9 Warner (p. 25, n. 1) states that no such work was written by Cassiodorus. Hibernia (Fides ak) cites: 'Fides religionis catholice lumen est anime, hostium vite, fundamentum salutis eterne' and attributes this to a similar work by Chrysostomus. In the edition of 1887, the reference is given as: 'Super illud Mat., XIII. Inventa una precio' but has not been found in Homily 47 (Migne, *Gr.* lviii. 481–6).

24/13–14 Hebr. xi. 6. In both S and M, the chapter number is given as 'six', apparently a misreading by Scrope or his source. This Biblical quotation also appears in *CdV* (M 771 under Prudence).

XIV

24/26 Pallaunce. See Warner's note (p. 25, n. 5). Orosius (sig. r7ᵇ) prints: 'la cite de pallance qui est present Romme appellee'.

> Et aussi Pallas appellerent
> Celle dame, que tant amerent,
> Pour une isle, qui est nommee
> Pallance, dont elle fu nee.
> (*Mutacion*, ll. 11999–12002)

Royal 16 (f. 35ᵇ) cites the island as Palerne, while Add. 19669 (f. 33) has Palene.

25/4 Hermes = *Dicts*, 14/5–6 and 15/5.

25/9–15 Quotation in Hibernia (Spes q), where it is attributed to Homily 9. Actually it is in the sixth Homily (Migne, *Gr.* xii. 336).

25/15–18 Hebr. vi. 18. Pigouchet, Le Noir, Wyer, and Bab. also have 'tenendum', but do not omit 'spem' as do Laud and Scrope.

XV

25/20 Christine writes (in *Mutacion,* ll. 339–40) of:

> Ma mere, qui fu grant et lee
> Et plus preux que Panthasellee.

The Amazon queen is cited as Panthaselee in MCG (ff. 135^b–138). On Penthesilea in illustrations in the French Orose, *Hist. anc.,* and Lefevre's *Recueil,* see Tuve's article referred to in the note on 14/21, pp. 157–61.

25/23 Dont si noble voix est semee (Fr.); Of whom is sowen so noble voyce and fame (Wyer, sig. D8^b).

25/25 This story also occurs in the *Hist. anc.* (Stowe, f. 186; Egerton, f. 93; Add. 19669, f. 88^b; Royal 16, f. 79; and Royal 20, f. 156^b, with a fine series of miniatures). See also the 1509 Orosius (sig. q1); Add. 9785 (f. 171^b); Lydgate, *Troy Book,* iv. 3804 sq.; and Gower (*Confessio Amantis,* iv. 2135–47—not all the analogous passages to the *Othea* found in this poem are cited in these notes). Christine also uses it in the *Cité* (Harley 4431, f. 305; so in the *Cyte of Ladyes,* i, ch. xix).

26/10 quant prouesse et valeur est amortie en chevalier (Laud, f. 40; similarly Pigouchet); when honour & prowes is dede in a knyght (Bab., p. 34).

26/11–12 A wiseman. Compare Ashby, *Dicta philosophorum,* st. 11, with the heading: 'Honoranti fit honor. Aristoteles.'

26/16–22 Cassiodorus, *Expositio in Psalmum XII* (Migne, lxx. 100). Compare Shakespeare, *Merchant of Venice,* iv. i. 194 sq.

26/18–19 soubz la quelle germe la bonne vertu la bonne volente (Laud, f. 40). Scrope obviously took 'germe' to be a noun (though it is a masculine one) instead of the 3rd pers. sing. pres. ind. of 'germer'. Apparently Scrope's exemplar, as other French texts, did not have 'la bonne vertu' which seems to be a slip peculiar to Laud.

26/23–6 I Cor. xiii. 4–5.

XVI

26/28–31   Refuse to ensewe, the fayre Narcisus
               As with great Pryde, to be accloyde
               For the Knyghte prowde, and surquydrous
               Of many graces / is destytute and voyde.

                                             (Wyer, sig. E2)

See Ovid, iii. 341 sq. and *Ovide*, iii. 1854–1902; also Prose Ovide (Royal 17 E. IV, f. 46ᵇ). Cf. Gower, *Confessio Amantis*, i. 2275 sq. and Chapter LXXXVI, below.

27/2 Narcisus fu vng damoisel (Laud and Pigouchet); Narcisus was a meyd (Bab., p. 35 and 'sche' below). Laud also has: 'il auoit en despit tous autres'.

27/7 oultre cuydance (Wyer, sig. E2ᵇ). The presence of the bracketed words in L suggests that they were present in Scrope's original translation and that L, consequently, here represents the original draft. It seems more likely that these words would have been omitted by a scribe than added by him. Laud (f. 40ᵇ) has: 'c'est a entendre l'outrecuidance de lui mesmes, ou il se mira' (similarly Pigouchet).

27/11–12 Socrates = *Dicts*, 98/34 and 99/37; cf. Campbell, p. 180.

27/14–15 Sentence omitted by Bab. (p. 35), though in Laud, Harley, and Pigouchet.

27/17–23 In Hibernia (Superbia aq, attributed to the first homily on Ezechiel. Actually in the ninth; cf. Migne, *Gr.* xiii. 734). This passage is also quoted, though not in the identical wording, in *CdV* (M 771, f. 42ᵇ under Orgueil): 'Origenes, parlant d'orgueil, dit ainsi: Pour quoy faire s'en orguillist terre ne cendre comme se ose la personne orguillir quant il ymagine sa nature, ne comment est venu au monde, ne qu'il deuendra, ne comme sa vie est contenue en foible vaisseau, ne quel ordure il gette hors par tous les conduis de son corps.' So in *Boke* (f. 97ᵇ), but not found, under Superbia, in any text of the Italian *Fiore* consulted.

27/20 al nakid] cf. Warner, pp. xl and 28, n. 3, Laud (f. 41) has 'contenue' as other French texts, while Scrope's source presumably read 'toute nue'.

27/23–5 Job. xx. 6–7 (though all French texts, and Wyer, give the tenth chapter and correctly have 'perdetur').

XVII

27/27–30   Athamas fullye enraged / and royde
          Caused his two chyldren, to be estraunged
          By the Goddesse of furye, that gladly ottroyde
          Therfore with Furye, be not newefangyled.
                                        (Wyer, sig. E3ᵇ)

With certain modifications (cf. Campbell, pp. 125–6; Gordon, p. 149; Warner, p. 29, n. 1), the source is *Ovide*, iv. 2804–2928 and 3834–3963. See also the Prose Ovide, f. 63ᵇ sq., and Chapter XCIX, below.

28/3 ble cuit (*Ovide*, ll. 2836 and 2843; Prose Ovide, f. 63ᵇ). The queen is Yvo in Bab. (p. 36).

28/4 par dons et par promesses aux prescheurs (Prose Ovide).

28/16 fumerell] 'A hole in the roof for the escape of smoke' (Warner, p. 30, n. 1); 'floure' (Wyer, sig. E4).

28/23-4 In *Ovide*, it is Ino who casts herself into the sea, with Melicerta, from 'une roche naïve' (l. 3957).

29/2-3 *CdV* (M 771, f. 17[b]) has 'Et dit: garde toy de ire car elle destourbe raison et trouble l'entendement' (so *Boke*, f. 42[b]). The previous philosopher named was Varro, but this saying is probably based on the Italian *Fiore*, where one finds (Venice, 1566, sig. A12[b]): 'Ira (secondo Aristotile) e turbamento d'animo.' Legrand, *Book of Good Manners* (*STC* 15398, sig. c1[b]) has: 'As Seneca sayth: Ire troubleth the vnderstandynge of the creatures' (PML 747). Not in the *Dicts*; see my paper in *PMLA*, lxii (1947), 39.

29/7-11 *CdV* (as above): 'Saint Augustin dit que, ainsy comme vng mauuais vin corrompt le vaisseau ou l'on le boute, ainsy ire corrompt le corps de l'omme se elle y demeure d'un iour a autre.' So *Boke*; Telin, f. 118[b]; and Hibernia (Ira b). From Augustinus, *Epistola CCX* (Migne, xxxiii. 958). Also cited by Bartolommeo da San Concordio, *Ammaestramenti* (Florence, 1840), pp. 440/1, no. 3.

29/12-13 Eph. iv. 26 (same Biblical quotation in *CdV*, following the extract from St. Augustine).

XVIII

29/17 The story of Aglauros (Ovid, ii. 737 sq.) is taken from *Ovide*, ii. 3777-4076, followed by a long 'explication' (4077-4566). See Campbell, p. 122, and Warner, p. 31, n. 2.

29/25 For Scrope's 'enforcyng', Wyer had 'brenned' as French (defrisoit, Laud).

29/26 discouloured and as pale as asshen (Wyer, sig. E6, who seems to have misunderstood his source (Le Noir, sig. b3[b]): 'et verte comme yerre'). Bab. (p. 38) omits 'as an ivi leef'.

30/4 sister] all French texts have 'serouge' (Bab. and Wyer = 'syster-in-law').

30/9-10 *CdV* (M 771, f. 14) has, under Envie: 'Socrates dit que celluy qui a le vaisseau d'enuie aura payne perpetuelle.' The English version (*Boke*, f. 33[b]) renders this as: 'Socrates sayth that he whiche beareth the vessel of enuy shal haue euerlasting paine.' See my article 'Christine de Pisan and a Saying attributed to Socrates', *Philological Quarterly*, xxxiii (1954), 418-20.

30/14-19 Saint Augustin . . . dit que envie est auoir doleur de la felicite d'aultruy. Et dit que l'enuieux n'a pas tant seulement enuie a plusgrant de soy mais a ceulx qui sont egaulx et maindres de luy. Il a enuye aux plusgrans de luy de ce qu'il n'est si grant ou si puissant comme ilz sont. Il porte enuie a ses pareilz de ce qu'il n'est plus grant que eulx. Et a enuie aux maindres de luy de paour qu'il a qu'ilz ne deuiengnent grans comme luy' (*CdV*, M 771, f. 13ᵇ and *Boke*, f. 33; also cited by Hibernia (Invidia d). From Augustinus, *De Genesi ad litteram*, xi. 14 (Migne, xxxiv. 436)).

30/16–17 ayens . . . thei] omitted by Pigouchet, Le Noir, and Wyer.

30/19–20 Eccli. xiv. 8 (same Biblical quotation by *CdV* under Envie. For 'invidi', Vulgate has 'lividi' and Pigouchet–Le Noir–Wyer have 'mundi').

XIX

30/24 For Ulysses and Polyphemus, compare Lydgate's *Troy Book* (v. 1959–61):

> Poliphemus þe geaunt, out of drede,
> Had an eye mydde of his forhede,
> Whiche Vlixes smot out at a stroke.

Cf. Campbell, pp. 128–9, and Gordon, p. 149.

30/31 Griffin–Columnis, p. 258; 'vnum sibi ex oculis eius euulsi.'

31/3 with the barates & yll inuasion of the malicious (Wyer, sig. E7ᵇ).

31/6 On Sloth, see Siegfried Wenzel, 'Sloth in Middle English Devotional Literature', *Anglia*, lxxix (1961), 287–318.

31/7–8 *CdV* (M 771, f. 15ᵇ) under Melencolie: 'Et Hermes dit: benoist soit celluy qui vse ses jours en bonnes occupacions, car il dit que la personne oysiue commet tous ses fais a l'auenture.' Similarly, *Boke* (f. 37ᵇ) has: 'And Hermes sayth, blessed is he that vseth good occupacyons in al his tyme.' There is a very similar saying in the *Dicts* (9/9–11), but it is there attributed to Sedechias.

31/12–16 Cited by Hibernia (Accidia f) from Bede, *Expositio super Parabolas*, ii. 13 (Migne, xci. 978).

31/17–18 Prov. xxi. 5. The same extract is cited by *CdV* under Melencolie (M 771, f. 16).

XX

31/22 The account of Latona (Ovid, vi. 313 sq.) is taken from *Ovide*, vi. 1581–1772 (with the attendant 'allégories'). See Campbell, p. 112.

32/18–22 Plato = *Dicts*, 126/3–6 and 127/2–6 (and note p. 351).

32/25 Bab. (42/5–8) here inserts a passage not in Scrope nor in the French texts. Compare Gordon, p. xl.

32/26–30 *Mutacion* (ll. 5745–9; cf. also *Chemin*, ll. 4617–21) has:

> . . . c'est la grant mare.
> Que saint Augustin accompare
> Au feu d'Enfer, qui, sanz sejour,
> Ne cesse de prendre et tousjour
> Reçoit, sanz ja estre assouvi.

Saint Augustin dit que l'auaricieux est semblant a l'enfer car iamais enfer n'est saoul pour ame qui y entre, ne aussi, se tout le tresor du monde estoit amasse en la possession de l'auaricieux, il ne seroit pas content ne saoul (*CdV*, M 771, f. 39ᵇ, under Avarice, a shortened version being in Telin, f. 119). Cf. Chaucer, *Tale of Melibee*, l. 1616 (with a reference to Prov. xxvii. 20 in Skeat, v. 221), where the saying is attributed to St. Austyn; also Hibernia (Avaritia c), with the attribution 'Augustinus, in Epistola ad comitem'. The same Latin quotation is found in Bouchet, *Les Regnards* (Paris, *c.* 1503), sig. rᵌ, together with the lines:

> De l'auoir peut on, par raison,
> Faire a enfer comparaison,
> Car ne scait d'ames trop auoir
> Aussi ne fait il auoir d'auoir
> Qu'il dye ia qui luy suffise
> Par l'ardeur de son auarice;
> Iamais suffisance n'aura
> Mais tousiours amasser vouldra.

Compare Bernardus, *De modo bene vivendi*, cap. xliv (Migne, clxxxiv. 1266).

32/31 Eccli. xiv. 9, the 'in patrem' being Scrope's error for the 'in partem' found in Laud (f. 44). Again *CdV* has the same Bible quotation, following directly on the saying from St. Augustine.

XXI

33/2 For Bacchus, see the account in *Ovide*, iii. 823–45 and 2528–76.

33/3–5
> Yvresce occit le scens, l'ame et le corps,
> Et fait cheoir l'omme en villains acors.
>   (Christine, *Prouverbes mouraulx*, no. 53)

33/13–14 Ypocras dit: L'abondance de vin et de viandes destruit le corps et l'ame et les vertus (*CdV* under Glotonnie, M 771, f. 27ᵇ; thus *Boke*, f. 65; not in the Italian *Fiore*). Note that the identical philosopher, Patristic and Biblical quotations appear in this chapter and in the chapter on Gluttony in *CdV*.

33/17–21 Saynte Gregorye saythe, that when the Vyce of Glotonye hath the domynacyon and power of the person, it shal cause him to lease all the goodnesse that euer he dyd. And that when the body of the person [le ventre de la personne, Fr.] is not gouerned by abstynence, al the Vertues of the same person be drowned (*Boke*, f. 65; so *CdV*, M 771, f. 27ᵇ; and Telin, f. 117ᵇ). Gregorius, *Moralia*, xxx. 18 (Migne, lxxvi. 556).

33/21–4 Phil. iii. 19. Laud, Pigouchet, and *CdV* have 'eorum' where Vulgate has 'ipsorum'.

XXII

33/26 The story of Pygmalion is in *Ovide*, x. 929–1074; cf. Caxton's *Ovyde*, pp. 7–8. See Campbell, pp. 127–8.

34/4 Cidoyne] see Warner's note, p. 35, n. 4. *Ovide* (l. 929) has: 'En cele terre d'Amatonte', which becomes Amaconte in the prose version (Royal 17 E. IV, f. 159).

34/10 In both the *Ovide* and the prose version, the statue was made of 'yvoire blanc' (l. 944). The source for Christine's statement that the statue was made of stone has not been found.

35/2–4 þe philosophre Aptalyn (Bab., p. 44). This saying is not found in the *Dicts* nor has the philosopher been identified.

35/9–12 O ignis infernalis, luxuria cuius natura [? materia] gula, cuius flamma superbia, cuius scintille praua colloquia, cuius fumus infancia [? infamia], cuius cinis inopia [? immundicia], cuius finis gehenna. Jhero. (Bouchet, sig. s3ᵇ; so Hibernia, Luxuria l, with variants as noted, also attributing this to some epistle of St. Jerome). Saint Gregoire dit, en parlant de luxure en vne histoire et epistre: O feu de luxure, du quel la bouche est glotonnie, la flame est orgueil, les flamettes sont paroles corrompues, la fumee est mauuais renom, les cendres sont pouurete, la fin est le tourment d'enfer (*CdV* under Luxure, M 771, f. 20ᵇ; similarly *Boke*, f. 50 and Telin, f. 117ᵇ; not in the Italian *Fiore*).

35/13–15 II Petr. ii. 13. In *CdV*, the same extract follows the passage above. Laud (f. 45) alone assigns this to 'Prima Petri'.

XXIII

35/17 Diana appears frequently in *Ovide* and elsewhere (e.g. *The Assembly of Gods*, etc.).

35/22–3 et comme il ne soit riens tant mauuais qui n'ait aucune bonne propriete (Laud, f. 45ᵇ; thus Harley, Pigouchet, and Wyer); wyche, though sche varyaunt & chaungeable be, yett (Bab., p. 45).

35/32   Dyane, c'est la Deïté
                 Qui regnoit en la Trinité. (*Ovide*, iii. 635–6)

36/3–5 For a discussion of this identification, see my 'The Apostles and the Creed', *Speculum*, xxviii (1953), 335–9, where fifteen different combinations are listed. To this may be added: no. 16 = I and II: James the Less; III: Thomas; IV: John; V: James; VI: Andrew; VII: Peter; VIII: Matthias; IX^1: Jude; IX^2–X^1: Simon; X^2: Matthew; XI: Bartholomew; XII: Philip (Max Lehrs, *Geschichte und kritischer Katalog des deutschen, niederländischen und französischen Kupferstichs im 15. Jahrhundert* (Vienna, 1908–34), iv. 83). Also no. 17 = I and II: Peter; III: John; IV: Andrew; V: Simon; VI: Matthew; VII: Bartholomew; VIII: James; IX: Jude and Philip; X: Thomas; XI: James the Less; XII: Matthias (Opicinus de Canistris, Cod. Pal. 1993 t. 5; courtesy of the late Richard G. Salomon). In Bodley 283 the order of the Apostles is as in no. 1, but the division of the sections differs. In *Auslegung des Glaubens* (Low German) [Magdeburg, 1493], there is a variant of no. 12. No. 6 is also found in Berno, *De officio missae* (Paris, 1510), ff. 16–17. To the bibliography may be added: Carl Wehmer, 'Zur Echtheitskritik der Metallschnittplatten Schreiber 2746a und Schreiber 2865', *Buch und Papier* (Leipzig, 1949), pp. 143–57; Robert H. Bowers, 'Three Middle English Poems on the Apostles' Creed', *PMLA* lxx (1955), 210–22; W. W. Williamson, 'Saints on Norfolk Rood-Screens and Pulpits', *Norfolk Archaeology*, xxxi^3 (1956), 303; Sister Mary Teresa, 'The Apostles and the Creed in Manuscripts of *The Pore Caitiff*', *Speculum*, xxxii (1957), 323–5; James D. Gordon, 'The Articles of the Creed and the Apostles', *Speculum*, xl (1965), 634–40; and the references cited there.

XXIV

36/7–10   Resemble well Ceres, the Goddesse bryght
             Whiche gyueth all men corne, and none doth denie
             So shulde hym selfe abandon, euery good knyght
             That well woll susteyne, the order of cheualrie.

                                              (Wyer, sig. F6)

Ceres appears in the fifth book of *Ovide*. See also the *Cité* (Harley 4431, f. 314^b; *Cyte*, i, ch. xxxv); *Chemin*, l. 2600; *Assembly of Gods* (l. 293); etc.

36/12   Ceres ara premierement,
             Et dona le cultivement
             De terre, et fist les blez semer.
             Cele devons nous tuit amer. (*Ovide*, v. 1846–9).

See *Mutacion*, ll. 12057–64.

36/13 les gaagnages (Laud, f. 46); les gaignages (Harley, f. 107^b).

36/15 Cerès, dame de blee (Machaut, *Font. amour.*, l. 1671; similarly *Ovide*, v. 3782 and *ME De claris mulieribus*, l. 552).

36/15–16 et la terre nommerent de son nom (Laud, and in all others except Bab., p. 47).

36/17–18 Laud has 'abandonnee' and 'abandonnez'. Scrope anglicizes the OFr 'abandoner' (lavish), no such sense being recorded by *OED*. Wyer also has 'abandoned'. Scrope seems to identify or confuse this with 'abundant'.

36/20 This saying is not in the *Dicts*. *CdV* (under Largesse, M 771, f. 38 = *Boke*², sig. K2ᵇ) has: 'Alexandre dit: donne et on te donnera' (a translation from the *Fiore*: 'Alessandro dice: Dona ad altrui, se tu vuoi che sia donato a te' (Florence, 1856, p. 39)). See also Legrand, *Book of Good Manners* (London, 1507), chap. xv: 'Lybralyte [*sic*] is the moyen for to gete frends'; Baldwin (p. 83): 'Give liberally for thy profit'; *Dits* (Paris, 1533), f. cxvᵇ: 'estre liberal, donner . . . font l'homme estre aime de chascun.'

36/25–7 See Chapter XXIII (Creed II). Bab. (p. 47) identifies this section with 'Seint Andrew'. Scrope belongs to my type no. 13, while Babyngton is the sole representative of no. 5.

XXV

36/29–37/2 In the Ulm, 1473 edition (f. xi) of the *De claris mulieribus*, she is described as 'Ysis cui antea nomen Yo . . . illos [the Egyptians] docuit terras colere, cultis commitere semina etc'. Here Isis, as no. 8, follows the account of Ceres (no. 5).

> A nobyll lady, an excellent pryncess,
> Now callyd Isys, toforne clepyd Io,
> Throught all Egypt souereyne goddess.
> > (*ME De claris m.*, ll. 835–7)
> Tawght them to sowe and to eyre the lonnd.
> > (Ibid., l. 897)

In her *Cité* (Harley 4431, ff. 314ᵇ–315), Christine is reminded, regarding Isis: 'si que toy meismes as touchie en ton liure de Othea' (thus also in the *Cyte of Ladyes*, sig. Mm5ᵇ). The goddess is also mentioned in the *Chemin*, l. 2600; and see *Mutacion*, ll. 11884–921. According to Add. 19669 (f. 30), Yo was worshipped as a goddess 'si l'apelerent Ysin'. Cf. also *The Assembly of Gods*, st. 48.

36/29 hiȝ] compare Warner, p. 39, n. 2. The first line in Laud (f. 46) reads: 'Toutes vertus hantes et plantes.' Apparently Scrope (or his original) read 'hautes'.

37/7–10 The quotation from Hermes has not been located; compare *Dicts*, 10/31.

37/18–20 See Chapter XXIII (Creed III).

XXVI

37/23–6 For this story, see Campbell, pp. 126–7, and Gordon's summary, p. 150; note the chapter in the Prose Ovide (Royal 17 E. iv,

f. 175) headed: 'Comment Mydas eut oreilles d'asne pour ce qu'il juga le son du flaiol Pan plus delicieux que la lyre Phebus.' See Ovid, xi. 146–93 and *Ovide*, xi. 651–770.

> Et d'autre part Pan freteloit,
> Qui dieu des bestes s'apelloit,
> Et Midos li sos desprisoit
> La harpe, et le fretel prisoit,
> Mais Phebus en prist grant vengence,
> Car il fist tant par sa puissance
> Que Midos d'asne oreilles ot.
> (Machaut, *Font. Amour.*, ll. 1691–7)

Compare Gower, *Confessio Amantis*, v. 141 sq., and Caxton's *Ovyde*, pp. 32–3.

37/28 Phebus et Pan le dieu des pastours (Laud, f. 46^b). Perhaps Scrope, or his source, originally read 'les dieux'.

> Pan fu, si com dist li auctours,
> Dieus des bestes et des pastours. (*Ovide*, i. 4033–4).

38/15 *CdV* (M 771, f. 30) sets forth a requirement of a good judge which is that 'il juge selon raison'.

38/16–17 Senecques dit que le foul est compare a la taulpe qui voyt [*sic*] et riens n'entent (*CdV* under Folie, M 771, f. 5); Senec saith that a foole may be compared to the Moldwarpe, whiche heareth but vnderstandeth not (*Boke*, f. 14).

38/18 Diogenes = *Dicts*, 66/21–3 and 67/23–5. 'Vng iour en passant par aulcun lieu, il [Diogenes] vit vng homme ydiot assis sus vne pierre; en le monstrant a ceulx qui auec luy alloient, l'en dit: "Ve la pierre sus pierre" ' (M 277, f. 50; on this manuscript see my note in *Speculum*, xii (1937), 450–1). See a perhaps related story under 'Pazzia' in the *Fiore di virtù*, there connected with Aristotle. Note also my 'Diogenes and *The Boke named The Governour*', *Modern Language Notes*, lxix (1954), 481–4.

8/21–3 qui le benoit Filz de Dieu iuga a prendre lier et pendre au gibet de la Croix (Laud, f. 47). Scrope, or his exemplar, may have read 'lire'.

38/26–7 See Chapter XXIII (Creed IV). Only Bab. (p. 49) connects this article with 'Seynt Jhon'; see notes to Chapter XXIV.

XXVII

38/29–32 Story is from *Ovide*, vii. 1681–1951. Compare Campbell, pp. 114–15, and especially Gordon, p. 150. See also Chapter III.

39/3 Proserpyne, þe feyre daughter off þe goddes Ceres (Bab., p. 50; the addition is peculiar to Bab.).

39/7 Et a Cerberus le portier d'enfer coppa les chaynes (Laud, f. 47ᵇ, though Gordon, p. xli, suggests this is not in the French). Probably Acerberus was Scrope's translation, partially corrected in L. For the chains of Cerberus, see *Ovide*, ix. 723–4:

> Et si trais Cerberon d'enfer
> En grosses chaënes de fer.

39/9–10 Compare *Dicts*, 65/19–20.

39/10–11 Et dist Pitagoras: Tu dois l'amour de ton amy garder diligamment (Laud, f. 47ᵇ; not found in French *Dits*). Compare *Dicts*, 56/25, 98/28, 272/26, etc.

39/12–18 The 'Mortalyte' (*sic*; cf. Gordon, p. 50) is again much extended in Bab.

39/18 See Chapter XXXIII (Creed V).

XXVIII

39/20 For Cadmus, see *Ovide*, iii. 1 sq. and iv. 5116 sq.; *Cyte of Ladyes* (sig. Cc1ᵇ); Chaucer, *Knight's Tale*, A 1547–9; Lydgate, *Siege of Thebes* [De Worde, 1496], sig. a6; etc. There is an account of Cadmus in the Prose Ovide (Royal 17 E. IV, f. 42ᵇ). Cf. Warner (p. 42, n. 1) and notes to Chapter XLVI (Constans).

39/25 Le Roy Cadmus qui premier fonda Thebes (Egerton, f. 64ᵇ; similarly, with Cadamus, in *Edipus*, sig. A2ᵇ).

39/26–7 Cadmus fu sages et soutis, | A philosophie ententis (*Ovide*, iii. 205–6; the founding of the university seems to be implied in the commentary, ll. 205–72).

39/28–9 Jadis Cadmus a moult grant paine
       Un grant serpent sus la fontaine
       Dompta . . . (*Chemin*, ll. 1075–7).

Very similarly, *Mutacion*, ll. 3187–91. See also the Prose Ovide: 'Comment Cadmus occyst le serpent a la fontaine ou les gens furent occys' (Royal 17 E. IV, f. 41).

40/1 For 'doute', Laud and Harley have 'dompter'. Scrope's exemplar, however, must have had the variant 'donter' which he read as 'douter'.

40/2–3 Cadmus, qui serpens devint (*Ovide*, iv. 5202). See also the chapter 'Comment Cadmus et sa femme deuindrent serpens' (Royal 17 E. IV, f. 70).

40/5 le bon cheualier doit amer et honnourer les clercs letrez (Harley, f. 109).

40/6–8 Aristotle = *Dicts*, 162/5–6 and 163/4–6.

40/15 wherof he had perfyte victory (Wyer, sig. G3ᵇ); of wyche lyffe he had perfyghte victorye (Bab., p. 52). For Scrope's text, see my note in *Scriptorium*, iii (1949), 124–5.

40/16–17 See Chapter XXIII (Creed VI).

XXIX

40/20 According to Campbell (pp. 129–30), this account comes from the *Hist. anc.*; see also Gordon, p. 151, and Chapter XXX, below.

40/24 Yo as daughter of Ynacus, see *Ovide*, i. 3450–4. According to Add. 19669 (f. 30): 'moult estoit la damoisele bele & saige . . . [and, as for the Egyptians] lor aprist la damoisele letres a lor guise & a lor menniere dont il onques n'auoient en nul usaige.' Similarly the 1509 Orosius (sig. e6) states: 'leur enseigna l'usaige des lettres que iamais n'auoient veu & leur aprint a lire et a escripre en tables.' The *ME De claris mulieribus* (ll. 902–3) has: ' . . . she gaf them a language | And ordeynd lettyrs and wrytyng to that vsage.' *Mutacion* (l. 11920) calls her: 'Yo la bien lettree.'

40/28 a womman] Scrope's source may have lacked 'commune' but it is required by the sense (see l. 14). Laud (f. 48) has 'puis femme commune fu', with which Harley, Pigouchet, and Le Noir agree. Bab. (p. 52) offers '& afterward a comon woman' and Wyer (sig. G4ᵇ) has 'and after was a common woman'. Warner (p. 43) suggests adding: '[this was not so]'. This, however, is not justified by any French text.

40/29 hath hidde = aient mucie (Laud, Harley, Pigouchet); haue cloked (Wyer, sig. G4ᵇ); have schewed (Bab., 52/23).

41/11–14 Hermes = *Dicts*, 18/25–8 and 19/24–7.

41/22 See Chapter XXIII (Creed VII).

XXX

41/24 This account comes from *Ovide*, i. 3408–3796; see also the Prose Ovide (Royal 17 E. IV, ff. 21–3ᵇ).

41/30 in a skye = en vne nue (Laud, Pigouchet); in a clowde (Bab.).

42/20–1 Hermes = *Dicts*, 12/35 and 13/34.

42/22 Bab. (p. 55) much enlarges his 'Moralyte' with material not found in Laud, Harley, or Pigouchet, nor, of course, in Scrope or Wyer.

42/27–8 See Chapter XXIII (Creed VIII).

XXXI

42/30 Pirrus le filz Achilles moult suer et hardi (Add. 9785, f. 176). He avenges his father's death (ff. 179ᵇ–180), slaying Panthasilee

(Egerton, f. 93ᵇ; cf. 1509 Orosius, f. 121). See E. Bagby Atwood, 'The Story of Achilles in the *Seege of Troye*', *Studies in Philology*, xxxix (1942), 489–501, and Rosemond Tuve, 'Spenser and some Pictorial Conventions with Particular Reference to Illuminated Manuscripts', ibid. xxxvii (1940), 149–76, especially pp. 160–1.

43/4–5 et bien ressembla son pere de force et de hardement (Laud, f. 49ᵇ = Harley, f. 110); force and hardines (Wyer); strenghthe & hardines (Bab.).

43/10–12 Not located. Compare *Dicts*, 192/13; possibly a reference to Alexander and Cahus (*Dicts*, pp. 178–9).

43/13 See the very brief Allegorie in Scrope and Harley (f. 110ᵇ) vs. the extended 'Moralyte' in Bab. (p. 56). Laud (f. 49ᵇ) has the same text as Harley, but the incorrect heading 'Prologue a Allegorie' which is *not* found in Scrope.

43/17 See Chapter XXIII (Creed IX). Wyer (sig. G7ᵇ) prints: 'as saith s. the lesse [*sic*].'

XXXII

43/19–22 For Cassandra, see Harley 4431 (f. 325ᵇ) and *The Cyte of Ladyes* (sig. A6). She also appears in *Lavision* (106/26).

43/24–5 Cassandra . . . la quelle estoit moult saige en diuiner les chouse [*sic*] qui auenir estoyent (Add. 9785, f. 19ᵇ). Stowe (f. 71ᵇ) says of Cassandra: 'en clergie fu sages a merueille'; see also f. 48.

44/2–3 Pictagoras = *Dicts*, 50/29 and 51/32. 'It is a ryght honourable and blessed thing to serue God, and sanctify his sainctes' (Baldwin, *STC* 1255, sig. K2). Warner (p. 46, n. 2) calls this 'a wrong translation', but see my note (*Dicts*, p. 334).

44/4 Bab. (p. 57) again enlarges his 'Moralyte' very extensively over Christine's text.

44/9–10 See Chapter XXIII (Creed X).

XXXIII

44/23 Christine could have obtained her knowledge of Neptune from innumerable sources. Neptune is, of course, included in the *Assembly of Gods*.

44/27–9 Dit vng sage: Je ne repute mie Dieu estre bien serui seulement par paroles mais par bonnes oeuures (Laud, f. 50ᵇ; compare L). See also *Dicts*, 52/12–13 and 53/13–15. Telin (f. 115ᵇ) has, also under Pithagoras: 'Le sage ne repute pas Dieu honnore par parolles mais par oeuures.' Baldwin (*STC* 1255, sig. K2) writes: 'The worship of God consisteth not in woordes, but in workes, Pitha.' See also Tilley W 820.

45/7–8 See Chapter XXIII (Creed XI). Assigned by Bab. (p. 58) to 'Sent Thadde thapostle'.

XXXIV

45/10 Atropos appears in Statius, *Thebais*, iii. 68, and (as Autropos) in Lydgate's *Siege of Thebes* (E.E.T.S., E.S. 108, 125, l. 734 and note, ii. 105); also in *The Assembly of Gods*, l. 419 sq. On the personification of Death, see Patch, *Fortuna*, pp. 117–20, and the extensive literature cited there. Christine mentions him in *Mutacion*, ii. 2771–2819 (Solente, i. 161, who calls attention to the comparable description of the 'femmina balba' in Dante, *Purg.* xix).

45/11 Atropos, though one of the Fates, is masculine here (cf. Warner, p. 47, n. 1).

> Ayes a toute heure regart
> Et a Atropos et a son dart. (Laud, f. 50ᵇ)

Scrope, or his exemplar, must have read 'son art'.

45/22–3 Pictagoras = *Dicts*, 52/9–11 and 53/10–12.

45/26 Accropos] one of the many examples of identical spelling at the same place in M and S, strongly suggesting a common prototype.

46/1–2 See Chapter XXIII (Creed XII).

XXXV

46/4 Warner (p. 48, n. 3) remarks on Bellerophon that his 'story is here confused with that of Hippolytus by making Anteia his stepmother'. Christine's source is *Ovide*, iv. 5892–5995; see also Campbell, pp. 113–4.

46/14–15 Quotation not found under Hermes in *Dicts*, but compare 94/10–11 (Socrates) and 163/22–3 (Plato). The Italian *Fiore* (under Tristezza) attributes to Jesus, son of Sirach: 'Meglio è la morte, che la amara vita.' Telin (f. 98ᵇ under Aristote): 'Mourir honnorablement vault mieulx que viure a deshonneur'; similarly, *CdV* under Crainte (M 771, f. 23).

46/16–19 The prologue is omitted by Bab. (p. 60). For Middle English texts on the Ten Commandments, see (for example): J. F. Royster, 'A Middle English Treatise on the Ten Commandments', *Studies in Philology*, vi, viii (1910–11); H. G. Pfander, 'Dives et Pauper', *The Library*, 4th ser. xiv (1933), 299–312, and the editions of 1493, 1496, and 1536 (*STC* 19212–14); *The Floure of the Commaundementes of God* (1510; as translated from the French (1496) edition by A. Chertsey (*STC* 23876)); *The Book of Vices and Virtues* (ed. W. Nelson Francis; E.E.T.S., O.S. 217 (1942), pp. 1 ff, and pp. 317 ff.); *Treatise on the Ten Commandments* (ed. G. C. Heseltine, *Selected Works of Richard Rolle* (London and New York, 1930)), pp. 75–8.

46/25 Augustinus, *De civitate Dei*, vi. Praefatio (Migne, xli. 173). For 'the decre', Bab. (p. 60) has 'þe deuocioun off þe hert' and Wyer has 'latria' (see also *Dives and Pauper*, First Commandment, chap. xi). Campbell (p. 164) remarks: 'Sur les 18 [citations des Pères] que nous n'avons pas pu trouver dans Thomas [Hibernicus], les 11 qui illustrent les Dix Commandements sont probablement tirées de quelque traité sur la Décalogue.' This seems highly probable, but the work has not, unfortunately, been identified.

46/29–30 Matth. iv. 10.

XXXVI

47/2–5   Maimon, ton loyal cousin,
        Qui a ton besoing t'est voisin
        Et tant t'aime, tu dois amer
        Et pour son besoing toy armer. (Laud, f. 51^b)

He is called Menymon by Wyer and Memynon (or Mymenon) by Bab. See Warner's note (p. 49) and Campbell (p. 107). His death is noted by *Ovide*, xii. 4508.

47/7–14 For Memnon helping Hector 'son chier cousin' (Stowe, f. 137^b); see also Add. 9785, f. 101, and *Hist. anc.* (BN fr. 301, ff. 98^b–99), where Hector and Memnon are called 'ses chiers cousins'. *Mutacion* (MCG, f. 126^b) has:

        Maimon, le loyal cousin
        Hector, qui en estoit voisin,
        Quant Achilles lanca ce coup
        Sur lui sault comme enragie loup.

47/11–14 For the battle between Achilles and Memnon, see Lydgate's *Troy Book*, iv. 2897–2968.

47/16–19 See *Dicts*, 163/27–30, on the importance of securing the friendship of relatives.

47/22–3 For the saying, cf. Zabion (*Dicts*, 42/16–17, 43/16–17, and notes). In the Arabic, this philosopher is Zeno of Elea; his *vita* and sayings, in Arabic with German translation, were printed by Franz Rosenthal (*Orientalia*, 1937, pp. 40 ff.).

47/30–48/1 As Warner points out (p. 50, n. 4), this view is expressed in St. Augustine's *Sermo CLXXX* (Migne, xxxviii. 972).

48/3–5 Ex. xx. 7. Laud (f. 52) alone has 'assumpsit'.

XXXVII

48/7–10 Compare *Ovide*, vii. 196–242. For short accounts of the Argonauts, see the Prose Ovide (Royal 17 E. iv, ff. 90 sq.); Add. 9785, ff. 1–9^b (incomplete at beginning); and 1509 Orosius (ff. 100 sq.). See also Chapters LXI and LXVI, and comment at LIV (below).

48/16 Consult the chapter 'De la parole du messaigier' (Stowe, f. 35). For Laomedon's inhospitality, compare *Mutacion* (MCG, f. 109^b).

48/24 Homer = *Dicts*, 36/2 and 37/2–3.

49/2 Bab. (p. 63) does not cite St. Augustine. Christine's source may have been his *Sermo CCLXXX* (*De Dominica*; Migne, xxxix. 2274). Bodley MS. 283 (ff. 5–6) cites: 'Seynt Austin setteth many tokens why þe Sonday sholde be worshiped . . . Whan the holy Sondaye cometh, we sholde haste vs to go to chirche, that is to seye, to praye to God, and leve alle erthely werkys, & doo non othir thynge on this holy Sondaye.'

49/6–7 Is. 1. 16–17. Neither Laud nor Scrope gives a full reference.

XXXVIII

49/9–12 As for the story of Pyramus and Thisbe, Christine says, in her *Cyte of Ladyes* (ii, chap. 56), that 'Ouyde telleth [it] in his booke of Methamorphoseos' (French in Harley 4431, ff. 352^b–353), and she probably obtained the details from *Ovide*, iv. 219–1169. See also Schick, *Lydgate's Temple of Glas*, p. 75; Gower, *Confessio Amantis*, iii, ll. 1331 sq.; and Lydgate, *Reson and Sensuallyte*, ll. 3952–4001.

49/15 Only Scrope sets Pyramus's age as eight, all the others (including Laud) giving it as seven. The age is given as 'sept ans' in the Prose Ovide (Royal 17 E. iv, f. 56, and De Boer, p. 134).

50/5 soubz vng meurier tout blanc (Laud, f. 53); vnder þe wyte walles (Bab., p. 64, who seems to confuse 'la mûre' with 'le mur' as Scrope does later, in 50/22). Wyer (sig. H8^b) has: 'whyte brere bery tre.'

50/22–3 Et dit la fable que pour ycelle [pitie, Harley] deuint lors la meure noire qui estre souloit blance (*sic*; Laud, f. 53^b). And the fable sayth that for this pytuous case þe beryes of the brere tre become blacke whiche ere were whyte (Wyer, sig. I1).

50/25 [il] ne doit donner grant foy (Laud, and all other texts).

50/26–8 This saying is apparently not in the *Dicts* (cf. 83/1 and 120/24). Compare:

> Estre avisié sur les choses doubtables
> Fait prendre soing sur les plus proufitables.
> > (Christine, *Prouverbes mouraulx*, no. 50)

50/33 For the omission of text common to Scrope and Laud, see my article *Fastolf's Manuscripts*, pp. 125–6. After 'mere', Harley 4431 (f. 113) correctly has: 'et pour les biens fais que nous de eulx receuons.' Bab. (p. 65) somewhat extends the text as given by Harley.

51/2–6 Saint Augustin dit que l'on doit honnourer son pere et sa mere en deux manieres, c'est assauoir leur porter honneur et reuerence et leur administrer ce dont ilz ont necessite. Et de cestuy propos dit le saige: Honora patrem, etc. (*CdV*, M 771, f. 10^b and *Boke*, f. 25^b).

51/4–6 Eccli. vii. 29 (both Laud and Scrope omit the name of the book).

XXXIX

51/8–11

Escupalius [*sic*] fu nommez.
Sages fu et de grant clergie:
Cil trouva l'art de sirurgie,
Et tant sot d'art de medecine. (*Ovide*, ii. 2426–9)

See also l. 2993 sq. The story of his saving Rome from the plague is told in xv. 1613–1898. The prose Ovide (f. 32^b) states: 'Esculapius lequel trouva l'art de geomancie et sauoit de medicine tant qu'il faisoit les mors resusciter.' Surely Christine would have used these statements if she had known or employed this text.

51/14 It is uncertain where Christine got the statement that he compiled books, though this may be implied in *Ovide*, ii. 3119–20: 'Mes sa science et sa clergie | Remest et l'art de sirurgie.'

51/22–6 Plato = *Dicts*, pp. 44–6 and 45–7.

51/30–2 For a very dissimilar extract, see *Dives and Pauper* (Westminster: De Worde, 1496 = PML 734), sig. 18^b: 'And yet as saynt Austen sayth . . . he that sleeth his brother with his honde, & he that hateth his brother, & he that bacbyteth his brother, all thre be mansleers.'

52/6–7 Apoc. xiii. 10 (though all texts ascribe this to Luke). Bab. (p. 67) has: 'Qui gladio percutit gladio peribit'; see Gordon's comment (p. 151).

XL

52/12 The story of Achilles and Polyxena is in *Ovide*, xii. 4305–4579. See also Chapter XCIII.

52/20–2

Entrez est ou temple Apolin.
Paris et plusieurs de son lin
Furent ou temple bien garni.
Achilles treuvent desgarni
Devant l'autier agenoullié.
Paris par la plante dou pié
L'ocist d'une fleche en traiant.

(*Ovide*, xii. 4573–9)

According to *Mutacion* (MCG, f. 134), Paris was accompanied by ten 'cheualiers moult bien armez'.

52/24–6 Compare Marcedarge/Magdarge in *Dicts*, 253/12–14: 'In what place soeuer thu be inne, be it in dysportynge or othirwise with thyne enemye, loke thu make euer good wacche'; also 26/30, 29/1, 64/22, 281/20, etc.

52/31 The omission of the negative in S recalls the 'Wicked Bible' (London: Barker and Assigns of Bill, 1631), where the Seventh Commandment (Ex. xx. 14) reads: 'Thou shalt commit adultery'.

53/1 For St. Isidore's views, see his *Sententiarum libri*, II. xxxix (Migne, lxxxiii. 640–3). See also Heseltine, *Richard Rolle*, p. 77.

53/3–4 Lev. xx. 10 (Laud, f. 55, and Scrope have 'moriatur' where Vulgate and all other texts have 'moriantur').

XLI

53/6 For the legend of Busiris, see Campbell (pp. 77–8) and *The Oxford Classical Dictionary* (Oxford, 1949), p. 150. He is also noted by Orosius, *Historiae adversum paganos* (i. 11. § 2—*Corpus scriptorum ecclesiasticorum latinorum*, v (Vienna, 1882)). See also Pauly–Wissowa, iii[1]. 1073–7. A fifteenth-century account is in Raoul Le Fevre, *Le Recueil des hystoires troyennes* (Lyons, 1529), ii. f. 2[b]. Compare the manuscript of this text (Royal 17 E. II; miniature on f. 151), with the chapter: 'Comment Juno enuoya Hercules en Egipte pour estre occis du tyrant Busire, et comment Hercules occist le tirant contre l'esperance de Juno' (f. 151). The first redaction of the *Hist. anc.* has the following comment on Busiris: 'qui estoit moult desloyaulx, car tous les hostes qui a lui venoient pour hebergier, il les faisoit occire si en prenoit le sang et en faisoit a ses dieux sacrifices' (Morgan MSS. M 516, f. 49[b] and M 212, p. 127).

53/17–18 Socrates = *Dicts*, 140/23 and 141/24–5 (under Plato).

53/23–6 This passage is very reminiscent of the discussion on the Seventh Commandment in Royster, pp. 29–30. Not located in the works of St. Augustine.

53/26–7 Eph. iv. 28.

XLII

53/32 Story is from *Ovide*, iv. 3150–3586 and (?) Guillaume de Machaut, *Jugement dou roy de Navarre* (*Œuvres* (Paris, 1908–11), i. 248, ll. 3221 sq.). Cf. Campbell, pp. 115–17. Also Christine's *Cité* (Harley 4431, f. 353—'Hero et Lehander') and the English *Cyte of Ladyes* (ii, chap. 57—'Hero and þe Hander').

54/4–6 For the omission in Laud, see my *Fastolf's Manuscripts*, p. 127.

54/13–14   Qu'entre les flos vit Leandon
       Qui floteloit a abandon. (Machaut, ll. 3289–90).

54/19–21 Compare *Dicts*, 34/15, 80/25, 252/26, and 268/16–22.

54/26 For St. Augustine against 'bacbiteres', see Royster, pp. 26–7.
Bodley MS. 283 (f. 10) cites: 'Seint Austin . . . conseilleth no man to
lye for no thyng, neythir for to save his bodily lif, ne for non othir
thyng.' Cf. Augustinus, *De mendacio* (Migne, xl. 487–548).

54/28–32 The quotation from St. Isidore is cited by Hibernia (Testi-
monium d). It occurs in the *Sententiae* (II. lv. 2—Migne, lxxxiii. 727).

54/32 The Bible quotation (Prov. xix. 5) is omitted in both S and M
and therefore, presumably, by Scrope. It is present in Bab. (p. 70),
Wyer (sig. I7) and Laud (f. 56), who has: 'Et pource dit l'escripture:
Testis falsus non erit impunitus et qui loquitur mendacium non
effugiet. Prouerbiorum xix° capitulo.'

XLIII

55/2–5   Rens Helayne son la demande
         Car en grant meffait gist amende
         Et mieulx vault tost paix consentir
         Que desloyaute ancourir. (Harley, f. 115)

         Yelde agayne Helayne, yf any man demaunde her
         For great offence well maye be reparable
         Better is consent to peace, than to withstande her
         And when the Stede is stolen, to close fast the stable.
                                            (Wyer, sig. I7ᵇ)

A marginal note to the last line of Harley reads 'Que tart venir au
repentir', which becomes line four in Pigouchet and subsequent
editions.

55/10–11 For the Greek ultimatum to Priam, see Add. 19669, ff.
80ᵇ–81, and the 1509 Orosius, sig. 04ᵇ; also Schick's note (p. 76) to
Lydgate's *Temple of Glas*, ll. 92–3.

55/17–19 Plato = *Dicts*, 144/3–6 and 145/4–6.

55/23–4 Since the Biblical extract in *CdV* corresponds to that in
Othéa, Christine may here simply have modified a passage in the *CdV*
(M 771, f. 12ᵇ—Amour de concupiscence): 'Saint Augustin dit que
pechie de fornication est clere perdition et clere dampnation de l'ame,
dont nostre Seigneur dit en l'Euuangile, Qui viderit mulierem [etc].'
See the quotation from St. Augustine in Chaucer's *Parson's Tale*
(l. 844), which, according to Robinson (p. 771), has not been traced.
Royster's text has (p. 33): 'And in þis commandement þe wille of þe
syn is forboden'; and Bodley MS. 283 (f. 10ᵇ): 'In this commande-
ment is forbedyn þe desire or the consentyng to haue flesshely feleship
with any woman oute of mariage.'

55/25 For the Fifth Commandment, read the Sixth, as in all texts
except S and M.

55/26–8 Matth. v. 28.

XLIV

56/2 For the story of Cygnus as here related, see Campbell, p. 104, and Gordon, p. 152. The deaths of both Cygnus and Memnon are recounted in Book xii of *Ovide* and Christine seems to have confused the two stories, thus making Aurora the mother of the former rather than of the latter. In the Prose Ovide (Royal 17 E. iv, f. 205), Cygnus is slain by Achilles and is changed by his father Neptune 'en oysel blanc qui ancoires porte le nom qu'il auoit lors'.

56/8 The weeping Aurora is in *The Assembly of Gods*, l. 255. Bab. (p. 72) expands his Glose with material not in Laud or Harley, nor (of course) in Scrope.

56/11–13 So *CdV* (M 771, f. 14ᵇ), which the *Boke* (f. 34ᵇ) translates thus: 'And Arystotyle saythe (to hys Dyscyple Alexaundre) what Angre, Rancoure, or Malyce soeuer that thou haste in thy hearte, thou ought alwayes to showe mery and Joyefull countenaunce, and there afore all folkes.' Compare *Dicts*, 60/24, and the saying in Chapter VI, above.

56/19–21 Cf. the quotation from St. Augustine in the *ME Treatise on the Ten Commandments* (Royster, pp. 34–5). Bodley MS. 283 (f. 11ᵇ) has: 'This commandement forbedith wylle to haue any other mannys goode wrongefully what-so-euer it be.'

56/21–3 Ps. lxi. 11, though chapter and verse are not cited in the other texts consulted.

XLV

56/25 The source is *Ovide*, viii. 617–986; cf. Campbell, p. 122.

56/30–57/1 Pasiphe . . . ama vng torel qui est a entendre que elle acointa vng homme de ville condicion (Laud, f. 57ᵇ; so Harley, f. 116). Pigouchet (sig. d1) and subsequent editions, as well as Bab. (pp. 73–4) and Wyer (sig. K2ᵇ), expand the text thus: 'thoreau et que mere fut Mynothaurus qui fut moitie homme & moitie thoreau qui est . . .' (Le Noir, sig. d1).

57/9–12 Galen = *Dicts*, 256/16–18 and 257/19–21. Note the name Cleopatrie in Scrope's translation of the *Dits* and Cleupare in the anonymous one. If *Othea* had been later than the *Dicts*, Scrope would probably have a spelling closer to Cleopatra than the Clempare of 57/10.

57/15–22 Quoted by Hibernia (Conversio q) from Gregorius, *Homiliae in Evangelia*, ii. xxxiv (Migne, lxxvi. 1248).

57/23–4 Jer. xxxvi. 3. Note that all texts read Chapter 26, a slip apparently made by Christine. Also all have 'ipsorum' except S and Bab. (p. 74), which read 'eorum' as the Vulgate.

XLVI

57/29 The source for the Story of Thebes was probably *Ovide*, ix. 1437–1838 (cf. Prose Ovide, Royal 17 E. IV, ff. 144^b sq.). The plot is outlined in the *Cyte* (II, xvi; sig. D2^b–D3), in the *Mutacion* (ll. 12421 sq.), and in *Les Enseignemens* (BN fr. 19919, f. 18). See further the account in the *Hist. anc.* (Royal 16, f. 54; Stowe, f. 1; Egerton, f. 64; Add. 19669, f. 62). Compare also the early printed *Roman de Edipus* (repr. Paris, 1858) and the discussion by Léopold Constans, *La Légende d'Œdipe* (Paris, 1881; especially pp. 301–74; for Christine and the *Othéa*, pp. 349–52). Cf. Chapters XXVIII, L, and XCIV, and notes thereto.

58/23–5 For the Expositour of Dremys, Campbell (p. 184) suggests Frere Nicole Saoul de S. Marcel, following an early rubric. For further notes on medieval dream-books, see my 'Two Middle English Texts of the *Somnia Danielis*', *Anglia*, lxxx (1962), 264–73. Hector dismisses Andromache's dream (Add. 19669, f. 83^b) with the remark: 'cele auision n'auoit fors que fantosme' which provides an opinion on dreams by one of Christine's sources. Compare *Dicts*, 48/26–8.

58/29–30 Compare Tilley M 535.

58/31 Probably a reference to Tobias and the Angel in the *Book of Tobit*; see *The Apocrypha of the Old Testament* (London, 1957), pp. 54–64.

58/33–59/2 Cited by Hibernia (Contemplatio b) but wrongly attributed, in the edition of 1483, to an *Epistola ad Paulinum*. Actually in the *Epistola ad Paulinam* (*Epistola CXLVII*; Migne, xxxiii. 597).

59/2–3 Ps. cxviii. 47, though most French texts (and Vulgate) have 'meditabar'.

XLVII

59/5–8   De Cupido, se ieune et cointes,
                          Es me plaist assez que t'acointes.
                          Par mesure, comment qu'il aille,
                          Il plaist bien au dieu de bataille. (Laud, f. 58^b).

59/10–15 Cupido is the God of loue, and forsomoch, as it is not vnsyttyng vnto a yonge knight, to be amorous vpon a Lady that is good, his condycions may therby become better. But bycause Othea knoweth that the hauntynge therof is withdrawynge a man, and a thynge moche anoyenge to Armes, she sayth to the good knyght, that she is well consentyng that he acqueynt him with Cupido (Wyer, sig. K6).

59/15–16 This saying has not been located elsewhere. It is quite possible, of course, that Christine occasionally composed her own 'dits', if no suitable ones were at hand. For contrast, compare *CdV* (M 771, f. 25ᵇ): 'Paour vient de ceur foible.'

59/25–30 The extract from St. Bernard has not been located, though the statement is quite commonplace. Compare, for example, the *Tractatus de charitate* (Migne, clxxxiv. 583–636; especially 616, 623).

59/28–9 Note the omission of 'take my . . . Sone seide' in Bab. (p. 77).

59/31–3 I Petr. i. 18–19.

XLVIII

60/2–5 The source is apparently *Ovide*, ii. 2121–2622; note the wood-cut in Vérard's edition of the French prose adaptation (1 March 1493/4), sig. C1ᵇ.

> N'occis pas Corinis, la belle,
> Pour le raport et la nouuelle
> Du corbel, car se l'occioies,
> Apres tu t'en repentiroies. (Laud, f. 59).

Apparently Scrope read the first word as the imperative of 'noter'.

60/8–15 lequel auoit lors vng blanc oizel nomme corbel . . . et en signe de doleur lui mua ses blancez plumes en noires (Prose Ovide, Royal 17 E. IV, ff. 31–32ᵇ). Compare also Chaucer's *Manciple's Tale* (ed. Robinson, pp. 225–7).

60/20–3 that he . . . be smale] þat he be no berer off no tythynges lest þat he repent hyt (Bab., pp. 78–9). Most French manuscripts have the full text as Scrope: 'le bon cheualier ne se doit auancier de dire a son prince nouuelles qui le meust a yre ne couroux par flaterie contre le bien d'autrui, car en la fin de telz rappors sont communement les guerdons petis' (Laud, f. 59ᵇ).

60/25–8 Hermes = *Dicts*, 20/17–20 and 21/16–18.

60/32 The quotation from St. Augustine has not been traced.

61/14–15 Prov. iv. 23. Laud and Harley have 'Cum', while Pigouchet, Le Noir, Wyer, and Bab. have 'Omni' as Vulgate.

XLIX

61/18 Se le noiel [vault] mieulx que l'escaille (Laud, f. 60). This proverb is not listed by G. L. Apperson, *English Proverbs and Proverbial Phrases* (London, 1929), but compare *ODEP*, p. 466: 'Not worth a nutshell', and Tilley N 360 and N 366.

61/22 De richesce et de seignorie
Est Juno deesse et roïne. (*Ovide*, i. 4110–11).

61/29–32 Hermes = *Dicts*, 14/22–4 and 15/20–2 (and note).

62/4–8 Bernardus Claraevallensis, *De adventu Domini sermo IV* (Migne, clxxxiii. 47).

62/15–17 Matth. xix. 24 (cf. Tilley C 26).

L

62/19 See Warner's note (p. 54, n. 3) on Amphiaraus, which is also the spelling in *Ovide* (e.g. ix. 1622).

62/24 According to Gordon (note under XLVI), only the *Hist. anc.* could have supplied the form Amphoras (thus in Stowe, f. 16ᵇ:, Add. 19669, f. 68; Royal 16, f. 62ᵇ). So also in the *Roman de Edipus* (sig. G2) and in Christine's *Mutacion* (ll. 12875–88). In the 1509 Orosius (sig. 14ᵇ–15), the name is Amphorus. See notes to XLVI for Constans.

63/3–4 This saying is not found in the *Dicts*, though it may simply be a revision of that attributed to Galen (Leber, f. 119): 'science ne peut profiter au fol ne a celuy qui n'en vse.' In Mansion's edition (Bruges, c. 1477, f. num. 94 in BN copy), one finds: 'En oultre dist Seneque, vse du conseil des saiges, affin que tu faces mieulx que tu dois faire.' Also in contrast, see Prov. xii. 15: 'qui autem sapiens est audit consilia.'

63/8–11 Gregorius, *Homiliae in Evangelia*, I. iv (not v as Warner; Migne, lxxvi. 1092).

63/13–14 car quant la parole ouye n'est retenue ou ventre de la memoire (Laud, f. 61; Scrope here either mistranslates or his exemplar omitted the negative).

63/18–19 Matth. iv. 4. Scrope and Laud (f. 61) have 'de omni', while other texts (and Vulgate) have 'in omni'.

LI

63/22–5   Ta langue si soit Saturnine
                Ne soit a nul male voisine.
                Trop parler est laide coustume
                Et qui l'ot folie y presume. (Laud, f. 61ᵇ).

Scrope apparently misunderstood the French phrase 'presumer folie' (points to madness, etc.) in l. 4, though he seems to have got it right in 64/1.

63/27 See VIII, Glose (18/27–8).

64/2–3 Compare Campbell, p. 183, and *Dicts*, 23/21, 36/13, 97/17, etc. Also, in contrast, Baldwin (*STC* 1255, sig. L3): 'A foole is knowen by his speche, and a wyse man by sylence, Pitha.' *CdV* (M 771, f. 44ᵇ) has: 'Et dit que la langue d'un homme monstre son sens ou sa foulie.' Similarly, the *Motz dorees* (sig. GG4ᵇ): 'Si un homme parle, on congnoist a sa parole s'il est sage ou non; et se il se taist, on doubte qu'il le soit.'

64/5 The long first sentence of the 'Moralyte' appears to be peculiar to Bab. (p. 83).

64/6–10 This quotation, also attributed to Hugo de S. Victore, will be found in Christine's *Livre de Prudence* (BR 11072, f. 237ᵇ; BN fr. 605, f. 6 and fr. 2240, f. 2).

64/10–13 Attributed by Hibernia (Liberalitas u; 1483, sig. m4) to Liber II (for III) of Hugo's *De anima* (printed as Bernardus, *Tractatus de interiori domo*; see Migne, clxxxiv. 537).

64/15–17 Ps. xxxiii. 13–14. Laud (f. 61ᵇ; so Pigouchet, Bab., etc.) has 'qui vult', as Vulgate.

LII

64/19–22 See Chapter XLVIII (*Ovide*, ii. 2160 sq.; see cut in Vérard's *Ovide*, sig. c1). Warner (p. 56, n. 5) quotes the 'texte' from Harley, which corresponds to that in Laud.

64/24–7 La corneille, ce dit la fable, encontra le corbel quant il portoit la nouuelle a Phebus de s'amie Corinis, qui se estoit meffaitte, et tant lui enquist que il lui dist la choison de son erre (Laud, f. 62).

64/27 iournay] Scrope confuses 'erre' (voyage) with 'erré' (error). Wyer (sig. L5ᵇ) has: 'of his erroure'. Scrope has also (and understandably) misunderstood the French and here should have 'she required' and 'told her'.

64/27–30 Warner (p. 56, n. 8) provides the necessary explanation: 'Literally translated, this sentence should read: "But she (the crow) dissuaded him from going by giving him an example of herself, who for a like case had been driven from the house of Pallas", etc.' See Ovid, ii. 542.

64/30–1   Je fui jadis dame et mestresse
               De l'ostel Pallas la deesse. (*Ovide*, ii. 2203–4).

65/3–4 Plato = *Dicts*, 132/24–6 and 133/23–5.

65/7–11 Compare Hibernia under Consilium (f) = Fortitudo (l). Laud and Scrope attribute the quotation to St. Gregory's *Homilies* (cf. Migne, lxxvi. 1017), while Pigouchet (so Wyer and Bab.) assigns it to the *Morals*, as does Hibernia (to Liber V).

65/12–14 Prov. ii. 10–11. Note that S and Wyer omit citing location. See Bible quotation in Chapter I.

LIII

65/19 For the narrative, see Warner (p. 57, n. 4), Campbell (p. 126) and Gordon (p. 153). That the story of Hyacinthus is here given to Ganymedes is no doubt due, as Campbell suggested, to the fact that one story follows the other in *Ovide*. There the account of Jacintus (x. 753–882 and 3425–3519) follows that of Ganimeden (x. 724–52 and 3362–3424).

65/23–6 The story of 'le palet' is told in *Ovide*, x. 787–817.

65/26–8 *CdV* (M 771, f. 16b) under Paix: 'Contendre contre plus grant que toy est forsennerie.' Cf. note to 75/1.

65/28–30 A wise man = *Dicts*, 285/8–9.

66/5–8 quia nimirum virtus abstinentiae aut omnino nulla est, si tantum quisque corpus non edomat quantum valet; aut valde inordinata est, si corpus atterit plus quam valet (Gregorius, *Moralia*, xx, xli; Migne, lxxvi. 185; Hibernia, Abstinentia m). For penance to be practised with restraint, cf. *Cloud of Unknowing*, ed. P. Hodgson (E.E.T.S., o.s. 218 (1943), notes to 38/16) and *Speculum sacerdotale* (E.E.T.S., o.s. 200 (1936), 75/23 and 87/11).

66/10–11 See my comment in *Fastolf's Manuscripts* (p. 125) and especially my 'Wirk alle thyng by conseil', *Speculum*, xxiv (1949), 410–12. Compare also Charity C. Willard, The *'Livre de la paix'* of *Christine de Pisan* (The Hague, 1958), p. 73 and notes (p. 189), as well as her comment on p. 45. Cf. Prov. xxiv. 6.

LIV

66/13–16 For the story of the Argonauts, see *Ovide*, vii. 8–646 and *Hist. anc.* (Stowe, ff. 33 sq. and short account in Royal 16, f. 70); also Griffin-Columnis (pp. 6 sq.); Gower, *Confessio Amantis* (v. 3247 sq.); and Schick's note (p. 74) to Lydgate's *Temple of Glas*, l. 62. Christine also tells the story in the *Cité* (Harley 4431, f. 352; English *Cyte*, Bk. ii, chap. 55) and in the *Mutacion* (MCG, ff. 109 sq.). See also *Les enseignemens* (BN fr. 19919, f. 17; Solente, p. 37) and Chapters XXXVII, LVIII, LXI, and LXVI of the present work.

66/20 [Son oncle] continuelment pensoit en quel maniere il le pourroit faire morir (Stowe, f. 33). In the *Mutacion* one reads:

> Et, com Peleus eust enuie
> Sus son nepueu, voulsist sa vie
> Apeticier, se il peust. (MCG, f. 109)

66/25–6 et moult est sages en l'art de nigromence (Stowe).

66/30 & loued anothir] see notes to LVIII.

67/8–10 Compare Baldwin (*STC* 1255, sig. M1b): 'Yf thou entende to doe any good, tary not tyll to morow, for þou knowest not what maye chaunce thee this nyght.' A number of similar sayings in the *Dicts*, none being identical with that in *Othea* (e.g. 142/33). The *Dits moraulx* (Leber, f. 13) has: 'et ne fais pas longe demeure en l'execution de ce qu'il te conuiendra faire; et soyez debonnaire pardonneur.' Compare Tilley T 95.

67/14–18 Sainte Bernarde saythe in his Cantikes, that ingratitude is enemye of the soule, and dyminysheth the vertues, and is perdycyon of merytes and benefytes; the sinne of ingratitude is lyke the wynde, whyche dryeth vp the water of the fountaines of pytie, the dewe and water of grace, and goodnesse of mercye, as the wyse manne saythe: Ingrati enim spes [etc.]. (*Boke*, f. 26; comparable French text in *CdV* M 771, f. 10ᵇ; Latin text in Hibernia (b) under Ingratitudo).

67/17 nought] comme vn vent sec (Harley, f. 120; so Pigouchet and Le Noir); as a drye wynde (Wyer, sig. M1ᵇ and Bab., p. 87). Laud (f. 63ᵇ) has 'comme ment sec', and this—or perhaps some variant derived from this—must account for the reading in Scrope.

67/19–21 Sap. xvi. 29. Note that this quotation also accompanies the extract from St. Bernard in *CdV*.

LV

67/23–6 Story from *Ovide*, iv. 5637–5713 (with Allégories, 5714–5891). See also Campbell, pp. 125–6, and Gordon, p. 153. The change from Perseus to Perceval seems to be Scrope's, unless it be due to his exemplar (see Chapter V). According to *Ovide* (iv, 5664) she 'ot non Gorgon ou Medusa', while the Prose Ovide (Vérard, sig. f7ᵇ; so Royal 17 E. IV, f. 71ᵇ) states that she 'auoit nom de Mogorgon ou Meduse'. See Gower, *Confessio Amantis*, i. 391 sq.

67/29–30   Pour ce qu'au temple la deesse [Pallas]
              L'ot desfloree Neptunus. (*Ovide*, iv. 5671–2)

So the Prose Ovide, and see Warner's note (p. 60, n. 1).

68/3–4 Perseus, le vaillant cheualier, ala pour combatre a la fiere beste (Harley, f. 120ᵇ). Laud (f. 63ᵇ) omits 'le vaillant cheualier' though the phrase is in Scrope. This again suggests that Scrope did not make his translation from Laud.

68/7 his hede] M appears to correct a slip by Scrope, as L and S agree in this reading.

68/23–5 Aristotle = compare *Dicts*, 156/29 sq.

69/1–7 Dist Crisostome que comme c'est impossible que le feu arde en l'eaue, aussi est ce impossible que compunction de cuer soit entre les delices du monde [etc.] (Laud, f. 64). See Warner's notes (p. 61, n. 3 and n. 4). From the variants it seems reasonable to conclude that

Scrope's original text had Aristotle and the omission, and that, there-
fore, the reading in M represents Scrope's final corrections. The Latin
text is cited by Hibernia (Delitie f) which is a translation of Chryso-
stomus, *De compunctione*, i. 7 (Migne, *Gr.* xlvii. 404): Ὥσπερ γὰρ
χαλεπὸν, μᾶλλον δὲ καὶ ἀδύνατον, ἀναμίξαι ὕδατι πῦρ, οὕτω, οἶμαι,
τρυφὴν καὶ κατάνυξιν εἰς ταυτὸ συναγαγεῖν· ἐναντία γὰρ ταῦτα, καὶ
ἀλλήλων εἰσὶν ἀναιρετικά· Ἡ μὲν γὰρ δακρύων ἐστὶ μήτηρ καὶ νήψεως,
ἡ δὲ γέλωτος καὶ παραφορᾶς· καὶ ἡ μὲν κούφην καὶ ὑπόπτερον ἐργά-
ζεται τὴν ψυχήν, ἡ δὲ αὐτὴν μολίβδου παντὸς βαρυτέραν καθίστησι.

69/7–8 Ps. cxxv. 5. As Warner remarks (p. 61, n. 5), this is the only
instance in L where the Biblical quotation has been supplied, and it is
noteworthy that the scribe has written the English text. Cf. Tilley
S 209.

LVI

69/10–13 The source is probably *Ovide* (iv. 1268–1371), though Phebus
is not mentioned there. See also Schick's note (pp. 79–80) to the
Temple of Glas, ll. 126–8. Phebus is described as the one responsible
for discovering the adultery in *Reson and Sensuallyte* (ll. 3766–7).

69/13 lyemes] this seems to be the most likely reading in all three
manuscripts, though both 'lyeines' and 'lyenies' are possible. Scrope
apparently misunderstood the French 'liens'.

69/19 Bab.'s Glose (p. 90) differs considerably from Scrope's. For
example, after 'braas' he here adds: 'as he wyche was chyeff ferrour
off goddes & goddesseȝ, by whom were forged in þe skye all thondreȝ
& lyghtenynges'.

69/22 ijᵒ] Scrope, or perhaps the scribe of his archetype, misread
'dieux' as 'deux'. The mocking by the 'goddys celestial' is mentioned
in Lydgate's *Reson and Sensuallyte*, ll. 3768–72.

69/26 Mars] a misreading for 'mais'.

70/1–2 Compare *Dicts*, 108/8–10 and Campbell's note, pp. 181–2.
See Luc. viii. 17 and Tilley N 330.

70/6–15 From Hibernia (Tentatio ak); see Leo Magnus, *Sermo XXVII*
(Migne, liv. 218).

70/12–15 Scrope, or his French manuscript, must have read: 'il
examine de toutes les coustumes, discute des cuers, coniecture les
affections et la quiert il cause de [iniure] ou il treuue la creature plus
encline et legiere et occupe' (Laud, ff. 64ᵇ–65, but with 'nuire' as other
French texts). Le Noir (sig. d6ᵇ; thus Wyer, sig. M4) has: '. . . et la
quiert il cause de nuyer ou il trouue la creature plus diligemment
enclinee & occupee.'

70/16–18 I Petr. v. 8. All texts assign this to the Second Epistle.

LVII

70/20 The probable source was *Hist. anc.* (Add. 19669, f. 125; Stowe, f. 260; etc.). Christine seems to have been very fond of this story; it appears in the *Mutacion* (ll. 9535–9802; esp. ll. 9772–93) and in the *Cité* (Harley 4431, f. 303ᵇ; English version, I. xvii). Compare also *Les Enseignemens* (BN fr. 19919, f. 7ᵇ), the 1509 Orosius (sig. x8), the ME *De claris mulieribus* (ll. 1529 sq.), the *Speculum humanae salvationis* (Lutz & Perdrizet, cap. xxx. 85–94 and comments, i. 223) and Warner (p. 63, n. 1).

71/7 et sa gent toute morte & prise (Laud, f. 65 and so other texts; omitted only by L).

71/18–19 Compare *Dicts*, 120/4–5 and 257/1–2. Laud (f. 65ᵇ) has: 'A ce propos dit Platon: ne desprises nul pour sa petite faculte [omission by Scrope or his source] car ses vertus peuent estre grandes.' This, in turn, was perhaps based on *CdV* (M 771, f. 40ᵇ, under Humilite): 'Cathon dit: donne lieu a plus grant de toy et ne mesprise nul pour petit qu'il soit; car ia soit ce que l'omme soit pouure, ses vertus peuent estre grandes.' However, the *Fiore* (under Humiltà; Venice, 1566, sig. C4) has only: 'Cato dice: da loco al tuo maggiore.'

71/24 Cassianus, *De coenobiorum institutis*, XII. xxxi (Migne, xlix. 472).

71/29–30 Eccli. iii. 20. Note that the same quotation from the Bible is also found in the chapter on Humility in *CdV*.

LVIII

72/7 See notes to LIV and the description of Medea in the *Cyte* (I. xxxii). Also Campbell (pp. 105–6, with wrong reference to the '67ᵉ *Histoire*') and Gordon (p. 153).

72/12 Medea giving Jason 'goodes' is also suggested in *Mutacion* (MCG, f. 113): 'Tout le tresor du roy emporte / Medee. . . .' For Medea, compare MCG, ff. 110–13: 'Le vj chapitre, de l'amour que Medee ot a Jason.'

72/13   [Jason] hathe for-sake ful vnkyndely
          þis Medea, in payne, sorwe, and wo.
                    (Lydgate, *Troy Book*, i. 3694–5)

          ȝytt afterworde Jason hir forsoke
          And oon Cerusa to his wife toke.
                    (*ME De claris mulieribus*, ll. 1357–8)

See Hoccleve, *Letter of Cupid* (E.E.T.S., E.S. 61 (1892)), 304 and *Ovide* (vii. 1365 sq.).

72/16–17 Plato = *Dicts*, 122/10–11; cf. Warner's note (p. 64, n. 5).

72/21–8 As Campbell points out (p. 165), this passage was probably taken by Christine from Hibernia (Voluntas x). The first part comes from Bernardus Claraevallensis, *Sermo in tempore resurrectionis*, iii (Migne, clxxxiii. 290); Bab. (p. 93) assigns the latter portion to the Bible ('as seyth Scripture'), but it has not been found there.

72/28–30 Prov. xxix. 15 (Warner remarking 'somewhat corrupted' in Harley 4431). Laud appears to have 'diunctum' as M, while H reads 'dimitum'.

LIX

73/4–5 See Warner (p. 65, n. 3) and *Ovide*, xiii. 3689 sq. (esp. 4092–4147).

73/8 Compare Warner, p. xl and p. 65, n. 4. Laud (f. 66^b) has 'qui Acys estoit nommez', which Scrope (or his French exemplar) misread as 'qui occis estoit'.

73/11–13 Scrope obviously misunderstood the French (Laud, f. 66^b): 'adonc [Polyphemus] fu surprins de soudaine rage et tellement escrolla la roche que tout en fu Acys acrauentez' (cf. Tobler–Lommatzsch, *acraventer*).

73/15–16 d'estre surpris de tel qui ait puissance et pouer & volente de lui greuer (Laud, f. 66^b; most French texts, as Scrope, omit 'et pouer').

73/22 St. Jerome's *Commentaria in Jeremiam Prophetam* is printed in Migne, xxiv. 679–900. However, if this passage is based on Hibernia (Gloria eterna z: 'Nullus labor durus, nullum tempus longum videri debet, quo gloria eternitatis acquiritur'), then it is there attributed to one of his epistles. Cf. 88/8.

73/25–6 Sap. v. 9. Laud, as S and M, has 'nam', where the other texts have 'omnia' as Vulgate.

LX

73/28–31 For source, see Campbell (pp. 97 sq.) and notes to Chapter LXXIII, below. Probably taken from *Ovide*, xi. 1242 sq. (esp. 1242–1315 and 1467–1842; see also Prose Ovide, Royal 17 E. IV, f. 177^b). Christine also recounts the events of the wedding in her *Chemin*, ll. 6149 sq., and the story further appears in Machaut's *La Fonteinne amoureuse*, ll. 1633 sq. See also the account in Caxton's *Book called Cathon* (*STC* 4853, sig. d3), giving a reference to St. Augustine's *City of God*. If based on the *De civitate Dei* (XVIII. x; Migne, xli. 567), this is a much-expanded version of that brief outline. Another English version is in Lydgate's *Reson and Sensuallyte* (E.E.T.S.) ll. 1847–2070; compare Caxton's *Ovyde*, pp. 36–47.

74/16 For Hecuba's dream, compare *Hist. anc.* (Stowe, f. 46).

74/19–20 Machaut (*Font. amour.*, ll. 1908–10) has Mercury tell Paris of his origin:

> Fils yes au Roy Priant de Troie,
> Et Ecuba, la noble dame,
> Est ta mere. . . . (*Œuvres*, iii. 211)

74/26–7 Pithagoras = *Dicts*, 56/24. Compare *CdV* (M 771, f. 16ᵇ), as below.

75/1–5 Et dit: fuy les lieux ou tu penses qu'il y aura riot et discencion, car de contendre contre ton pareil ⟨Scrope or his source read 'paix'⟩ est folie, contendre contre maindre de toy est vergogne, contendre contre plus grant que toy est forsennerie. Saint Paul [*as below*] (*CdV* under Paix; cf. 65/26 note). This is cited by Hibernia (Discordia q), as: 'Sumopere iurgia fuge; nam contra parem contendere anceps est, cum superiore furiosum, cum inferiore sordidum [etc.].' Although taken directly from Seneca (*De ira*, ii. 34, 1; *Opera*, I (Leipzig, 1905), 103), it is here attributed to the *Commentary* on the Psalter by Cassiodorus. See Chaucer's *Tale of Melibee* (Robinson's 2nd edn. (1957), p. 180, 1486), where the saying is assigned to Seneca; it is attributed to Sidrac by the *Boke* (f. 40ᵇ).

75/4 Rom. xiii. 13 (*CdV* also having this extract under Paix).

LXI

75/12 For Laomedon's refusal to welcome the Argonauts, compare *Ovide*, vii. 196–249. See also *Hist. anc.* (e.g. Stowe, ff. 31 sq.) and notes to XXXVII and LXVI.

75/13 After 'Grece', Bab. (p. 96) expands his Glose with material not found in the usual French texts.

75/20–1 Hermes = *Dicts*, 26/27–8 and 27/33–4.

75/27–76/2 Hibernia (Iudex t) attributes the following to Gregory's Homily 32: 'Presentis temporis ita agenda est letitia, ut numquam amaritudo sequentis iudicij recedat a memoria.' Not traced.

76/3–4 Joel. ii. 13. Scrope follows Laud (f. 68) in omitting 'Convertimini' and in ascribing the extract to the third chapter of Joel. Cf. my note in *Fastolf's Manuscripts*, p. 126, n. 24. Bab. (p. 97) here supplies a portion of Joel. iii. 4.

LXII

76/10 For Semele, see *Ovide*, iii. 701–810 (from Ovid, iii. 253–315) and Warner's note (p. 69, n. 2).

76/13–25 [Juno] auoit prins la forme de Berre, la vielle nourrisse de Semelle (Prose Ovide, Royal 17 E. IV, f. 44). She then suggested to

Semele that: 'requiers lui qu'il t'embrasse ainsy comme il fait Juno sa femme, quant elle se deduist' (f. 44ᵇ).

76/19 loue of hir loue] de l'amour de son amy (Laud, Pigouchet, etc.). Cf. Warner's note 3, with the text of Harley.

76/23 Juno halsed his wijf] for this curious passage, see my explanation in *Fastolf's Manuscripts*, p. 128. Wyer (sig. N6) has: 'that he wold accoll and embrace her in such maner as he dyd his wyfe Juno . . . she myght apperceyue the loue of her paramour' (similarly Bab., pp. 97–8).

77/2–4 This exposition is wanting in Bab. (p. 98; see Gordon, p. xxxix).

77/9–10 Hermes = *Dicts*, 28/9–10 and 29/8–11 (cf. Campbell, p. 180).

77/15–20. Augustinus, *Sermo XLVII—De ovibus*, *Ez. xxxiv. 17–31* (Migne, xxxviii. 303). Bab. (p. 98) merely cites Seynt Austeyn.

77/20 to oure stedfast breþir] a noz freres enfermes (Fr, except Le Noir, who omits 'enfermes', sig. e1ᵇ; cf. Warner, p. 70, n. 2). Wyer (sig. N7) has: 'against our brethren, or euyn Christen'.

77/21 Tit. ii. 7.

LXIII

77/25 For Diana, see Chapter LXIX, below.

78/1–2 *CdV* (M 771, f. 15ᵇ), under Melencolie: 'Aristote dit: Oysiuete fait et amaine moult d'inconueniens.' For this, the English translation (*Boke*, f. 37ᵇ and *Boke²*, sig. E2ᵇ) has: 'Arystotyle saythe, that slepe bringeth much inconuenyence.' This is not found in the Italian *Fiore*.

78/6–8 Hieronymus, *Epistola CXXV ad Rusticum* (Migne, xxii. 1078): 'Facito aliquid operis, ut te semper diabolus inveniat occupatum.' Thus, in the *Pilgrimage of Perfection* of 1526 (*STC* 3277, sig. AA4, with a marginal note citing this letter), we read: 'Therfore in your solytarinesse be euer wele occupyed that, as Saynt Jerome sayth, the enemye fynde you nat ydell but outher doing some good or thynking on some good.' A similar ascription is in Bartolommeo da San Concordio, *Ammaestramenti* (Florence, 1840), pp. 488–9, no. 4. The saying is given to St. Jerome in the *Speculum Christiani* (E.E.T.S., 65/14 and 107/14), in Caxton's *Golden Legend* (*STC* 24873, prologue, f. 2), in the *Book of Vices and Virtues* (E.E.T.S., 228/24), in the *Ayenbite of Inwyt* (E.E.T.S., p. 206), in the *Chastising of God's Children* (*STC* 5065, sig. F4ᵇ), etc. On the other hand, the *Treatise of Love* (*STC* 24234, sig. F5ᵇ) simply assigns it to 'an holy fader'.

Chaucer uses this saying ('seith Seint Jerome'; it is anonymous in

Sec N Prol. 6–7, Robinson, p. 207) in his *Tale of Melibee* (Robinson, p. 182, 1595, and note on p. 744: 'The reference . . . has not been traced'). It was included in his French source but not in the Latin original (see J. Burke Severs, 'The Source of Chaucer's Melibeus', *PMLA* l (1935), 94, no. 5). According to the *Sources and Analogues* (p. 602), it was attributed to St. Innocent in one manuscript and to St. 'Jerosme' in some others. The Morgan MS. (M 39, f. 18ᵇ) ascribes it to St. Gerosme; on this manuscript, see my article, 'The Morgan Manuscript (M 39) of "Le livre de Melibee et de Prudence" ', *Studies in Language and Literature in Honour of Margaret Schlauch* (Warsaw, 1966), pp. 49–54.

The saying is, perhaps, here attributed to Gregory through confusion with some such saying as: 'And þer-fore seiþ Seynt Gregorie, "No mane", he seyþ, "shuld be ydell in þis liffe, þat he lese not is stede of reste in þe liffe þat euermore shall laste in þe blisse of heven" ' (*M.E. Sermons*, E.E.T.S., o.s. 209 (1938), p. 75 and note, p. 349). Compare also Isaac Watts, *Divine Songs* (London, 1728), p. 29, Song XX: 'For Satan finds some Mischief still | For idle Hands to do.' Cf. Tilley, I 13.

78/8–10 Prov. xxxi. 27 (though Laud, f. 69, has 'occiosa' as Vulgate's 'otiosa').

LXIV

78/12–15 Source is *Ovide*, vi. 1–318. See the account in the *Cyte* (i. xxxix); also Campbell (p. 111) and Warner (p. 71, n. 3); and the miniature in MS. Royal 17 E. iv, f. 87ᵇ.

78/13 A yraignes (Laud, f. 69). Scrope's French text may have read (or appeared to read): 'L yraignes.'

78/22–5 For the lacuna in Laud (f. 69ᵇ), see my *Fastolf's Manuscripts*, p. 127.

78/25–7 By þis fable mey be vnderstand euery woman [Fr. = aucune] þat auanteth her-selfe ageyn her bettre, wherthoro sche hathe harme þerby (Bab., p. 100). Wyer (sig. N8ᵇ) confusedly has: 'So maye it be that some Handemanne auaunted hym-selfe agaynst her maystres, wherby euyll vnto her came by some maner.'

79/1–3 Plato = *Dicts*, 132/27–30 and 133/27–31. For this quotation and the following Allegorie, compare *CdV* (M 771, f. 42ᵇ under Orgueil): 'Senecques dit que quant tu feras vne chose mieulx que vng autre ne t'en vante pas car, se tu le fais, Platon [*Boke* = Cato] dit que tu en seras mesprise. Saint Augustin dit, ou liure de la Cite de Dieu, que vantance est vice paruers de l'ame, et celluy qui ame loange humaine mesprise le vray tesmoingnaige de sa propre conscience. Et pource dit Salomon: Quid profuit [etc.].' See *Boke*, f. 97.

79/6–10 Augustinus, *De civitate Dei*, XII. viii (Migne, xli. 356; cited by Hibernia, Iactantia b).

79/8–9 mais est vice de l'ame peruerse (Laud and Harley); mais est vice de l'ame parfaite (Pigouchet and Le Noir); but it is a perfyte vyce of the soule (Wyer, sig. O1).

79/11–12 Sap. v. 8. Both M and S (consequently Scrope) have 'vobis' where all other texts have 'nobis' as Vulgate. Here again, Othea and *CdV* have the same philosopher's maxim, theological quotation, and Biblical extract in similar chapters.

LXV

79/16–17 Compare *Ovide*, x. 1960–2093 (Venus and Adonis) and 2438–93 (death of Adonis). M and S certainly read 'Dadomus' and so may L, though Warner preferred the reading 'Dadonius'. French manuscripts vary; Le Noir and Wyer have 'Adonius'.

79/27–9 Sedechias = *Dicts*, 4/17–22 and 5/16–21. Bab. (p. 101) has 'Sedechre þe prophete'.

80/5–8 II Petr. ii. 19.

80/9–10 Apoc. xiii. 7.

LXVI

80/15 For the story of the Argonauts, see notes to XXXVII, LIV, LVIII, and LXI, and the accounts in *Hist. anc.* (Stowe, ff. 33–44) and in the 1509 Orosius (sig. n6–7).

80/19 According to Stowe (f. 41), Laomedon gathered together 'tant de gens comme il ot et yssirent dehors la ville'. *Mutacion* (MCG, f. 113^b) states:

> En la cite ne remaint homme,
> Si en yssi si tresgrant somme
> De gent que merueilles estoit.

80/22 Stowe (f. 217^b) has the similar form 'Thalamon aiax'.

80/22 Most 'authorities' credit Hercules with the plan and Ajax with the execution of the ambush; thus *Hist. anc.* (Royal 20, f. 35, with illustrations), Lydgate (*Troy Book*, i. 4020 sq.), Columnis (*Historia Troiana*, Strassburg, 1486, sig. b4^b and Griffin, p. 36), *Ystoire de Troye* (Add. 9785, f. 5^b), etc. See also *Mutacion* (MCG, f. 114) and:

> Vne part de l'ost est alee
> S'embuschier es courtilz d'entour
> Troie, pour jouer d'un faulx tour. (MCG, f. 113^b).

80/23 Rex Thelamon in vrbem ipsam primus victor intrarat (Columnis, sig. b6^b; similarly *Hist. anc.* (Royal 16, f. 70^b and Add, f. 77^b) and

Ystoire de Troye (f. 8ᵇ)). For this deed, Hercules gave him Esiona (thus in *Mutacion*); note also Caxton's *Ovyde*, p. 34, and Chapter LXXX, below.

80/26–7 This dictum is not found under Hermes in the *Dicts*. Compare *CdV* (M 771, f. 26): 'Salomon dit que l'on doit doubter son ennemy pour sa mauuaise subtilite et pour son engin.' See also the quotation in XL. For the misreading of 'l'agait' as 'la gent' by Scrope (or his French original), see Warner (p. xl and p. 73, n. 3).

81/1–6 *CdV* (M 771, f. 26ᵇ under 'L'ennemy d'enfer'; also *Boke*, f. 62ᵇ) has: 'Saint Augustin dit que, ainsy comme en la guerre les gens ne se despoullent point des armes de iour ne de nuit, especialement quant ilz ont leurs ennemis pres, ainsi durant le temps de ceste presente vie ne nous deuons point despoullier des vertus, et comme celluy qui son aduersaire trouue desarme, dont l'Euuangile fait mencion disant: Fortis armatus [etc.].'

81/6–7 Luc. xi. 21. M and S follow Laud (f. 70ᵇ) in having 'custodiet'.

LXVII

81/9–12 The source here is almost certainly *Ovide*, x. 708–17 and xi. 1–10; see also Chapter LXX.

> Trop ne t'assotes de la lire
> Orpheus, se tu veulx eslire
> Armes pour principal mestier;
> D'instrumens suiure n'as mestier. (Laud, f. 70ᵇ).

81/24–5 Compare Bab., p. 104; 'For as Scripture seyth: þe sounde of þe instrument is þe meyte of þe deuel.' Is this identification based on Jer. xlvi. 22: 'Vox ejus quasi aeris sonabit'? The Hebrew has 'of the serpent', but Christine could hardly have known this, though Laud (f. 71; so other French texts) has: 'A ce propos dit vne auctorite. Le son de l'instrument est le las du serpent.'

81/25–7 Quotation not under Plato in *Dicts*; but see under Tholomee: *Dicts*, 226/27–9 and 227/29–31.

82/1–5 Augustinus, *De singularitate clericorum* (Migne, iv. 838; in the *Opuscula supposita* of Cyprianus: 'Minus voluptatibus stimulatur, qui non est ubi frequentia est voluptatum. Et minus avaritiae molestias patitur, qui divitias non videt'). See Warner, p. 75. n. 1.

82/5–6 Bible reference [Ps. ci. 8] omitted in all texts.

LXVIII

82/11 For the 'ravysshement of Dame Helayne by Parys', with an account of the Trojan war, see Book XII of *Ovide* and Caxton's *Ovyde*.

82/13 For Paris dreaming of his adventure, see Gordon (p. 154). According to Columnis (Strassburg, 1486, sig. c6ᵇ; Griffin, p. 61), Paris dreamed that Venus had promised him a beautiful lady.

82/18-19 Compare Warner (p. 75, notes 3 and 4) for the Greek settlements in Italy. An account of Greece, Sicily, Calabria, Apulia, etc. will be found in the *Hist. anc.* (Stowe, f. 32ᵇ, in the story of the Argonauts). Here is provided the interesting note, apparently from personal experience: 'encores parle on en ce pais [Sicily] en pluseurs lieux Gregois' (Stowe, f. 32ᵇ). See also Christine's *Faits d'armes* (cf. Paulin Paris, *Les Manuscrits françois de la Bibliothèque du Roi* (Paris, 1836–48), v. 135, MS. 7087 [now fr. 603]). This passage is omitted by Bab. (p. 105). St. Jerome correctly calls the district 'Magna Graecia' (Migne, xxii. 540).

82/26-7 Plato = *Dicts*, 138/13-14 and 139/14-15.

83/1 Laud (f. 71ᵇ) has: 'Et dit Saint Gregoire es Omelies', where all the other texts, French and English, have 'es Morales'. If Scrope had been translating from Laud, one would expect to find Homilies as the reference. The first 'spice' (espece) reads in Laud: 'La premiere que [quant, Pigouchet] le bien que ilz ont, ilz reputent que ilz l'ont d'eulx meismes.' Compare Telin (ff. 117ᵇ–118) and below. From Gregorius, *Moralia*, xxiii. vi (Migne, lxxvi. 258).

83/1-8 *CdV* (M 771, ff. 42ᵇ–43, under Orgueil): 'Saint Gregoire, parlant d'arrogance, dit ou Liure des Moralitez que quatre manieres sont esquelles toutes les manieres et enfleures des arrogans sont demonstrees. La premiere est quant le bien qui est sien cuide et repute l'auoir de soy mesmes. La seconde si est s'ilz croyent auoir de Dieu le bien qu'ilz ont toutesfois cuident que ce soit par leurs merites et qu'envers Dieu l'ayent bien desserui. La tierce est quant ilz s'en vantent du bien et ilz n'en ont point. La quarte est quant en eulx mesmes ilz mesprisent autruy et desirent que les gens saichent le bien qui est en eulx. De cest vice parle le saige en ses Prouerbes disant: Arroganciam [etc.].'

83/9-10 Prov. viii. 13, as in *CdV*.

LXIX

83/12-15 The source for the story of Actaeon is *Ovide*, iii. 337–570 (cf. Ovid, iii. 131–252). See also Campbell (p. 123), Gordon (p. 154), and Warner (p. 76, n. 3). Antheon appears briefly in *Mutacion* (ll. 4847–54). The story is also told by Gower (*Confessio Amantis*, i. 333 sq.).

84/7 et tantost fu acueilli de ses propres chiens (Laud, f. 72). Scrope, apparently, misunderstood the meaning of 'acueillir' here (Godefroy, i. 91 = 'assaillir'; so Wyer).

84/11–12 And the harte rothyth, cryeth & wepyth whan he is take (Bartholomaeus Anglicus, *De proprietatibus rerum* [English]; *STC* 1536, sig. cc2). The Latin text reads: 'quando autem capitur, mugit & lacrimatur' [Cologne, 1472, XVIII. xxx]. Compare *Hamlet* (III. ii. 259) and *As you like it* (II. i. 41). This belief does not appear to be listed by Hanns Bächtold-Stäubli, *Handwörterbuch des deutschen Aberglaubens* (Berlin and Leipzig, 1927–41) and has not been traced through Stith Thompson, *Motif-Index of Folk-Literature* (Copenhagen, 1955–8), Bab. (p. 106) has: '& so þer began fyrst wepyng at deth, as þe fable seyth.'

84/12–14 La fu Antheon occiz et martirez a grant douleur de sa mesgnie mesmes qui en poux d'eure l'orent [tout, *om*. Laud] deuoure (Laud, f. 72ᵇ and others; sentence omitted by Bab., p. 106).

84/22 The anonymous saying comes from the *Dicts*, 290/19–20 and 291/21–2. It also occurs in Nicholas Ling, *Politeuphuia* (London: for N. Ling, 1597; *STC* 15685, f. 56ᵇ): 'Idlenes ingendereth ignorance, and ignoraunce ingendereth error' (thus in Baldwin (*STC* 1255, sig. N5ᵇ) attributing it to Plato). Scrope preserves the slip found in Laud (f. 72ᵇ): 'Et dit vng sage: oysiuete engendre oysiuete et erreur.' See my *Fastolf's Manuscripts*, p. 126.

84/27–85/2 Quoted by Hibernia (Penitentia h): 'Jugum meum leue est et sarcina mea leuis [Matth. xi. 30]; hec sarcina non est pondus onerati, sed ale sunt volatori; habent enim et aues pennarum suarum sarcinas et quidem portant illas in terra, portantur ab illis in celum. Augustinus, Super Psalmo.' However, this will be found in his *Sermo CLXIV* (Migne, xxxviii. 898).

85/2–3 Matth. iii. 2. S and M follow Laud in the reading 'appropinquabit'.

LXX

85/6–9 See *Ovide*, x. 1–195 and Caxton's *Ovyde*, pp. 1–3 (with Erudice as M); also Campbell (pp. 119–21) and Gordon (pp. 154–5). The latter, in his extract from *Ovide*, has accidentally combined ll. 29–30 into one, thus 'D'amour et sa grace a doner.' Text should read:

> D'amours, mes ele li noia
> S'amour et sa grace a doner.

Also, in line 26, read 'pastours', and 'sivoit' in line 34. See Chapter LXVII, above.

85/13–17 For the text in L, see my *Revisions*, p. 267.

85/24 The four are not named by Bab. (p. 108). Warner (p. 79, n. 1) has a note on Acharon.

86/5–8 Sentence omitted by Bab. (p. 108). Wyer, like S, has (sig. P3):

'one had his loue taken from hym & after rendred to hym agayne, and sythen he lost her againe.'

86/11–12 Salamon] this is, perhaps, a revision of the saying attributed to Solon in the *Dicts*, 38/27–8, though there are a number of similar apophthegms to be found there (e.g., 145/18, 247/19, 290/9). Note further *CdV* (M 771, f. 24ᵇ) under Seurte: 'Fole chose est craindre la chose que on ne peut escheuer.' The following is attributed to Chilo in the collection of French *dits* found in Morgan MS. M 277 (f. 10ᵇ): 'Non point desirer choses impossibles.' *Boke*² (sig. L4ᵇ) has: 'Barbalicus saith, a man of good discrecion ought not to exercise him in thinges unuailable.'

86/17–22 Perhaps based on Augustinus, *In Joannis Evangelium tractatus LXXIII* (Migne, xxxv. 1824–6).

86/24–6 Jac. iv. 3.

LXXI

87/1 Compare the account of Achilles given in *Ovide*, xii. 1101–63 (cf. Campbell, pp. 101–3 and the story, with woodcut, in Vérard's edition of the Prose Ovide, sig. r8). Further Robert Holcot's *Convertimini* (MS. Royal 7 C. I, f. 118; H. L. D. Ward and J. A. Herbert, *Catalogue of Romances in the Department of Manuscripts in the British Museum* (London, 1883–1910), iii. 133), the *Gesta Romanorum* (trans. Charles Swan (London, 1905), p. 334, story CLVI), Gower's *Confessio Amantis* (v. 2961 sq.), etc. The chapter-heading in Caxton's *Ovyde* (p. 73) reads: 'How Ulixes by hys subtylte had knowleche of Achilles amonge the ladyes & broughte hym in to the Oost.'

87/7–8 Son fil mist en une abeïe
De nonains, en habit de fame.
(*Ovide*, xii. 1106–7)

Sy le mist en vne abbeye de leur loy en abit de dame (Prose Ovide; Royal 17 E. IV, f. 200ᵇ); wherfore she put hym in an Abbaye of theyre lawe in habyte of a mayde (Caxton's *Ovyde*, p. 73).

87/21 Compare Chaucer, *Squire's Tale* (ll. 608–9; Robinson, p. 134): '. . . alle thyng, repeirynge to his kynde, | Gladeth hymself.' From Boethius, *De philosophiae consolatione* (III. met. ii. 34–5), which Chaucer translates thus (Robinson, p. 343): 'Alle thynges seken ayen to hir propre cours, and alle thynges rejoysen hem of hir retornynge ayen to hir nature.'

87/27–8 Legmon (Leguroun, Bab.) = *Dicts*, 248/24 and 249/25–6, and notes.

87/28–30 Hermes = *Dicts*, 18/6 and 19/5–6; see Tilley F 718.

88/6-8   No goode dede vnrewardid is, or quytte;
          Ne euyl vnpunysshid, seith Holy Writte.
                        (Hoccleve, *Regement of Princes*, ll. 2890-1)

88/8-10 Nullus labor durus, nullum tempus longum videri debet, quo gloria eternitatis acquiritur. Hieronymus in epistola (Hibernia, Gloria eterna z; the reference has not been traced). Cf. 73/22.

88/10 quant ilz attendent la gloire pardurable en loyer (Laud, f. 74ᵇ).

88/11-12 II Par. xv. 7, but all other texts correctly have 'vestre' as Vulgate.

LXXII

88/15-18 The tale of Atalanta comes from *Ovide*, x. 2094-2437. Compare the texts listed in the *Catalogue of Romances*, iii: p. 111 (Holcot; Arundel 384, f. 89ᵇ), p. 174 (moralized tale; Harley 7322, f. 97ᵇ), and p. 190 (*Gesta Romanorum*; Harley 5369, f. 38); also Neville, *Castell of Pleasure* (E.E.T.S., o.s. 179 (1928), ll. 418 sq.). Cf. Frederic Madden, *The Old English Versions of the Gesta Romanorum* (London, 1838), pp. 104, 288 and (notes), 512-13; also the additional story printed on pp. 429-30 of the E.E.T.S. edition of the *Gesta*.

88/18 De tel cours tu n'as nul mestier (Laud, f. 74ᵇ); And vnto suche a course, thou no mestier haste (Wyer, sig. P6).

88/20-2 Athalenta fu vne nimphe de grant beaute mais diuerse estoit sa destinee, car pour cause d'elle, plusieurs perdirent la vie (Laud, f. 74ᵇ; thus other texts, though Pigouchet, Le Noir, and Wyer read 'dure' for 'diuerse'. Sentence omitted by Bab., p. 110).

89/2-6 Perhaps based on *Dicts* (24/1-3): 'And he saithe: who-soo that laborith in that the whiche profitith not, he lesethe therefore that the whiche profitithe.'

89/6-8 Thessille = *Dicts*, 252/30-2 and 253/34-6. Bab. (p. 111) gives the author's name as Thesaly.

89/12-16 Cf. Hibernia (Mundus a), attributing the extract to 'Augustinus ad Diascorum'. Actually it will be found in St. Augustine's *Epistola CXLV ad Anastasium* (Migne, xxxiii. 593). Scrope's translation is not very clear; Laud (f. 75) has: '. . . mais plus le voit on moleste et moins s'en doit on empescher, et moins quant il attrait a son amour que quant il donne occasion d'estre despite.'

89/17-18 I Joan. ii. 15; see Biblical quotation in XCIII.

LXXIII

89/21 See notes to Chapter LX, and *Ovide* (xi, especially 1830-2189); also *Hist. anc.* (Stowe, f. 47). Paris tells the story as a vision in a dream, inspired by Mercury, in *Confessio Amantis* (v. 7225 sq.) and so in *Hist. anc.* (Royal 16, f. 71 and Add., f. 78^b). See also E. Bagby Atwood, 'The Judgment of Paris in the *Seege of Troye*', *PMLA* lvii (1942), 343–53, with extensive annotation.

89/24 S and M alter (? improve) the rhyme-word in L. 'Plusieurs en ont eu mal louyer' (Laud, f. 75); 'Many men haue receyued an euyll wage' (Wyer, sig. P7^b).

90/1–2 Paris voult diliganment enquerre la force & puissance de chascune a par soy (Laud, f. 75^b; similarly other texts; omitted by Bab., p. 112).

90/22–3 Pictagoras = *Dicts*, 54/15–16 and 55/18–19.

90/26–91/1 Quoted by Hibernia (Iudex b), attributing it to the second book of St. Augustine's *Against the Manichaeans*. Thus in the French manuscripts, though Wyer and Bab. omit the title. The quotation actually comes from Augustinus, *De sermone Domini in monte* (II. xviii; Migne, xxxiv. 1297). Telin (f. 119) quotes this as from St. Augustine: 'On se doit bien garder de iuger rien contre autruy, car on n'est pas certain se celluy, qui faict la chose, la faict a bonne intention ou mauuaise' (so *CdV*, M 771, f. 43^b).

91/2–3 Matth. vii. 1–2 (with French texts, and Bab., as Scrope; cf. Warner, p. 84).

LXXIV

91/6 Many citations of Christine's use of Fortune are given by Howard R. Patch, *The Goddess Fortuna in Mediaeval Literature* (Cambridge, Mass., 1927). See also Alfred Doren, 'Fortuna im Mittelalter und in der Renaissance', *Vorträge der Bibliothek Warburg*, ii^1 (1922–3), 71–144, and Ernst Cassirer, *Individuum und Kosmos in der Philosophie der Renaissance* (*Studien der Bibliothek Warburg*, x (1927)), pp. 77 ff. For ME texts, see (for example) Lydgate, *Troy Book*, ii. 1 ff and elsewhere; *Assembly of Gods*, l. 316 and notes, pp. 69–70; and countless others. Illustrations of the Wheel of Fortune occur in *Hist. anc.* (Stowe, f. 197 and Royal 20, f. 163^b).

91/17–18 The quotation from Socrates does not appear to come from the *Dicts*; compare Warner (p. 84, n. 4). Bab. (p. 113) has: 'þe wheel of fortune is lyke a ingyne made to take fysche'. Apparently, neither he nor Scrope understood the French 'engins'.

91/22–7 Concerning the extract from Boethius, Campbell (p. 185, n. 1) remarks that he has not been able to find it; but see the *De philosophiae consolatione*, III. prose ii (Vienna and Leipzig, 1934, pp. 47–9). Note also Chaucer's use of this belief in *Gen. Prol.*, 336 sq.; *Merch. T*, 2021; and *TC*, iii. 1691. Cf. Dante, *Convivio* (iv. 6 and 22; *Opera* (Florence,

1960), pp. 242 and 274). Bab. (p. 114) alone omits the 'des Epicuriens' of the other texts. Scrope literally translates the text of Laud (f. 76ᵇ): 'lesquelles condicions ne resistent point les choses'. Most French texts (e.g. Harley and Le Noir) have 'present', for which Wyer (sig. Q2) supplies 'gyue' and Bab. 'have'.

91/28 Is. iii. 12. Note that Laud (f. 76ᵇ) has 'decipient' as M, while S and all the other texts agree with Vulgate in having 'decipiunt'.

LXXV

92/2-5   Pour guerre emprendre ou commencier
                Ne fais pas Paris auancier
                Car mieulx sauroit, ie n'en doubt mie,
                Soy deduire es beaulx bras s'amie. (Laud, f. 76ᵇ)

It is noteworthy that Scrope agrees with the other French texts here used in having the French rhyme-words of lines 1–2 read 'auancer | commencer'. The second line reads in Wyer (sig. Q2ᵇ): 'Make not of Paris, thy pryncipall Capytayne.'

92/7 The 1509 Orosius (sig. o1) suggests that Paris 'auoit le couraige leger'.

92/9 cheuetain de son ost ne de ses batailles (Laud).

92/10-12 This saying is not in the *Dicts* (cf. 230/21-5 and 218/10). Campbell (pp. 183-4) could find no source for the four Aristotle to Alexander quotations; compare Chapters XXVIII, XLIV, and XC and my notes to these.

92/17-22 Hibernia (Contemplatio k) cites this extract, taking it from Gregorius, *Homiliae in Ezechielem*, I. iii (Migne, lxxvi. 809). Compare the reference in the *Book of Vices and Virtues* 221/1-2): 'þe lif of bisynesse of þe world, þat clerkes clepen actif lif, as seynt Gregorie seiþ'. An analogous extract from St. Gregory was used in Nicholas Love's translation of the *Meditationes vitae Christi* wrongly ascribed to St. Bonaventura (*The Mirrour of the Blessed Lyf of Jesu Christ* (Oxford, 1908), p. 161).

92/23-4 Luc. x. 42. Only M and S omit 'sibi Maria'.

LXXVI

92/29 The story of Cephalus and Procris is taken from *Ovide*, vii. 2759-3282 (Ovid, vii. 661-865). Line 4 reads in Laud (f. 77): 'Le t'aprent et la femme Loth.'

93/11 þe leves] la fueille (Laud and other French manuscripts); the leues of a busshe (Wyer, sig. Q4ᵇ); þe booes of þe vnderwood (Bab., p. 115).

93/17 et pource fu tantost muee en vne mace de sel (Laud, f. 77ᵇ; thus other French texts have 'en vne masse de sel' as Pigouchet, sig. e8ᵇ). Lot's wife is omitted by Bab. (p. 116) and was changed 'into a salte stone' in Wyer (sig. Q4ᵇ). Similarly, *Hist. anc.* (Royal 16, f. 26ᵇ and Add., f. 22) states that she became 'une pierre salee'. The *Speculum humanae salvationis* (ll. 93–4, p. 65) has 'versa est in lapidem', which Jean Mielot (p. 149) and the 1509 Orosius (sig. d7ᵇ) render as 'en une pierre'; see also Lutz and Perdrizet, Cap. xxi. 87–94 and comment, i. 223. Josephus (*Ant. Jud.* i. xi; Franz Blatt, *The Latin Josephus* (Copenhagen, 1958), i. 150) has 'in statuam salis' as Gen. xix. 26.

93/21–5 Hermes = *Dicts*, 10/35–6 and 14/2–5. Compare Campbell (p. 181) and *ODEP*, p. 148: 'Do as you would be done by.'

93/30–94/8 Saynt John Crisostome, speaking against them which do iudge other folkes and saithe, howe doest se so many litle faultes in the dedes of another man, and dothe let pas so many great faults in thine owne dedes, thou ought to be dylygent to consydre thyne owne dedes, more then the dedes of other men. For oure Lorde saithe in the Gospell: Quid autem [etc.] (*Boke*, f. 100; thus *CdV*, M 771, f. 44). Hibernia (Consideratio sui y) attributed this to 'Chrisostomus super illud Matthei. 7: Quid autem vides fetuscam [*sic*] in oculo &c', but not found in Migne, *Gr.* lvi. 725–9 or lvii. 307–20.

94/6–8 Matth. vii. 3. Only Bab. (p. 116) has 'non consideras'. A modification of this verse is in the *Fiore di virtù* (Venice: [Jenson], 1474, f. 63ᵇ); 'Aristotile dice: tale ha la traue nel suo occhio che dice al compagno che si leue la fistuga del suo.' Compare, *ODEP*, p. 435, and Tilley M 1191.

LXXVII

94/10 Helenus (so other French and English texts) was 'le quart frere' among Priam's sons (1509 Orosius, sig. 01ᵇ). M confuses Helayne, the beloved of Paris, with his brother Helenus.

94/16–17 et plain de science. Si desconseilla tant comme il pot (Laud (f. 78), Harley, Pigouchet, Le Noir, etc.; cf. M).

94/17 The warning of Helenus is in Stowe (f. 54), Add. (f. 78ᵇ), and Royal 16 (f. 71). Add. 9785, ff. 17ᵇ–18, has: 'Et je vous dy certeynement que, se Paris ameyne femme de Gresce, Troye en sera destruicte.' In the *Mutacion* (MCG, f. 115ᵇ), Helenus (and 'les anciens') warn against the Trojan war because of 'les escrips de Sebille . . . et autres anciens escrips'.

94/20–2 Hermes = *Dicts*, 18/25–8 and 19/24–7. 'Et dist Hermes: qui honnoure les sages et vse de leur conseil est perpetuel' (Laud, f. 78).

94/25–9 According to Campbell (p. 156), this passage comes from St. Augustine's commentary on the Psalter, but this is apparently a slip and the reference is proper to Chapter LXXVIII. Compare Hibernia (Diabolus b) and the *Speculum Christiani* (201/26): 'Augustinus. Nemo potest a diabolo decipi, nisi qui prebere uoluerit sue uoluntatis assensum; Augustinus. No man may be bygylede of the feende, bot he that wil ȝeuen assent of hys wyl' (200/31–3).

94/29–32 I Cor. x. 13 (Laud has 'prime', and Bab. alone has 'resistere' for 'sustinere').

LXXVIII

95/4 Morpheus appears in *Ovide*, xi, and widely elsewhere (e.g. *Assembly of Gods*). In Machaut, *Font. amour*. (ll. 669–79), he reveals to Alchion (see next chapter) the death of Ceys.

95/8 et est dieu de songe et fait songer (Laud, f. 78ᵇ; thus Pigouchet, sig. f1ᵇ; cf. text of L).

95/18–19 Socrates; compare *Dicts*, 90/3–4 and 91/4–6.

95/25–96/4 Hibernia (Patientia d): 'Fili, si ploras, pie plora: noli cum indignatione, noli cum typo superbie. Vnde plangis? quod pateris medicina est, non pena; castigatio, non damnatio. Noli repellere flagellum, si non vis repelli ab hereditate; noli attendere quam penam habeas in flagello, sed quem locum in testamento. Aug. sup. Ps. 99.' The edition of Paris, 1887 (p. 517) ascribes this to the commentary on Psalm XCVI [*sic*]. Not found in Augustinus, *Enarrationes in Psalmos*, 36, 96, 99, 9r 116 (Migne, xxxvi-xxxvii).

96/5–6 'Esse' is found in all texts except Bab. (p. 118), which has 'omne' as Vulgate. Scrope's quotation is identical with Laud and Pigouchet. Bible location (omitted in M and S) is given correctly (Eccli. ii. 4) by Laud, Harley, Pigouchet, Le Noir, and Wyer.

LXXIX

96/10–11 Story taken from *Ovide*, xi. 2996–3393 (cf. Prose Ovide, Royal 17 E. IV, ff. 186ᵇ sq. and Caxton's *Ovyde*, pp. 48–59). See also Chaucer, *Book of the Duchess*, ll. 62–269 (Robinson, pp. 268–9) and Gower, *Confessio Amantis*, iv. 2927 sq. Allusions to Alchion will be found in Christine's *Mutacion* (ll. 1257–9) and Machaut, *Font. amour*. (ll. 543–698). *ME Sermons* (327/21–7) notes that, according to St. Ambrose, the sea is always calm when the bird nests (cf. Warner, p. 90, n. 1). For the unusual details in *Othea*, see Campbell, pp. 130–1. Bab. (p. 119) says nothing about Alchion getting into the ship.

96/23 Laud (f. 79) has 'eolus', which might easily be misread as 'colus' and thus have lead to Scrope's reading. *Ovide* has 'rois Eolus' (l. 3787) and the *Assembly of Gods* provides Eolus.

96/26–7 Juno . . . En deus oisiaus mua leurs corps humains (Machaut, *Font. amour*., l. 691).

96/29 vpon the see (Wyer, sig. R1; so Bab.); sus la mer (Harley, f. 131; omitted in Laud, f. 79).

97/5–7 Assaron = *Dicts*, 232/11–12 and 233/10–11.

97/12–13 Seynt Ambrose in þe fyrst boke of Officez (Bab., p. 120; all others refer to the second book).

97/12–17 See the quotation in Hibernia (Consilium d), taken from Ambrosius, *De officiis ministrorum*, II, xv (Migne, xvi. 122–3).

97/18 But compare 'In trust is treason', *ODEP*, p. 673.

97/20–1 Prov. iii. 21–2.

LXXX

97/24 For the debate between Helenus and Troylus (taken from the *Hist. anc.*), see also Chapter LXXVII. According to the 1509 Orosius (sig. o1ᵇ), Troylus was the 'cinquiesme frere'.

98/3 For Hesione, see Warner (p. 91, n. 1). See also *Hist. anc.* (Stowe, f. 217ᵇ; Add. f. 78; Royal 16, f. 70ᵇ), 1509 Orosius (sig. n8ᵇ) and note to LXVI.

98/3 Thalamon Aiax (Stowe, f. 217ᵇ); Thelamonaiaux (Laud, f. 80).

98/5 In the *Ystoire de Troye* (MS. Add. 9785, f. 18), the prophecies are ridiculed: 'car ce est manyere de preuoyre, d'estre tousiours en doubte de chouse qui touche peril et honneur.'

98/14–15 Warner (p. 91, n. 4) refers to Eccl. x. 16: 'Vae tibi, terra, cujus rex puer est.' The *Fiore di virtù* (M 770, f. 13) has: 'Egli [Salamone] si dice: dolente la terra che a il giouane re' (which is usually assigned to Seneca in the printed editions). *CdV* (M 771, f. 31) includes, under Iniustice: 'Senecques dit que dolente est la terre de qui le seigneur est jeune'; *Boke²* (sig. H8) renders this as: 'Senec saythe, that muche sorowe and trybulacyon, is in the Lande wherof the Lorde and Gouernoure, is a yong man.' This apophthegm is not found in Chaucer's *Tale of Melibee*, though it does occur in the French original (*Sources and Analogues*, p. 581, ll. 381–2, attributed to Solomon). See also Shakespeare, *Richard III*, II. iii. 18 (Variorum edn. (Philadelphia, 1908), p. 178), and A. C. Friend, 'The Proverbs of Serlo of Wilton', *Mediaeval Studies*, xvi (1954), 217–18. There is a reference to this *dictum* appearing in the *Summa virtutum et vitiorum* (ii. 35 and 202) of Peraldus by C. Frati, 'Ricerche sul "Fiore di Virtù"', *Studi di filologia romanza*, vi. 365. See Tilley W 600. Sir David Lindsay (*The Poetical Works* (Edinburgh, 1881), i. 40) writes in *The Dreme* (ll. 1010-11):

> I see rycht weill, that proverbe is full trewe,
> Wo to the realme that hes ouer young ane king.

98/20–3 Pessime matris ignorantie, pessime ibidem due filie sunt,

scilicet falsitas & dubietas; illa miserior, ista miserabilior, illa perni-
tiosior, ista molestior (Hibernia, Ignorantia b; Campbell, p. 156,
ascribes this to Augustinus *super Joannem*). Scrope must have mis-
understood the French 'moleste' (Godefroy, p. 373 = désagréable,
furieux), taking it to be 'moleste = mollete' (Godefroy, p. 375 = mou).
Pierre Gringore (*Les Abus du monde* (Paris, 1509), sig. H3) cites this
saying: 'Aristoteles; Ignorantia mater viciorum.'

98/24-6 Sap. x. 8 (though Gordon (p. 155) follows Warner (p. 91, n. 6)
in citing this as the fifth verse). Scrope follows the text of Laud (f. 80)
except for 'fuerunt' instead of 'sue relinquerunt' (cf. Vulgate).

LXXXI

98/28 The account of Calchas (see Warner, p. 92, n. 2) comes from the
Hist. anc. See also the 1509 Orosius (sig. 04) and the prose *Ystoire de
Troye* (Add. 9785, ff. 31ᵇ–33).

98/30 Trayssent regnes et empires (Laud, f. 80ᵇ; thus Harley and
Pigouchet).

99/4 *Cyte* (sig. A2) reads: 'The thyrde [Sibyl] of Delphe engendred
in the temple of Appolyn & was named Delphyca. And this lady
preched the destruccyon of Troye longe tyme before & Ouyde put
many verses of her in his boke.' [Note the 'verses' which suggests that
Christine thought instinctively of the versified, rather than the prose,
Ovide]. Apollo also appears as Appolyn in the *M.E. Sermons* (316/15).
Mutacion (MCG, f. 122) notes: 'Car en Delphos lui dist li dieux |
Apolin. . .'

99/15-16 This saying, attributed to Plato, has not been located.
Perhaps based on *Dicts* (136/11–12): 'noise not thyne ennymye for
litille though he be litille, for he may noy the more than thou thinkist'.
Compare also *Dicts*, 118/18–21.

99/20-5 *CdV* (M 771, f. 33ᵇ), under Faulsete: 'Saint Augustin [thus
Le Noir (sig. e2ᵇ) and *Boke* (f. 80); also Telin (f. 118ᵇ)] dit que le
traistre ne se adoulcist iamais par familiarite de compaignie ne pour
priuete de boyre ne de mangier ne pour nul seruice ne pour dons de
beneffices. Dont Saint Paul en fait mencion, disant: Erunt homines
&c. (as *Othea*).' The attribution to St. Jerome is possibly based on the
lines in *Epistola CXXV ad Rusticum monachum* (Migne, xxii. 1073,
3–6).

99/24-5 II Tim. iii. 2–4, with Scrope following Laud (f. 81) in omitting
'tumidi'. Laud also has Ethimologeum.

LXXXII

99/29 Christine apparently took the fable of Hermaphroditus from
Ovide, iv. 1997–2223 (cf. Ovid, iv. 285–388). Compare the Prose Ovide

(Royal 17 E. IV, f. 63, and De Boer, p. 145, both with Hermofroditus).

100/2–3 vne nimphe (Laud, f. 81); a grett ladye of hye parage (Bab., p. 123).

100/6–7 arriua adonc a la fontaine de Salmacis (Laud, f. 81); than arriued he at the fountaine of Salenaxis (Wyer, sig. R5^b; Salmaxis, Bab., p. 123).

100/8 adonc lui prist talent de soy baigner (Laud); than he toke talent [etc]. (Wyer). *OED* has last use of *talent* in sense 2 (wish, desire) in 1530.

100/13–14 Adonc la nimphe plaine de deul pria aux dieux (Laud; cf. omission in M).

100/18–22 liche as . . . maistris seith] omitted only by Bab.

100/29–30 Hermes = *Dicts*, 28/16–17 and 29/17–18. Compare also 160/26–7.

101/4–10 Hibernia (Consolatio g) from Gregorius, *Moralia*, III. xii (Migne, lxxv. 609).

101/11–12 Is. xxxv. 3.

LXXXIII

101/23 According to the *Hist. anc.* (Stowe, f. 50^b), chess was invented during the siege of Troy. See the miniature of Achilles playing the game in Royal 20 (f. 128) and consult Lydgate, *Troy Book*, ii. 806–23. Christine may well have obtained the idea that Ulysses invented chess from the Pseudo-Ovidian *De vetula*, a tract which 'is with much probability ascribed to Ricardus de Furnivalle, who flourished about the year 1250' (BMC vi: 877). See the lines in the edition [Perugia: Petri & Nicolai, *c.* 1475], f. 11:

> Est alius ludus scachorum ludus Ulixis
> Ludus Troyana quem fecit in obsidione.

For a contrary view, see Caxton's *The Game of Chess* (Bruges, a. 31 Mar. 1474/5), f. 4: 'Trewe it is that some men wene that this playe was founden in the tyme of the bataylles & siege of Troye but that is not soo.'

101/25 suyche maner game as be nott contrarius to verteu (peculiar to Bab., p. 125).

101/25–6 The saying ascribed to Solin cannot be traced (but see *Dicts*, 140/13–14). The corresponding sentence in Bab. (p. 125, re-checked with manuscript: 'Al thyng sotyl & honest schold þe ydle doo') seems even more obscure.

101/31–102/4 Quotation is assigned to 'Saint Gregoire' in Laud

(f. 82) and to St. Jerome in all other texts. From Gregorius, *Moralia*, II. i (Migne, lxxv. 553); also quoted by Abelard, *Epistola VIII ad Heloissam* (Migne, clxxviii. 306).

102/2 nous y voyons l'enterine face de nostre ame (Laud, f. 82). See Warner's note (p. 118) under 'herdly', and note 2 on p. 95. Wyer has (sig. R7ᵇ): 'we may se therin the face of our Lorde' (so Le Noir, sig. f4).

102/2-3 la pouons nous veoir nostre bel; la pouons nous veoir nostre lait (Harley, f. 133; so Bab., p. 125, but first half omitted by Laud, Pigouchet, Le Noir, Wyer, and Scrope).

102/5-6 Joan. v. 39. Scrope has the same text as Laud, while the other French and English texts have 'in quibus putatis' for the 'quia vos putatis in ipsis' of the Vulgate.

LXXXIV

102/10 The account is taken from the *Hist. anc.* (see the miniatures of Calchas greeting his daughter in Royal 20, ff. 101ᵇ and 102). See also the *Ystoire de Troye* (Add. 9785, ff. 78ᵇ–85), and the plots of the versions by Chaucer and Shakespeare. Bab. has Cryseyde, thus suggesting that both he and Scrope knew Chaucer's poem. Wyer (sig. R8ᵇ) has: 'Bryseyde (whom mayster Chaucer calleth Cressayde, in his Boke of Troylus).' The French texts, of course, have the 'B' form of the name. For this story, compare *Mutacion* (MCG, ff. 123ᵇ–124).

102/29-20 Hermes] not under Hermes in *Dicts*, but compare Leginon (245/19–20: 'Fellaship nat with euell folkes leste thu be oon of hem') and Plato (138/15: 'Felawship not with shrewis þat þi nature takithe not of theirs'). Walter Burley, *De vita et moribus philosophorum* [German] (Augsburg, 1490, f. 98) has under Hermes: 'Hüte dich vor der geselschaft der bösen.' Compare also Tilley C 570.

103/3 Cf. my note in *Fastolf's Manuscripts* (p. 127, n. 31).

103/5-9 Hibernia (Gloria vana b) from Augustinus, *Enarratio in Psalmum VII* (Migne, xxxvi. 100). Compare also *CdV* (M 771, f. 29; from *Fiore di virtù* under Vanagloria): 'Et en la somme des vices ce lit que quant la personne a vaincu les vices que encore luy demeure vayne gloyre.' So *Boke*, f. 61.

103/10-11 I Cor. i. 31, the 'secundem' being apparently Christine's slip.

LXXXV

103/13 The death of Patroclus is probably from *Ovide*, xii. 3514 sq.

103/23 sa grant force (Laud); his great puyssaunce (Wyer).

103/25–6 Since the *Epistle of Othea* is both addressed to Hector and his death is there related (Chapters XC–XCII), Christine seeks to avoid the resulting anachronism by relating Hector's death as a prophecy of things to come.

104/1–3 Magdarge = *Dicts*, 252/12–14 and 253/12–15; see Campbell, p. 180.

104/8 Solin, not in *Dicts*; Bab. has: 'þe doctour Solin.' Pigouchet, Le Noir, and Wyer attribute the quotation to Job (cf. Job vii. 1, and the various commentaries thereon).

104/8–11 and in sygne therof, this present lyfe is called melitant to the difference of the lyfe aboue, whiche is called tryumphaunt, for that hath the vyctory of Enemyes (Wyer, sig. S2^b).

104/11 Compare M and L. Laud has: 'car elle a ia victoire des ennemis' (so Harley, Pigouchet, and Le Noir). Cf. Introduction, p. xxii, note 2.

104/12–13 Eph. vi. 11. All French texts have 'armatura' except Harley ('armatum'). Bab. (p. 127) has a different quotation = Gal. iv. 26 (not 'vi' as stated by Gordon, p. 156).

LXXXVI

104/15 The account of Echo is taken from *Ovide*, iii. 1292–1463; see Campbell, p. 112. Note the masculine adjective in the second and third lines of S and L, Scrope having (perhaps) been misled by the 'son vueil' of the third French line. The readings in M are obviously corrections of an earlier slip.

104/25 Narcysus (Bab., p. 128). Cf. Ovid, iii. 339–401.

105/5 les dieux (all French texts); see variants to 104/28.

105/12–15 Zaqualcum = *Dicts*, 34/18–21 and 35/22–5 (and notes).

105/19–24 Augustinus, *De sermone Domini in monte* (Migne, xxxiv. 1229–1308, especially 1234); quotation is in Hibernia (Misericordia d). Scrope gives a poor rendering of the French, which reads in Laud (f. 84): 'car ilz desseruent que la misericorde de dieu les deliure de leurs miseres'. Possibly Scrope's exemplar was at fault, since the French is perfectly clear.

105/25–6 Prov. xxii. 9, though all French texts (and Bab.) have 'pronus' as Vulgate.

LXXXVII

106/1 The fable of Daphne and Phoebus is in Ovid, i. 452–567, and *Ovide*, i. 2737–3064. Compare Campbell, pp. 121–2; Gordon, p. 156; and Schick's note on *Temple of Glass*, ll. 112–16.

106/7 In the Prose Ovide of MS. Royal 17 E. IV (f. 20ᵇ), Daphne appeals to Diana for help, whereas in *Ovide*, (l. 3020) one finds: 'Biaus douz peres, secorez moi.' Similarly, in De Boer's edition of the *Ovide moralisé en prose* (p. 67), she appeals to 'son dit pere'.

106/9 M and L have 'lorier' as Laud (f. 84ᵇ), and this must have been the form first chosen by Scrope. Harley, Pigouchet, and Le Noir have 'laurier' and Bab. has 'laurer'.

106/13–18 This exposition is omitted by Bab. (p. 130).

106/22–3 Omere dit: par grant diligence vient l'omme a parfection (*CdV*, M 771, f. 16, under Melencolie; not in Italian *Fiore*). *Boke* (f. 38ᵇ) similarly has: 'Homer saythe that by greate dylygence, a man commeth to perfeccyon.' The French *Dits* has 'a son intencion' (Royal 19 B. IV, f. 11ᵇ), and the Latin *Dicta* 'quod vult' (p. 419). Christine here used *CdV*, not *Dicts* (cf. 38/12 and 39/14–15).

106/29 Gregorius, *Homilia XXXVII in Evangelia* (Migne, lxxvi. 1275). The omission noted by Warner (p. 100, n. 2) is not Scrope's error but is peculiar to L. Compare *Speculum Christiani* (118/16–120/3): 'Augustinus. What tonge may seye, what witte may thynke, or what mynde may esteme hou many ioyes ben to haue al-way God presente, al-way to see hym, al-way to sitte be-for hym in worschipe?' (with Latin equivalent on 119/14–121/3).

107/1 Scrope misunderstood the French (Laud, f. 85): 'auec les benois esperis assister a la gloire du conditeur [the Creator].' Wyer has (sig. S6): 'to be assystynge with the blyssed sprytes, in the glory of the maker.'

107/5 Ps. lxxxvi. 3 (location also omitted by Laud, Pigouchet, etc.).

LXXXVIII

107/8 For Andromache's 'vision', see also Chapter XC and the accounts in the 1509 Orosius (sig. p1) and in the *Seege or Batayle of Troy* (E.E.T.S., p. 109, ll. 1363 sq.). Her name appears as Andromata (Add. 9785, f. 92ᵇ) and Eudromada or Eudomada in Royal 16 (f. 75).

107/21–4 Un proverbe, dont me recorde,
Qui dit auques pareillement:
Ne desprises l'enseignement
De nul, posé q'un enfent fust,
Qui te monstrast, s'aucun bien sceust!
(*Mutacion*, ll. 6612–16; also MCG, f. 49)

Solente (ii. 350) calls attention to a similar passage in Hugo de S. Victore cited in Hibernia (Auditor l), but this is not as close as *Dicts*, 149/11–14, 136/4 and 120/1 sq. The French in Leber (sig. I4) partly agrees word for word with *Othéa*. Under Socrates, the *Mer des histoires* (ii. 22ᵇ) cites: 'N'as tu point honte de estudier et aller a l'escole en ta viellese.' See also Tilley L 153.

107/29–108/5 Porro ad faciendum bonum quid in nobis bonus spiritus operatur: profecto monet. mouet & docet. monet memoriam. mouet voluntatem & docet rationem. nec minimam paleam intra cordis quod possidet habitaculum patitur residere. sed statim igne subtilissime circumspectionis & compunctionis exurit spiritus dulcis & suauis. (Hibernia, Spiritus sanctus d; also attributing this to the *Moralia* of St. Gregory).

108/2–5 þe spirite . . . circumspeccion] omitted only by Bab. (p. 132).

108/4 du cuer ou il s'inspire (Laud, f. 85ᵇ; so Harley, Pigouchet, and Le Noir); wherin he hym-self enspireth (Wyer, sig. S7ᵇ).

108/6 Despite the assertion in Laud, Pigouchet, and elsewhere, this extract does not come from the *Epistle to the Hebrews*. The correct reference is I Thess. v. 19.

LXXXIX

108/9–12 See *Ovide*, i. 2425 sq. and *Hist. anc.* (Egerton, ff. 17 and 20ᵇ; Royal 16, ff. 16 and 19ᵇ; and Add., f. 9ᵇ [De Nembron le iaiant] and f. 13ᵇ [Ninus]); also 1509 Orosius (ff. 11–12 and 22ᵇ–23). In *Lavision* (133/9), 'Nambroth le jeant' is mentioned, and he (and Ninus) are discussed at length in the *Mutacion* (ll. 8443–8730 and 8781 sq.).

108/11 The French texts all have Ninus (Nynus, Bab., p. 132).

108/14 In the *Cyte* (sig. Ll3ᵇ), 'Nembroche the gyaunt' is cited as the inventor of 'Pyromancye'. There is a miniature of Nambroth and the Tower of Babel in Heineman, MS. 1, f. 24ᵇ (*Hours*, Use of Rouen, c. 1500).

108/20–1 Plato] the quotation is apparently based on *Dicts*, 118/18–21 (see also 269/10–11). *Motz dorees* (in 1509 Orosius, sig. DD5ᵇ) has: 'En toutes tes entreprises, metz plus grande fiance en ta puissance et science qu'en ta force.'

108/25–109/3 Augustinus, *De singularitate clericorum* (cf. notes to LXVII; Migne, iv. 837).

108/29 M. R. James says that three folios of S are missing here, but only one is wanting according to my collation. See Introduction, p. xiv, n. 2.

109/6 For the omission of the Biblical quotation in Laud and M, see my *Fastolf's Manuscripts*, p. 126, n. 24. Harley (f. 136) reads: 'Pour ce dit Dauid: Bonum est confidere in Domino quam confidere in homine' (Ps. cxvii. 8; and so Pigouchet, Le Noir, Wyer, and Bab.). Laud

(f. 86) has a blank space after 'dit' and L (uniquely) supplies: 'Spera in domino etc.' (Ps. xxxvi. 3).

XC

109/8–11   Hector, noncier m'estuet ta mort,
                 Dont grant douleur au cuer me mort.
                 Ce sera quant le roy Priant
                 Ne croiras, qui t'ira priant.   (Laud, f. 86)

Compare Campbell, pp. 106–7 and 140, and Gordon, p. 157. See also Chapter LXXXVIII and XCII (and notes). Christine also recounts 'Adromatha's' vision in the *Cyte* (sig. F3) and in the *Mutacion* (MCG, f. 124ᵇ).

109/17–19 Minerva and Mars are not named as responsible for Andromache's vision in the *Hist. anc.* (Add., f. 83ᵇ: '[elle] uit endormant une uision'; Stowe, f. 133: 'elle vit par signes et par auisions'). They are implied, however, in Stowe (f. 133ᵇ) where she says: 'les dieux . . . m'ont monstrez en ceste nuit'. In the *Mutacion* (MCG, f. 124ᵇ), Minerva, Mars, and (especially) Venus warn Andromache.

109/17–18 and . . . armes] omitted by Bab. (p. 133) and by Pigouchet, Le Noir, and Wyer; present in Laud (f. 86) and Harley (f. 136).

109/21 The Prose Ovide (De Boer, p. 317) has 'par une sousterne', while Vérard's *Ovide* (sig. s8) has 'par vne posterne' (as Bab.); similarly Caxton's *Ovyde* (p. 95) 'by a posterne'. The *Ystoire de Troye* (Add. 9785, f. 99) offers the chapter-heading: 'Si dit que la presse estoit si grant que Hector ne pouoit saillir hors'; while the *Hist. anc.* (Royal 20, f. 112ᵇ) simply observes: 'que a paine pot il issir hors.' According to the *Mutacion* (MCG, f. 125ᵇ), Hector left Troy 'par vne estroite soubsteraine'.

109/25 his souereyne] omitted by Pigouchet, Le Noir, Wyer, and Bab.; in Laud and Harley.

109/27–9 Aristotle to Alexander] this maxim does not appear to be in the *Dicts*, though it may be based on 163/2–9. See my note in *Fastolf's Manuscripts* (p. 127, n. 31).

110/4–9 From Bernardus Claraevallensis, *Sermo de conversione ad clericos*, cap. viii (Migne, clxxxii. 843). It seems difficult to believe that the omission in Laud and M of 'ne moins certain que l'eure de la mort' (Harley, f. 136ᵇ and all others) could be purely coincidental. But see *CdV* (M 771, f. 23ᵇ): 'Saint Bernart dit qu'il n'est plus chose commune que la mort, car la mort n'a mercy du pouure ne ne porte honneur au riche; elle n'espargne ne foul ne saige, jeune ne viel' [and adds Bible quotation as *Othea*]. *Boke* (f. 56ᵇ) renders this thus: 'Saynte Austyne saythe, that there is nothyng so sure as death, for deathe hathe no mercye of the poore, nor beareth no honoure to the ryche, and so spareth no maner of folkes' (cf. Augustinus, *De contritione cordis* (Migne, xl. 943) and *M.E. Sermons*, 276/26). On the other hand, Hoccleve (*De regimine principum*, no. 81 (E.E.T.S., E.S. 72 (1897), p. 21): 'No thyng is more certein than dethe is, | Ne more uncertein than the tyme ywis' (with marginal note apparently attributing this to Seneca *ad Lucillum*: 'Nil certius morte' etc.). So Petrarca, *Historia Griseldis* [German] (Ulm, 1473), f. 1ᵇ: 'Vnd alss gewiss ist das er komme, so vn-gewiss ist die stund seiner zukunfft.' Note also Anselmus, *Meditatio VII* (Migne, clviii. 741). See Tilley N 311 and N 316 (citing Caxton's translation of Alain Chartier's *Curial*, c. 1484).

110/9 medwis] see Warner's note on p. 120 ('mydwes'). Laud has 'espies' which Scrope may have read as 'en pres'.

110/10–11 Eccli. xiv. 12. For the omission of this in Laud and Scrope, see my *Fastolf's Manuscripts* (p. 126, n. 24). All texts have 'tardabit' for the 'tardat' of the Vulgate.

XCI

110/18 See notes to Chapters XC, XCII, and XCIV (with the comment by Constans on Ajax being unarmed). Caxton's *Ovyde* (p. 97) states that Hector 'caste hys shelde behynde hys backe and hys breste was al bar & dysgarnysshyd'. Vérard's *Ovide* (sig. s8ᵇ) records: 'Et tandis qu'il estoit a ce faire occupe [the despoilment of Polibetes], il getta son escu derriere son dos & sa poictrine demoura desgarnie. Adonc Achiles, voiant que Hector de nul ne se gardoit, print vng fort et court espieu, et courut de randonne a Hector, & le ferit en sa poictrine par si grande vertu qu'il le perca tout oultre le corps du vaillant Hector, dont il tumba mort de son cheual.' This is, of course, taken from the narrative of Guido de Columnis (Strassburg, 1486, sig. i6). See also Christine's *Mutacion* (MCG, f. 126ᵇ).

110/21–2 Hermes = *Dicts*, 20/12–14 and 21/11–13 (and note). Bab. (p. 134) thus revised the quotation from Hermes: 'þe lyff & deth of a man is but as þe strooke of an arew.' *CdV* (M 771, f. 23ᵇ) has under Crainte: 'Hermes dit que la mort est commune et est comme le cop d'une fleche, et la vie de l'omme est comme le cop flechie qui met long temps a venir' (not in Italian *Fiore*).

110/26 as seyth Seynt Gregor in hys Moralyes (Bab., p. 135; thus Pigouchet, Le Noir, and Wyer; title of work not cited by Laud or Harley). This saying has not been traced through the indexes of Migne nor through those attached to the English translation by James Bliss (*Morals on the Book of Job by S. Gregory the Great*, Oxford, 1844–50).

111/3–4 Matth. vi. 6; 'in abscondito' being omitted by M. Since the location is also wanting, both may have been omitted by Scrope's French exemplar—or his 'working copy' may have been unfinished.

XCII

111/6–9 The plot apparently comes from the *Hist. anc.* (Royal 16, f. 75ᵇ; Add., f. 84; Egerton, f. 88ᵇ, with miniature). See also 1509 Orosius (sig. p1ᵇ–p2) and Lydgate's *Troy Book* (iii. 5332–5406, with his comments on covetousness). Consult the notes to LXXXVIII, XC, and XCI, as well as Georges Chastellain, *La complainte d'Hector* (*Œuvres* (Brussels, 1863–6), vi. 167–202).

111/11 Polibetes, according to Warner (p. 105, n. 1), is 'the Politenes of Benoît de Ste. Maure (l. 16105) and Guido delle Colonne'.

111/14 Hector . . . estoit aclinez seur le col de son cheual (*Hist. anc.*, Royal 16, f. 75ᵇ; Egerton, f. 89; and Add., f. 84); and stouped doun ouer his stedes mane (*Seege or Batayle of Troye*, l. 1497); and enclyned him vpon the necke of his horse (Wyer, sig. T4). Similarly *Mutacion* (MCG, f. 126ᵇ): 'Sus le corps se baisse et se prent | A lui [Polibetes] despouillier.'

111/21–2 Attributed to Democritus in Bab. (p. 136). Not found in *Dicts* (but see 156/11 and 25). Compare *CdV* (Le Noir, sig. f2ᵇ) under Avarice: 'Senecque dit que l'auaricieux est cause de sa destruccion; et dit que [l'auarice] est le chemin de la mort espirituelle & souuent aussi de la mort temporelle' (similarly, Telin, f. 106ᵇ).

111/26–112/6 Innocentius, *De contemptu mundi*, II. vi (Migne, ccxvii. 719–20), which Bab. (p. 136) cites as 'þe boke of þe fylthe of condicioun of man'. For the inexplicable 'sauce-makers' ('sancsues' misread as 'saussieurs'?), see Warner (p. xl and p. 105, n. 5). Compare *ODEP*, p. 130: 'The daughter of the horse-leech' (Prov. xxx. 15).

112/6–7 See extract from *CdV* cited above.

112/7–8 I Tim. vi. 10. Compare *Dicts*, 42/19 and note; *Fiore* (Venice, 1566, sig. B2ᵇ: 'San Paulo dice: L'auaritia e radice di tutti i mali'); and Chaucer, *Tale of Melibee* (Robinson's edn., p. 187, l. 1840: 'Coveitise is roote of alle harmes'). Cf. Tilley C 746.

XCIII

112/16 For the story of Achilles and Polyxena (here probably taken from the *Hist. anc.*), see also the 1509 Orosius (sig. p3–p8), *Ovide* (xii. 4305–4579), Schick's note to *Temple of Glass*, ll. 94–5, and notes to Chapters XXXI and XL, above.

112/18 The 'anniuersarium' of Columnis (Griffin, p. 183) becomes the 'anniuersaire' of some manuscripts of the *Hist. anc.* (Add., f. 85), the Prose Ovide (Royal 17 E. iv, f. 218), the *Ystoire de Troye* (Add. 9785, f. 110ᵇ) and Lydgate's *Troy Book* ('anyuersarye', iv. 528). In Vérard's *Ovide* (sig. t1), it is 'enniuersaire', while other manuscripts of the *Hist. anc.* (Royal 16, f. 76ᵇ and Royal 20, f. 120ᵇ) have 'uniuersaire', with Wyer (sig. T5^b) providing 'vnyuersarie'. Laud (f. 88) has: 'a l'uniuersaire du chief de l'an des obseques Hector', while Pigouchet and Wyer omit the 'du chief de l'an.' *Mutacion* (MCG, f. 128) speaks of the 'obseques du chief de l'an' and Caxton's *Ovide* (p. 99) has: 'The yere passed and the day cam on whiche was doon the servyse of Hector.' Bab. (p. 136) says 'to se þe burying of Ectour'.

113/7–8 The 'dit' of the wise man has not been identified, but it is a very commonplace observation.

113/10–12 See my note in *Fastolf's Manuscripts* (p. 126, citing Harley, Wyer, and Bab.).

113/12–13 Toute estrange c'est le monde qu'il doit fouir (Laud, f. 88). Toute chose estrange c'est le monde doit fuyr (Harley, f. 138). Toute chose estrange c'est que le monde doibt fuyr (Pigouchet, sig. g3). Euery straunge thyng (that is to say the world) he ought to flye (Wyer, sig. T6). Estraung love is þe world wyche oweth to be hated & fled (Bab., p. 137).

113/14–18 Augustinus, *In epistolam Joannis ad Parthos tractatus*, II. ii (Migne, xxxv. 1994). Laud (f. 88^b) has: 'le monde passe & sa concupiscence' (but, in place of 'aimer Jesuchrist' [as Pigouchet and Harley] has 'auec Jhesucrist' [as Scrope]).

113/19 I Joan. ii. 15; see Bible quotation in LXXII.

XCIV

113/25 See the different account in *Ovide*, xiii. 1255–89. In the 1509 Orosius (f. 120^b), Paris and Ajax kill each other, there being no mention of Ajax as unarmed; so also in Egerton (f. 89^b) and Royal 16 (f. 78^b) of the *Hist. anc.*, and in the *Ystoire de Troye* (Add. 9785, f. 168^b). In Royal 20 (f. 150^b), Ajax goes to fight Paris 'sans hautere & sans heaume & armeures'. Constans (*Œdipe*, pp. 351–2), in remarking that Ajax was killed when unarmed, suggests: 'il pourrait bien y avoir ici un souvenir de la fatale imprudence d'Athon (l'Atys de Stace), qui, se trouvant hors des murs sans armure, fut tué par Tydée.' Compare notes to XLVI, Constans (pp. 349–52) finding other 'allusions au roman de Thèbes' in XXVIII and L. *Mutacion* (MCG, f. 135), noting that Ajax and Paris 's'occirent', maintains:

> Ayaux, qui trop n'estoit amez,
> Par la bataille desarmez
> D'un bras aloit, par grant orgueil.

In the *Boke of Noblesse* (ed. J. G. Nichols, London, 1860), p. 63, Ayax is called 'the best fighter amonge the Grekis ayenst the Trojens'.

114/4–6 Aristotle] compare *Dicts*, 172/10–11 and 173/9–11.

114/9–15 Hibernia (Confidentia c) quotes from Augustinus, *Sermo CCLXXVI: In festo Vincentii* (Migne, xxxviii. 1256).

114/16–18 II Cor. iii. 4–5. Bab. (Harley 838, f. 90ᵇ) apparently also has 'sumus' as Scrope and the other texts, instead of the 'simus' of the Vulgate. S, M, Laud and Harley read 'Secundem'.

XCV

114/25 The story of Antenor's betrayal is in the *Hist. anc.* (Royal 16, ff. 80–1 and Add., ff. 89ᵇ–90); also *Ystoire de Troye* (Add. 9785, ff. 181ᵇ sq.) and the 1509 Orosius (sig. q2). Laud has the name as Anthenor, as has the *Mutacion* (MCG, f. 138ᵇ) where his betrayal is judged to be comparable 'tout aussi comme Judas fist'. See the chapter in MS. Add. 9785, f. 217ᵇ: 'Comment Anthenor et les siens firent les cites de Venise et Padoa.'

114/26 et quant vint a la fin des grans batailles Troyennes (Laud, f. 89; the text in M is obviously a later emendation of that in S and L).

114/29–30 See my remarks in *Fastolf's Manuscripts*, p. 127.

115/6–7 Plato = *Dicts*, 146/22–3 and 147/25–6. Bab. (p. 139) provides: 'Fyghtyng is þe capteyn & gouernoure of ille people.' Wyer (sig. T8ᵇ) has 'barate' as French.

115/11–16 The quotation from St. Augustine has not been traced. Scrope must have read 'tres' (or 'iij') where all French texts have 'les inconueniens'.

115/13–15 Le papillon se brûle à la chandelle, continua le prince, comparaison vieille comme le monde (Stendhal, *Le Rouge et le noir*, chap. liv (Paris, 1870, ii. 143). Compare the πυραύστης of Aeschylus (Augustus Nauck, *Tragicorum Graecorum fragmenta* (Leipzig, 1856), p. 72, no. 280) and Lactantius, *Phoenix*, ll. 107–8 (Migne, vii. 281); also *Ayenbite of Inwyt* (E.E.T.S.) 206/16, the *Hecatomgraphie* of Gilles Corrozet (Paris, 1543, sig. L2ᵇ), Petrarch's Sonnet XIX 'Sono animali al mondo' (*Le rime* (Florence, 1899), pp. 19–20), Bacon's *Sylva sylvarum* (London, 1631, p. 171, § 696), Shakespeare's *Merchant of Venice* (II. ix. 82) and countless other works down to modern times (cf. Anthony Trollope, *The Small House at Allington* (London, 1964), p. 99). The motif was used as the device of the calligrapher Giovanbattista Palatino; see James Wardrop, 'Civis romanus sum', *Signature*, N.S. xiv (1952), 15. Compare also *ODEP*, p. 212 and Tilley (F 394): 'The fly (moth) that plays too long in the candle singes its wings at last.'

115/19 Prov. iv. 15.

XCVI

115/22–5

    Au temple Minerue souffrir
    Ne dois tes ennemis offrir;
    Mire toy ou cheual de fust;
    Encore ert Troye, s'il ne fust. (Laud, f. 89ᵇ)

Note that S and M follow the French rhyme-words in lines 1–2, though L seems to make better sense. Wyer (sig. U1) has for the first line·'Suffre none offeryng to come to the Temple.'

The first redaction of the *Hist. anc.* (Egerton, f. 95) gives only a short account of the horse, as does the 1509 Orosius (sig. q3); Royal 16, f. 81 (for example) supplies brief details as an alternative explanation for the fall of Troy. The second redaction (e.g. Stowe, ff. 201^b sq.) gives a quite detailed account, as does Royal 20 (ff. 167^b sq.) with a fine sequence of miniatures.

> Le cheual de bois fu parfait,
> Mais tant l'orent grant & haut fait
> Que le mur couuint de la porte
> Rompre, pour celle offrande torte
> Mettre ens. . . .   (*Mutacion*, MCG, f. 139)

116/1 Usually described as a 'cheual de fust' (*Hist. anc.*, Add., f. 91^b) but appears also as a 'cheual de cuyure' (Add. 9785, f. 198) and a 'cheual d'arain' (*Histoire de la destruction de Troie* (Geneva, *c.* 1481), f. 55^b). Columnis (Strassburg, 1486, sig. m5) has 'magnum equum ereum' and Lydgate's *Troy Book* (iv. 6052) 'a stede . . . of coper & of bras'.

116/4–5 See my note in *Revisions and Dedications*, pp. 267–8.

116/8–10 A wise man = *Dicts*, 280/17–19. Compare *CdV* (M 771, f. 26): 'Salomon dit que l'on doit doubter son ennemy pour sa mauuaise subtilite et pour son engin; et se ton ennemy charnel est saige, doubte le pour sa subtilite, et s'il est foul pour sa mauuaistie.'

116/13–17 Hibernia (Ecclesia a) cites this from Augustinus, *De fide ad Petrum*, § 44 (Migne, xl. 768).

116/16 le giron de l'eglise (Laud, f. 90; still a proper form for 'the bosom of the Church'). Wyer (sig. U2) renders this as 'the circuite of the churche', while Bab. (p. 141) translates the phrase as 'þe werkyng of þe chyrche'.

116/17–18 Ps. xxi. 26.

XCVII

116/20–3
> Ne cuides auoir seur chastel,
> Car Ylion, le fort chastel,
> Fu pris & ars; aussi fu Thune.
> Tout est entre les mains fortune.   (Laud, f. 90)

Warner suggested (p. 110, n. 3) that Thune was 'perhaps a corruption for Thyre or Tyre', but all French texts have the rhyme *Thune:fortune*. The siege of Tyre is, however, related in the *Hist. anc.* (Add. f. 145; compare D. J. A. Ross, 'The History of Macedon in the "Histoire ancienne jusqu'à César" ', *Classica et Mediaevalia*, xxiv (1963), 191–2). Name omitted by Bab. (p. 141), who apparently read it as Troye.

117/2–3 Ptolemy = *Dicts*, 226/29–30 and 227/31–3.

117/8–13 Hieronymus, *Epistola CXVIII ad Julianum* (Migne, xxii. 965). Compare *Speculum Christiani* (224.29–31): 'Ieronimus. It is ryght harde, 3e impossible, that thou ioye here in this worlde and that thou regne wyth Criste, that thou fille here thi wombe and ther thi mynde, and that thou appere oueral, in both places, gloryos and ioyful.' A very similar rendering is in Earl Rivers's translation of the *Cordiale* (Westminster, Caxton, 1479, Part IV, chap. 3): 'Seint Jherom saith, in a pistle þat he sent vnto Julyan, how it was a greet difficulte, and a thing as impossible, a man to vse & haue the welthe and playsier of this world pure [for "here"] & also of that to come, and þat the filling of his bely here shulde fede his sowle, & that he shulde, from delites and playsirs here, go to delites & playsirs there, and þat he shulde appere glorified in bothe worldes.' The quotation also appears (in brief) in Caxton's own translation of the *Doctrinal of Sapience* (Westminster, 1489, sig. A7ᵇ).

117/14–16 Apoc. xviii. 7.

XCVIII

117/18 The fable of Circe is in *Ovide*, xiv. 2355–2562; cf. Campbell, pp. 104/5. It is also told in Christine's *Mutacion* (ll. 1043–54) and in her *Cité* (Harley 4431, f. 312ᵇ), as well as in the *Book callid Caton* (Westminster, Caxton, 1483, sig. h8ᵇ). Compare the *M.E. De claris mulieribus* (ll. 1222 sq.) and Ward and Herbert, *Catalogue of Romances*, iii. 112, 166, and 176.

118/2–3   . . . puis nous bailla boivre
                La poison, qui tel force avoit
                Que nulz homs morteulz n'en bevoit
                Que truie ou pors ne devenist.   (*Ovide*, xiv. 2448–51)

118/4–6 This comparison is wanting in Bab. (p. 142).

118/6 The variant 'voydenes' of M seems to be an unsatisfactory attempt to find a better equivalent for the French 'vaguete', which Godefroy defines as 'inconstance dans les sentiments' and cites Christine's use of it elsewhere.

118/11–12 Aristotle = *Dicts*, 166/22–4 and 167/26–7.

118/15–19 Gregorius, *Moralia*, xv. vi (Migne, lxxv. 1084). *CdV* (M 771, f. 29; similarly Telin, f. 117ᵇ) has: 'Saint Gregoire blasme trop la vaine gloire des ypocrites, et dit que leur vie n'est sinon vne vision fantasmatique qui monstre par dehors vng ymaige qui n'est pas dedans. Jhesucrist, parlant en l'euangile, des ypocrites dit: Ve vobis ypocrite [etc.]' (same Bible quotation as in *Othéa*).

118/20–2 Matth. xxiii. 27, omitted by Scrope and Laud (f. 91). Cited here from Harley (f. 140, with 'qui' for 'quia'; thus in other French texts, Wyer, and Bab.).

XCIX

118/24 See the notes to Chapter XVII. The first line reads: 'Tu ne dois belles raisons tendre' (Laud, f. 91). Wyer (sig. U5) has 'parables' for Scrope's 'reson(s)'.

118/29 For the sowing of the 'ble cuit' by the 'puissans [*sic*] du pays', see Vérard's *Ovide* (sig. f2), with cut on sig. f1^b.

118/30–119/2 *Dicts*, 34/14, suggests that it is foolish to teach a fool.

119/2–4 Aristotle = *Dicts*, 166/29–31 and 167/35–7.

119/9–14 Bernardus Claraevallensis, *Tractatus de gradibus humilitatis*, cap. vi (Migne, clxxxii, 951–2). The omission noted by Warner (p. 113, n. 2) is peculiar to L. Bab. (p. 144) does not give the title of St. Bernard's treatise.

119/16 I Cor. xiv. 38.

C

119/23 This story probably comes from Jacobus de Voragine, *Legenda aurea* (ed. Th. Graesse (Dresden and Leipzig, 1846), p. 44; cf. Warner, p. 113, n. 5). So, of course, in Caxton's translation (Westminster, 1483, f. 5). without mention of a mountain; similarly Telin (f. 52), who apparently also used Voragine's account, as did the *Speculum humanae salvationis* (facs. ed. by J. Ph. Berjeau (London, 1861), f. 22 and fig. 32). For date of composition of this work (perhaps 1324) and for the possible author (? Ludolphus de Saxonia), see Paul Perdrizet, *Étude sur le Speculum humanae salvationis* (Paris, 1908); for the Sibyl, cf. pp. 60–3, giving numerous other examples of the literary and artistic occurrence of this legend. See further Lutz and Perdrizet (cap. viii, 85–98, and extensive comment, i. 192–4). Additional information on Augustus and the Sibylla Tiburtina is set forth in the *Lexikon für Theologie und Kirche* (Freiburg, 1957–64), ix. 727. The Sibyls are described (as 'Propheciens de Jhesucrist') in *Ovide*, xiv. 1067 sq. and in the *Cyte of Ladyes* (Bk. ii, chaps. 1–3). Abelard (*Epistola VII*; Migne, clxxviii. 247), citing Virgil, states that it was the Cumaean Sibyl that foretold the coming of Christ.

119/24–6 Thenne was so grete peas in therthe that alle the world was obeyssaunt to hym, and therfore our Lorde wold be born in that tyme, that it shold be known that he brought peas fro heuen (Caxton, *Legenda aurea*, f. 4^b; compare Orosius, *Historiarum adversum paganos libri* (*Corp. scrip. eccl. lat.*, *v*; Vienna, 1882), vi. 22, § 5).

120/1c–12 Hermes = *Dicts*, 106/18–20 and 107/20–2 (but under

Socrates). Compare Campbell, p. 181. The variant 'of a woman' is not found in the other texts and was probably added to M because of the dedication of this version to a lady. See Tilley W 670 and C 690.

120/17–24 Hugo de S. Victore, *Didascalicon*, III. xiv (Migne, clxxvi. 774; ed. Charles H. Buttimer (Washington, 1939), p. 62). Buttimer prints: 'indifferenter ab omnibus quod sibi deesse videt quaerit'. Christine (Pigouchet, sig. g6ᵇ) has: 'il quiert indifferenment par tout & tout ce que il voyt dont il a deffaulte'.

120/25–6 Eccli. iii. 31.

INDEX OF BIBLICAL QUOTATIONS

WRONGLY CITED IN THE *OTHEA*

IX	Scrope has 'secundi Esdre' for III
XXXIX	from Apoc. xiii. 10; attributed to Luc. xiii
LIII	from Prov. xxiv. 6; garbled version
LXXXVIII	from I Thess. v. 19; Scrope has 'Ad Hebreos xj' (Fr., Harley 4431, f. 135[b], has 'xij').

INDEX OF PATRISTIC (AND OTHER RELIGIOUS) QUOTATIONS

GLOSSARY

This Glossary is a selective list rather than a complete record of the words and forms found in the *Othea*, the reader's working knowledge of Middle English being presumed. It seems worth noting, however, that Scrope had command of a very extensive vocabulary; over 2,025 separate words (excluding the usual particles, familiar pronouns, and the like) appear in this work. Since it is a relatively late text, the meanings frequently correspond closely to those of our own day. These have been but sparingly recorded, though words judged not to be immediately intelligible have been included. Inflexional forms of a few select words have been cited, so that readers concerned with grammar may have ready access to them. Unusual or particularly noteworthy idiomatic phrases are included, though not all those phrases have been recorded that were obviously familiar and common-place then, and are so now.

The arrangement is alphabetical. Normally only a single example is given. The abbreviations used are those found in *OED*. Asterisks are provided for reasons set forth in the Introduction (p. xxxi), and a superior 'v' indicates that the word will be found among the variants. It should be pointed out that initial **i**, when representing **j**, follows the normal **i**; internal **y** (= **i**) is treated as **i**, and **u** (= v) as **v**; similarly initial **v** (denoting **u**) is alphabetized under **u**. Initial **y** is here retained as the last letter, since it seemed pointless to scatter the **y**- words under **e**, **g**, **h**, **i**, and **y**.

a *v.* (a worn-down form of **have**) 15/19, 39/4, 97/16, 117/26.

abatyng *pr. p.* diminishing 121/11.

abaundon *v.* surrender 18/6; **abaundoned** *ppl. a.* given to 18/3 (see also **habandoned** and 36/17 n).

abbey *n.* nunnery 87/8.

abesse *v.* degrade 78/29.

abhominable *adj.* repulsive 32/8.

abide *pr. 3 s. subj.* should remain 29/10; **abidith** *ind.* 21/11; **abide** *inf.* 32/7; **abood** *pt. 3 s.* 60/12; **abiden** *pp.* 105/10; **abiding** *ppl. a.* patient 12/15.

absence *n.* separation 49/25.

abstinence *n.* self-denial 33/20, 66/7.

abusion *n.* wicked practice 47/32.

accorde *n.* agreement 50/2.

accorde *imp.* agree 33/2; **accordid** *pp.* 55/19 (*ppl. a.* 58/7); **according** *ppl. a.* harmonious 15/8 (possibly *a* [*indef. art.*] + *cording*; see *MED* s.v. **Cordinge**).

accusacions *n. pl.* indictments 54/27.

accusid *pt. 3 s.* indicted 69/17; **pp.* disclosed 49/19 (first ex. *MED* this sense).

acomen *pp.* reached 47/14.

acte *n.* deed 76/2; **actis** *of armis* deeds of arms 121/5.

actijf *adj.* worldly (Eccl.) 92/19.

addynge *pr. p.* joining 32/21.

admonestith *pr. 3 s.* exhorts 108/1.

aduersarie *n.* opponent 8/3, 81/5.

aduersite *n.* misfortune 12/24, 26/20.

affeccion *n.* love of noble deeds 121/14; *pl.* emotions 70/13.

affliccions *n. pl.* miseries 26/21.

affraide *pt. 3 s.* frightened 39/6; *ppl. a.* alarmed 101/5 ('afflict', Laud).

afore *adv.* before 31/23; above 40/26; ahead 85/27.

afore *prep.* rather than 5/33; into the presence of 13/21; ~ *er* before 77/6.

aftir *prep.* according to 6/32; ~ **that** *conj.* according as 13/22.

age, aage *n.* phr.: *of* ~ old 49/15; *yong* ~ youth 113/1; **agys** *pl.* 121/16 (see also **first age**).

aȝens *prep.* in respect to 53/22; against 54/26.

agid *ppl. a.* old 97/25, 110/9.

agre *v.* consent 106/3; *refl.* give assent 98/17.

agreable *adj.* pleasant 15/27; acceptable 36/2.

a-gree *adv.* favourably, in a friendly manner 119/19.

ayre *n.* air 81/16; **eire** 5/20.

alchiones *n. pl.* halcyons (species of kingfisher) 96/30.

a-legge *simple inf.* (or *imp.*) cite 11/26 (see note).

algatis *adv.* in any case 79/25.

all and some *phr.*: entirely 3/13 (cf. **hooll**).

allegorie *n.* spiritual interpretation 9/27; *pl.* 123/30.

aloone *adj.* alone 50/6; **al-oonly** *adv.* by itself (himself) 44/27-8.

alowed *pp.* praised 26/11, 118/12.

amende *v.* rectify 8/20.

amendis *n. pl.* reparations 52/24, 55/11.

amyable *adj.* friendly 17/1.

amorous *adj.* amorous 18/2; enamoured 27/5.

anamly *adv.* namely 6/23ᵛ.

angil *n.* angel 70/7; **aungelis** *pl.* 106/32.

anguishous *adj.* apprehensive 96/22.

appere *v.* come into view 4/16;

aperid *pt. 3 s.* 120/4; **apperid** *pt. 3 pl.* 109/19.

appese *v.* placate 10/1.

appetite *n.* inclination 3/29.

*****applique** *v.* apply (first ex. *MED*) 7/26; **appliking** *pr. p.* 27/14.

*****apte** *adj.* skilled, qualified 92/10 (first ex. *MED*).

aqueinte *inf. refl.* become acquainted 103/2; **aqueynted** *pt. 3 s. refl.* 99/7; *phr.*: *was* ~ *with* 56/32.

araieth *pr. 3 s.* adorns 5/36; **araide** *pp.* 7/10 (arayed 22/30).

argumentis *n. pl.* reasonings 119/4.

arived *pt. 3 s.* reached (a place) 31/30; *pp. were* ~ 48/14.

arme *n. phr.: ~ of the* see estuary 54/3; **armys** *pl.* human arms 54/16.

armee, armye *n.* military force 55/9, 82/14.

armys *n. pl.* weapons 111/13 (*MED* cites only pl. as distinct from *arm*).

armure *n.* armour 23/20, 87/18.

arowe, arwe *n.* arrow 110/22, 64/11.

arrant (*theef*) *adj.* (or *n.* ?) roving robber, outlaw 53/7 (see also **errant**).

arrogance *n.* haughtiness 27/18; **arrogansis** *pl.* 83/2.

articule *n.* statement in Apostles' Creed 36/4.

ashamed *pp.* full of shame 107/23.

asked *pp.* asked for 55/2.

a-slepe *adv.* asleep 42/8.

a-sondir *adv.* to pieces 73/13.

aspie *inf.* search out 70/9; **aspiyng** *vbl. n.* action of spying 93/24.

assaied *pp.* tested 103/6.

assaile *pr. 3 s. subj.* attacks 80/12; **assailid** *pp.* 71/6.

assautes *n. pl.* temptations 8/2.

assay *n.* experience 5/28.

asschis *n. pl.* ashes 27/18.

asse *n.* ass 37/25.

assemble *imp.* gather 62/22; *pr. 2 s. subj. refl.* 18/21 ('t'assembles', Laud).

assembles *n. pl.* meetings 50/1.

assistid (*to*) *pp.* helped towards 107/1.

assotte *inf. refl.* become infatuated 35/3; **assottith** *pr. 3 pl.* besot 81/20; ~ *in* 112/11; ~ *of* 34/31; ~ *on* 35/3; ~ *vpon* 113/5.

***assottid** (*of himself*) *ppl. a.* infatuated with oneself 27/5 (first ex. *MED* this const.).

attende *v.* pay heed to 108/25.

***auctorised** *pp.* given validity 39/21, 122/12 (first ex. this sense *MED*).

auctorite *n.* doctrine 39/13; right to rule 52/3; **auctoritees** *n. pl.* authoritative statements 7/15.

auctours *n. pl.* writers 16/29.

aument *inf.* increase 3/26.

auncient *adj.* aged 76/14; ~ *age* old age 122/1–2.

availe *n.* benefit 79/3.

availe *v. intr.* prosper 25/9; *trans.* benefit 90/15.

auante *imp. refl.* boast 78/12.

avaunce *v. refl.* move forward 13/7; **avaunced** *pp.* raised in rank 29/24; successful 64/30.

auenterous *adj.* doubtful 8/31.

aventure *n.* jeopardy 54/18; **aventuris** *pl.* 121/24; phr.: *at* ~ on a quest 58/4; outcome 96/25; *do* ~ put oneself in danger 57/20.

auenture *inf. refl.* venture to go 11/1.

avice *n.* opinion 107/19.

avise *v.* counsel 107/24; *imp. refl.* consider 48/7.

avisement *n.* forethought 18/22.

avision *n.* prophetic dream 82/29.

auoutrie *n.* adultery 52/32.

avowed *pp.* made a vow 115/28.

awayte (*lay in*) *n.* ambush, lay in 104/23.

a-werke *adv.* phr.: *sette . . .* ~ use 23/29 ('mettre en œuure', Fr).

bachelere *n.* youth 27/2.

bad see **biddith.**

badly *adv.* improperly 55/5.

bakbityngis *n. pl.* slanders 54/27.

bake *n.* back 62/11.

balaunce *n.* phr.: *right* ~ proper deliberation 9/7; *grete* ~ jeopardy 53/30.

banke-side *n.* coast of the sea 54/5–6.

bapteme *n.* baptism 116/15.

bare see **bere.**

bare-fote *adj.* barefoot 85/13.

***barke** *n. fig.* superficial part 100/25 (last ex. *MED*).

barre *n.* metal bar 65/23.

bataile *n.* armed conflict 4/33; **bataillis** *pl.* battalions 92/9.

batailled *pt. 3 s.* fought for a cause 22/5.

be *prep.* by 5/24, 5/28, 6/26, 9/9 (*passim*).

be *inf.* 7/3; **am** *pr. 1 s.* 3/16; **arte** *2 s.* 13/8; **is** *2 & 3 s. & 3 pl.* 4/32, 3/10, 98/23; **be** *1, 2 & 3 pl.* 50/32, 121/29, 7/11; **be** *pr. subj. 2 & 3 s. & 3 pl.* 11/15, 8/31, 82/10; **was** *pt. 3 s. & pl.* 4/5, 103/20 (**were** 6/24); **were** *pt. subj. 1 & 3 s.* 3/23, 9/11; **be** *imp.* 3/2; **being** *pr. p.* 7/27; **ben** *pp.* 6/21; phr.: ~ *evill goon* fared badly 39/4; **were** *nede for* would be necessary 103/27.

beaute *n.* spiritual goodness 8/4; physical attractiveness 27/3.

become, becam *pt. 3 s.* became 40/2, 50/23, 40/27^v.

begynner *n.* promoter 92/3.

begynnyng *n.* creation 45/22; start 112/17.

behauynge *vbl. n.* behaviour 22/28; *pr. p. refl.* comporting himself 56/10–11.

beholde *v.* observe 10/11; **biholdiþ** *pr. 3 s.* 70/10; **bihelde** *pt. 3 s.* 68/2; **biholding** *pr. p.* 68/22; **beholden** *pp.* 27/6.

behoueli *adj.* suitable 7/22, 23/1.

behoueth *pr. 3 s.* properly belongs 10/8.

beleuers *n. pl.* faithful Christians 70/9.

beli *n.* stomach 33/20.

***bellue** *n.* sea monster, whale 14/27, 15/17 (last ex. *MED*; OED 1474–1572).

benefete *n.* profit 47/27; **beneficis** *pl.* 67/14.

benygne *adj.* gracious 3/12, 4/8.

bere *inf.* carry 38/11; **berith** *pr. 3 s.*

57/21; **we bere** *pr. 1 pl.* 85/1;
berith (*wittenes*) *pr. 3 pl.* testify
4/7; **bare** *pt. 3 s.* 15/14, gave birth
to 31/27; **borne** *pp.* 15/25; ~
thorugh stabbed 113/30.

berere *n.* one who speaks gossip
64/21.

beres *n. pl.* bears 11/8.

besi *adj.* useful 5/19; occupied
65/29; demanding attention 108/9;
bisily *adv.* 96/18.

beste *n.* beast 50/12; **bestis** *pl.*
46/13.

betokenyth *pr. 3 s.* presages 106/19.

be-traye *inf.* dupe 103/24; **be-
traieth** *pr. 3 pl.* lead astray, ruin
98/30.

beuteuous *adj.* handsome 100/2
(*MED* c. 1438).

bewaylid *pt. 3 s.* grieved over
56/8.

bi- see also **be-**.

biddith *pr. 3 s.* suggests 95/4; **bad**
pt. 3 s. requested (something from
some one) 119/30.

bie *inf.* buy 59/27; **bye** *imp.* 59/30;
bouȝt *pt. 3 s.* 70/23.

birde see **brid**.

birneth see **brenne**.

bisines *n.* business, work 61/24;
effort 96/16; exertion 82/24; **be-
synessis** *pl.* efforts, anxieties
44/26.

***bitingis** *n. pl. fig.* bitings, afflictions
108/29 (first ex. *MED*; 'morsures',
Laud).

bitith *pr. 3 s.* bites, eats into 109/9;
biten *wiþ pp.* bitten by 85/16.

blame *inf. intr.* complain about
34/5; *be gretli to* ~ be greatly at
fault 43/31.

blaspheme *n.* slander 48/2.

blewe *pt. 3 s.* blew (played on a flute)
42/7.

blody *adj.* bloodstained 50/11.

***bocche** *n.* camel's hump 62/10
(last ex. *MED*).

bodily *adj.* physical 112/7.

boistous *adj.* powerful, fierce 48/16.

bolnyngis *vbl. n. pl.* puffings up
(with arrogance) 83/2.

bonde *adj.* enslaved 81/26.

bord *n.* table (dining) 74/8.

bore *n.* boar 79/17; **boores** *pl.*
11/8.

bothom *n.* bottom 64/9.

botirflie *n.* (butterfly), moth 115/13.

bounte *n.* goodness 10/12, 26/11;
praise, honour 53/16; knightly
prowess 78/29; **bounteis** *pl.*
perfect goodnesses 37/16.

bowe *inf.* be submissive 104/7.

***braynge** *vbl. n.* croaking 32/10
(first ex. *MED* 1440).

breed *n.* bread 4/23.

breke *inf.* break, shatter, crush
48/27; **brekith** *pr. 3 s.* 21/6;
brak *pt. 3 s.* 47/11; **broken** *pp.*
12/23.

brenne *inf.* burn 69/2; **brenneth** *pr.
3 s.* 115/14 (**birneth** L); **brent** *pt.
3 s. & pl.* 51/22, 116/5; **brennyng**
ppl. a. 70/11.

brennynge *vbl. n.* being burnt
109/3.

briboure *n.* impostor 38/23.

brid, birde *n.* bird 84/30, 115/15;
briddis *pl.* 81/16.

bridell *n.* bridle 64/9.

bright *adj.* shining 87/19.

brightnes *n.* light 49/27; brilliance
(? reflection) 68/5.

bringer *n.* bearer 60/16.

brithir see **brothir**.

broileþ *pr. 3 s.* burns 108/4; **broiled**
pp. burnt 76/30.

brokith *pr. 3 s.* retains, digests
63/16.

bronde *n.* firebrand, torch 34/13.

***broth** *n.* water in which frogs or
toads have been 32/7; **brothis** *pl.*
31/21 (only ex. *MED*).

brothir *n.* brother 58/11; **brithir,
breþir** *pl.* 58/16, 77/20.

brought, (*hard*) *pp.* brought (to
nought) 89/22.

busch *n.* thicket 50/8; **busschis** *pl.*
84/6.

busschementis *n. pl.* troops lying
in ambush 71/5.

caas *n.* phr.: *in* ~ in the event 52/3;
in liche ~ in similar circumstances
30/3.

calle v. appeal 45/2; ~ *ayen* recall 76/27.

camell n. camel 62/10.

can see **conne.**

cappiteyne, capteyn n. military leader 57/17; *fig.* chief 115/7.

carles n. pl. knaves 32/2.

caste *inf.* excrete 27/22; **castith** *pr. 3 s.* vomits 63/15; **keste** *pt. 3 s.* threw 28/21, 87/19 (**caste** *refl.* 54/15); **caste** *pp.* 32/12.

casting *vbl. n.* throwing (a bar) 65/22.

cause see **maner.**

*****certainte** n. assurance 49/9 (first ex. this sense *MED c.* 1450).

certeyne n. assurance 90/31; knowledge (?) 110/8; *phr.: in* ~ in certainty 50/30.

certeyne *adv.* surely 38/31.

cesse v. cease 8/20; **sece** *inf.* 112/25; **cecith, seceth** *pr. 3 s.* 27/22, 70/8; **cecid** *pt. 3 pl.* 32/8; *pr. 3 s. subj.* yielded (?) 72/22; **cessing** *pr. p.* 49/4.

ceteseyns, citesyns n. pl. citizens 5/4, 52/14.

chaf n. *fig.* something evil 108/3.

chaiere n. *phr.: in* ~ in the office of a professor 6/2.

chambirs n. pl. *phr.: schette hire in* ~ confined her to quarters 49/20–1.

champions n. pl. warriors 25/13.

chapelet n. wreath 106/10.

charge n. burden 84/28.

chargid *pp.* weighed down, experienced (?) 97/26.

charmys n. pl. magic spells 51/19.

chaufed *pp.* heated 83/22.

*****chaunge** n. *phr.: in a* ~ in exchange 98/2 (this phrase not in *MED*).

*****chaungeabilnes** n. inconstancy 116/29–30 (first ex. *MED*).

chaungeable *adj.* unstable 20/20.

chef bailie n. chief bailiff 13/21.

cheyne n. chain 69/19.

chepe n. sheep 66/21ᵛ.

chese *inf.* choose 46/13, 92/17.

cheualerous, chevalroures n. chivalry 8/30, 8/30ᵛ.

cheuentayne n. chieftain 92/9.

chide *inf.* scold 32/3.

chidynge *vbl. n.* scolding, quarrelling 32/9.

childe n. shield 68/29ᵛ.

childer n. pl. two children 27/29; several children 52/15.

chippe n. ship 64/9ᵛ.

circumspeccion n. careful consideration 108/5.

clamoures n. pl. complainings 34/9.

clave *pt. 3 s.* split 73/12.

clennes n. sinlessness 107/4.

clyme v. climb 6/3, 41/19.

cloos n. close (monastic) 86/29.

cloos *ppl. a.* concealed 110/26 (**cloosed** *pp.* 61/3).

clotheth *pr. 3 s.* envelopes 72/26.

cofre n. treasure chest 60/33.

coloure n. disguise 47/31.

come v. 42/1; **cometh** *pr. 3 s.* 43/9; **comyth** *pr. 3 pl.* 58/24; **come** *pr. 3 s. subj.* 83/15; *pt. 3 s.* 43/6 (**came** 60/11); **come** *pt. 3 pl.* 99/3; **comyng** *pr. p.* 55/32; **comyn** *pp.* 27/19 (**comen** 71/3).

*****commytteþ** *pr. 3 s.* appraises (?) 70/13 (cf. *MED* 5ᵇ only ex.; 'coniecture', Laud & Harley; 'coniectureth or gessyth', Wyer); **commyttid** *pp.* appointed to office 13/29.

communes n. pl. common people 32/11.

*****communiall** *adj.* generous 26/22 (only ex. *MED*:, cf. Godefroy II, 199 s.v. 'communicaire'; thus Laud & Harley).

*****communyon of seintes** n. fellowship of the faithful 44/8 (first ex. this sense *MED*).

comon womman n. prostitute 41/5.

comparison n. *phr.: be of no* ~ *to* be unequal to 8/9.

complexion n. constitution 17/1.

compunccioun n. contrition, repentance 69/5.

conceytys n. pl. ideas, opinions 122/14, 123/21.

conceyved *pt. 3 s.* became pregnant with 57/1; **conceived** *pp.* made pregnant 31/28.

conclucion *n.* successful outcome 114/28.

conclude *inf.* be concluded 66/8.

concupiscence *n.* carnal desire 10/1, 113/15.

condicioned *ppl. a.* adjusted, accustomed 92/7; phr.: *wel* ~ well tempered 107/20.

condites *n. pl.* ducts (of the body) 27/22.

*conditoures *n. s. fem.* leader 8/15ᵛ (in L, only ex. *MED*); *n. pl.* guides 8/15 (first use *MED* 1460).

confoundid *pt. 3 s.* harassed 82/21.

conne *inf.* know (how to) 119/13; can *pr. 1 s.* 4/2; *pr. 3 s.* 120/24; couthe *pt. 3 s.* 23/28 (coude 92/4).

connyng *vbl. n.* wisdom, knowledge 3/28, 4/25, 5/28.

connynge *adj.* wise 43/29; connyngist *adj. superl.* 72/7.

*conquest *n.* struggle, effort to conquer 66/22 (first ex. this sense *MED*).

conseruacyon *n.* maintenance 123/11.

consideracion *n.* contemplation 61/12.

constable *n.* chief military officer 92/11 (connestable 92/11ᵛ).

constreined *pp.* oppressed 50/2; moved 54/9.

contemplacion *n.* religious meditation 41/20, 92/23.

contemplatijf *adj.* devout 92/18.

continuance (*of tyme*) *n.* duration 121/3.

contrarious *adj.* adverse 8/20.

contrariousnesses *n. pl.* adversities 11/23.

contreuour *n.* prevaricator 60/26.

conveid *pp.* accompanied 4/5; conducted, guided 8/1.

conveyng *vbl. n.* conduct 48/19.

conuersant *adj.* on familiar terms 17/6.

corage *n.* inclination 3/33; disposition 16/10; spirit 30/1; heart 72/16.

cordith *pr. 3 s. refl.* reconciles 101/7

corn *n.* grain 36/8; cornys *pl.* 36/15.

corners *n. pl.* remote regions 13/5.

correccion *n.* phr.: *be vndir* ~ be under discipline, punishment 50/32, 95/26.

correcter, correctoure *n.* one who rebukes 13/18, 40/4.

corrumpe *v.* corrupt spiritually 70/9; corrumpith *pr. 3 s.* ruins, rots 29/8; corrumped *pt. 3 s.* corrupted by bribery 28/4.

corrupcion *n.* moral disintegration 80/6, 69/1ᵛ.

cosin *n.* kinsman 47/2; phr.: ~ germayn *fig.* first cousin, relative 9/2.

cours *n.* way 23/15; flow of water 81/16.

couthe see conne.

covenaunte *n.* agreement 88/24.

couered *pp.* covered (with armour) 110/24.

*couertli *adv.* ambiguously, not plainly 12/4 (first ex. this sense *MED*).

couerture *n.* concealment 19/27 ('couuerture', Laud); *vnder (the)* ~ *of poetis (fable)* in the manner of poets (fable) 13/19–20, 18/29–30 (first ex. these phrases *MED*).

crafte *n.* art 45/11 (see note); craftis *pl.* handicrafts 24/28.

*crased *pp.* crushed in spirit 12/27 (this sense not in *MED*); perforated 49/27 (first ex. *MED*).

crevice *n.* crack 49/29; fissure of a rock 73/10.

crommes *n. pl.* crumbs 4/19.

crouned *pp.* phr.: ~ *in blis* 'crowned in glorye' (Wyer) 8/10.

cruel *adj.* taking pleasure in giving pain 53/11; inhuman 16/10 ('cruel' Laud f. 34ᵇ).

cuirboille *n.* cuir-bouilli, boiled leather 23/27.

curteys *adj.* courteous 83/17; curtesie *n.* 118/1.

custom *n.* habit, conduct 3/7.

dampnacion *n.* damnation 96/1.

dampned *pp.* damned 59/26, 75/26.

damysell *n.* young girl 49/17.

darte *n.* dart, metal-pointed missile 93/4; Cupid's dart 49/16; **dartes** *pl. fig.* spears 109/1.

daungere *n.* reluctance 100/28.

debate *n.* dispute 55/15; phr.: *to make* ~ 32/7; [*be*] *at* ~ 58/16.

debatour *n.* one who stirs up fights 74/25.

debonayre *adj.* humble 58/34.

deceite *n.* stratagem, trick 76/18; **deceytis** *pl.* 31/3.

deceyuable *adj.* unreliable, deceptive 8/6, 61/32.

deceyved (*wiþ*) *pp.* deceived (by) 80/25.

decre *n.* (see note to 46/26).

deede *n.* action 55/9; **deedis** *of armes pl.* feats of arms 4/34.

deede *n.* (the dead) 42/27; *adj.* 26/1.

deedid *pp.* deadened 26/10 (so *MED*; 'amortie', Laud).

deedli *adj.* mortal 25/11; ~ *aduersarie* mortal foe 8/3.

defaute *n.* fault 29/1; lack 111/17ᵛ; **defautis** *pl.* sins 53/1.

*defauty *adj.* faulty 38/16 (first ex. this sense *MED* 1449).

defence *n.* prohibition 53/21; warding off 88/31; defence 108/19.

defendant *n.* phr.: *in his body* ~ defender of himself 52/4–5.

defende *pr. 1 s.* forbid 27/30; **defendith** *pr. 3 s.* 30/12; **defended** *pp.* forbidden 27/9.

defoule *imp. refl.* pollute 31/21.

degre *n.* social rank 36/10; **degrees** *pl.* stages of development 103/7.

degree *n.* decree (?) 18/13.

*delaiynge *ppl. a.* postponing 67/8 (not as *adj.* in *MED*).

dele *n.* part 9/6; amount, value 33/27.

delectacions *n. pl.* pleasures 61/5.

deliberacion *n.* careful consideration 11/22, 82/25.

delicious *adj.* delightful to drink 118/2 (so as *adv.* **deliciously** in M).

delitable *adj.* delightful, pleasing 100/23.

delite *n.* pleasure 54/18.

delite *inf. refl.* take pleasure in 45/18; *imp. refl.* 40/19; **deliteth** (*in*) *pr. 3 s.* delights in 3/5; **delited** *pt. 3 s. refl.* 53/11.

delyuered *pt. 3 s.* rescued 14/27 (*pp.* 109/3;) ~ *to pp.* bestowed upon 24/6, restored to 85/30.

deme *n.* judgement 64/22ᵛ.

*demene *n.* bearing, behaviour 64/22 (first ex. *MED c.* 1450).

demene *v. refl.* behave 90/22.

demurely *adv.* quietly 61/7.

denying *vbl. n.* refusal 99/30; *pr. p.* refusing 105/14.

departe *v.* go away 45/17; **departith** *pr. 3 s.* drives away 110/27; **departid** *pt. 3 s.* separated 58/6; *pp.* allotted 90/7.

departing *vbl. n.* separation 96/20.

derke *adj.* obscure, unclear 95/10.

desertes *n. pl.* good deeds 15/24.

desirous *adj.* eager 3/22.

despisith *pr. 3 s.* scorns (?) (see 72/25 and variant).

despite *n.* contempt 38/7.

*despite *inf.* belittle 10/3 (first ex. *MED*); **despiteth** *pr. 3 s.* 16/9, despises 54/30; **despited** *pp.* despised 8/21; **dispite** *imp.* 107/9.

destenye *n.* fate, that which will come about 88/21.

destroied *pt. 3 pl.* overthrew 75/16.

determyned *pt. 3 s.* ended 113/12 ('*soit terminee*', Fr).

deuice *n.* heraldic design 106/17.

*deuocion *n.* devout impulse 96/14 (first ex. this sense *OED* 1489; not in *MED* ?), reverence 44/7, 44/24.

deuoured *pp.* eaten 15/19; phr.: *be* ~ *with* be eaten by 46/13, 50/14 (use of 'with' not in *MED*).

dewe *n.* dew; phr.: ~ *of grace fig.* blessing 67/18.

dewe *adj.* proper, due 9/24 (**dwe** 101/24).

dictis *n. pl.* dicts, sayings 123/21.

dide *pt. 3 s.* died 17/17 (**dyed**, **dyyed** 17/17ᵛ; **diede** 85/17); **deying** *pr. p.* 50/17.

diffence *n.* act of defence 11/15.

difference *n.* phr.: *in* ~ *of* in contrast to 104/10.

di3t *pp.* reared, taught 86/29.

diligence *n.* effort 45/29 (**diligent** *adj.* 94/4; **diligentlye** *adv.* 39/11).

dyner *n.* dinner 74/8 (**dynne** L).

dis- see also **des-**.

discerne *v.* perceive 19/15.

discolourid *ppl. a.* changed in colour 29/26.

disconfited *pp.* vanquished 15/16.

disconfort *v.* dishearten 91/16.

discorde *n.* contention 38/3.

discouered *pp.* revealed 76/9; exposed 103/24; bare, unarmed 110/15.

*discouerte *adj.* unarmed 111/16 (not as *adj.* in *MED*; 'dyscouerte', Wyer).

discute *inf.* discuss 19/17; ***discutith** (*of*) *pr. 3 s.* examines 70/13 (first ex. this const. *MED*).

disealowid *pt. 3 s.* censured, reproved 64/27 (**dissalowed** L).

disherite *v.* disinherit 28/3.

dishoneste *n.* sexual indulgence 35/20.

dishonestli *adv.* dishonourably, shamefully 47/30.

disordenat *adj.* excessive 53/2, 111/21.

disparbelid *pp.* distracted 65/11.

dispendith *pr. 3 s.* spends wastefully 84/16.

displesire *n.* annoyance 30/5.

dispoile *inf.* strip of armour 111/15; **dispoilleth** *pr. 3 s.* pillages 72/25ᵛ; **dispoilid** *pp.* stripped 81/4.

*dispoiling *vbl. n.* stripping off of arms 111/8 (this sense not in *MED*).

disport *n.* pleasure 4/1.

disporte *inf.* entertain 101/21; *intr. for refl.* 101/30; **disportynge** *pr. p.* making merry 85/13 ('esbanoiant', Laud).

*disportefull *adj.* agreeable 59/13 ('aduisant', Fr; cf. Godefroy I, 118; this sense not in *MED*).

disposed *pp.* inclined 54/32.

*dispraise *n.* contempt 27/4 (only ex. in *MED*; 'en despris', Harley).

dispraised *pp.* blamed 4/11.

dispreisinge *vbl. n.* disapproval 34/22; ***diminution** 67/16 (first ex. this sense *MED*).

dispurveide *ppl. a.* unprepared 75/16.

dissalowed see **disealowid**.

dissymilacions *n. pl.* dishonesties 54/28.

dissolucion *n.* dissoluteness 56/31.

distincciones *n. pl.* classifications 100/23.

distourbled *pt. 3 s.*; ~ *þe peas* disturbed the peace 99/10–11 (**distourbid** 10ᵛ).

distres *n.* affliction (?) 70/23 (**distrus** L; 'despris', Laud).

distroccion, destruccion *n.* destruction 48/19, 30/28.

distroubleth *pr. 3 s.* impedes 29/3; prevents 8/3–4.

ditee *n.* treatise 8/13.

diuerse *adj.* disagreeing 21/11; various 24/24; vicious 28/25.

do *inf.* 3/20; **doost** *pr. 2 s.* 79/1; **doith** *3 s.* 54/29 (**doot** 54/29ᵛ); **dooth** *3 pl.* 38/29 (**doo** 59/1); **do** *pr. subj. 2 s.* 79/3; **dede** *pt. 3 s.* 38/32; **dide** *pt. 3 s. & pl.* 12/3, 55/9; **do** *imp.* 78/6; **doynge** *pr. p.* 51/3; **do** *pp.* 75/23 (**doon** 3/18); *phr.*: ~ *amys* done wrong 64/26; ~ *armes* perform feats of arms 11/6; ~ (*hir*) *bisines* earnestly tried 96/16; ~ (*his*) *diligence* seeks 97/6; ~ *harme* hurt 79/26; ~ *of* took off 100/9; ~ (*gret*) *payne* tried hard 112/27; ~ (*hir*) *power* sought earnestly 107/16; ~ *so moche* went so far 46/12; ~ *þingis* perform tasks 82/23; ~ *vntrouth* do something dishonourable 46/14; ~ *velony* offends 54/29; ~ *worshipe* respects 110/6–7.

doctrine *n.* body of precepts 123/31.

doers *n. pl.* phr.: *yvell* ~ wicked people 52/2.

dome *n.* phr.: *day of* ~ Last Judgement 16/1.

dominacion *n.* rule, control 8/22, 72/21.

dongeon *n.* keep, donjon 116/25.

dorst *pt. 3 s.* dared 42/3.

dotid *pp.* bewildered, doting 76/7.

doubilnes *n.* instability 102/11.

douȝtles *adv.* surely 87/2.

doute *n.* fear 42/4; phr.: *in ~* dubious 50/27; *wiþouten ~* surely 107/14.

***doute** *v.* tame, conquer (?) 40/1 (see note).

doute *pr. 1 s.* mistrust 21/17; **doutede** *pt. 3 s.* feared 39/28.

***doutousli** *adv.* ambiguously, uncertainly 18/24 (first ex. *MED*; 'en doubtance', Laud).

drawe *v.* draw 39/17; **druwe** *pt. 3 s.* 28/20 (**drewe** 39/15); **drawe** *dovne pp. + adv.* dragged down (by dogs) 84/9.

drempte *pt. 3 s.* dreamed 58/21.

dresse *v. refl.* apply oneself 5/18, 53/9; **dressid** *pt. 3 s. refl.* proceeded 73/13.

drie *adj.* dry, apathetic 29/25 ('seiche', Laud).

drieth *pr. 3 s.* dries up 67/17.

drynke *inf.* drink 32/5; **dronken** *pp.* 33/9.

drive *v.* 115/10; **drof** *pt. 3 s.* 19/2 (**drwe** L); **driven** *away* *pp. + adv.* 60/14.

dronkenes *n.* drunkenness 33/11.

drounyd *pp.* drowned 32/13; **drowned** *fig.* overwhelmed 33/21.

dulle *adj.* insensible 26/10 (cf. **deedid**).

durable *adj.* permanent 27/12.

dured *pt. 3 s.* lasted 49/24 (**duryd** 54/8); *euer* **duryng** *ppl. a.* not transitory 5/31.

dwellinge place *n. fig.* seat 23/14.

e- see also **y-**.

edificacion *n.* enlightenment 7/26.

***edifice** *n. fig.* structure 71/25 (not in fig. sense in *MED*).

edifie *v.* prosper spiritually 37/2.

eell *n.* eel 64/10.

eese *n.* phr.: *be at ~* rest undisturbed 55/18; **eesi** *adj.* not oppressive 84/28.

effecte *n.* intended result 4/16; result 4/25; phr.: *sette in ~* put into action 107/29.

eire see **ayre**.

***embaundoned** *pp. refl.* devoted yourself 121/24 (first ex. this sense *MED*).

embrace *v. fig.* enfold, surround 70/10.

embuched *pp.* hidden in ambush 80/22.

***empechist** *pr. 2 s.* disparage 94/3 (first ex. this sense *MED*); **empechid** (*wiþ*) *pp.* hindered 97/10.

***emplye** *v.* make use of 99/28 (first ex. this sense *MED*).

emprice *n.* enterprise, martial deed 63/2; **emprises** *pl.* 82/10.

emprideth *pr. 3 s.* makes proud 72/25.

***enamoured** (*on*) *pt. 3 s. refl.* fell in love with 34/23 (only ex. *MED*); *ppl. a.* 100/3.

enchaunte *inf.* bewitch 66/26; **enchaunteth** *pr. 3 s.* 41/27; **enchauntid** *pt. 3 s.* 78/15.

enchauntement *n.* witchcraft 66/22; **enchauntementis** *pl.* magic powers 51/19.

enchaunteresse *n.* sorceress 51/10, 117/24.

enclyned *ppl. a.* yielding 70/14.

encrees *n.* increase by propagation 36/8.

ende *n.* conclusion 12/1; death 45/23; objective 112/2; phr.: *made an ~* died 105/4.

endite *v.* compose 6/7.

enemye, ennemyes *n.* (*pl.*) phr.: *olde ~* the devil 42/24, 70/7; *gostly ~* evil spirits 122/27.

enflamme *v.* incite with lust 70/11.

enforce *pr. 2 s. refl.* strive 65/16; **enforceth** *pr. 3 s. refl.* undertakes 41/12.

***enforcyng** (*in*) *vbl. n.* being compelled into 29/25 (this sense not in *MED*).

enforme *inf.* instruct 123/31; **enformed** (*to*) *pp.* trained 79/29.

engendrith *pr. 3 pl.* bring forth 69/6.

engins *n. pl.* snares 91/18.

enhaunce *v.* exalt 13/6.

enlumyned *ppl. a.* enlightened 6/26.

enorte *v.* exhort 5/14; enortid *pp.* tempted 72/2; urged 72/9.

*enorting *vbl. n.* urging 66/19 (only ex. in *MED*).

enquere *inf.* ask 93/29.

entent *n.* intention 3/27; understanding 18/7; phr.: *to the* ~ for the purpose 8/26, 49/29.

*enterpryse *n.* warlike expedition 63/2ᵛ (entreprises *pl.* 121/23); *pl.* labours (of Hercules) 12/7 (first exs. in *MED*).

entierly *adv.* wholeheartedly 112/14.

entre *n.* opportunity to enter 29/28.

envirouned *pp.* surrounded 83/25, 109/2.

ere *n.* ear 42/8 (eeris *pl.* 63/12).

ere *inf.* plough 36/12; eried *pp.* 36/14.

ere *prep.* before 18/23.

errant *adj.* phr.: ~ *knyghte* knight in quest of adventure 14/29; ~ *theef* outlaw 53/7ᵛ (see also arrant).

erthly *adj.* worldly (?) 102/2 (see note).

eschewe *v.* shun 37/7, 115/12.

escuse *pr. 3 pl. refl.* excuse themselves 119/10 (ascuse L).

especiall *adj.* phr.: *in* ~ chiefly 9/4.

euerlastinge *adj.* continuing 24/11; perpetual 45/31; constant (?) 94/22.

euerychone *pron.* every single one 58/15.

evill *adv.* disastrously 39/4.

evinli *adj.* equal (in rank) 30/16.

examyneth (*of*) *pr. 3 s.* scrutinizes 70/12–13.

*exaunced *pp.* exalted 86/18 ('exaulcee', Laud; first ex.; cf. *MED* s.v. *exhauncen* and *exaucen*).

excedede *pt. 3 s.* surpassed 18/1.

excusacion *n.* excuse 94/26, 119/15.

execucion *n.* phr.: *to put in* ~ perform 100/30.

exempled *ppl. a.* exemplified 122/13, 123/26.

*exhauncid *pp.* granted 17/19; *exhaunsing *vbl. n.* exalting 11/25 ('exaussement', Laud; first ex. *MED* under *exaucen* and *exaucing*; see exaunced).

exilynge *vbl. n.* banishment 28/10.

exortacion *n.* admonition 23/15.

exposicion *n.* explanation 28/24, 42/9.

expositour *n.* interpreter 58/23; *pl.* 95/12.

expounyng *pr. p.* interpreting, expounding 113/14.

expresse *adj.* evident 15/1; *adv.* quickly 98/30.

fable *n.* fiction, legend 12/4, 40/29.

face *n.* appearance 102/2; person 9/9.

*ffadyrhode *n.* step-fatherhood 122/7 (this precise sense not in *MED*).

fayne *adv.* eagerly 69/23.

faireste *superl. adj. as n.* (the) most beautiful 74/11.

fairye *n.* supernatural creature 73/7.

falle *v.* suffer misfortune 69/24; come to pass 6/15; fallith *pr. 3 s.* 20/12; felle *pt. 3 s.* fell down 50/9 (fel happened 69/16).

familiarite *n.* intimacy 99/21.

famyn *n.* famine 97/17.

fantesie *n.* untruth 118/17; *pl.* imaginations 58/24; illusions 116/7.

fardel *n. fig.* bundle 30/9.

fast by *adv. phr.* nearby 50/8.

fauchon *n.* sword, falchion 15/5.

faucon *n.* appearance (?) 22/21 ('faconde', Laud; cf. *MED facioun*).

faute *n.* want, lack 111/17.

fauour *n.* sympathetic regard 25/20.

fawty *adj.* mistaken 38/16ᵛ.

febilnesse *n.* worthlessness 4/11; infirmity 121/11.

fedris *n. pl.* feathers 60/14 (federis 115/16).

feend (*of hell*) *n.* Satan 16/3 (fende 59/27).

feerful *adj.* reverent 19/18; terrifying 28/14; frightened 50/7.

feersly *adv.* savagely 27/29.

feest *n.* banquet 74/11; celebration (?) 101/16; **fest** feast day 44/14.

feynyng *pr. p.* pretending 4/4; **feyned** *ppl. a.* false 5/6.

feint *adj.* false, deceptive 115/27.

feire *adj.* excellent 24/28; beautiful 54/2; *adv.* carefully 65/18.

feithful *adj.* trustworthy 44/7.

fel *see* **falle.**

felauschip *n.* band 32/2; armed band 52/20; comradeship (**feleship**) 99/22.

felauschip *v. refl.* associate 58/30.

felawe *n.* equal 7/5, 14/9; *pl.* companions 38/29.

felde *n.* phr.: *in the* ~ in battle 22/11; **feldes** *of bataile* joustings 31/16.

*****fele** *n.* feeling 6/6 (last ex. *MED* 1400).

fele *inf.* touch 61/10; experience 24/18; enjoy 33/26; **felest** *pr. 2 s.* suffer 95/26; **felith** *pr. 3 s. refl.* regards as 47/19.

felicite *n.* happiness 30/14; pleasure 61/28; prosperity 106/12.

felle *adj.* cruel, savage 11/3.

ferforth *adv.* phr.: *so* ~ *þat* so far that 71/6–7.

*****ferre** *adj.* prolix 30/22 ('prolixe', Laud; this sense not in *MED*); distant 113/6.

ferre *adv.* *fig.* far, profoundly 4/12.

fersnes *n.* ferocity 13/28.

fest *see* **feest.**

*****ficcion** *n.* invention of the mind 57/5 (first ex. *MED c.* 1450).

fighte *inf.* contend 12/5 (**feight** 11/7; **fiʒt** 68/4); **feightith** *pr. 3 s.* 72/24 (**feythyt** 24ᵛ); **faughte** *pt. 3 s.* 12/6; *pl.* 57/33.

fiʒtteris *n. pl.* warriors 82/21.

ffyghtyng *vbl. n.* moral struggle 122/2.

figure *n.* appearance 68/1; parable 15/9.

*****figure** *ppl. a.* disposed 17/1 (only ex. *MED*).

file *v. refl.* befoul 32/14ᵛ.

filþe *n.* sinfulness 53/1.

fire *n.* phr.: *to take* ~ to catch fire 34/14.

first age *n.* youth 5/12 (*MED* only cites 'the Golden Age').

flaterie *n.* coaxing speech 60/21.

flaume *n.* flame 34/14; **flawmes** *pl.* 109/2.

flee *v.* flee 20/9; **fle** *imp.* 68/23 (**fleeth** 73/28); **fledde** *pt. 3 s.* 50/8; **fleyng** *pr. p.* 84/6; **fled** *pp.* 74/29.

fleese *n.* fleece 48/14.

fleith *pr. 3 s.* flies 15/14; **flawe** *pt. 3 s.* 15/12; **fleyng** *pr. p.* 5/20.

flesch *n.* human body 27/22.

fleschli *adj.* carnal 10/3.

fletyng *pr. p.* floating 54/14.

floyte *n.* flute 38/1; *pl.* 41/25.

florisschid *pt. 3 s.* prospered 6/33.

floterith *pr. 3 s.* vacillates 21/11.

flowrid *pt. 3 s.* throve 123/5.

foli *adj.* foolish 78/21.

*****folich** *adj.* foolish 108/28 (first ex. *MED*).

folily *adv.* stupidly 38/9, 90/25.

folke *n.* troop of soldiers 73/31.

folowe *v.* follow 36/24 (**folwe** 105/30); **folowith** *pr. 3 pl.* 48/23; **folwe** *imp.* 68/24; **folowyng** *pr. p.* 3/3.

fonde, foonde *pt. 3 s.* invented 23/25, 24/27; discovered 25/30.

forbi *adv.* going past 68/13 (**forthbi** M).

force *n.* violence 53/25; (**forse**) superior strength 96/21; fortitude (cardinal virtue) 122/13.

fordide *pt. 3 s.* discarded 51/25; **fordon** *pp.* overcome 13/17.

foreine *adj.* foreign 22/11; distant 61/6.

fornicacion *n.* lechery 52/32, 118/12.

forsweryng *pr. p.* renouncing, repudiating 54/30.

fortefie *imp.* reinforce 40/7.

forthe *adv.* phr.: *puttith* ~ advances 4/15.

forþwiþ *adv.* immediately 69/17.

fortune *v.* fare, conclude 99/5.

foryete *imp.* forget 75/7; **forʒate** *pt.*

3 s. 75/15; *pl.* 75/14; **foryeten** *pp.* 9/14.

forʒetilnes *n.* oblivion 69/28.

fouled *pp.* befouled 50/11; *ppl. a.* defiled 36/1.

foundement *n.* basis 71/26.

***fragilite** *n.* frailty 114/9, 119/10 (first ex. *MED c.* 1439).

***fraudelouse** *adj.* deceitful, deceptive 99/19, 118/17 (only exs. in *MED*).

***fre** *inf.* 81/12ᵛ [Warner suggests 'follow' but this sense not in *MED* or *OED*; did scribe misread the original 'fue'?].

freel *adj.* frail 27/20; unstable 119/11.

freilnes *n.* spiritual weakness 19/16; frailty 77/18.

fryst *ord. num.* first 122/12.

fro, from *prep.* phr.: ~ *that* from the time that, 49/15; ~ *him-silf* out of his wits 97/13.

frosschis *n. pl.* frogs 31/20 (**frosses** L).

froward *adj.* unkind 100/12.

***fructifie** *imp.* flourish 37/1; **fructifieth** *pr. 3 s.* 26/19 (cited as earliest ex. *MED*).

ful *adv.* completely 34/7.

fulfille *v.* complete 3/32; **fulfilled** *ppl. a.* perfect 9/3.

fumerell *n.* smoke-hole in roof 28/16.

g- see also **y-**.

***gaineryes** *n. pl.* farmers 36/13 (**gaineyers** L; first ex. *MED*).

garmentes *n. pl. fig.* attires 12/25.

geaunt, giaunt *n.* giant 30/29, 73/3; **geauntes** *gen.* 30/24.

gebet *n.* gallows phr.: *~ of the Crosse* 38/23 (first ex. *MED* ?).

gedered *pt. s.* gathered 4/19.

gelozie *n.* jealousy 76/13.

gete *inf.* get 5/19; earn 68/13; **gete** *pr. 3 s.* 40/2; **gate** *pt. 3 s.* 10/14; **geten** *pp.* 15/30 (**gete** 86/7); **gotyn** *ppl. a.* 61/31.

getynge *vbl. n.* acquiring 31/5; *pl.* possessions 84/17.

geyne-sey *v.* contradict 42/4; **geyn-seyng** *vbl. n.* 20/12.

girde *pp.* girded 111/18.

girdell *n.* belt 49/28; *pl.* 87/17.

gise *n.* behaviour 43/21; phr.: *for no* ~ under no circumstances 110/14.

gladde *adj.* jolly 17/1.

glayue *n.* sword 15/15.

glewe *n.* birdlime 115/15.

glose *n.* explanatory comment 6/17; *pl.* 123/24.

glotonye *n.* gluttony 33/16, 70/12.

go *inf.* 11/7; *pr. 1 s.* 5/8 (**goo**); *2 s. subj.* 11/4; *3 s.* 45/2–3 (**gooþ** 75/28); *3 pl.* 61/8 (**gooth** 23/12); **wente** *pt. 3 s.* 12/5; *pl.* 116/5; **goon** *pp.* 39/4; **go** *imp.* 62/20; phr.: ~ *be the* go by 45/3; ~ *vppon* attack 62/25–6; ~ *seking* continually seek 5/8.

gobet *n.* lump, mass 93/17.

goddes *n. s.* goddess 27/28, 31/25; *pl.* gods 16/20, 28/5; *s. gen.* God's 63/12; **goddessis** *pl. fem.* 74/4.

goyng *vbl. n.* journeying 14/26.

good *n. coll.* property 40/20; *pl.* possessions 61/23.

goodli *adj.* valiant, noble 32/14.

goodnes *n.* excellence 25/27; kindness 67/3; piety, spiritual virtue 107/30.

goostli *adj.* spiritual 8/17, 122/2.

gouernaunce *n.* administration 70/27.

gouernoure *n.* commander 115/7.

grace *n.* admirable quality 26/31; material favour 99/23; phr.: *moder of all* ~ applied to the Virgin Mary 37/15.

gracious *adj.* fortunate 3/23; generous 105/14.

graciouslye *adv.* benevolently 17/5.

graffis *n. pl.* grafts, shoots 37/4 **griffes** M)

grauntyng *vbl. n.* gift 89/23.

greete *adj.* great 70/27; mighty 74/21; phr.: ~ *wiþ* pregnant with 74/16.

greine (cf. note to 26/18); **greynes** *n. pl.* species of cereals 37/1.

greuaunces *n. pl.* physical damages 26/4.

greve inf. injure, harass 73/16; imp. refl. worry 6/14; greued pp. angered 38/7.

greving vbl. n. anger 97/29.

greuous adj. unpleasant 89/24; greuously adv. severely 76/1.

grounde n. basis 22/24; foundation 24/11.

grounde imp. establish 82/8; groundid (in) pp. based on 21/12; ~ (vp-on) 122/12.

growinge vbl. n. capacity to grow 37/5 ('croissance', Laud.)

grucchinges n. pl. complaints 54/27.

guerdon n. reward 60/13; v. repay 67/7 (gwerdon 47/27).

h- see also y-.

habandoned ppl. a. lavish (?) 36/17ᵛ (see note; Godefroy I, 16. b; MED, I, 7 'abandonen', sense 2c).

habill adj. able 5/25.

habitacion n. fig. abode 108/4.

habundaunte adj. productive 36/17; habundantly adv. abundantly 57/21.

halowe inf. honour 44/3.

*halowid (wiþ) pp. hallooed by 84/7 (no ex. use of 'wiþ' in MED).

halse inf. embrace 76/23.

hande n. phr.: of his ~ of valour 113/28.

happe v. fare 71/16; pr. subj. 3 s. happen 58/30; happith pr. ind. 3 s. 47/19; 3 pl. 50/24; happed pt. 3 s. 54/9.

harde adj. callous (?) 14/23; harsh 66/16; obstinate 30/1; hard (firm) 30/2.

hardi adj. fearless 12/27.

hardines n. boldness 25/26, 43/5.

harlotries n. pl. sinful acts 27/21.

harneis n. armour 110/15ᵛ.

harpid pt. 3 s. played the harp 85/11.

harpour n. harp player 85/25.

hast n. urgent need 88/18; phr.: in ~ speedily 48/18.

hasti adj. quick 63/29; hastili adv. 111/6.

hauȝteyn adj. haughty 26/30.

haunte inf. frequent 77/27; imp. 43/19; haunted pt. 3 s. 43/26.

hauntyng vbl. n. visiting 49/18.

haue inf. 7/7; pr. 1 s. & pl. 4/2, 7/13; hast(e) 2 s. 19/8, 84/2; hath 3 s. & pl. 4/23, 74/23 (haue 57/16); haue subj. 2 3 s. 24/18, 14/16; hadde 3 pl. subj.15/21; had(de) pt. 1 3 s. & 3 pl. 3/21, 37/25, 6/29; haddist 2 s. 113/16; haue imp. 67/25; hauyng pr. p. 6/20; had(de) pp. 5/12, 86/12; phr.: ~ despite of held in contempt 38/7; ~ fauour vn-to favour 25/20; ~ guerdon be rewarded 60/12–13; ~ heuene win Paradise 45/29–30; ~ (a) liste wished 100/8; ~ (to) mariage married 34/29; ~ (to) marye eligible for marriage 57/26; ~ (in) mynde recall 112/12; ~ mysdoon mistreated 52/9; ~ nede need 44/21; ~ (in) suspecion suspected 41/29–30; ~ tyme and place have proper occasion 75/19–20; ~ (the) victorie conquered 40/15; ~ werre with war on 22/10; ~ wil is determined 17/17

hede n. phr.: take ~ pay attention 58/21.

hede n. head 42/9; pl. 42/17.

hedid pp. decapitated 71/10.

heelde pt. 3 pl. 16/21 (held 16/23); see holde.

heete n. heat 83/23.

helle n. hell 61/13.

*helly adj. infernal 85/19, 85/25 (first ex. OED 1532).

helme n. helmet 13/8.

helpely adj. serviceable 44/23.

helpid pt. 3 s. helped 99/9; holpen pp. 105/23.

helthe n. salvation 24/12, 116/17; physical soundness 51/8.

hepid (to) pp. amassed 32/29.

*herdly adj. earthly 102/2ᵛ (cf. Warner, p. 118, and MED 'erdli', with inorganic h not in OED).

herdman n. herdsman 74/15.

here inf. hear 8/13; hire pr. 2 s. subj. 6/8; herith pr. 3 s. 63/17; here pr. 2 pl. 63/12; herde pt. 3 s. 50/7; hering pr. p. 63/11; herde pp. 63/13; phr.: ~ tolde hear related 41/10.

heres n. pl. hairs 28/15.

hering *vbl. n.* hearing 59/2.
heritage *n.* inheritance 96/2.
hert *n.* stag 83/14; hertys *pl.* 84/12.
herte *n.* heart 44/26; hertis *pl.* 3/34; hertily *adv.* 25/28.
hete *n.* heat 32/3; see heete.
heuy *adj.* despondent 26/1; grave 18/28.
heuynes *n.* sadness 21/8, 56/12; grief 101/7('douleur', Fr & Wyer).
hiȝ *adj.* weighty 11/30; exalted 25/27; hiȝer *comp.* loftier 117/2.
highnes *n.* high rank 11/30.
hire *n.* reward 88/10.
hire see also here.
hires *poss. fem. pron.* hers 56/3.
holde *adj.* old 122/22.
holde *v.* accept 98/12; holdith *pr. 3 s.* considers 32/20; ~ *me dere* esteems me 6/1; held *pt. 3 s.* kept possession 58/12; holding *pr. p.* 120/5; holden *pp.* accepted 98/11; judged 123/16.
hole see hooll.
Holy Writte *n.* Holy Scriptures 41/18; holy-day 48/29; holi-chirche 51/21.
homely *adj.* domestic, native 22/12 ('priuees', Laud; 'pryuy', Wyer).
homlynes *n.* intimacy 99/22.
honeste *adj.* commendable 101/17.
honeste *n.* phr.: ~ *of the bodi* chastity 35/26.
honged *pp.* hanged 38/23.
hooll, hole *adj.* whole 3/17; healthy 51/20; phr.: ~ *and som* wholly 5/30; ~ *sovne* 3/10; ~ *and sounde* 22/23; hoolly *adv.* 37/17, 66/31.
hoost *n.* host (of retainers) 26/1.
*hoote *adv.* lustfully 46/10 (as adj. first ex. this sense *OED* 1500); *adj.* heated 83/22.
houndis *n. pl.* dogs 83/12.
housbonde *n.* husband 31/29.
huge *adj.* immense 30/30 (hooges L).
hundrith *card. num.* hundred 120/14.
hunte *v.* hunt 79/25; huntid (*at*) *pt. 3 s.* 79/23; huntyng *vbl. n.* 77/29.
hurte (*of*) *n.* damage to 48/15; *pl.* blows 51/32.

*hurtith *pr. 3 s.* vexes 54/31 (first ex. this sense *OED* 1526); hurted *pt. 3 s.* inflicted injury on 43/6.

i- see also y-.
idill *adj.* idle 79/28.
iȝe *n.* eye 29/15 (yȝe 62/9); yen *pl.* 42/5.
*ignorant *n.* ignorant person 107/24 (first ex. *OED c.* 1480; ingnorant L); *adj.* 98/18.
ile *n.* isle 24/25.
illusiones *n. pl.* delusions 82/9.
*inaduertance *n.* inattention, carelessness 77/4 (first ex. *OED* 1568; 'inaduertence', Laud).
*in-certayne *adj.* uncertain 108/29 (first ex. *OED* 1491).
inclynacion *n.* disposition 5/24.
inconueniencie *n.* harm 37/8; misfortune 65/28; *impropriety 115/18 (first ex. this sense *OED c.* 1460); *pl.* 31/6, 115/12.
indifferently *adv.* indiscriminately 120/20.
indignacion *n.* disdain, wrath (?; thus Laud & Wyer) 95/28.
infelicite *n.* misery 91/24ᵛ.
influence *n.* occult force 17/30, 20/27 (astrol.).
infortunes *n. pl.* misfortunes 11/24.
ingnorant see ignorant.
iniure *n.* damage 70/15.
innocent *n.* guiltless person 38/26.
inspiriþ *pr. 3 s. absol.* animates (?) 108/4.
instavnce *n.* entreaty 122/34.
instrumentis *n. pl.* musical instruments 81/12.
intrayle *n.* entrail 50/12.
isse *v. intr.* issue 80/13; issed *pt. 3 s.* 80/19.
i-wis *adv.* certainly 9/2.

iangeling *vbl. n.* chatter 104/22.
iangilloure *n.* chatterer 65/3 (iangeler 104/21).
*iaueloth, iauelott *n.* small javelin 92/29, 93/12 (first ex. *OED* 1489).
ielous (*ouer*) *adj.* jealous (of) 93/8; ielousie *n.* 104/22.
ient- see gent-.

iewellis see iuellis.

iogeloure n. jester 110/28 (iowgo-lowre L).

joyne imp. ally 24/16; ioyned pp. met in conflict 38/4.

ioli adj. amorous 79/19 (so Wyer; 'cointe', Laud).

iolynes n. joviality 18/2; wantonness 90/11.

*iourneyer n. traveller 12/2 (first ex. OED 1566; 'voyager', Laud).

ioye n. happiness 54/8; ioies pl. 106/28.

joyous, ioyeux adj. joyful 26/21, 91/25.

iuellis, iewellis n. pl. jewels 87/18, 87/22.

*iusticere n. judge 13/4 (first ex. this sense OED 1481).

iustifie v. refl. judge 13/14.

kepe v. keep 37/18; kepte pt. 3 s. 51/25; kepyng pr. p. 14/15; kepte pp. phr.: armes be ~ be armed 25/2–3; yvill ~ uncontrolled 64/10.

keperes n. pl. keepers, guardians 42/15.

keping vbl. n. custody 64/7; herding 74/20.

kercheues n. pl. kerchiefs 87/17 (keurcheffes L).

keste see caste.

kyn n. coll. relatives 47/17; ancestral stock 49/17.

kinde, kynde n. variety 112/11; phr.: in ~ in proper manner 19/24; in no ~ improperly 45/12.

knyvis n. pl. knives 53/13.

knowe inf. 57/11; knewe pt. 3 s. 62/27; knowing pr. p. 56/25; knowe, knowen, knowin pp. 25/22, 49/10, 76/17; phr.: ~ of have had intercourse with (?) 76/17 ('conioye', Laud).

knowing vbl. n. knowledge 114/4; adj. instructed 98/19.

knowlech n. knowledge, perception 95/15.

knowliched pt. 3 s. confessed 76/16.

lacchesse n. slackness 31/7.

lak n. fault, shame 4/13.

*langage n. talk 23/3 (first ex. this sense OED c. 1450).

lappe n. fig. protective cover 116/16; n. pl. laps 28/21.

largeli adv. liberally 36/24; copiously 40/22.

largenes n. liberality 3/13.

laste n. phr.: at the ~ in the end 28/28.

lastith pr. 3 s. continues 105/4; lastid pt. 3 s. extended, reached 82/18.

laude n. praise 11/18.

laugh (on) pr. 3 s. subj. may smile upon 109/4.

laughingis n. pl. laughter 69/6 ('ris', Laud; see lawyng).

launchid pt. 3 s. hurled 65/25.

laurere see lourere.

lawe n. religious system 28/4, 43/25; the Scriptures 48/2.

lawyng vbl. n. joy, rejoicing 69/8ᵛ ('exultatio', Latin).

leche n. doctor 51/28; pl. 51/17.

lechecrafte n. art of medicine 57/10.

leder n. leader (? God; cf. notes) 107/1.

leef adv. willingly 53/6.

leeful adj. lawful 101/26 ('loisible', Laud).

leerith pr. 3 s. teaches 92/30.

leest n. phr.: at þe ~ at all events 76/8.

lefte see leve.

leyde pt. 3 s. refl. laid (herself) down 50/8.

*leiser n. phr.: at longe ~ at length 38/4–5 (this phr. not in OED).

leke blade n. fig. leek's leaf (something of little value) 9/12.

lene v. lend 105/14.

lepe inf. leap 117/10; lepte pt. 3 s. 28/24; pt. 3 pl. 116/5.

lerne v. acquire knowledge 40/21; imp. 56/26; lerned pt. 3 s. 57/9; taught 57/11.

lese v. lose 85/29; lesith pr. 3 s. 115/16; lesing vbl. n. 67/16.

*leser n. destroyer 67/16 (only ex. OED Wycliffe).

lesynge n. lying, falsehood 43/29; pl. 54/31.

lessith *pr. 3 s. intr.* decreases 21/9.

lessons *n. pl.* lectures 6/2.

lete *inf.* permit 116/3; *phr.*: ~ *kepe him* let him keep himself 79/25–6.

lette *v.* hinder 89/15; **lettith** *pr. 3 pl.* 10/2; **letted** *pt. 3 s.* 3/19; **lettid** *pp.* 89/11.

lettingis *n. pl.* hindrances 74/30.

lettred *ppl. a.* educated 39/27.

leve *inf.* leave, stop 55/15; **lefte** *pt. 3 pl.* 85/22.

leve *pr. 2 s. subj.* believest 103/15.

leuer *adv. comp.* more gladly 46/6, 113/16; see **leef**.

leves *n. pl.* leaves 93/11.

lewde *adj.* unchaste 34/23; poor 43/30; foolish 108/27.

lewdenes *n.* wickedness 34/3.

lewedly *adv.* ignorantly 38/10; wickedly 61/30.

lie (*with*) *v.* have intercourse 60/9; **lay** (*bi*) *pt. 3 s.* 67/29.

***lieme** *n.* shackle 69/19; **lyemes** *pl.* 69/13 ('liens', Fr; cf. note. Not in *OED*).

liȝt *n. phr.*: *angil of* ~ one who dwells in Heaven 70/7–8.

light, lite *adj.* slight 98/13, 3/28; frivolous 102/27; wanton 70/14; **lightli** *adv.* easily 8/20.

lightnesse *n.* brightness 55/31.

liȝne *n.* line (lineal descent) 62/5.

lijf *n.* life 18/6.

likenyth *pr. 3 s.* compares 38/18; **likened** *pp.* 118/6.

likerousnes *n.* keen desire 70/12.

lymytte *inf.* restrict 9/29.

linage *n.* lineage 10/13 (**lenage** L).

lynes *n. pl.* strings, bonds 73/29 ('liens', Fr; cf. **lieme**).

lyon *n. fig.* lion (fiercely brave person) 3/4; (animal) 50/7.

***liquour** *n. fig.* liquid, essence 100/26 (first ex. fig. sense *OED* 1526).

liste *v. phr.*: *him* ~ *pt. 3 s.* (*with dat.*) he chose 104/27.

lite see **light**.

litell *adj.* undistinguished 47/17.

lyuyng *ppl. a. absol.* living (those alive) 5/32.

lodging *n.* encampment 58/2.

loke *v.* look 85/27; *imp.* take care 26/28; **loked** *pt. 3 s.* 30/25; **lokinge** *pr. p.* 86/2.

longeth *pr. 3 s.* belongs 3/9; **longyng** *pr. p.* 19/7; *ppl. a.* *appropriate 87/18 (this sense not in *OED*).

lourere, laurere, lorier *n.* laurel tree 106/9 & 9ᵛ, 106/13.

loue *v.* love 40/5; *imp.* 39/20; **louest** *pr. 2 s.* 62/5; **loued** *pt. 3 s.* 41/1.

loueable *adj.* deserving of being loved 44/3 (see Glossary of *Dicts*, p. 394; 'louable', Laud; 'lowable', Wyer).

lowable *adj.* praiseworthy 4/8.

luste *n.* inclination 42/3, 46/13.

***mace** *n.* sceptre of office 61/12; *pl.* 61/9 (first ex. this sense *OED c.* 1440).

***made** *ppl. a.* artificially produced 34/32 (first ex. this sense *OED c.* 1578).

maister *n.* overlord 40/4; *pl.* teachers 40/8; ***maastres** *of iustice pl.* legal functionaries 52/1 ('maistres de Justice', Laud; not in *OED*); *phr.*: ~ *dongeon* chief dungeon 116/25.

***maistres** *n.* woman who has mastered an art 66/26 (first ex. this sense *OED* 1484).

maistried *pp.* overcome 72/11.

make *inf.* 55/15; *pr. 1 s. & 3 pl.* 3/24, 3/31 (**makeþ** 116/26); **makith** *3 s.* 12/15; **make** *subj. 3 s.* 69/10; **made** *pt. 3 s. & pl.* 30/4, 34/20; **make** *imp.* 39/20; **makynge** *pr. p.* 38/11; *vbl. n.* 34/2; **made** *pp.* 51/23; *phr.*: ~ *amendis* make restitution 55/11; ~ (*the*) *cours* prepare the way 23/15; ~ (*a*) *covenaunte* reached an agreement 88/24; ~ *debate* quarrel 32/17; ~ *delay* tarry 100/29; ~ *dye* slew 30/4–5; ~ *heuynes* sorrow 101/5–6; ~ *iournaye* undertake a trip 3/31–2; ~ *mencion* report 111/19; ~ *noise* rustle 93/11; ~ *pleies*

make (*cont.*):
contend 65/17; ~ *prayers* prayed 34/12; ~ *present* give 3/16; ~ (*to be*) *prisoned* imprisoned 30/4–5; ~ *sacrifices* sacrificed 53/13; ~ *schorte* shortens 69/10; ~ *viagis* travel 96/9; ~ *werre* fight 10/20–1; ~ (*the*) *weye* prepares the way 23/13; ~ *yifte* present 3/24.

makere *n.* God 45/5; phr.: ~ *of hevyn and of erthe* 36/3.

malencolyous *adj.* gloomy 20/22.

malice *n.* ill-will 28/26; power to harm 87/17; malicious *adj.* evil-disposed 31/3.

man *n. s.* 13/16; mannys *gen.* 63/3; men *pl.* 13/18; mennes *gen.* 13/12.

manace *n.* menace 48/21.

manace *inf.* threaten 48/17; manacynges *vbl. n. pl.* 48/8.

maner *n.* variety, kind 56/12; *pl.* 40/26; phr.: *no* ~ *of* periphrastically for 'no' 38/8–9; with ellipsis of 'of' 46/27; *no* ~ *cause* no reason whatever 95/23.

maners *n. pl.* habitations 54/3.

*mankyndli *adj.* human 8/4, 12/23, 53/15; humane 79/8 (so Fr & Wyer); manlike 17/12 (not in *OED*).

*mankyndlynes *n.* manhood 4/14 (not in *OED*; cf. Glossary of *Dicts*, p. 394).

manly *adj.* valiant 43/10.

*manslaughter *n.* destruction of human life 53/12 (first ex. this sense *OED c.* 1450; *manslaughte M, no ex. this sense *OED*).

mansleer *n.* homicide 53/20.

marchis *n. pl.* border districts 68/12.

mariage *n.* phr.: *hadde hire to* ~ married her 34/29.

maryners *n. pl.* seamen 96/30.

martired *pp.* slain (by a cruel death) 84/13.

materis *n. pl.* phr.: *vnclene* ~ excrements 27/21.

may see mowe.

medewe *n.* meadow 85/13; medwis *pl.* 110/9 (see note).

meyne *n.* retinue 84/13.

membres, membris *n. pl. phr.*: *preuy, secrete* ~ private parts 19/1, 53/2–3 (first ex. **secret* ~ *OED* 1644).

*memorie *n.* phr.: *for* ~ as a memorial 105/5 (first ex. this sense *OED c.* 1470).

mendes *n. pl.* reparations 55/3 ('amende', Laud).

mene *n.* agency 19/26, 115/1.

*menewey *n.* midway, middle course 59/13 (not in *OED*).

mente *ppl. a.* meant 55/5.

meritis *n. pl.* excellence, esteem 67/16.

merveil *n.* wonder 86/16; *v. pr. 1 s.* I wonder 54/19.

merueilous *adj.* remarkable 11/31; wonderful 19/19; merveilously *adv.* 93/4.

messangeris *n. pl.* messengers 48/16 ('messages', Fr; 'messagers', Wyer).

mesure *n.* phr.: *out of* ~ excessively 26/1, 50/13; *be good* ~ largely 59/8.

meve *v.* move 60/22; mevith *pr. 3 s.* 108/2; meved *pt. 3 s.* 70/28; *pp.* (~ *with*) 85/23; meving *vbl. n.* 71/3.

mychel *adv.* greatly 77/24.

myddes *n.* phr.: *in the* ~ *of* in the middle of 30/30.

myȝte *n.* virtue 90/2; myghti *adj.* powerful 38/11.

mynde *n.* phr.: *have* ~ *vppon* think of 67/25 (with *on* 110/3–4).

mynystres *n. pl.* ecclesiastical ministers 44/2.

myrrour *n.* mirror 102/1 (merowre L).

mysbeleue *n.* heresy 42/24; *mysbeleuers *n. pl.* infidels 119/26 (first ex. *OED* 1470–85).

myschaunce *n.* misfortune 98/22 (so Wyer; 'meschance', Fr).

myschefe *n.* trouble 32/6; *wickedness 52/31 (first ex. *OED* 1470–85); myschevis *pl.* calamities 74/23.

mysdon *pp.* done ill 43/8.

*myspent *ppl. a.* wasted 3/18 (first ex. *OED* 1500–20).

*myster *n.* need 10/26 (Fr 'mestier').

mystooke *pt. 3 s. refl.* offended 78/13 (last ex. *OED c.* 1425).

mys-wroughte *pp.* done amiss 75/8.

*moderate *v.* render less violent 53/18; moderatith *pr. 3 s.* abates 9/25 (first ex. *OED* 1432–50).

molle *n.* mole 38/17.

*mone-schyne *n.* moonlight 50/10 (first ex. *OED* 1468).

monstre *n.* monster 15/18.

moralizacions *n. pl.* moral interpretations 123/30.

*moralized *pp.* interpreted morally 123/30 (first use of verb *OED c.* 1450).

moralli *adv.* in a moral sense 7/7.

mote *pr. 3 s. subj.* must 29/30; *3 pl.* 32/7; most *pt. 2 s. (used as pr.)* 10/10; *3 s.* 22/9 (muste 43/27); most(e) *2 pl.* 13/3; phr.: *me* must it behoves me 109/8; *nedes* ~ are obliged to 13/3.

mountaigne *n.* mountain 120/3; mountaynes *pl.* 71/4.

mowe *inf.* be able 84/1; may *pr. 1 s.* 4/22; *2 s.* 99/28 (maiste 64/22); *3 s.* 4/1; *1 pl.* 6/27; *3 pl.* 3/34; myȝt *pt. 3 s.* 28/13; *3 pl.* 69/20; phr.: myȝt *be* could exist 39/9; *as myche as he* ~ to the greatest extent possible 94/16–17.

*muse (in) *v.* take amusement in 77/31, 81/23 (not in *OED*; 'amuser', Fr).

must see mote.

name *n.* phr.: *of grete* ~ distinguished 39/26.

*name *inf.* allege 108/27 (first ex. this sense *OED* 1470–85); *pp.* designated 5/33.

namely *adv.* especially 7/4, 32/17.

necessite *n.* dire need 52/3; *pl.* difficulties, being in straits 51/4 (first ex. this sense *OED c.* 1475).

nede *n.* necessity 113/8; phr.: *at*

(theire) ~ in (their) necessity 38/32, 44/22–3.

nedi *adj. absol.* the indigent 101/3; nedis *adv.* necessarily 54/12.

nedillis *n. gen.* needle's 62/9.

neghbourgh, neiȝebore *n.* neighbour 16/9, 54/26; neghboris *gen.* 55/23.

nere hande *adv.* almost 10/33, 28/18.

newfangilnes *n.* tendency towards novelties 102/10.

nyce *adj.* stupid, senseless 48/8 ('nice', Fr.)

nygromancye *n.* necromancy 100/21.

nobles *n.* noble condition 10/16; nobleness 32/19.

noblith *pr. 3 s.* ennobles 120/11.

*noyse *pr. 1 s.* hold 44/27 (this sense not in *OED*; 'repute', Fr & Wyer); *pr. 3 pl. refl.* boast 83/3; noised *pp.* 73/23.

nonne *n.* nun 87/8.

noon *adv.* phr.: *or* ~ or not 62/7.

norisschynge *ppl. a.* affording nourishment 41/3.

note *n.* nut 61/18.

note *v.* perceive 19/6 (not 50/31); mark carefully 41/18; *pr. 1 pl.* set down as having a bad character 21/2 (first ex. *OED* 1526); noted *pp.* ~ *for the good name* known for a good character 15/22–3.

notifie *pr. 1 pl.* denote, indicate 20/7.

nought *n.* nothing 67/17; phr.: *sette at* ~ disregard 107/28; *brouȝt to* ~ destroyed 116/27–8; *adv.* not at all 60/2.

novn-power *n.* impotence, weakness 14/14.

noye *subj. pr. 3 s.* annoy, vex 69/11.

noyous *adj.* vexatious 111/20; troublesome 118/9 (noyens L).

O *int. (voc.)* 5/7; *prep.* of (apocopate form) 13/27.

obeisaunce *n.* deference 14/10.

obserued *pp.* kept, honoured 5/10 (Fr rhyme: 'preseruee: obseruee').

occasion *n.* cause 50/24.

occupacion *n.* task 78/8; *pl.* 31/8.

occupieþ *pr. 3 s. refl.* busies himself 70/15; *occupied *ppl. a.* engaged 78/7 (first ex. *OED* 1483).

offende *v.* attack 11/14.

office *n.* duty 74/7; *pl.* functions 19/6.

officers *n. pl.* officials 85/25 ('offices', Laud).

offre *inf. absol.* to present a sacrifice 115/23.

offringis *n. pl.* sacrifices 116/7.

ofte tymes *adv.* frequently 112/6.

onappy see vnhappy.

onys *adv.* once 105/1.

oo *num.* one 18/2, 21/6, 39/9.

ooste *n.* armed company 58/13.

oppressid (*with*) *pp.* borne down in battle (by) 47/9.

or *prep.* before 3/18; ∼ *that conj.* before 19/12.

ordeyned *pt. 3 s.* appointed 60/16.

ordre *n.* confraternity 121/1; ordris *pl.* ranks, classes (?) 14/4 ('tout ordre', Fr); *phr.*: ∼ *of aungelis* nine grades of angels 106/32.

ordure *n.* filth 19/26.

othir *adj.*, otiose in idiomatic *phr.*: *of all* ∼ *thinges* 7/21.

*ouctrecuidez *adj.* cocksure 27/7 (not as adj. in *OED*).

ought *n.* aught, anything whatever 6/8.

ought *v.* (*as pr. 1 s.*) 5/30; *2 s.* 47/4 (ouȝtist 96/3); *3 s.* 84/29; *1 pl.* 19/18; *3 pl.* 52/16.

oure *n.* hour 110/4.

outhir . . . outhir *conj.* either . . . or 60/26–7.

outragious *adj.* unusual 65/29ᵛ; outragiousli *adv.* excessively 32/18.

oueral *adv.* everywhere 87/14.

ouercomyng *vbl. n.* conquering 16/3.

ouer-goo *inf.* overwhelm, surmount 103/7 (so Wyer).

*ouir-hope *n.* presumption 48/27 (last ex. *OED c.* 1440).

ouer-leid *pp.* oppressed (?) 69/13; *surprised 69/28, 73/15 ('surpris', Fr & Wyer; this sense not in *OED*).

ouer-ranne *pt. 3 s.* outran 88/25.

*ouerseen *pp.* examined mentally 82/27 (only ex. *OED c.* 1477).

ouertooke *pr. 3 s. subj.* overcomes 31/2.

*ouerthrowe *n.* deposition from power 117/3 (first ex. *OED* 1513).

*ouer-trusting *ppl. a.* excessively trustful 71/15 (not in *OED*).

ouer-wenyng *ppl. a.* conceited 26/30, 27/10.

paas *n.* rate of movement 75/28.

palais *n.* palace 28/16, 58/1.

paramoures *adv.* passionately 60/8, 69/15.

parceyve *v.* observe 49/30; parceyued, perceyved *pp.* discovered 49/19, 54/6.

parde *adv.* indeed 53/31; *int.* 11/6.

parfit *adj.* perfect 8/9.

parte (*fro*) *v.* separate (from) 50/4.

partye *n.* side 71/6; *plight, predicament 117/21 (first ex. *OED c.* 1440); *pl.* respects 54/29; regions (of the world) 25/29; *phr.*: *bettir* ∼ (so Wyer) favourable side 90/31.

passage *n.* sea voyage 96/14; *pl.* mountain passes 71/4.

passe *v.* pass over, ignore 94/2; (*intr.*) die *or* continue (?) 113/17 ('passer', Laud); passid *pt. 3 s.* spent his life 40/14; crossed 54/4.

passeris forbi *n. pl.* passers-by 68/13.

passing *ppl. a.* ephemeral 117/7.

pasturis *n. pl.* grass lands 37/28.

*payment *n.* pay, wages 25/12 (first ex. *OED c.* 1449).

paynymes *n. gen. pl.* pagans' 44/17.

peas *n.* peace 28/27; pesibilly *adv.* peacefully 119/25.

peyne *n.* distress 30/10; trouble 39/23; *pl.* torments (of hell) 85/25.

peyne (*him*) *v. refl.* exert himself 93/28.

peise *v.* ponder 19/4; peysid *pp.* 48/22.

pendant *n.* ornament, tassel (?) 49/28.

*penurie *n.* want 105/21 (first ex.

OED 1432–50; **penowrye, pen-
uery** L).

per- see also **par-**.

perceth *pr. 3 s.* pierces 64/11.

perell *n.* danger 113/23, 80/4; *pl.*
54/19.

perfiȝtli *adv.* perfectly 26/16; **perfit**
adj. 21/11.

*****perfitith** *pr. 3 s.* perfects, makes
faultless 9/25 (first ex. *OED* 1494).

perych *v.* perish 54/12; **perisschid**
pt. 3 s. 53/32; *****perisched** *ppl. a.*
dead 54/16 (first ex. *OED* 1538).

perlous, parlious, perlyous *adj.*
perilous 17/26, 117/27, 54/11;
perlioser *comp.* 117/3.

perpetuel *adj.* eternal 30/10, con-
tinuous 96/28; **perpetuelly** *adv.*
113/17.

perseueraunce *n.* persistence 80/4,
106/27.

phayrie *n.* fairy-folk 88/20, see
fairye.

phesik *n.* medicine 51/14; **phisi-
cien** *n.* medical practitioner 51/28.

pyll *inf.* plunder 68/12ᵛ (cf. **pulle**).

pistell *n.* epistle 3/1.

pite (*of*) *n.* pity (on) 32/5; **pitous** *adj.*
mournful 34/9; **pitously** *adv.*
54/12.

plantere *n.* sower of seeds (fem.)
37/13.

pleies *n. pl.* games 65/17.

pleyne *adv.* expressly 27/30.

pleinly *adv.* completely 51/9.

pleyntes *n. pl.* lamentations 34/25.

plenere *adj.* full 5/5.

plenteuouslye *adv.* abundantly
36/14.

plesaunce *n.* pleasure 16/5; enjoy-
ment 53/29; *pl.* 87/25.

plite *n.* unfortunate state 69/19.

plongeth (*in*) *pr. 3 s.* sinks (into)
21/7; *pp.* fallen (into) 27/21.

*****poetikly** *adj.* poetical 74/22; *****adv.*
poetically 7/14 (not in *OED*).

police *n.* diplomacy 123/10; **policie**
n. government 7/11; ∼ **gouern-
aunce** political sagacity 122/11.

*****pontificalle** *adj.* dignified 22/28
(first ex. this sense *OED* 1589;
'pontifical', Laud).

ponysschid *pt. 3 s.* punished
38/11.

porter *n.* watch-dog 10/27 (so *OED*);
porterys *gen.* 39/7.

possibilite *n.* capability 12/10.

possid *pp.* knocked about 54/11.

postyle *n.* apostle 22/16ᵛ, 108/5ᵛ.

*****potage** *n.* drink 118/2 (this sense
not in *OED*; first ex. 1567;
'drinke', Wyer; 'beuurage', Laud).

poundered *pp.* thought over 121/22.

power *n.* ability 3/26; control 64/14;
might 68/17; *phr.*: *dide hir* ∼ did
her best 107/16.

praid *pt. 3 s.* begged 79/22; *pp.*
invited 74/5; **prayinge** *pr. p.*
beseeching 109/11.

prechinge *n.* preaching 23/13; *pl.*
23/8; **prechoures** *pl.* preachers
23/10.

prees *n.* throng 61/9; **precis** *pl.*
47/11.

preise *n.* laud 78/29 ('not common
till after 1500' *OED*).

preiudice *n.* injury 100/28.

premisses *n. pl.* propositions 122/5.

prerogatif *n.* superiority 6/30.

present *n. phr.*: *to make* ∼ to make
a gift 3/16.

present *adj.* actual 81/3; being at
hand 107/2; *phr.*: *to be* ∼ *wiþ* to
be among 106/32.

preson *n.* imprisonment 49/24.

prestis (*of the lawe*) *n. pl.* pagan
priests 28/4.

presume *inf.* venture upon (?)
63/25 (see notes); be presump-
tuous 114/10; *phr.*: *****∼ *folye* raise
a presumption to foolishness 64/1
(Fr *phr.* 'presumer folie'; not in
MED or *OED*).

presumpcion *n.* assumption 49/11,
90/30.

presumptuous *adj.* arrogant 78/19.

preuy members see **membres**.

price *n.* renown, glory 12/19, 23/2.

prided *ppl. a.* filled with pride
12/24 (only exs. *OED* c. 1400 &
1883).

prikkinges *n. pl.* incitements 82/2.

prime-temps *n.* springtime 26/17.

prynspally *adv.* primarily 122/16.

prisoned *pp.* incarcerated 30/5 (presound L).

prolouge *n.* preface 3/1, 7/24.

promesse *n.* promise 91/7; **promysses** *n. pl.* 91/16.

pronounce *v.* proclaim 109/8; **pronounceth** *pr. 3 s.* 114/11.

propirly *adv.* correctly 29/5.

propirte *n.* distinctive quality 35/23; **propirteis** *n. pl.* 57/12.

prove *v.* experience 105/2; **proueth** *pr. 3 s.* endeavours 12/24; **proued** *pp.* tested 77/10.

prouost *n.* provost, overseer 13/21.

prudens *n.* wisdom 4/29, 97/15; **prvdently** *adv.* wisely 122/18.

pulle *inf.* plunder 68/12 (cf. **pyll**).

purchase *inf.* procure 11/6; *imp.* 93/23; **purchaced** *pt. 3 s. intr.* strove 114/21.

purpose *v.* propose, present 70/12.

***pursewe** *inf.* continue 55/16 (first ex. this sense *OED* 1456); **pursuwyng** *pr. p.* 17/4; **pursuyng** *vbl. n.* pursuit 61/28.

pursuet *n.* pursuit 100/5 (**purswte** L).

purueid (*for*) *pp.* provided (for) 97/16; ~ (*of*) supplied (with) 108/19.

purviaunce *n.* provision 54/20.

put (*to*) *v.* bring (into) 43/1; ~ (*it oute*) *pt. 3 s.* blinded (an eye) 31/1; ~ (*to deth*) *inf.* execute 52/1; **puttith** (*me forthe*) *pr. 3 s.* thrusts me forward 4/15; **put** (*þe from*) *subj.* disinherit 96/2; **puttynge** *vbl. n.* 52/1ᵛ.

***quantite** *n.* number 82/21 (first ex. this sense *OED* 1456).

quarter *n. phr.*: *first* ~ first fourth 50/3.

queint *adj.* clever 102/14.

queynte *pr. 2 s.* acquaint 59/6.

quenchid *pt. 3 s. intr.* went out 49/25.

quyk *n.* the living 42/27 (*the* ~ *and the deede*).

quyk siluere *n.* mercury (metal) 22/26.

qwythe *adj.* white 50/5ᵛ.

raffe *pt. 3 s.* split, clove 73/12ᵛ.

rage *n.* storm (? ; *OED* 4c) 73/11; *pl.* sudden risings of the sea 30/28.

ramping *ppl. a.* rearing 11/8.

raveine *n.* rapine 53/24, 56/20.

rauenous *adj.* voracious (?) 17/25 ('vexatious', Warner, though this sense not in *OED*; 'trauailleux', Fr & Wyer).

rauysch *inf.* carry off 94/18; entrance 34/7; **rauysschid** *pt. 3 s.* violated 10/25; carried off 39/3; **rauishing** *vbl. n.* carrying away 98/6.

reaume *n.* realm 6/22, 13/9.

reboundyng *vbl. n.* bounding back 65/24.

receyue *imp.* accept 63/13; **resceyved** *pt. 3 s.* greeted 117/30; ***receyved** (*wiþ*) *pp.* assailed by 84/7 (this sense & const. not in *OED*; see note).

recomfort *v.* relieve 101/6.

recommended *pp.* praised 7/19.

recompence *v.* requite 76/1; ***n.* repayment 89/24ᵛ (first ex. this sense *OED* 1473).

recoueryd *pt. 3 s.* regained 34/18.

rede *inf.* read 41/18; *pr. 1 s.* 6/2; **here . . . redde** hear read 41/10; **reding** *pr. p.* 101/30; *vbl. n.* 59/1.

redemptoure *n.* redeemer 59/24.

redoubted *ppl. a.* distinguished 3/8.

redresse *v.* reform 101/9.

***reduce** *inf.* translate 122/9 (first ex. this sense *OED* 1484).

reede *adj.* red 83/28.

***refeccion** *n. phr.*: *take his* ~ partake of food 63/9–10 (first ex. this phr. *OED c.* 1440).

refreyne *inf.* restrain 9/31.

refresch *inf. refl.* rest or restore oneself 48/15.

refuse *inf.* reject 100/27; **refused** *pp.* rejected (as a lover) 105/3.

regarde *n.* account 73/24; *phr.*: *to* ~ *of* in regard to 8/9–10.

reighne, regne *v.* reign 109/29, 31/14.

reyne *n.* rain 26/17, 119/3.

reisith (*him*) *pr. 3 s. refl.* exalt

20/15; **reised** *pt. 3 s. refl.* 27/3;
pp. elevated 117/2.

reioiced *pt. 3 s.* exhilarated 56/7;
pp. 56/9.

rekeles *adj.* ungrateful 67/5 (*OED*
1c).

*remedied *pp. absol.* provided with
a remedy 96/18 (first ex. this use
OED c. 1440).

remembre (*of*) *inf.* have in mind
67/9; ~ *the imp. refl.* reflect on
14/21.

reneye *inf.* abjure 115/18.

rengnyd *pt. 3 s.* reigned 123/5.

renne *inf.* run 88/17; **ranne** *pt. 3 s.*
85/14; **ran** *pt. 3 pl.* 75/15; **ronne**
pp. 28/19.

rennyng *vbl. n.* running 88/18.

renomme, renovnne *n.* renown
122/4, 123/1.

renommeed *ppl. a.* celebrated
121/1.

repaired *pp.* restored, rebuilt 97/28.

reporte *n.* account 60/3; phr.: *make
good* ~ *of* report favourably on
16/1; (*fals*) **reportes** *pl.* evil
rumours 54/28.

reprove *inf.* censure 53/8; **reproved**
pt. 3 s. 51/23; **repreuede** *pp.*
35/4.

*repuignand *ppl. a.* (or *adj.* ?)
resisting, repelling 122/27 (first
exs. *OED c.* 1440 or 1460).

require *v.* request 86/16; **requireth**
pr. 3 s. needs 105/8; **requyred** *pt.
3 s.* demanded 46/11; inquired of
64/26; *pt. 3 pl.* demanded (as a
condition) 55/10.

rescuwe *inf.* rescue 39/3.

resemble (*to*) *v.* compare, be like
36/22.

reserued *pp.* saved (from death)
66/29.

*resist *pr. 3 pl.* oppose 91/26 (first
ex. this sense *OED* 2c 1483; see
note).

resistence *n.* act of resisting 75/25,
88/31.

reson *n.* reason 28/30, 38/15;
resonable *adj.* rational 51/25,
113/15; **resonabli** *adv.* with
reason 7/29.

reste *inf.* desist from 98/10; **restith**
pr. 3 s. remains 20/26; reposes
61/1; **restid** *pt. 3 pl.* stood still
81/17; *~ (*vppon*) *pp.* founded
on 65/9 (first ex. this sense *OED*
1530).

restore *v.* refresh, invigorate 8/28;
*restored (*to*) *pp.* returned to
(a place) 55/11 (first ex. this sense
OED c. 1450).

retorik *n.* rhetoric 22/29.

reued *pp.* delivered, rescued 14/28.

reuerence *n.* deference 14/10.

*reuerende *adj.* worthy of deep
respect 91/25 (first ex. *OED* 1449).

reuolucion *n.* phr.: *by* ~ in due
course of time 121/9.

reward *n.* recompense 72/13; retri-
bution 75/9.

richesses *n. pl.* riches 61/23, 82/4.

ryght *n.* law 52/4; phr.: **in the* ~ *of*
in title to 58/11 (first ex. this phr.
OED 1472); *ful* ~ *adv.* exceed-
ingly 26/31.

rightwis *adj.* virtuous 4/8; **riȝt-
wislye** *adv.* justly 14/2; ***right-
wisman** *n.* righteous person 57/17
(not in *OED* as comb. n.).

riȝtwisnes *n.* righteousness 88/6.

rigoure *n.* strict enforcement 13/28.

rynnyng *adj.* running 81/15.

rioterys *n. pl.* dissolute persons
69/23.

riotis *n. pl.* tumults 74/26.

rise *inf.* get up from sleep 93/7; ~
ayen return to life 45/31; ***riseth**
pr. 3 s. flows up 39/30 (first ex.
this sense *OED* 1530; 'sourt',
Laud); **roos** *pt. 3 s.* arose 40/16,
54/7.

ryuer *n. fig.* river 67/18; **ryver-side**
n. bank of a river 54/14; *pl.*
(*with gen.*) 32/10–11.

roche *n.* rocky height 28/24; huge
mass of stone 73/11.

*rollid *pt. 3 pl.* moved by means of
rollers 116/4 (first ex. this sense
OED 1513).

roted *pp.* rooted 21/12.

rothir *n.* rudder 64/10.

*rotters *n. pl.* rioters 69/23ᵛ (not in
OED).

routhe *n.* occasion of sorrow 114/23.
rowe *n.* phr.: *on the good mennes* ~ in the category of good men 13/11–12.
royde *adj.* strong, stout 12/27.
rude *adj.* big and coarse 38/8; uncultured 100/24; imperfect 119/1; **rudeli** *adv.* violently 50/7.

saaf *adj.* safe 108/28.
Sabaoth (*day*) *n.* Saturday 49/1 & 3.
sacrilege *n.* theft of religious objects 53/24.
*****sad** *adj.* mature, serious 67/25, 62/19 (first ex. this sense *OED* 1485); **sadli** *adv.* soberly 48/22.
sadnes *n.* staidness 64/6.
safegard *n.* (? *adj.*) protection (? protecting) 122/27.
salewes *n. pl.* sallows, willows 100/7 (see note).
sangwen *adj.* sanguine (one of the four 'complexions') 17/1.
*****satisfied** *pp.* contented 32/30 (first ex. this sense *OED c.* 1489).
saugh see **see.**
*****saus makers** *n. pl.* sauce-makers (?) 112/4 (not in *OED*; see note).
saue *quasi-prep.* except 52/3.
sauoure *n.* flavour 92/21.
say *n.* test, assay (aphetic form) 87/1.
scape *v.* escape (aphetic form) 106/7.
schal(le) *pr. 1 & 3 s. & pl.* 6/15, 15/31, 7/9, 47/22; **schalte** *2 s.* 5/31 (**schall** 5/33ᵛ); **schulde** *pt. 1 s.* 5/35; *2 s.* 44/13 (**schuldest** 44/14); *3 s.* 45/5 (**shoult** 113/10); *1 pl.* 8/7; **scholde** *3 s. & pl.* 13/16, 23/8.
schaping *n.* shaping, creating 78/18.
scharpe *adj.* acute 34/21; **scharpir** *comp.* more severe 66/7; **scharpeli** *adv.* vigorously 43/6.
scharpenes *n.* harshness 57/4; painfulness, bitterness 105/2 ('asprete', Laud).
scheep *n.* sheep 66/21.
schelde *n.* shield 15/3.
schell *n.* shell (of a nut) 61/18.
schette *pt. 3 s.* shut 49/20.

schewe *inf.* show 5/13; **schewid** *pp.* 3/21; stated 48/7; **schewing** *vbl. n.* manifesting 7/3; phr.: *in* ~ *therof* in proof of this 34/13.
schewer *n.* displayer 9/21; *pl.* those who show 23/9.
schynyng *ppl. a.* bright 15/3; distinguished 15/26.
schippe *n.* ship 30/29, 64/9.
schive *n.* slice of bread 4/23.
scholde see **schalle.**
schorte *pr. 3 s.* curtail 70/4.
scilence *n.* silence 19/19.
sclaundrous *adj.* defamatory 64/12.
sclave *n.* slave 81/27.
scool *n.* school 56/26; **scolis** *pl.* 90/10.
scourge *n.* whip, lash 96/3.
scriptures *n. pl.* writings 41/8, 98/5.
sece see **cesse.**
secrete *adj.* hidden 70/1; see **membres.**
secretnes *n.* that which is secret 77/9.
sectes *n. pl.* sexes 100/17.
see *n.* sea 44/12; fig. phr.: ~ *of the worlde* overwhelming mass of existence 45/4.
see *inf.* 61/10; **se** *pr. 1 s.* 54/19; **saugh** *pt. 3 s.* 41/31 (**sawe** 54/13; *pt. 3 pl.* 56/7); **seen** *pp.* 40/26.
seege *n.* siege, beleaguering 25/30; seat 65/11; *****sege** camp (?) 102/21 (so Warner; this sense not in *OED*).
seek *adj.* sick 63/15; **seeknessis** *n. pl.* 51/19.
seers *n. pl.* observers 42/13 (if **clere-seers,** *not* in *OED*).
see-side *n.* edge of the sea 96/29 (see note).
sei *pr. 1 s.* say 9/1; **seith** *pr. 3 s.* 39/2; **sey** *pr. 3 pl.* 101/22 (**seith** 37/4, **seyne** 38/32); **seide** *pt. 3 pl.* 57/5; **seiyng** *pr. p.* 61/14; **seide** *pp.* 37/16.
seke *inf.* seek 85/7; **sekiþ** *pr. 3 s.* 70/15; **souȝt** *pp.* 87/13.
sekir, sikir *adj.* sure 75/18, 96/31.
semblable *adj.* similar 115/5.
sen *prep.* subsequent to 84/11.

sentence *n.* order 15/19; judgement 18/23.

serche (*for*) *inf.* make a search for 119/14; **serchid** *pt. 3 pl.* 84/8.

sere *adj.* divers, various 95/5.

*serpently *adj.* serpent-like 28/15 (not in *OED* as adj.).

serue *inf.* do reverence 44/21; deserve 16/7 (*OED* v²).

seruyce *n.* employment 4/9; assistance 99/23; religious performance 112/18.

sette *imp.* set 6/6; *pr. 2 s. subj.* 10/9; **settith** *pr. 3 s.* 4/30; **sette** *pp.* 36/29; *ppl. a.* 3/27; phr.: ~ *bi* assess 62/2; value 89/14.

sette *pt. 3 s. refl.* sat 28/15.

sewe see **sowe, suwe.**

shame *n.* shamefastness 119/14.

shelde *n.* shield 113/24.

shewe *v.* show 118/24.

shotte *inf.* shoot 110/22.

shoult see **schalle.**

shrewednes *n.* wickedness 116/9.

sich *adj.* such 50/3.

sighte *n.* view 65/25.

signe *n.* insignia 38/12; indication 104/26; phr.: *in* ~ *of* as evidence of 106/17.

signed *pp.* attested (?), assigned (?) 23/22.

sikir see **sekir.**

silf *n.* self 90/2.

sylyd *pp.* soiled, befouled 50/11ᵛ.

simpeler *adj. comp.* more humble 105/23.

singulere *adj.* special 44/7.

sister germayn *n.* full sister 9/18.

sittith *pr. 3 s.* fits 59/10; **sittyng** *ppl. a.* suitable 24/19.

skye *n.* cloud 41/30.

slake *pr. 3 s.* lessen 80/14.

slee *v.* slay 51/30; *pr. 2 s. subj.* 60/4; **slewe** *pt. 3 s.* 28/29 (**slowe** 28/23); **slayne** *pp.* 47/12 (~ *with* 79/24; **sleyn** 60/30).

smerte *adj.* painful 109/8.

smyteth *pr. 3 s.* smites 45/12; **smote** *pt. 3 s.* 39/7; **smytyng** *pr. p.* 58/5; **smyten** *pp.* 42/17.

snare *n. fig.* trap 81/25; *pl.* 70/8.

socoure *n.* succour 15/21; *v.* 15/20; **socourable** *adj.* helpful 44/23.

sodein, sothen *ppl. a.* boiled 118/29, 28/3.

sodeinly, sodenly *adv.* suddenly 118/3, 68/2.

softe *adj.* gentle 9/5; pleasant 14/23; *adv.* not loudly 41/26 (**softely** 42/7).

softith *pr. 3 s.* eases 25/12; **softid** *pp.* softened 101/10.

soioure *n.* sojourn, respite 101/22.

soiourne *v.* remain 63/23; abide 118/9; **soiournyng** *vbl. n.* 118/11.

sokeþ *pr. 3 s.* sucks 100/26 (**souketh** 100/26ᵛ).

solas *n.* consolation 25/11; *v.* console 101/14; *refl.* 76/24.

solempne *adj.* solemn 91/25; **solempneli** *adv.* 49/3.

*sollennes *n.* unusual behaviour 113/29 (**soleynnesse** 29ᵛ; this n. not in *OED*; cf. s.v. 'solein').

som *n.* phr.: *hooll and* ~ entirely 5/30 (cf. **all and some**).

somtyme *adv.* in the past 64/30.

sondri *adj.* various 54/29.

soolde *pp.* sold 59/26, 81/27.

sooþe *n.* truth 96/11.

*sore, soore *adv.* greatly 34/16, 49/16 (first ex. this sense *OED* c. 1440); strongly 31/22; grievously 47/13; earnestly 64/26; **sorer** *comp.* more grievously 57/19.

sores *n. pl.* afflictions 95/26 ('maulx', Fr).

sorowe *n.* regret 28/11; distress 50/13.

sothen see **sodein.**

*sotted *pt. 3 pl.* made foolish 81/20ᵛ (first ex. aphetic form of 'assot' *OED* c. 1400–50).

*sovne *n.* safety phr.: *with hole* ~ in full security 3/10 (last ex. *OED* 1400; as trans. of Fr 'arroy').

souplid *pp.* mollified 99/21.

soutil see **subtile.**

souereyne *n.* superior 14/9, 75/2; *adj.* supreme 34/6, 66/26; **souereynly** *adv.* preeminently 69/25.

sowe, sowen *pp.* spread about 25/23; planted 119/3; **sowith** *pr.*

sowe (*cont.*):
> *3 s.* 64/12; **sowyn** *pr. 3 pl.* 69/7ᵛ;
> **sewe** *pt. 3 pl.* 36/13.

sowle-hele *n.* salvation 122/11.

sowne *n.* sound 37/29 (see *Dicts* Glossary).

sownynges *vbl. n. pl.* swoonings 50/21ᵛ (cf. *OED* 'sounding³').

spaas *n.* phr.: *tyme &* ~ opportunity 101/15, 75/20ᵛ.

sparke *n. fig.* flame (of love) 49/24; *pl.* sparks 35/11.

speche *n.* speech 64/6.

specyall *adv.* phr.: *in* ~ especially 9/4ᵛ; **specialli** *adv.* 103/8.

*****spede** *n.* power, might (?) 45/11 (but *OED* not after 1250); *v.* prosper 81/11.

speke *inf.* speak 61/10; ~ (*vnto*) 50/19–20; **spekith** *pr. 3 s.* 120/22; **spak** *pt. 3 s.* 71/11; *pl.* 12/4; **spokyn** *pp.* 48/22; (*wel*) **spekyng** *ppl. a.* 30/4.

speking *vbl. n.* discoursing 91/11.

spere *n.* sphere 16/24.

spices *n. pl.* kinds, varieties 83/2.

*****spies** *n. pl.* spyings 116/9 (first ex. this sense *OED* c. 1450; 'agais', Laud) spies 22/12.

spynne *v.* spin 78/23; **spynnyng** *vbl. n.* 78/22.

spotte *n.* moral stain 30/7; blemish 36/1.

spring *n.* phr.: ~ *of the day* dawn 56/2.

stabilnes *n.* stability 11/21.

stale *pt. 3 s.* stole 30/25; ~ (*fro*) withdrew secretly 109/20.

*****standyng** *ppl. a.* understanding, supposing 8/6, 48/21, 88/9, 119/10. (aphetic form, not in *OED*; see *Dicts* Glossary).

stanke *n.* pond 100/8 (stangne M).

staunch *inf.* quench 32/1; *****staunchid** *pp.* put out (fire) 111/27 (first ex. this sense *OED* c. 1450).

stede *n.* horse 7/4.

stered *pp.* moved 4/20, 82/4.

sterte, stirte *pt. 3 s.* started 109/21, 96/20.

*****stinging** *ppl. a.* biting (serpents) 11/7 (this specific meaning not in *OED*).

stodiere *n.* student 40/1.

stoon *n.* stone 29/18, 68/3.

store *n.* phr.: *sett* ~ want 77/16; *set no* ~ value lightly 37/24; *sette more* ~ value more highly 45/18.

stouped (*doun*) *pt. 3 s.* stooped down 111/14.

streyned *pp.* stretched (as strings) 38/22; distressed 54/14.

streite *adj.* rigorous 68/14; narrow 71/3.

*****strengthe** *n.* potency 33/8 (first ex. this sense *OED* [1. l] 1588); vigour 37/5; bodily power 65/8; power 90/2.

strengthe *inf.* strengthen 87/13.

stretche, strech *inf.* extend 70/8, 7/29 (*****~ *to* catch up to 88/27 [this precise sense not in *OED*]); **stretchith** (*ayens*) *pr. 3 s.* strains against 30/15; **strecchid** *pt. 3 s.* extended 28/16.

strif *n.* phr.: *take* ~ contend 10/21.

stryue *inf.* contend, quarrel 32/17; **striue** *imp.* 31/20; **stroof, strove** *pt. 3 pl.* 37/29, 65/22.

strok, strook *n.* stroke, blow 110/21, 111/17; *pl.* 51/32.

strong *adj.* eminently able 26/8; difficult 66/22; difficult to invade 71/4; **strengir** *comp.* 65/17; **strengist** *superl.* 108/15; **strongeli** *adv.* forcibly 22/13.

stroof see **stryue.**

stuf *n.* material 4/22.

subiecte *n.* inferior 14/10; **suget** *adj.* 73/2.

submittith *pr. 3 s.* subjects 72/27.

subtile, soutil, sutile *adj.* cleverly designed 24/28; clever 99/2; refined 100/25; **subtilli** *adv.* cunningly 34/7; dexterously 69/21; cleverly 69/26.

subtilte *n.* craftiness 30/31; **sotiltees** *pl.* guiles 116/9.

successyon *n.* successive passage (of time) 121/10.

suerte *n.* phr.: *be in* ~ be in certainty 107/2–3.

suffice (*to*) *v.* be adequate to 106/30.

suffraunce *n.* permission 122/5.

suffre *v.* endure 32/15; permit 29/29;

suffriþ *pr. 3 s.* 52/4; **suffrid** *pp.*
54/20.

suget see **subiecte.**

superfluyteis *n. pl.* excesses 9/29,
33/13.

supposed *pt. 3 s.* believed 93/8.

suremounted *pp.* raised 123/16.

*surnamed *pp.* given a surname
24/25 (first ex. *OED* 1512).

suspecion *n.* suspicion 42/4; phr.:
had him in ~ suspected him
41/29–30.

suspecte *n.* suspicion phr.: *holde in*
~ be suspicious of 104/2.

sustene *v.* maintain 57/8; *pp.* sup-
ported 63/9.

suwe, sewe *inf.* pursue 105/31;
occupy oneself with 81/12; **suweth**
pr. 3 s. 21/25; **suwed** *pt. 3 pl.*
111/9; **suwing, sewing** *pr. p.*
118/7, 7/12.

swerde *n.* sword 50/16, 111/19.

swere *v.* swear 47/30; **swore** *pt. 3 s.*
103/22.

*sweuenyng *vbl. n.* dream 58/25
(last use *OED* 1423).

swolowe *v.* swallow 32/27 (**swolve**
L).

swovnyngis *n. pl.* swoonings, faints
50/21 (see **sownynges**).

take *inf.* 4/24; *pr. 1 s. & 3 pl.* 4/22,
100/25; **takist** *2 s.* 94/1; **takith** *3 s.*
120/23; **take** *pr. 2 & 3 subj.* 45/10,
63/9; **took** *pt. 3 s. & pl.* 7/8 (**toke**
30/31), 90/1; **take** *imp.* 59/28;
taking *pr. p.* 54/16; **taken** *pp.*
6/18 (**take** 69/12); phr.: ~ *a-gree*
received favourably 119/19; ~ *at*
worthe (see **worthe**); ~ *(the)*
barke (see **barke**); ~ *(a) deuocion*
vowed 96/14; ~ *example* take as
precedent 80/15; ~ *fire* catch
fire 34/14; ~ *for* undertaken
because of 82/29; ~ *harme* suffered
78/27; ~ *haven* seek refuge 117/
30; ~ *hede* take care 45/10; ~ *him*
brought to him 85/26; ~ *in his*
(hir) armys embraced 87/23, 100/
11; ~ *loue* fell in love 66/24; ~
on hande undertake 5/25; ~ *(þe)*
see set sail 96/15; ~ *strif* quarrel

10/21; ~ *to* susceptible of 24/24; ~
vengeaunce be avenged 28/12; ~
(the) watir plunged into water
54/10; ~ *with the deede* take in
guilt 41/31; ~ *wreke* (see **wreke**).

*talent *n.* power of body 88/16
(first ex. *OED* c. 1430).

targes *n. pl.* light shields, bucklers
62/22.

tarye *(of) v.* delay, put off 76/2.

tastid *pp. fig.* tried, examined 71/26.

tatchis *n. pl.* vices 33/3 (**tacches** M).

teche *v.* teach 107/23; **techeþ** *pr. 3*
s. 108/1; **taught** *pt. 3 s.* 119/21.

teching *n.* instruction 120/11; *pl.*
23/8.

teid *pp.* tied 69/12.

teynte *ppl. a.* attainted (aphetic
form) 28/30.

tell *inf.* 60/21; **tellith** *pr. 3 s.* 52/12;
toolde *pt. 3 s.* 64/27; **tolde** *pp.*
41/10.

temperell *adj.* transitory 113/16.

temperid *adj.* phr.: ~ *full wele*
well-tempered 9/5.

temporat *adj.* temperate, moderate
26/20.

*temptyng *ppl. a.* enticing to evil
94/27 (first ex. *OED* 1546).

*tending *vbl. n.* attention, regard
99/29 (not in *OED*).

tendyng *pr. p.* having regard 17/8;
attending to 92/15.

terme *n.* duration 73/25; *pl.* con-
ditions, limits 16/27.

texte *n.* short passage setting forth
a theme for further discussion
8/25; **textys** *pl.* 123/21.

thik *adj.* dense 83/19.

thyng *n.* composition 4/24; **þingis**
pl. affairs, matters 82/23, 7/31
(**thing** old neut. *pl.* 6/29, 12/11;
note use in *Dicts*).

þinke *v.* think 67/7; **thinkith** *imp.*
42/30; **thouȝt** *pt. 3 pl.* 119/26;
thought *pp.* 88/9.

tho, thoo *pron.* those 8/13, 5/36;
adj. 8/28.

thornes *n. pl.* thorn-bushes 57/21
('espines', Fr).

thorugh *adv.* through 3/29; see
wherþorugh.

thoughte *n.* anxiety 54/13; contemplation 55/24.

thraldom *n.* servitude 49/4; captivity 72/27.

thredde *ord. num.* third 123/13.

thresscholde *n.* threshold 29/27 (thresshefolde *ML*).

tydyngis *n. pl.* news 60/10.

tierment *n.* burial 112/20 (terment M).

tyme *n.* phr.: **in ~* seasonably 43/19 (first ex. this phr. *OED* c. 1450).

tising *vbl. n.* instigation 114/29 ('enditement', Laud).

tobbe *n.* tub 71/9ᵛ.

toolde see tell.

toon, tone *pron.* (the) one 57/32, 58/1.

torned *pp.* antagonized 64/11; **tourned *ppl. a.* perverse 79/8 (this sense not in *OED*; cf. v. sense 14b; 'peruerse', Laud).

tothir *pron.* (the) other 57/33; totheris *gen.* 58/1.

touche *v.* relate to 69/25; touchith (*to*) *pr. 3 s.* 11/28.

transfigurid *pt. 3 s. refl.* transformed (himself) 70/7.

**transquillite *n.* tranquillity 123/12 (var. sp. not in *OED*).

trauailed *pp.* harassed 31/29.

tre *n.* tree 106/10; wood 115/24.

treson *n.* treachery 47/12, 52/18; *pl.* trickeries (?) 99/13.

trespace *n.* transgression 55/3.

**trompresse *n.* female deceiver 51/11 (not in *OED*; 'tromperresse' Laud).

**troubelous *adj.* vexatious 95/10 (first ex. this sense *OED* 1463).

trouble *v.* perplex 42/31; troubleth *pr. 3 s.* disturbs (mentally) 29/2; troubled *pt. 3 s.* stirred physically 31/23.

**trowe *pr. 1 s.* suppose 118/27 (first ex. this expletive *OED* c. 1491).

trust *v.* 51/15; *imp.* 49/9 (troste 108/11); trustith *imp. pl.* 108/12; trustid *pt. 3 s.* 52/17.

trwes *n. pl.* truce 101/16; trewes *gen.* 112/18.

turment *n.* torment 35/12; *pl.* 85/21

(tormentis 117/27; turnementes 35/12ᵛ).

tweyne *adj.* two 27/29.

vmbethinke *imp. refl.* bethink thyself 6/10, 49/1, 57/29.

**vnbehouely *adj.* unsuitable 33/12 (only dated ex. *OED* 1390; last use ?).

vnbounde *ppl. a.* unbounded 117/12 ('deliee', Fr.)

**uncloþid *ppl. a.* naked 100/10 (first ex. *OED* 1440).

vncouerid *ppl. a.* unarmed (?), unprepared (?) 75/16.

vncunnyng *ppl. a.* ignorant 67/13ᵛ.

vnderstande *inf.* comprehend 15/20; vnderstode *pt. 3 s.* 50/17; vndirstandin *pp.* 80/2.

vnderstandynge *n.* comprehension 23/16; *pl.* meanings 24/24.

vndertake *inf.* engage in 31/16.

vndirstandis *n. pl.* understandings 68/21.

vndoon *pp.* ruined 60/19.

**vnfelicite *n.* state of being unhappy 91/24 (not in *OED*; 'infelicite', Fr, Wyer, Bab. & M).

vngraciose *adj.* wicked, rude 65/29 ('malgracieux', Laud).

vnhappy *adj.* wretched 98/15 (onappy L); associated with misfortune 111/7.

vnknowing *vbl. n.* ignorance 67/15; *ppl. a.* ignorant, uninformed 67/13.

vnkunnyng *vbl. n.* ignorance 67/15ᵛ.

vnleifful *adj.* lawless 53/23.

vnnethe *adv.* scarcely 70/1.

vnponysschid *ppl. a.* unpunished 88/7.

**vnscribeable *adj.* undescribable (?) 107/2 (this word not in *OED*; 'incirconscriptible', Fr and Wyer = 'uncircumscribable'.)

**vnsent (*fore*) *ppl. a.* unsummoned 74/6 (first ex. with 'for' *OED* 1501).

vnsesid *ppl. a.* bereft (of) 81/2 (onsesyde L; 'dyssease', Wyer).

vnstedfastnes *n.* unsteady conduct 20/27.

vntrouth *n.* disloyalty 46/7; **false

statement 55/5 (first ex. this sense *OED* c. 1449).

unware *adj.* off guard 75/16ᵛ.

vnwurschipful *adj.* devoid of honour 17/26.

vsages *n. pl.* usings 53/2.

vse *pr. 3 pl.* engage in, play 65/29 (cf. *Dicts* Glossary).

vsschere *n.* usher 61/11; *pl.* 61/8.

vsurpacion *n.* unlawful seizure 53/24.

vagaunt *adj.* roaming 111/1.

vailable *adj.* advantageous 11/25, 41/11.

vaile *n.* veil 87/8.

vayle *v.* be of use 116/16; **valith** *pr. 3 s.* profits 65/8.

valew *n.* value 72/26, 112/5.

valey *n.* vale (of misery) 11/1 (**vale** 11/1ᵛ; **vaylie** 13/22ᵛ).

valure *n.* worth, merit 26/10.

*****vaunte** *v. refl.* boast 83/30; **vauntid** *pt. 3 s. refl.* boasted 76/17 (perhaps first ex. this constr.).

vaunting *vbl. n.* boasting 79/8.

*****vauntour** *n.* braggart 78/29 (first ex. *OED* 1456).

veyne *n. fig.* vein 18/16.

veine *n.* advb. phr.: *in* ~ vainly 20/10–11.

veinglorie *n.* inordinate pride 16/6; *fig.* 103/3.

velony *n.* villainy 54/29; **velyens** *adj.* villainous 48/21ᵛ.

venge *v.* avenge 43/2; **venged** *pt. 3 s.* 26/2.

vengeaunce *n.* revenge 43/11; punishment 52/30; phr.: *take* ~ 28/12.

venymose *adj.* venomous 68/11.

vertuous *adj.* righteous (?) 3/7; chaste 26/5.

vessell *n.* container 29/8, 64/8; *fig.* 27/20.

vexid *pp.* troubled 34/9.

viage *n.* voyage 96/17; **viages** *pl.* 12/3.

victorie *n.* conquest 40/15; **victorious** *adj.* successful 12/21; *****victoriousli** *adv.* triumphantly 22/5 (first ex. *OED* 1502).

vileine *n.* villainy 100/27 (**vilony** 32/15; **vilenye** 54/29ᵛ).

vileyns, vileynes *adj.* villainous 35/19, 118/5.

vilonous, vilenous, vileynose *adj.* villainous 32/18, 48/21, 67/4 see *Dicts* Glossary).

vynegre *n.* vinegar 29/8.

violence *n.* violent conduct 51/32.

visage *n.* countenance 17/7; face 107/2.

vision *n.* dream 107/8; *pl.* 107/19.

voide *adj.* destitute 26/31; empty 61/32 ('vaines', Fr); vacant (?) 110/26 ('vagues', Fr; 'vagaunt', Wyer).

voide *v.* clear away 29/7; drive away 48/16; **voided** *pt. 3 s.* 18/14.

voydenes *n.* vanity 118/6ᵛ.

*****voluptuosenesses** *n. pl.* wantonnesses 82/3 (first ex. *OED* 1508).

*****vomyted** *pp. trans.* spewed out 50/11 (first ex. this sense *OED* 1560).

vouche-saaf *v.* deign 76/23.

wacche *n.* phr.: *to make* ~ keep under observation 42/11; **wacchis** *pl.* guards 42/12; plots 52/25 (**watches** 8/2).

wagis *n. pl.* rewards 12/20.

*****waisch** *n.* wash, ford 31/30 (first ex. this sense *OED* c. 1440; 'gue', Fr).

wan *conj.* when 55/8.

wanne see **wynne** *v.*

ware *imp.* beware 103/14; *adj.* watchful 120/1.

watir *n.* body of water 54/7; **watris** *pl.* 81/15.

watir-side *n.* margin of the sea 80/20.

wawes *n. pl.* waves 54/11.

waxe *v.* become, increase 30/18; **wexeth** *pr. 3 s.* 112/5; **wex(e)** *pt. 3 s. & pl.* 29/30, 49/24 (**waxe** 28/22).

weddid *pt. 3 s.* married 74/3.

weel *n.* profit 16/11 ('le bien', Fr).

*****weight** *n. fig.* importance, claim to consideration 9/11 (first ex. this sense *OED* 1521; see note).

welbeloued *ppl. a.* dearly loved 76/17.

***wele-spekinge** *ppl. a.* well-spoken 42/14 (not in *OED*).

welle-spring *n.* source of a spring 100/7.

welwillyng *adj.* benevolent 26/21.

wene *v.* think, judge, suggest 117/5; **wenith** *pr. 3 s.* 50/30; **weneth** *pr. 3 pl.* 117/13 (**wene** 83/4); **wende** *pt. 3 s.* 32/4; **wenyng** *pr. p.* 74/18.

wepe *v.* cry 56/16; **wepeth** *pr. 3 s.* 56/15; **wepte** *pt. 3 s.* 84/10; **wepyng** *vbl. n.* 55/33.

were *v.* wear 87/8; phr.: *an helme to* ~ *to don* armour 13/8.

werke *v.* shape 4/22.

werking *vbl. n.* performance 88/4.

werkis *n. pl.* undertakings 61/6 ('operacions', Wyer & Fr).

werrant *adj.* (?) warring (?) 28/18ᵛ (cf. Warner's note, p. 30).

werre *inf.* make war on 122/3, 22/13; *n.* 10/21; **werrys** *pl.* 87/12.

wery *adv.* truly 122/30; *adj.* weary 100/5.

weve *v.* weave 78/23; **weving** *vbl. n.* 78/18.

wexe see **waxe**.

wey *n.* conduct (of life) 10/18; means 46/7; phr.: *hiʒ* ~ ideal conduct 92/28; *in the* ~ in course of action 50/8–9.

weymentacions *n. pl.* lamentations 50/20.

what *pron.* how much 37/9; *adj.* whatever 41/24.

whelis *n. pl.* wheels 116/3.

wherþorugh *adv.* through which 77/3.

whete-corne *n.* grain of wheat 12/12.

which *pron.* phr.: *the* ~ that 6/30; who 7/1–2, 54/5 (in oblique cases usually **whom(e)** 43/16, 60/27); *in that the* ~ in regard to that which 24/29; *to that the* ~ to that one who 67/3.

white-thorn *n.* common hawthorn 50/5.

who *pron.* 106/29 (see also **which**); **who-so** whoever 16/9, 94/21.

wich-crafte *n.* witchcraft 117/25.

wighte *n.* person 65/16.

wildenes *n.* eagerness 11/10.

wiles, willes *n. pl.* trickeries 31/3, 93/24.

will(e) *pr. 1 & 3 s., 1 & 2 pl.* 5/14, 13/11, 101/4, 13/2; **wul(l)** *1 s. & 3 pl.* 6/7, 83/30; **wilte** *2 s.* 13/6 ; **wold(e)** *pt. 1 & 3 s., 3 pl.* 4/9, 40/4, 55/13; **woldest** *2 s.* 37/10.

wille *n.* wish 3/33; carnal desire 46/12; intent 106/15; phr.: *at his* ~ voluntarily 34/29 (*atte þe owne* ~ 72/9–10); *come to his* ~ achieve his desire 106/15.

willfare *n.* welfare 60/22.

***willyngly** *adv.* voluntarily 105/20 ('voluntarily', Wyer, 'volentiers', Laud; first ex. this sense *OED* 1552).

wilne *v.* desire 16/4.

wympil *n.* wimple, veil 50/9.

wynde *imp.* wrap up 26/29 ('affubler', Laud).

wynne *v.* win 100/13; **wan(ne)** *pt. 3 s.* 15/11, 39/23.

***wynneris** *n. pl.* winners, victors 10/30 (first ex. this sense *OED* 1456; see note).

wise *n.* phr.: *in no* ~ under no circumstances 31/20, 37/22.

wite *inf.* learn 98/1, 117/29; **wote** *pr. 1 s.* know 11/9; *pr. 3 pl.* 114/5; **woste** *pr. 2 s.* 104/18; **wist** *pt. 3 s.* 76/28; **wiste** *pt. 3 pl.* 114/27 (**wost** L).

wiþ-all *adv.* therewith 93/23.

***with-draughte** *n.* retreat phr.: *chambre of* ~ private chambers 61/2 (phr. not in *OED*; first ex. this sense *OED* 1480).

withdrawe *inf.* draw back 61/4; *imp. refl.* remove thyself 65/18.

withoute *prep.* outside 50/4.

withstand *v.* oppose 65/23.

witnes *n.* evidence 79/10; one who gives evidence 47/32; phr.: *I take* ~ I note 92/4.

witte *n.* wisdom 4/12; intellectual ability 26/8; *pl.* 110/26, (five) senses 61/3.

woke *n.* week 16/22.

woman *n.* 6/19; wommen, wemen
pl. 107/10 & 10ᵛ; wommenys
gen. 71/6.

wombe *n.* uterus 31/27; belly
117/11; **fig.* place of development
63/14 (first ex. this sense *OED*
1593).

wondirful *adv.* exceedingly 53/11.

wont *pp.* accustomed 50/5, 84/25.

woo *n.* physical pain 25/14; grief
25/21; wois *pl.* 34/9; woful *adj.*
grieving 26/9.

wood *adj.* mad 28/20; woodnes *n.*
madness 27/28, 75/2.

wor- see also wur-.

wordly *adj.* worldly 122/11, 7/6ᵛ.

worth *adj.* of value 66/7.

worthe *n.* phr.: *take at* ∼ be con-
tent with it 4/14.

worthines *n.* excellent character
102/16; *worthinesses *pl.* worthy
deeds 26/3 (this sense not in *OED*;
'prouesses', Fr & Wyer).

wreke *n.* phr.: *take any* ∼ take any
vengeaunce 10/29.

wronge *n.* unfairness 20/22; mis-
chief 55/17.

wrongeful *adj.* unjust 48/19, 82/16.

wroughte *ppl. a.* fashioned 33/28.

wurschipfull *adj.* distinguished
8/30; reputable 114/2.

wurthi *adj.* worthy 12/14; wur-
thynes *n.* 4/6; *pl.* 3/27; worthy
deeds 26/3.

y *pron.* I 54/19.

yaf see yeue.

yate *n.* gate 6/25; yatis *pl.* 10/17.

ydelnes *n.* indolence 17/30, 118/7.

ydolatrie *n.* idolatry 46/29.

yeftis *n. pl.* gifts 122/16 (see yifte).

yelde *imp.* yield 55/2; yolden,
ʒolden *pp.* 55/21, 94/28; repaid
114/23.

yen see iʒe.

yere *n.* year 49/15; phr.: yeris
mynde anniversary 112/18.

yeue, yif *inf.* give 14/7, 45/6; yeue
imp. 14/8; *pr. 2 s.* 18/23; *pr. 3 s.*
19/13 (yeueth 17/30); yaf *pt. 3 s.*
42/4; *pt. 3 pl.* 16/26; yevyng *pr.
p.* 123/11; yoven, yovyn, yofe
pp. 16/30, 121/24, 20/2ᵛ; phr.: ∼
wey let pass 115/2.

yeuere *n.* giver 36/17.

yifte *n.* gift 3/24; phr.: *of* ∼ as a
gift 42/2; yiftis *pl.* 7/4 (see yeftis).

ymage *n.* statue 33/26; mental
picture 118/18.

ymagin *pr. 2 s.* picture 11/9;
*ymagened *ppl. a.* conceived
118/17 (first ex. *OED* 1509).

ymaginacion *n.* fancy 73/20.

ynough, ynowe *adv., n.* enough
32/28, 105/10.

yode *pt. 3 s.* went 80/19ᵛ.

yonghthe, yougth *n.* youth 7/1,
27/12.

yoven see yeue.

ypocrisye *n.* hypocrisy 118/14;
ypocrites *n. pl.* hypocrites 118/
15–16.

yraigne *n.* spider 78/21 (*MED* s.v.
'arain').

yrin, iryn *n.* iron 21/23, 65/23.

yvill *n.* evil 90/23; *adj.* 52/2.

yvi *n.* ivy 29/17.

*yvilknowing *ppl. a.* 'evil knowing',
ungrateful (?) 67/5 (not in *OED*;
'mal congnoissant', Laud).

ywis *adv.* certainly 56/28.

INDEX OF PROPER NAMES

EVERY variant spelling found in the manuscripts has been recorded once in the *variae lectiones* and is given below. Following the first entry for each name, there is enclosed in parentheses (where deemed necessary) a modern or more familiar form for the corresponding name in Scrope's text. Names used as adjectives or in the titles of books have usually not been included.

Pollinites (Polynices), **Polimites**: XLVI.

Priant (Priam), **Priaunt, Pryant, Pryaunt**: XI, XXXII, XXXVII, XL, LXXVII, LXXX, LXXXI, LXXXIV, XC, XCV.

Proserpin, Proserpine, Proserpyne, Proserpyng: III, XXVII, LXX.

Protheus, *see* **Pirotheus.**

Prudence, goddess of = Othea.

Ptholome, *see* **Tholome.**

Puille (Apulia): LXVIII.

Pymalion(Pygmalion), **Pymalyon, Pimalion, Pilamyon**: XXII.

Rabion (philosopher), **Rabyon**: XXXVI.

Romaynes: I, LXXXVII, C.

Salamon (Solomon; *see also* **Solin**), **Salomon**: IV.

Saturne, Satorne: VI, VIII, LI.

Sedechias (philosopher): LXV.

Semelle: LXII.

Sephalus, *see* **Cephalus.**

Serebrus, *see* **Cerebrus.**

Sibille, Sebille: C.

Signus (Cygnus; cf. Tinus): XLIV.

Socrates: App. A, XVI, XVIII, XLI, LXXIV, LXXVIII.

Solin (Solon), **Solyn, Soleyne, Salamon**: App. A, L, LXX, LXXXIII, LXXXV.

Stafford, Homfray (Duke of Buckingham, etc.): Prologue.

Stevyn (Scrope): App. A.

Symond (St. Simon), **Symonde**: XXXII.

Tawstyn, *see* **Austin.**

Thamarus (Tomyris), **Thamaris**: LVII.

Thebes: XXVIII, XLVI, L.

Thelamen Ayaux (Ajax Telamonius; *see* Aiaux), **Thelomonaialles, Thelomonailes, Thelomonailles**: LXXX.

Theocles (Eteocles): XLVI.

Theseus, Thesus: III, XXVII.

Thessille (philosopher): LXXII.

Thetis: LX, LXXI.

Tholome (Ptolemy), **Ptholome**: App. A, XCVII.

Thomas (St.): XXVIII.

Thune (Tunis?): XCVII.

Tidius (Tydeus): XLVI.

Tinus(Cygnus; cf. Signus), **Tynus**: XLIV.

Tisbe (Thisbe), **Tysbe, Thesbe, Tesbe, Tesbi**: XXXVIII.

Tobie (Tobias), **Tobi**: XLVI.

Troilus, Troyles, Troylus: XL, LXXX, LXXXIV, XCIII.

Troy, Troye, Troie: I, XIII, XV, XIX, XXXI, XXXVII, XLIII, XLIV, LX, LXI, LXVI, LXVIII, LXXIII, LXXVII, LXXX, LXXXI, LXXXIII, LXXXIV, XCIII, XCV, XCVI, XCVII, XCVIII.

Troyens: I, XXXI, XLIII, LIII, LXXI, LXXVII, LXXXI, XCIII, XCVI.

Venus: VII, XXII, LVI, LX, LXV, LXXIII.

Vlixes (Ulysses), **Vlyxes**: XIX, LXXI, LXXXIII, XCVIII.

Vulcans, Vulcanes, Vlnecans: LVI.

Vyrgyl (Virgil): App. A.

Ylion (Ilium), **Ylyon**: XCVII.

Ynacus (Inacus): XXIX.

Yno (wife of Athamas), **Ino**: XVII, XCIX.

Yoo (Io, daughter of Inacus), **Yo**: XXIX, XXX.

Ypocras (Hippocrates), **Ipocras**: XXI.

Yragnes (Arachne): LXIV.

Ysaie, *see* **Isaie.**

Ysidre, *see* **Isodore.**

Ysis, Isis, Ysys: XXV.

Ytalie, Ytaly, Ytaile, Ytailie, Itaille: LXVIII, XCVIII.

Zaqualcum (philosopher), **Zaqualcuin, Zaqualquin**: LXXXVI.

EARLY ENGLISH TEXT SOCIETY

THE Subscription to the Society, which constitutes full membership for private members and libraries, is £3. 3s. (U.S. and Canadian members $9.00) a year for the annual publications in the Original Series, due in advance on the 1st of JANUARY, and should be paid by Cheque, Postal Order, or Money Order made out to 'The Early English Text Society', to Dr. A. M. Hudson, Executive Secretary, Early English Text Society, Lady Margaret Hall, Oxford.

The payment of the annual subscription is the only prerequisite of membership.

Private members of the Society (but not libraries) may select other volumes of the Society's publications instead of those for the current year. The value of texts allowed against one annual subscription is 100s. (U.S. members 110s.), and all such transactions must be made through the Executive Secretary.

Members of the Society (including institutional members) may also, through the Executive Secretary, purchase copies of past E.E.T.S. publications and reprints for their own use at a discount of one third of the listed prices.

The Society's texts are also available to non-members at listed prices through any bookseller.

The Society's texts are published by the Oxford University Press.

The Early English Text Society was founded in 1864 by Frederick James Furnivall, with the help of Richard Morris, Walter Skeat, and others, to bring the mass of unprinted Early English literature within the reach of students and provide sound texts from which the New English Dictionary could quote. In 1867 an Extra Series was started of texts already printed but not in satisfactory or readily obtainable editions.

In 1921 the Extra Series was discontinued and all the publications of 1921 and subsequent years have since been listed and numbered as part of the Original Series. Since 1921 just over a hundred new volumes have been issued; and since 1957 alone more than a hundred and thirty volumes have been reprinted at a cost of £65,000. In 1970 the first of a new Supplementary Series will be published; books in this series will be issued as funds allow.

In this prospectus the Original Series and Extra Series for the years 1867–1920 are amalgamated, so as to show all the publications of the Society in a single list.

From 1 April 1969, since many of the old prices had become uneconomic in modern publishing conditions, a new price structure was introduced and the new prices are shown in this list. From the same date the discount allowed to members was increased from 2d. in the shilling to 4d. in the shilling.

LIST OF PUBLICATIONS

Original Series, 1864–1970.   Extra Series, 1867–1920

O.S. 104. The Exeter Book (Anglo-Saxon Poems), re-ed. I. Gollancz. Part I. (*Reprinted* 1958.) 55s. £2·75 — 1895

105. The Prymer or Lay Folks' Prayer Book, Camb. Univ. MS., ed. H. Littlehales. Part I. (*Out of print.*) — ,,

E.S. 67. The Three Kings' Sons, a Romance, ed. F. J. Furnivall. Part I, the Text. (*Out of print.*) — ,,

68. Melusine, the prose Romance, ed. A. K. Donald. Part I, the Text. (*Out of print.*) — ,,

O.S. 106. R. Misyn's Fire of Love and Mending of Life (Hampole), ed. R. Harvey. (*Out of print.*) — 1896

107. The English Conquest of Ireland, A.D. 1166–1185, 2 Texts, ed. F. J. Furnivall. Part I. (*Out of print.*) — ,,

E.S. 69. Lydgate's Assembly of the Gods, ed. O. L. Triggs. (*Reprinted* 1957.) 42s. £2·10 — ,,

70. The Digby Plays, ed. F. J. Furnivall. (*Reprinted* 1967.) 30s. £1·50 — ,,

O.S. 108. Child-Marriages and -Divorces, Trothplights, &c. Chester Depositions, 1561–6, ed. F. J. Furnivall. (*Out of print.*) — 1897

109. The Prymer or Lay Folks' Prayer Book, ed. H. Littlehales. Part II. (*Out of print.*) — ,,

E.S. 71. The Towneley Plays, ed. G. England and A. W. Pollard. (*Reprinted* 1966.) 45s. £2·25 — ,,

72. Hoccleve's Regement of Princes, and 14 Poems, ed. F. J. Furnivall. (*Out of print.*) — ,,

73. Hoccleve's Minor Poems, II, from the Ashburnham MS., ed. I. Gollancz. (*Out of print.*) — ,,

O.S. 110. The Old-English Version of Bede's Ecclesiastical History, ed. T. Miller. Part II, 1. (*Reprinted* 1963.) 55s. £2·75 — 1898

111. The Old-English Version of Bede's Ecclesiastical History, ed. T. Miller. Part II, 2. (*Reprinted* 1963.) 55s. £2·75 — ,,

E.S. 74. Secreta Secretorum, 3 prose Englishings, one by Jas. Yonge, 1428, ed. R. Steele. Part I. (*Out of print.*) — ,,

75. Speculum Guidonis de Warwyk, ed. G. L. Morrill. (*Out of print.*) — ,,

O.S. 112. Merlin. Part IV. Outlines of the Legend of Merlin, by W. E. Mead. (*Out of print.*) — 1899

113. Queen Elizabeth's Englishings of Boethius, Plutarch, &c., ed. C. Pemberton. (*Out of print.*) — ,,

E.S. 76. George Ashby's Poems, &c., ed. Mary Bateson. (*Reprinted* 1965.) 30s. £1·50 — ,,

77. Lydgate's DeGuilleville's Pilgrimage of the Life of Man, ed. F. J. Furnivall. Part I. (*Out of print.*) — ,,

78. The Life and Death of Mary Magdalene, by T. Robinson, c. 1620, ed. H. O. Sommer. 30s. £1·50 — ,,

O.S. 114. Ælfric's Lives of Saints, ed. W. W. Skeat. Part IV and last. (*See* O.S. 94.) — 1900

115. Jacob's Well, ed. A. Brandeis. Part I. (*Out of print.*) — ,,

116. An Old-English Martyrology, re-ed. G. Herzfeld. (*Out of print.*) — ,,

E.S. 79. Caxton's Dialogues, English and French, ed. H. Bradley. (*Out of print.*) — ,,

80. Lydgate's Two Nightingale Poems, ed. O. Glauning. (*Out of print.*) — ,,

80A. Selections from Barbour's Bruce (Books I–X), ed. W. W. Skeat. (*Out of print.*) — ,,

81. The English Works of John Gower, ed. G. C. Macaulay. Part I. (*Reprinted* 1957.) 60s. £3 — ,,

O.S. 117. Minor Poems of the Vernon MS., ed. F. J. Furnivall. Part II. (*Out of print.*) — 1901

118. The Lay Folks' Catechism, ed. T. F. Simmons and H. E. Nolloth. (*Out of print.*) — ,,

119. Robert of Brunne's Handlyng Synne, and its French original, re-ed. F. J. Furnivall. Part I. (*Out of print.*) — ,,

E.S. 82. The English Works of John Gower, ed. G. C. Macaulay. Part II. (*Reprinted* 1957.) 60s. £3 — .,

83. Lydgate's DeGuilleville's Pilgrimage of the Life of Man, ed. F. J. Furnivall. Part II. (*Out of print.*) — ,,

84. Lydgate's Reson and Sensuallyte, ed. E. Sieper. Vol. I. (*Reprinted* 1965.) 50s. £2·50 — ,,

O.S. 120. The Rule of St. Benet in Northern Prose and Verse, and Caxton's Summary, ed. E. A. Kock. (*Out of print.*) — 1902

121. The Laud MS. Troy-Book, ed. J. E. Wülfing. Part I. (*Out of print.*) — ,

E.S. 85. Alexander Scott's Poems, 1568, ed. A. K. Donald. (*Out of print.*) — ,

86. William of Shoreham's Poems, re-ed. M. Konrath. Part I. (*Out of print.*) — ,

87. Two Coventry Corpus Christi Plays, re-ed. H. Craig. (*See under* 1952.) — 1903

O.S. 122. The Laud MS. Troy-Book, ed. J. E. Wülfing. Part II. (*Out of print.*) — ,,

123. Robert of Brunne's Handlyng Synne, and its French original, re-ed. F. J. Furnivall. Part II. (*Out of print.*) — ,,

E.S. 88. Le Morte Arthur, re-ed. J. D. Bruce. (*Out of print.*) — ,,

89. Lydgate's Reson and Sensuallyte, ed. E. Sieper. Vol. II. (*Reprinted* 1965.) 35s. £1·75 — ,,

90. English Fragments from Latin Medieval Service-Books, re-ed. H. Littlehales. (*Out of print.*) — ,,

O.S. 124. Twenty-six Political and other Poems from Digby MS. 102, &c., ed. J. Kail. Part I. 50s. £2·50 — 1904

125. Medieval Records of a London City Church, ed. H. Littlehales. Part I. (*Out of print.*) — ,,

126. An Alphabet of Tales, in Northern English, from the Latin, ed. M. M. Banks. Part I. (*Out of print.*) — ,,

E.S. 91. The Macro Plays, ed. F. J. Furnivall and A. W. Pollard. (*Out of print; see* 262.) — ,,

92. Lydgate's DeGuilleville's Pilgrimage of the Life of Man, ed. Katherine B. Locock. Part III. (*Out of print.*) — ,,

93. Lovelich's Romance of Merlin, from the unique MS., ed. E. A. Kock. Part I. (*Out of print.*) — ,,

O.S. 127. An Alphabet of Tales, in Northern English, from the Latin, ed. M. M. Banks. Part II. (*Out of print.*) — 1905

128. Medieval Records of a London City Church, ed. H. Littlehales. Part II. (*Out of print.*) — ,,

129. The English Register of Godstow Nunnery, ed. A. Clark. Part I. 63s. £3·15 — ,,

E.S. 94. Respublica, a Play on a Social England, ed. L. A. Magnus. (*Out of print. See under* 1946.) — ,,

95. Lovelich's History of the Holy Grail. Part V. The Legend of the Holy Grail, ed. Dorothy Kempe. (*Out of print.*) — ,,

96. Mirk's Festial, ed. T. Erbe. Part I. (*Out of print.*) — ,,

O.S. 130. The English Register of Godstow Nunnery, ed. A. Clark. Part II. 55s. £2·75 — 1906

131. The Brut, or The Chronicle of England, ed. F. Brie. Part I. (*Reprinted* 1960.) 55s. £2·75 — ,,

132. John Metham's Works, ed. H. Craig. 50s. £2·50 — ,,

E.S. 97. Lydgate's Troy Book, ed. H. Bergen. Part I, Books I and II. (*Out of print.*) — ,,

98. Skelton's Magnyfycence, ed. R. L. Ramsay. (*Reprinted* 1958.) 55s. £2·75 — ,,

99. The Romance of Emaré, re-ed. Edith Rickert. (*Reprinted* 1958.) 30s. £1·50 — ,,

O.S. 133. The English Register of Oseney Abbey, by Oxford, ed. A. Clark. Part I. 50s. £2·50 — 1907

134. The Coventry Leet Book, ed. M. Dormer Harris. Part I. (*Out of print.*) — ,,

Forthcoming volumes

Other texts are in preparation.

Supplementary Series

The Society will issue books in the Supplementary Series from time to time as funds allow. These will nc
be issued on subscription but members will be able to order copies before publication at a reduced rate; detai
will be circulated on each occasion. The books will be available to non-members at listed prices. The fir
volume, which will appear in 1970, is a completely revised and re-set edition of the texts in Extra Series 10
with some additional prices.

February 1970.

Publisher: LONDON · THE OXFORD UNIVERSITY PRESS, ELY HOUSE, 37 DOVER ST., W. 1